REVISED PRINTING

Grade Aid Workbook with Practice Tests

for

Berk

Development Through the Lifespan

Third Edition

Prepared by

JoDe Paladino
Illinois State University

Laura E. Berk
Illinois State University

Sara Harris
Illinois State University

PEARSON

Boston   New York   San Francisco
Mexico City   Montreal   Toronto   London   Madrid   Munich   Paris
Hong Kong   Singapore   Tokyo   Cape Town   Sydney

ISBN: 0-205-43042-2

Printed in the United States of America

10 9 8 7 6 5 4 3   07 06 05 04

CONTENTS

PREFACE

As you embark on the fascinating journey of studying human development, it is our hope that this workbook will help you master the material in your text, *Development Through the Lifespan,* by Laura E. Berk. Our intention in preparing the workbook is to provide you with active practice in learning the content in your textbook and thought-provoking questions that help you clarify your own thinking. Each chapter in the workbook is organized into the following six sections:

CHAPTER SUMMARY

We begin with a brief summary of the material, mentioning major topics covered and general principles emphasized in text discussion. Each text chapter includes two additional summaries: an informal one at the beginning of the chapter, and a structured summary at the end of the chapter. Thus, the summary in the workbook will be your third review of the information covered in each chapter. It is intended to remind you of major points in the text before you embark on the remaining activities in the workbook.

LEARNING OBJECTIVES

We have organized the main points in each chapter into a series of objectives that indicate what you should be able to do once you have mastered the material. We suggest that you look over these objectives before you read each chapter. You may find it useful to take notes on information pertaining to objectives as you read. When you finish a chapter, try to answer the objectives in a few sentences or a short paragraph. Then check your answers against the text and revise your responses accordingly. Once you have completed this exercise, you will have generated your own review of chapter content. Because it is written in your own words, it should serve as an especially useful chapter overview that can be referred to when you prepare for examinations.

STUDY QUESTIONS

The main body of each chapter consists of study questions, organized according to major headings in the textbook, that assist you in identifying main points and grasping concepts and principles. Text pages on which answers can be found are indicated next to each entry. The study question section can be used in a number of different ways. You may find it helpful to answer each question as you read the chapter. Alternatively, try reading one or more sections and then testing yourself by answering the relevant study questions. Finally, use the study question section as a device to review for examinations. If you work through it methodically, your retention of chapter material will be greatly enhanced.

ASK YOURSELF . . .

In each chapter of the textbook, critical thinking questions appear at the end of each major section. Answering these questions will help you analyze important theoretical concepts and research findings. Three types of questions are included: *Review* questions, which assist with recall and comprehension of information in the text; *Apply* questions, which encourage application of your knowledge to controversial issues and problems; and *Connect* questions, which help you integrate what you have learned across age periods and aspects of development, thereby building an image of the whole person. Each question is answered on the text's companion website, where you may compare your reasoning to a model response.

PUZZLES

To help you master the central vocabulary of the field, we have provided crossword puzzles that test your knowledge of important terms and concepts. Answers can be found at the back of the workbook. If you cannot think of the term that matches a clue in the puzzles, your knowledge of information related to the term may be insecure. Reread the material in the text chapter related to each item that you miss. Also, try a more demanding approach to term mastery: After you have completed each puzzle, cover the clues and write your own definitions of each term.

PRACTICE TESTS

Once you have thoroughly studied each chapter, find out how well you know the material by taking the two 20-item multiple choice practice tests. Then check your answers using the key at the back of the workbook. Each item is page-referenced to chapter content so you can look up answers to questions that you missed. If you answered more than a few items incorrectly, spend extra time rereading the chapter, writing responses to chapter objectives, and reviewing the study questions in this workbook.

Now that you understand how the workbook is organized, you are ready to begin using it to master *Development Through the Lifespan.* We wish you a rewarding and enjoyable course of study.

JoDe Paladino
Laura E. Berk
Sara Harris

CHAPTER 1
HISTORY, THEORY, AND RESEARCH STRATEGIES

BRIEF CHAPTER SUMMARY

Human development is the study of all aspects of constancy and change throughout the lifespan. Theories lend structure and meaning to the scientific study of development. This chapter provides an overview of philosophical and theoretical approaches to the study of human development from medieval to modern times and reviews major research strategies used to study human behavior and development.

When compared and contrasted, historical philosophies and contemporary theories raise three basic questions about what people are like and how they develop: (1) Is development a continuous or discontinuous process? (2) Is there one course of development or many? (3) Are genetic or environmental factors more important in determining development? Although some theories take extreme positions on these issues, many modern ones include elements from both sides. The lifespan perspective recognizes that great complexity exists in human change and the factors that underlie it.

Research methods commonly used to study development include systematic observation, self-reports, clinical or case studies of single individuals, and ethnographies of the life circumstances of specific groups of people. Investigators of human development generally choose either a correlational or an experimental research design. To study how their subjects change over time, they apply special developmental research strategies—longitudinal, cross-sectional, and longitudinal-sequential designs. Each method and design has both strengths and limitations. Conducting research with human subjects also poses special ethical dilemmas.

Theory and research are the cornerstones of the field of human development. These components are helping us understand and alleviate many pressing problems faced by children and adults in today's world.

LEARNING OBJECTIVES

After reading this chapter, you should be able to:

1.1 Explain the importance of the terms *interdisciplinary* and *applied* as they help to define the field of human development. (p. 5)

1.2 Explain the role of theories in understanding human development, and describe three basic issues on which major theories take a stand. (pp. 5–7)

1.3 Describe factors that sparked the emergence of the lifespan perspective, and explain the four assumptions that make up this point of view. (pp. 7–12)

1.4 Trace historical influences on modern theories of human development, from medieval times through the early twentieth century. (pp. 13–15)

1.5 Describe theoretical perspectives that influenced human development research in the mid-twentieth century, and cite the contributions and limitations of each. (pp. 15–20)

1.6 Describe recent theoretical perspectives on human development, noting the contributions of major theorists. (pp. 20–25)

1.7 Identify the stand that each contemporary theory takes on the three basic issues presented earlier in this chapter. (p. 26)

1.8 Describe the research methods commonly used to study human development, citing the strengths and limitations of each. (pp. 27–30)

1.9 Contrast correlational and experimental research designs, and cite the strengths and imitations of each. (pp. 31–34)

1.10 Describe three research designs for studying development, and cite the strengths and limitations of each. (pp. 34–37)

1.11 Discuss ethical issues related to lifespan research. (pp. 37–39)

STUDY QUESTIONS

Human Development as a Scientific, Applied, and Interdisciplinary Field

1. Human development is an *interdisciplinary field.* Explain what this means. (p. 5)

_____

_____

Basic Issues

1. What are the three elements of a good theory? (p. 5)

   A. _____   B. _____

   C. _____

2. Cite two reasons why theories are important to the study of human development. (p. 5)

   A. _____

   B. _____

3. True or False: Theories differ from opinion and belief in that they are subject to scientific verification. (p. 5)

4. Match each theoretical approach with the appropriate description: (pp. 6–7)

   _____ Considers development to be universal
   across individuals and across cultures
   _____ Views development as a process of
   gradually building on preexisting skills
   _____ Regards the environment as the most
   important influence on development
   _____ Considers human development in light of
   distinct contexts
   _____ Views development as a progression through
   a series of qualitatively distinct stages
   _____ Views heredity as the most important
   influence on development

   1. Multiple courses of development
   2. Single course of development
   3. Continuous development
   4. Discontinuous development
   5. Nature
   6. Nurture

The Lifespan Perspective: A Balanced Point of View

Development as Lifelong

1. True or False: Most modern theories of development take a strong position on controversial issues such as the nature–nurture debate. (p. 7)

2. Explain how gains in the average life expectancy have altered our view of human development. (pp. 7–8)

_____

_____

_____

3. Describe the lifespan perspective, noting four assumptions that make up this broader view of development. (pp. 8–12)

   A. _____

   B. _____

   C. _____

   D. _____

4. List the eight periods of the human development covered in your text. (p. 8)

   A. _____

   B. _____

   C. _____

   D. _____

   E. _____

   F. _____

   G. _____

   H. _____

5. Cite the three broad domains of development in which change takes place across the lifespan. (p. 8)

   A. _____   B. _____

   C. _____

Development as Multidimensional and Multidirectional

1. Explain how human development is both multidimensional and multidirectional. (p. 9)

   Multidimensional: _____

   _____

   Multidirectional: _____

   _____

Development as Highly Plastic

1. True or False: Lifespan researchers emphasize that development is highly plastic at all ages. Briefly explain your response. (pp. 9–10)

   _____

   _____

Development as Embedded in Multiple Contexts

1. Events that are strongly related to age and therefore fairly predictable in when they occur and how long they last are called _____ -*graded influences*. (p. 10)

2. _____ -graded influences explain why people born around the same time tend to be alike in ways that set them apart from people born at other times. Provide three examples of such influences. (p. 11)

   A. _____

   B. _____

   C. _____

3. What are *nonnormative influences*? (p. 11)

_____

_____

4. True or False: In contemporary adult development, nonnormative influences have become less powerful while age-graded influences have become more so. (pp. 11–12)

5. True or False: The lifespan perspective emphasizes multiple potential pathways and outcomes of development. (p. 12)

Biology & Environment: Resiliency

1. What is *resiliency*? (pp. 10–11)

_____

_____

2. Briefly list and describe four broad factors that appear to offer protection from the damaging effects of stressful life events. (pp. 10–11)

   A. _____

_____

_____

   B. _____

_____

_____

   C. _____

_____

_____

   D. _____

_____

_____

Historical Foundations

Philosophies of Childhood

1. Explain the concept of *preformationism*. (p. 13)

_____

_____

2. Describe the influence of Puritanism on child-rearing values and practices during the Reformation. (p. 13)

_____

_____

3. During the Enlightenment, the British philosopher John Locke regarded the child as a *tabula rasa,* which means
_____. Briefly explain his view. (p. 13)

_____

_____

_____

4. Summarize Locke's stance on each of the three basic issues of human development. (p. 13)

Continuous or discontinuous development? _____

_____

One course of development or many? _____

_____

Nature or nurture as more important? _____

_____

5. Jean Jacques Rousseau, a French philosopher during the Enlightenment, introduced the notion of children as *noble savages.* Explain what he meant by this term. (p. 13)

_____

_____

_____

6. Cite two influential concepts included in Rousseau's philosophy. (p. 13)

A. _____

B. _____

7. Describe some of the key differences in the theories put forth by John Locke and Jean Jacques Rousseau. (p. 13)

_____

_____

_____

Philosophies of Adulthood and Aging

1. What three areas of adult development were addressed by German philosopher John Nicolaus Tetens? (p. 14)

A. _____

B. _____

C. _____

2. Name the four periods of human development identified by German philosopher Friedrich August Carus. (p. 14)

A. _____   B. _____

C. _____   D. _____

3. True or False: Tetens and Carus viewed aging not only as decline, but also as progression. (p. 14)

Scientific Beginnings

1. Explain the two principles emphasized in Darwin's theory of evolution. (p. 14)

   A. _____

   _____

   B. _____

   _____

2. _____ is generally regarded as the founder of the child study movement. (p. 14)

3. The _____ *approach* to child development uses age-related averages to represent typical development. (pp. 14–15)

4. Who constructed the first successful intelligence test? (p. 15)

   _____

5. A translated version of this test was developed for use with American children. What is the name of this instrument? (p. 15) _____

Mid-Twentieth-Century Theories

The Psychoanalytic Perspective

1. True or False: The psychoanalytic perspective emphasizes understanding the unique life history of each person. (p. 15)

2. Summarize the basic tenants of the *psychoanalytic perspective.* (p. 15)

   _____

   _____

   _____

3. Freud's _____ *theory* emphasized that how parents manage their child's sexual and aggressive drives in the first few years of life is crucial for healthy personality development. (p. 15)

4. Name and briefly describe the three components of personality outlined in Freud's theory. (pp. 15–16)

   A. _____

   _____

   B. _____

   _____

   C. _____

   _____

5. Match each of the following stages of psychosexual development with the appropriate description: (p. 16)

_____ During this stage, sexual instincts die down   1. Genital
_____ Stage in which the infant desires sucking activities   2. Anal
_____ Stage in which the Oedipal and Electra conflicts take place   3. Oral
_____ Stage marked by mature sexuality   4. Latency
_____ Stage in which toilet training becomes a major issue   5. Phallic
            between parent and child

6. Cite two contributions of Freud's theory. (p. 16)

   A. _____

   B. _____

7. Discuss some of the criticisms of Freud's theory. (p. 16)

   _____

   _____

   _____

   _____

8. In what way did Erikson build upon and improve Freud's theory? (pp. 16–17)

   _____

   _____

   _____

9. Match each of Erikson's stages with the appropriate description: (p. 17)

_____ Successful resolution of this stage depends on the adult's   1. Industry vs. inferiority
            success at caring for other people and productive work   2. Autonomy vs. shame and doubt
_____ The primary task of this stage is the development of a sense of self   3. Intimacy vs. isolation
            and a sense of one's place in society   4. Identity vs. identity diffusion
_____ Successful resolution of this stage depends on a warm, loving 5. Basic trust vs. mistrust
            relationship with the caregiver   6. Generativity vs. stagnation
_____ In this stage, children experiment with adult roles through make-   7. Initiative vs. guilt
            believe play   8. Ego integrity vs. despair
_____ Successful resolution of this stage depends on parents granting the
            child reasonable opportunities for free choice
_____ In this stage, successful resolution involves reflecting on life's
            accomplishments
_____ The development of close relationships with others helps ensure
            successful resolution of this stage
_____ Children who develop the capacity for cooperation and productive
            work will successfully resolve this stage

10. Why is psychoanalytic theory no longer in the mainstream of human development research? (p. 17)

   _____

   _____

Behaviorism and Social Learning Theory

1. True or False: Behaviorism focuses on the inner workings of the mind. (p. 18)

2. Watson's study of little Albert, an 11-month-old baby who was taught to fear a white rat by associating it with a loud noise, supported Pavlov's concept of _____

   _____ . (p. 18)

3. Skinner, who proposed _____ *conditioning theory,* believed that behavior could be increased by following it with _____, such as food or praise, and decreased by following it with _____, such as disapproval or withdrawal of privileges. (p. 18)

4. Albert Bandura's *social learning theory* posits that children acquire both favorable and unfavorable behaviors through the process of _____, also known as imitation or observational learning. (p. 18)

5. Bandura's theory has been revised to include the importance of cognition, or thinking. Based upon this change, the theory is now referred to as a _____ *approach* rather than a social learning approach. Briefly explain this view of development. (pp. 18–19)

   _____

   _____

   _____

6. What two procedures are combined in *behavior modification* in order to eliminate undesirable behaviors and increase socially acceptable ones? (p. 19)

   A. _____

   B. _____

7. Discuss two limitations of behaviorism and social learning theory. (p. 19)

   A. _____

   _____

   B. _____

   _____

Piaget's Cognitive-Developmental Theory

1. Summarize the basic principles of Piaget's *cognitive-developmental theory.* (p. 19)

   _____

   _____

   _____

2. Define Piaget's notion of *adaptation.* (p. 19)

   _____

   _____

3. Match each of Piaget's stages with the appropriate description: (p. 20)

_____ During this stage, thought becomes more complex, and children develop the capacity for abstract reasoning
_____ This stage is characterized by the use of eyes, ears, and hands to explore the environment
_____ During this stage, children develop the capacity for abstract thought
_____ This stage is marked by the development of logical, organized reasoning skills

1. Sensorimotor
2. Preoperational
3. Concrete operational
4. Formal operational

4. What was Piaget's chief method for studying child and adolescent thought? (p. 19)

_____

5. Describe two major contributions of Piaget's theory. (p. 20)

A. _____

_____

B. _____

_____

6. Describe three recent challenges to Piaget's theory. (p. 20)

A. _____

_____

B. _____

_____

C. _____

_____

Recent Theoretical Perspectives

Information Processing

1. Briefly describe the *information-processing view* of human development. (p. 21)

_____

_____

_____

2. Information processing theorists use _____ to map the precise steps that individuals use to solve problems and complete tasks. (p. 21)

3. In what basic way are information processing and Piaget's theory alike? In what basic way are they different? (p. 21)

Alike: _____

Different: _____

4. Cite one strength and two limitations of the information-processing approach. (pp. 21–22)

Strength: _____

Limitation: _____

Limitation: _____

Ethology and Evolutionary Developmental Psychology

1. *Ethology* is the study of _____

_____ . (p. 22)

2. Name the two European zoologists who laid the modern foundations of ethology. (p. 22)

   A. _____

   B. _____

3. Contrast the notion of a *critical period* with that of a *sensitive period*. (p. 22)

   Critical period: _____

   _____

   _____

   Sensitive period: _____

   _____

   _____

4. Explain how John Bowlby used the principles of ethology to understand the infant-caregiver relationship. (p. 22)

   _____

   _____

   _____

   _____

5. Briefly explain what is studied in the field of *evolutionary developmental psychology*. (pp. 22–23)

   _____

   _____

   _____

Vygotsky's Sociocultural Theory

1. Cite one benefit of cross-cultural and multicultural research. (p. 23)

   _____

   _____

2. Explain the importance of social interaction according to Vygotsky's *sociocultural theory*. (p. 23)

   _____

   _____

   _____

3. Compare and contrast the theories of Piaget and Vygotsky. (p. 23)

_____

_____

_____

_____

_____

4. True or False: Because cultures select tasks for their members, individuals in every culture develop unique strengths not present in others. (pp. 23–24)

5. Vygotsky's emphasis on culture and social experience led him to neglect _____ contributions to development. (p. 24)

Ecological Systems Theory

1. Briefly explain Bronfenbrenner's *ecological systems theory*. (p. 24)

_____

_____

_____

2. Match each level of ecological systems theory with the appropriate description or example: (pp. 24–25)

_____ Relationship between the child's   1. Exosystem
            home and school   2. Microsystem
_____ The influence of cultural values   3. Mesosystem
_____ The parent's workplace   4. Macrosystem
_____ The child's interaction with parents

3. Provide examples of factors in each system that can enhance development. (pp. 24–25)

Microsystem: _____

Mesosystem: _____

Exosystem: _____

Macrosystem: _____

4. Describe Bronfenbrenner's notion of *bidirectional relationships* within the microsystem. (pp. 24–25)

_____

_____

_____

5. Bronfenbrenner's _____-*system* refers to temporal changes that affect development, such as the timing of the birth of a sibling. (p. 25)

6. True or False: In ecological systems theory, development is controlled by the interaction of environmental circumstances and inner dispositions. (p. 25)

Comparing and Evaluating Theories

1. Identify the stand that each of the following modern theories takes on the three basic issues of childhood and child development: (p. 26)

Theory	One Course of Development versus Many Courses of Development	Continuous versus Discontinuous Development	Nature versus Nurture
Psychoanalytic theory	_____	_____	_____
Behaviorism and social learning	_____	_____	_____
Piaget's cognitive-developmental theory	_____	_____	_____
Information processing	_____	_____	_____
Ethology	_____	_____	_____
Vygotsky's sociocultural perspective	_____	_____	_____
Dynamic systems theory	_____	_____	_____

Studying Development

1. Research usually begins with a _____, or a prediction about behavior drawn from a theory. (p. 27)

2. Distinguish between research methods and research designs. (p. 27)

    Research methods: _____

    _____

    Research designs: _____

    _____

Common Research Methods

1. Compare and contrast *naturalistic* and *structured observation* techniques, noting one strength and one limitation of each approach. (pp. 27–28)

    Naturalistic: _____

    _____

    Strength: _____

    Limitation: _____

Structured: _____

_____

   Strength: _____

   Limitation: _____

2. Explain how *clinical interviews* differ from *structured interviews,* and note the benefits of each technique. (pp. 28–29)

Clinical: _____

_____

   Benefits: _____

_____

Structured: _____

_____

   Benefits: _____

_____

3. Summarize the limitations of the clinical interview technique. (p. 29)

_____

_____

_____

4. True or False: Researchers can eliminate problems with inaccurate reporting (on the part of interviewees) by conducting structured interviews rather than clinical interviews. (p. 29)

5. Cite the primary aim of the *clinical method.* (p. 29)

_____

6. The clinical method has been used to find out what contributes to the accomplishments of _____ — extremely gifted children who attain the competence of an adult in a particular field before age 10. (p. 29)

7. Discuss the drawbacks of using the clinical method. (p. 29)

_____

_____

_____

8. _____ is a research method aimed at understanding a culture or distinct social group. This goal is achieved through _____, a technique in which the researcher lives with the cultural community and participates in all aspects of daily life. (p. 30)

9. Cite two limitations of the ethnographic method. (p. 30)

A. · _____

_____

B. _____

_____

1. What is the primary aim of the Access Program? (p. 28)

_____

2. Explain how the program uses collaboration between schools, students, and parents to meet its objectives. (p. 28)

_____

_____

_____

_____

_____

3. True or False: Research findings show that the program was effective in helping participating adolescents gain access to a college education. (p. 28)

4. Explain how the Access Program illustrates the ability of researchers to assist communities in making programs more effective. (p. 28)

_____

_____

_____

_____

Cultural Influences: Immigrant Youths: Amazing Adaptation

1. True or False: Students who are first-generation (foreign-born) and second-generation (American-born with immigrant parents) achieve in school as well or better than do students of native-born parents. (p. 30)

2. Compared with their agemates, adolescents from immigrant families are (more / less) likely to commit delinquent and violent acts, to use drugs and alcohol, and to have early sex. (p. 30)

3. Discuss two ways in which family and community exert an influence on the academic achievement of adolescents from immigrant families. (pp. 30–31)

   A. _____

   _____

   B. _____

   _____

General Research Designs

1. Describe the basic features of the *correlational design.* (p. 31)

_____

_____

_____

2. True or False: The correlational design is preferred by researchers because it allows them to infer cause and effect. Explain your answer. (p. 32)

_____

_____

_____

3. Investigators examine relationships among variables using a(n) _____, a number that describes how two measures, or variables, are associated with one another. (p. 32)

4. A *correlation coefficient* can range from _____ to _____. The magnitude of the number shows the (strength / direction) of the relationship between the two variables, whereas the sign indicates the (strength / direction) of the relationship. (p. 32)

5. For a correlation coefficient, a positive sign means that as one variable increases, the other (increases / decreases); a negative sign indicates that as one variable increases, the other (increases / decreases). (p. 32)

6. A researcher determines that the correlation between warm, consistent parenting and child delinquency is -.80. Explain what this indicates about the relationship between these two variables. (p. 32)

_____

_____

7. If the same researcher had found a correlation of +.45, what would this have indicated about the relationship between warm, consistent parenting and child delinquency? (p. 32)

_____

_____

8. What is the primary distinction between a *correlational design* and an *experimental design*? (pp. 32–33)

_____

_____

9. The _____ *variable* is anticipated by the researcher to cause changes in the _____ *variable.* (p. 33)

10. What feature of an experimental design enables researchers to infer a cause-and-effect relationship between the variables? (p. 33)

_____

_____

11. By using _____ *assignment* of participants to treatment conditions, investigators are able to control for characteristics that could reduce the accuracy of their findings. (p. 33)

12. In _____ *experiments,* researchers randomly assign people to treatment conditions in natural settings. (p. 33)

13. True or False: Natural experiments differ from correlational research in that groups of participants are carefully chosen to ensure that their characteristics are as much alike as possible. (p. 33)

Designs for Studying Development

1. In a _____ *design,* a group of participants is studied repeatedly at different ages, and changes are noted as the participants mature. (p. 34)

2. List two advantages of the longitudinal design. (p. 34)

A. _____

_____

B. _____

_____

3. Describe three problems in conducting longitudinal research. (p. 35)

A. _____

_____

B. _____

_____

C. _____

_____

4. Describe the *cross-sectional design.* (p. 35)

_____

_____

5. In cross-sectional designs, researchers (do / do not) need to worry about participant dropout and practice effects. (p. 35)

6. Describe two problems associated with conducting cross-sectional research. (p. 35)

A. _____

_____

B. _____

_____

7. In the _____ *design*, researchers merge longitudinal and cross-sectional research strategies. List two advantages of this design. (p. 35)

A. _____

_____

B. _____

_____

A Lifespan Vista: The Impact of Historical Times on the Life Course: The Great Depression and World War II

1. During the Great Depression, adolescent (boys / girls / boys and girls) became increasingly focused on college and career aspirations. (p. 36)

2. Cite evidence suggesting that cultural-historic events have a differential impact, depending on the age at which they take place. (p. 36)

_____

_____

_____

1. Describe participants' research rights. (p. 38)

    A. Protection from harm: _____

    _____

    B. Informed consent: _____

    _____

    C. Privacy: _____

    _____

    D. Knowledge of results: _____

    _____

    E. Beneficial treatments: _____

    _____

2. For children _____ years and older, their own informed consent should be obtained in addition to parental consent prior to participation in research. (p. 38)

3. True or False: Like children, most older adults require more than the usual informed consent procedures. (p. 38)

4. In _____, the investigator provides a full account and justification of research activities to participants in a study in which deception was used. (p. 39)

ASK YOURSELF...

For *Ask Yourself* questions for this chapter, please log on to the Companion Website at www.ablongman.com/berk.

1. Select the Companion Website for *Development Through the Lifespan*, Third Edition.

2. Use the "Jump to" menu to go directly to this chapter.

3. From the menu on the left side of your screen, select *Ask Yourself*.

4. Complete questions and choose "Submit answers for grading" or "Clear answers" to start over.

SUGGESTED STUDENT READINGS

Cavanaugh, J. C., & Whitbourne, S. K. (1999). *Gerontology: An interdisciplinary perspective.* New York: Oxford University Press. Provides a thorough, broad-based survey of current knowledge on aging. Includes chapters on theory, research methods, physical changes, physical and mental health, cognition, self and personality, work and retirement, and dying and bereavement.

Goldhaber, D.E. (2000). *Theories of human development: integrative perspectives.* Mountain View, CA: Mayfield. Presents an extensive summary and critique of historical and current developmental theories, including Bandura's social–cognitive theory, Piaget's cognitive–developmental theory, Freud's and Erikson's psychoanalytic theories, social learning theory, information processing, ethology, Vygotsky's sociocultural theory, and the lifespan perspective.

Werner, E. E., & Smith, R. S. (2001). *Journals from childhood to midlife: Risk, resilience, and recovery.* New York: Cornell University Press. One of the most comprehensive studies of resiliency to date, this book presents findings from 40 years of data collection on a group of 700 infants born in 1955. Results indicated that although one-third of the participants experienced poverty, domestic conflict, and prenatal drug abuse in childhood, only one-sixth had severe psychological problems in adulthood. Factors related to resiliency included continuing education, vocational training, military service, religious affiliation, and a satisfying marital relationship.

PUZZLE 1.1 TERM REVIEW

Across

4. _____ savage: Rousseau's view of the child as naturally endowed with a sense of right and wrong and an innate plan for orderly, healthy growth
5. Freud's _____ theory emphasizes management of early sexual and aggressive drives.
6. Piaget's _____-developmental theory suggests that children actively construct knowledge as they manipulate and explore their world.
8. _____ influences: events that are irregular in that they happen to one or a few people and do not follow a predictable timetable
9. In ecological systems theory, temporal changes in children's environments
12. View of development in which new ways of understanding and responding to the world emerge at specific times
13. _____ perspective: approach to personality development introduced by Freud; assumes that children move through a series of stages in which they confront conflicts between biological and social expectations
14. Approach that emphasizes the study of directly observable behavior
16. Nature- _____ controversy: disagreement about whether genetic or environmental circumstances are more important determinants of development

Down

1. Erikson 's _____ theory of development focuses on resolution of psychological conflicts over the lifespan.
2. _____ approach: age-related averages are computed to represent typical development
3. View of development as gradually adding on more of the same types of skills that were there to begin with
5. Medieval view of the child as a miniature adult
7. _____ perspective: assumes that development is lifelong, multidimensional, highly plastic, and embedded in multiple contexts
10. _____-graded influences: explain why people born around the same time tend to be alike in ways that distinguish them from people born at other times
11. Genetically determined, naturally unfolding course of growth
15. _____ development: field of study devoted to understanding constancy and change throughout the lifespan

PUZZLE 1.2 TERM REVIEW

Across

1. In ecological systems theory, cultural values, laws, customs, and resources that influence experiences and interactions at inner levels of the environment

4. In ecological systems theory, activities and interaction patterns in the child's immediate surroundings

7. _____ systems theory: views the child as developing within a complex system of relationships affected by multiple levels of the environment

8. _____ learning theory: emphasizes the role of modeling in the development of behavior

10. In ecological systems theory, connections between the child's immediate settings

11. Approach concerned with the adaptive value of behavior and its evolutionary history

15. Participant observation of a culture

16. Tabula _____: Locke's view of the child as a blank slate whose character is shaped by experience

17. _____ interview method: uses a flexible, conversational style

Down

2. Vygotsky's _____ theory focuses on how social interaction contributes to development.

3. A qualitative change in thinking, feeling, and behaving that characterizes a specific period of development

5. _____ period: time that is optimal for certain capacities to emerge and in which the individual is especially responsive to environmental influences

6. In ecological systems theory, social settings that do not contain children but nevertheless affect their experiences in immediate settings

9. Information _____: approach that views the human mind as a symbol-manipulating system through which information flows

12. The ability to adapt effectively in the face of threats to development

13. An orderly, integrated set of statements that describes, explains, and predicts behavior

14. Effects of cultural-historical change on the accuracy of findings

PUZZLE 1.3 TERM REVIEW

Across

2. Variable expected to be influenced by the experimental manipulations
5. A number describing how two variables are related is called a correlation _____ .
7. Structured _____: research method in which the researcher evokes the behavior of interest in a laboratory setting
8. _____ observation: researcher goes into the natural environment to observe the behavior of interest
10. Design in which the researcher randomly assigns participants to two or more treatment conditions; permits inferences about cause and effect
12. Design in which one group of paticipants is studied repeatedly at different ages
13. Unique combinations of genetic and environmental circumstances that can result in markedly different paths of development
14. Design in which the researcher gathers information without altering the participants' experience

Down

1. Variable manipulated by the researcher
3. _____ assignment: even-handed procedure for assigning participants to treatment conditions
4. Longitudinal- _____ design: participants born in different years are followed over time
6. _____ - _____ design: groups of people differing in age are studied at the same point in time
9. Interview method in which the researcher asks all participants the same questions in the same way
11. _____ , or case study, method

PRACTICE TEST #1

1. Our knowledge of human development is *interdisciplinary*. What does this mean? (p. 5)
   a. Our knowledge of human development is based exclusively on research conducted by people in the field of human development.
   b. Human development is not recognized as a distinct field of study.
   c. Individuals from diverse fields have contributed to our knowledge of human development.
   d. Human development is part of a larger discipline known as developmental psychology.

2. An orderly, integrated set of statements that describes, explains, and predicts behavior is a (p. 5)
   a. strategy.
   b. theory.
   c. hypothesis.
   d. design.

3. According to the lifespan perspective (p. 8)
   a. early childhood has a supreme impact on the life course relative to all other periods of development.
   b. development is limited to improved performance (with no consideration of decline).
   c. development is plastic at all ages.
   d. pathways of developmental change are universal across individuals and cultures.

4. Rousseau's theory, which regarded children as noble savages, stressed that (pp. 13–14)
   a. children are blank slates to be filled with adult instruction.
   b. children do little to shape their own destiny.
   c. parents should use harsh, restrictive parenting practices to manage child behavior.
   d. children are innately endowed with a sense of right and wrong and a plan for orderly, healthy growth.

5. Which of the following theorists emphasized the concepts of natural selection and survival of the fittest? (p. 14)
   a. Locke
   b. Rousseau
   c. Gesell
   d. Darwin

6. In the normative approach to child study, researchers (pp. 14–15)
   a. jot down day-to-day descriptions and impressions of a youngster's behavior beginning in early infancy.
   b. take measures of behavior on large numbers of children and then compute age-related averages to represent typical development.
   c. investigate children's cognitive development through the use of clinical interviews, in which children describe their thinking.
   d. use flowcharts to map the precise steps that individuals take to solve problems and complete tasks.

7. Which of the following theories is noted for its focus on the unique developmental history of each individual? (p. 15)
   a. behaviorism
   b. social learning theory
   c. psychoanalytic theory
   d. information processing

8. Erikson's psychosocial theory (p. 17)
    a. strictly refuted Freud's psychosexual theory.
    b. emphasized that the ego acquires attitudes and skills that make the individual an active, contributing member of society.
    c. failed to account for the influence of culture on developmental outcomes.
    d. focused on modeling, or imitation, as a powerful source of development.

9. During Piaget's _____ stage, children's reasoning becomes logical, and they develop the ability to organize objects into hierarchies of classes and subclasses. (p. 19)
    a. sensorimotor
    b. preoperational
    c. concrete operational
    d. formal operational

10. New evidence challenging Piaget's theory suggests that he (p. 20)
    a. overestimated the competencies of young children.
    b. underestimated the competencies of young children.
    c. overestimated the importance of direct teaching in cognitive development.
    d. used overly simplified measures in his studies of cognitive development.

11. Which of the following theories is concerned with the adaptive value of behavior and its evolutionary significance? (p. 22)
    a. ethology
    b. ecological systems theory
    c. sociocultural theory
    d. bioecological theory

12. Evolutionary developmental psychology is the study of (p. 22)
    a. wide diversity in pathways of change.
    b. the adaptive value of species-wide cognitive, emotional, and social competencies as those competencies change over time.
    c. how culture is transmitted from one generation to the next.
    d. children's ability to adapt in the face of threats to development.

13. According to _____, cognitive development is a socially mediated process. (p. 23)
    a. Piaget
    b. Vygotsky
    c. Freud
    d. Bowlby

14. To understand human development at the level of the *microsystem,* one must keep in mind that all relationships are (p. 24)
    a. universal.
    b. unidirectional.
    c. predetermined.
    d. bidirectional.

15. Jennifer's mother volunteers as a room mother. This connection between home and school illustrates Bronfenbrenner's (pp. 24–25)
    a. mesosystem.
    b. exosystem.
    c. microsystem.
    d. macrosystem.

16. A researcher interested in the development of aggression in young children goes into a preschool. She keeps a record of all aggressive acts occurring during her time in the classroom. This is an example of (p. 27)
    a. structured observation.
    b. naturalistic observation.
    c. case study
    d. field experiment.

17. Ethnography aims to understand a culture or distinct social group through (p. 30)
    a. structured observation.
    b. case study reports.
    c. participant observation.
    d. clinical interviews with members of the group.

18. In a correlational design, researchers (p. 31)
    a. gather information on already existing groups of individuals, generally in natural life circumstances.
    b. randomly assign participants to various treatment groups.
    c. examine the behavior of interest in a laboratory setting.
    d. establish causal associations between variables.

19. In a study of the association between parental warmth and children's mental health, an investigator finds a correlation of +.31. What does this correlation coefficient indicate about the relationship between these two variables? (p. 32)
    a. As parental warmth increases, children's mental health also increases.
    b. As parental warmth increases, children's mental health decreases.
    c. There is a strong relationship between parental warmth and children's mental health.
    d. There is almost no relationship between parental warmth and children's mental health.

20. An experimental design permits inferences about cause and effect because (p. 33)
    a. experimental studies are conducted in natural settings rather than laboratory settings.
    b. the researcher controls changes in the independent variable.
    c. the researcher controls changes in the dependent variable.
    d. the researcher systematically assigns participants to specific treatment conditions based on their known characteristics.

PRACTICE TEST #2

1. Stage theories conform to which of the following perspectives on development? (p. 6)
    a. nature
    b. nurture
    c. continuous
    d. discontinuous

2. Tetens was ahead of his time in recognizing that (p. 14)
   a. intellectual declines in old age may reflect hidden gains.
   b. events occurring during childhood have little influence on adult development.
   c. aging is a process of progression in all domains.
   d. adult's thinking is qualitatively different than children's.

3. Which of the following is an example of a history-graded influence on development? (p. 11)
   a. The Great Depression of the 1930s
   b. an inspiring teacher
   c. menopause
   d. getting a driver's license at age 16

4. An important concept emphasized by Darwin that eventually found its way into important mid-twentieth century theories is that of (p. 14)
   a. natural, instinctive mother-infant bonding.
   b. the tendency of animal species to become extinct over time.
   c. the adaptive value of physical characteristics and behavior.
   d. the lack of variation within each species which enables it to survive.

5. The first successful intelligence test, developed by Alfred Binet, was important because it (p. 15)
   a. resolved the nature versus nurture debate on human intelligence.
   b. increased interest in individual differences in development.
   c. was a culturally unbiased measure of intellectual ability.
   d. showed that intelligence is a poor predictor of school achievement.

6. An approach that emphasizes the role of modeling, or observational learning, in the development of behavior is known as (p. 18)
   a. psychosocial theory.
   b. social learning theory.
   c. cognitive-developmental theory.
   d. behaviorism.

7. According to Piaget's theory, each stage of development is characterized by (p. 19)
   a. advances in motor development.
   b. increased capacity to process information.
   c. a distinct psychosocial crisis.
   d. qualitatively distinct ways of thinking.

8. Information processing is interested in (p. 21)
   a. the stages through which all people acquire cognitive skills.
   b. reinforcement and modeling to promote learning.
   c. the precise series of steps people use to solve problems and complete tasks.
   d. concepts of assimilation and accommodation to explain cognitive change.

9. _____ observation permits greater control over the research situation than does naturalistic observation. (p. 27)
   a. Clinical
   b. Correlational
   c. Longitudinal
   d. Structured

10. The clinical, or case study method (p. 28)
    a. asks each participant the same set of questions in the same way.
    b. brings together a wide range of information on one person.
    c. is well suited to studying large numbers of individuals.
    d. targets observable behaviors rather than subjective reports of thoughts, feelings, and experiences.

11. One strength of ethnography is that it (p. 30)
    a. provides a more thorough and accurate description of a culture than can be derived from a single observation.
    b. reduces the extent to which the researchers' presence alters the research situation.
    c. relies on careful, systematic experimentation.
    d. yields results that can be generalized to many cultures.

12. A major limitation of correlational research is that it (p. 32)
    a. rarely examines behavior in natural contexts.
    b. does not provide information about the strength of the relationship between the variables under study.
    c. relies heavily on random assignment of participants to treatment conditions.
    d. does not enable the researcher to infer cause and effect.

13. A number that describes how two variables are related is called a (p. 32)
    a. correlation coefficient.
    b. summation.
    c. standard deviation.
    d. variance.

14. In which of the following research designs do investigators capitalize on rare opportunities to randomly assign people to treatment conditions in natural settings? (p. 33)
    a. field experiments
    b. natural experiments
    c. laboratory experiments
    d. cross-sectional studies

15. A researcher is interested in studying peer relationships. He recruits a sample of kindergarten children and examines changes in their relationships with peers over the next ten years. This is an example of a (p. 34)
    a. cross-sectional design.
    b. longitudinal-sequential design.
    c. microgenetic design.
    d. longitudinal design.

16. A researcher concludes that 5-year-olds in the 1950s learned more slowly than 5-year-olds today. Which of the following is responsible for this finding? (p. 35)
    a. biased sampling
    b. investigator bias
    c. cohort effects
    d. selective attrition

17. In a _____ design, groups of people differing in age are studied at the same point in time. (p. 35)
    a. longitudinal
    b. cross-sectional
    c. longitudinal-sequential
    d. microgenetic

18. An advantage of the longitudinal-sequential design is that it (p. 35)
    a. allows researchers to infer cause-and-effect relationships.
    b. eliminates problems caused by practice effects.
    c. allows researchers to determine the presence of cohort effects.
    d. prevents participants from dropping out of the study.

19. How did the Great Depression of the 1930s affect development? (p. 36)
    a. Adolescent boys spent more time close to home.
    b. Adolescent girls were more likely to postpone marriage.
    c. Children showed a higher rate of emotional difficulties.
    d. More adolescents of both sexes were likely to enroll in college.

20. Which of the following is true of research rights involving informed consent? (p. 38)
    a. The right to informed consent applies to all research participants except young children and elderly people with mental impairments.
    b. In most cases, researchers need only obtain the child's consent; parental consent is not required.
    c. For children 7 years and older, their own informed consent should be obtained in addition to parental consent.
    d. Unless the research obviously risks harm to the participant, researchers are not required to obtain informed consent.

CHAPTER 2
BIOLOGICAL AND ENVIRONMENTAL FOUNDATIONS

BRIEF CHAPTER SUMMARY

This chapter takes a close look at the foundations of development: heredity and environment. The discussion of development begins at the moment of conception, an event that establishes the hereditary makeup of the new individual. At conception, chromosomes containing genetic information from each parent combine to determine characteristics that make us human and contribute to individual differences in appearance and behavior. Several different patterns of inheritance are involved, ensuring that each individual will be unique. Serious developmental problems are often caused by the inheritance of harmful recessive genes and chromosomal abnormalities. Fortunately, genetic counseling and prenatal diagnostic methods make early detection of genetic problems possible.

Just as complex as heredity are the environments in which human development takes place. The family has an especially powerful impact on development, operating as a complex social system in which members exert direct, indirect, and third-party influences on one another. Family functioning and individual well-being are influenced considerably by child-rearing practices as well as poverty and homelessness. The quality of community life in neighborhoods, schools, towns, and cities, also affects children and adults' development. Cultural values, as well as laws and government programs, shape experiences in all of these contexts.

Some researchers believe it is useful and possible to determine "how much" heredity and environment contribute to individual differences. Others think that the effects of heredity and environment cannot be clearly separated. They want to discover how these two major determinants of development work together in a complex, dynamic interplay.

LEARNING OBJECTIVES

After reading this chapter, you should be able to:

2.1   Describe the relationship between phenotypes and genotypes. (p. 44)

2.2   Explain the function of chromosomes. (p. 44)

2.3   Describe the structure of the DNA molecule, and explain the process of mitosis. (pp. 44–45)

2.4   Explain the process of meiosis. (p. 45)

2.5   Explain how the sex of the new individual is determined. (p. 46)

2.6   Identify two types of twins, and explain how each is created. (p. 46)

2.7   Describe basic patterns of genetic inheritance, and indicate how harmful genes are created. (pp. 46–50)

2.8   Explain genetic imprinting, noting how it helps researchers understand certain puzzling genetic patterns. (p. 49)

2.9   Describe Down syndrome and common abnormalities of the sex chromosomes. (pp. 50–52)

2.10 Discuss reproductive choices available to prospective parents and the controversies surrounding them. (pp. 51–57)

2.11 Explain genetic counseling, and indicate who is likely to seek this service. (p. 52)

2.12 Describe prenatal diagnosis and fetal medicine. (pp. 52–53)

2.13 Summarize research on adoption. (pp. 56–57)

2.14 Describe family functioning from the perspective of ecological systems theory, including direct and indirect influences and the family as a dynamic, changing system. (pp. 58–59)

2.15 Discuss the impact of socioeconomic status and poverty on family functioning. (pp. 59–61)

2.16 Summarize the roles of neighborhoods, towns, and cities in the lives of children and adults. (pp. 61–62)

2.17 Explain how cultural values and practices, public policies, and political and economic conditions affect human development. (pp. 62–66)

2.18 Describe and evaluate methods researchers use to determine "how much" heredity and environment influence complex human characteristics. (pp. 66–68)

2.19 Describe concepts that indicate "how" heredity and environment work together to influence complex human characteristics. (pp. 68–71)

STUDY QUESTIONS

1. _____ are directly observable characteristics that depend in part on the individual's
_____, the complex blend of genetic information that determines our species and influences
all of our unique characteristics. (p. 44)

Genetic Foundations

1. Rodlike structures in the nucleus of a cell that store and transmit genetic information are called
_____. (p. 44)

The Genetic Code

1. Chromosomes are made of a chemical substance called _____ . It looks like a twisted ladder and is
composed of segments called _____ . (p. 44)

2. A unique feature of DNA is that it can duplicate itself through a process called _____. (p. 45)

The Sex Cells

1. New individuals are created when two special cells called _____, or
_____ combine. (p. 45)

2. Gametes are formed through a cell-division process called _____, which ensures that a
constant quantity of genetic material is transmitted from one generation to the next. (p. 45)

3. A _____ is the cell that results when a sperm and ovum unite at conception. (p. 45)

4. True or False: Sex cells are unique in that they contain only 23 chromosomes. (p. 45)

Male or Female?

1. The 22 matching pairs of chromosomes are called _____ . The 23rd is made up of the
_____ *chromosomes*. (p. 46)

Multiple Births

1. Match each of the following terms with the appropriate description. (p. 46)

    _____ The frequency of this type of multiple birth is about 3 out of every 1000 births

    _____ The most common type of multiple birth

    _____ Genetically no more alike than ordinary siblings

    _____ Genetically identical

    1. Fraternal or dizygotic twins
    2. Identical or monozygotic twins

2. True or False: Children of single births are often healthier and develop more rapidly than twins in the early years. (p. 46)

Patterns of Genetic Inheritance

1. If the genes from both parents are alike, the child is _____ and will display the inherited trait. If they are different, then the child is _____, and relationships between the genes determine the trait that will appear. (p. 46)

2. Give an example of a characteristic representing dominant–recessive inheritance. _____ (p. 46)

3. One of the most frequently occurring recessive disorders is _____, which affects the way the body breaks down proteins contained in many foods. What determines how well children with this disorder develop? (p. 47)

    _____.

4. Why are serious diseases only rarely due to dominant genes? Explain why Huntington disease is a dominant disorder which has survived. (p. 47)

    A. _____

    _____

    B. _____

    _____

5. _____ is a pattern of inheritance in which both genes influence the individual's characteristics. Under what conditions is the sickle cell trait expressed by heterozygous individuals? (p. 47)

    _____

    _____.

6. True or False: Males are more likely to be affected by X-linked inheritance than are females. (p. 49)

7. Name two X-linked disorders. (p. 49)

    A. _____   B. _____

8. Describe *genetic imprinting.* (p. 49)

    _____

    _____

9. How are harmful genes created? (pp. 49–50)

    _____

10. Characteristics, such as height, weight, intelligence, and personality reflect _____, in which many genes determine the characteristic in question. (p. 50)

Chromosomal Abnormalities

1. _____, the most common chromosomal abnormality, often results from a defect in the 21st chromosome. (p. 50)

2. List the consequences of Down syndrome, and cite factors that promote favorable development among children with Down syndrome. (pp. 50–51)

    A. _____

    _____

    B. _____

    _____

3. In contrast to autosomal disorders, sex chromosomal disorders often go undetected until _____ . (p. 51)

4. Describe one myth about individuals with sex chromosomal disorders. (p. 51)

    _____

    _____

Reproductive Choices

Genetic Counseling

1. What is the purpose of genetic counseling, and who is most likely to seek this service? (p. 52)

    _____

    _____

    _____

2. What is the function of a pedigree in genetic counseling? (p. 52)

    _____

    _____

Prenatal Diagnosis and Fetal Medicine

1. Which two prenatal diagnostic methods are frequently used with women of advanced maternal age? (p. 52)

    A. _____

    B. _____

2. What complications are frequently associated with prenatal diagnosis and fetal medicine? (p. 53)

    _____

    _____

    _____

3. Advances in genetic _____ offer hope for correcting heredity defects. (p. 53)

Genetic Testing

1. Describe the risks and benefits associated with genetic testing. (p. 56)

    Risks: _____

    _____

    Benefits: _____

    _____

2. True or False: Experts in medical ethics recommend that genetic testing be offered to all individuals planning to conceive. (p. 56)

Adoption

1. List three possible reasons that adopted children have more learning and emotional difficulties than other children. (pp. 56–57)

    A. _____

    B. _____

    C. _____

2. True or False: Most adoptees appear well adjusted as adults. (p. 57)

Social Issues: The Pros and Cons of Reproductive Technologies

1. Explain the following reproductive technologies. (p. 54)

    Donor Insemination: _____

    _____

    _____

    In Vitro Fertilization: _____

    _____

    _____

2. Discuss some of the concerns surrounding the use of donor insemination and in vitro fertilization. (p. 54)

    _____

    _____

    _____

    _____

3. Cite at least two risks involved with surrogate motherhood. (p. 54)

_____

_____

_____

_____

_____

Environmental Contexts for Development

The Family

1. Distinguish between direct and indirect family influences. (pp. 58–59)

   Direct: _____

   _____

   Indirect: _____

   _____

2. Explain how important events and historical time period contribute to the dynamic, ever-changing nature of the family. (p. 59)

   _____

   _____

Socioeconomic Status and Family Functioning

1. What are the three interrelated variables that define socioeconomic status (SES)? (p. 59)

   _____

2. How does SES affect the timing and duration of phases of the family life cycle? (p. 59)

   _____

   _____

   _____

3. Describe the influence of SES on parenting practices and parent–child interaction. (pp. 59–60)

   _____

   _____

   _____

4. Explain how life conditions, such as parental stress and education, contribute to SES differences in family interaction. (pp. 59–60)

   _____

   _____

   _____

The Impact of Poverty

1. What two groups are hit hardest by poverty? (p. 60)

    A. _____   B. _____

2. Summarize developmental consequences associated with homeless children. (p. 61)

    _____

    _____

Beyond the Family: Neighborhoods, Towns, and Cities

1. True or False: Dissatisfaction with one's community is associated with increased child abuse and neglect. (p. 61)

2. Explain why neighborhood resources have a greater impact on economically disadvantaged than well-to-do children and adolescents. (p. 61)

    _____

    _____

    _____

3. Describe how neighborhoods affect adult's well-being (p. 61)

    _____

    _____

    _____

4. Summarize the benefits and drawbacks of living in a small town (p. 62)

    Benefits: _____

    _____

    Drawbacks: _____

    _____

5. Why is community life especially undermined in high-rise urban housing projects? (p. 62)

    _____

    _____

    _____

    _____

The Cultural Context

1. What are *subcultures*? (p. 62)

    _____

    _____

2. In _____ societies, people define themselves as part of a group and stress group over individual goals. In _____ societies, people think of themselves as separate entities and are largely concerned with their own personal needs. (p. 63)

3. What are public policies? How does the United States compare to other industrialized nations in terms of public policies designed to protect children and the elderly? (pp. 63–65)

   A. _____

   B. _____

4. List three reasons that the United States has not yet created conditions that protect the development of children. (p. 64)

   A. _____

   B. _____

   C. _____

5. True or False: Among developed nations, the United States serves as a forerunner in the development of public policies for the elderly. (p. 64)

6. Explain why many senior citizens experience substantial economic difficulties. (p. 65)

   _____

   _____

   _____

7. How has the number of aging poor changed since 1960, and how are the elderly in the United States faring in comparison to those in Australia, Canada, and Western Europe? (p. 65)

   A. _____

   B. _____

8. List the activities of the Children's Defense Fund. (p. 65)

   _____

   _____

   _____

9. List the activities of the American Association of Retired Persons. (p. 66)

   _____

   _____

   _____

Cultural Influences: The African-American Extended Family

1. Cite characteristics of the African-American extended family that help reduce the stress of poverty and single parenthood. (p. 63)

   _____

   _____

   _____

2. How does the extended family help transmit African-American culture? (p. 63)

    _____

    _____

    _____

Understanding the Relationship Between Heredity and Environment

The Question, "How Much?"

1. Describe two methods used to infer the role of heredity in complex human characteristics. (p. 67)

    A. _____

    _____

    B. _____

    _____

2. Heritability estimates are obtained from _____ *studies,* which compare characteristics of family members. (p.67)

3. True or False: Among children and adolescents, heritability estimates for intelligence and personality are approximately .50, indicating that genetic makeup can explain half of the variance in these traits. (p. 67)

4. A concordance rate of 0 means that if one twin has a trait, the other one (always / never) has it. A concordance rate of 100 means that if one twin has a trait, the other one (always / never) has it. (p. 67)

5. List three limitations of heritability estimates and concordance rates. (p. 68)

    A. _____

    B. _____

    C. _____

The Question, "How?"

1. Describe *range of reaction* and *canalization.* (pp. 68–69)

    A. Range of reaction: _____

    _____

    _____

    B. Canalization: _____

    _____

    _____

2. Match the following types of genetic–environmental correlations with their appropriate descriptors. (p. 69)

_____ Children increasingly seek out environments that fit their genetic tendencies (called niche-picking).

_____ A child's style of responding influences others' responses, which then strengthen the child's original style.

_____ Parents provide an environment consistent with their own heredity.

1. Passive correlation
2. Evocative correlation
3. Active correlation

3. True or False: Partially as a result of niche-picking, identical twins become more similar and fraternal twins and adopted siblings become less similar in intelligence with age. (p. 69)

4. _____ means development resulting from ongoing, bidirectional exchanges between heredity and all levels of the environment. (p. 71)

5. What is the major reason that researchers are interested in the nature–nurture issue? (p. 71)

Biology & Environment: Uncoupling Genetic–Environmental Correlations for Mental Illness and Antisocial Behavior

1. According to research, under what circumstances are adoptees likely to develop mental illness? (p. 70)

ASK YOURSELF...

For *Ask Yourself* questions for this chapter, please log on to the Companion Website at www.ablongman.com/berk.

1. Select the Companion Website for *Development Through the Lifespan,* Third Edition.

2. Use the "Jump to" menu to go directly to this chapter.

3. From the menu on the left side of your screen, select *Ask Yourself.*

4. Complete questions and choose "Submit answers for grading" or "Clear answers" to start over.

SUGGESTED STUDENT READINGS

Bornstein, M. H. (Ed.). (2002). *Handbook of parenting: Volume 4: Social conditions and applied parenting (2nd ed.).* Mahwah, NJ: Lawrence Erlbaum Associates. A collection of chapters focusing on social conditions, such as cultural values and beliefs, that influence parenting practices. In addition, this book presents practical and applied advice for successful parenting.

Elder, K., & Dale, B. (2000). *In vitro fertilization.* New York: Cambridge University Press. Describes the most recent additions to the range of current assisted reproductive technology (ART) clinical treatments, including the use of testicular and epididymal sperm, blastocyst stage transfer, and new perspectives on cryobiology and cryopreservation techniques.

Segal, N. L. (1999). *Entwined lives: Twins and what they tell us about behavior.* New York: Dutton/Penguin Books. Presents a compelling account of the unique behavioral and physical development of twins. The author covers topics, such as the unusual language patterns of twins, the role of fertility treatment in twin conceptions, the loss of a twin through death, and how conjoined twins interact on a daily basis.

PUZZLE 2.1 TERM REVIEW

Across

2. The genetic makeup of an individual
6. The process of cell duplication
8. Human sperm and ova
12. Pattern of inheritance in which, under heterozygous conditions, the influence of only one allele is apparent
13. Long, double-stranded molecules that make up chromosomes (abbr.)
14. A segment of DNA along the length of a chromosome
15. The process of cell division
16. Directly observable characteristics
17. _____ chromosomes: the 23rd pair of chromosomes; XX in females, XY in males
18. A sudden but permanent change in a segment of DNA
19. The 22 matching chromosome pairs in each cell

Down

1. Pattern of inheritance in which many genes determine the characteristic in question
3. Development resulting from ongoing bidirectional exchanges between heredity and all levels of the environment
4. Pattern of inheritance in which both alleles influence the person's characteristics
5. Pattern of inheritance in which a recessive gene is carred on the X chromosome.
7. Rodlike structures in the cell nucleus that store and transmit genetic information
9. Genetic _____: alleles are chemically marked in such a way that one pair member is activated, regardless of its makeup
10. Having two identical alleles at the same place on a pair or chromosomes
11. Having two different alleles at the same place on a pair of chromosomes

PUZZLE 2.2 TERM REVIEW

Across

2. _____ policies: laws and government programs aimed at improving current conditions

4. _____ diagnostic methods are medical procedures that permit detection of developmental problems before birth.

6. In an _____-family household, the parent and child live with one or more adult relatives.

9. Each person's unique, genetically determined response to a range of environmental conditions (3 words)

13. Genetic- _____ correlation: idea that heredity influences the environments to which individuals are exposed

14. _____ counseling: helps couples assess the likelihood of giving birth to a baby with a hereditary disorder and choose the best course of action in light of the risks and family goals

15. Group of people with beliefs and customs that differ from those of the larger culture

16. In _____ societies, people define themselves as part of a group and stress group over individual goals.

18. _____ estimate: statistic that measures the extent to which individual differences in complex traits in a specific population are due to genetic factors

19. The tendency of heredity to restrict the development of some characteristics to just one or a few outcomes

Down

1. The percentage of instances in which both twins show a trait when it is present in one twin is referred to as a _____ rate.

3. Twins that result from the release and fertilization of two ova; genetically no more alike than ordinary siblings; also known as dizygotic twins.

5. Twins that result when a zygote that has started to duplicate separates into two clusters of cells that develop into two individuals with the same genetic makeup; also known as monozygotic twins

7. A heterozygous individual who can pass a recessive trait to his or her offspring

8. In _____ societies, people think of themselves as separate entities and are largely concerned with their own personal needs

10. The tendency to actively choose environments that compliment our heredity (two words; hyph.)

11. A measure of a family's social position and economic well-being (abbr.)

12. _____ studies compare the characteristics of family members to determine the importance of heredity in complex human characteristics

17. Cell resulting from the union of the sperm and ova at conception

PRACTICE TEST #1

1. Directly observable physical and behavioral characteristics are called (p. 44)
   a. phenotype.
   b. genotype.
   c. alleles.
   d. chromosomes.

2. A molecule of DNA resembles _____ . (p. 44)
   a. a globe or sphere
   b. a twisted ladder
   c. either an X or a Y
   d. no one knows what it looks like

3. A unique feature of DNA is that it can duplicate itself through a process called _____ . (p. 45)
   a. meiosis
   b. mitosis
   c. imprinting
   d. codominance

4. A person whose 23rd pair of chromosomes is XY (p. 46)
   a. has Turner syndrome.
   b. has Down syndrome.
   c. has PKU.
   d. is male.

5. Serious diseases are only rarely due to dominant alleles because (p. 47)
   a. dominance requires that the same allele be inherited from both parents.
   b. other genes usually alter the effects of dominant alleles.
   c. children inheriting the harmful dominant allele would always develop the disorder and seldom live long enough to pass on the trait.
   d. recessive genes usually overtake the harmful dominant allele.

6. The case of PKU demonstrates that (p. 47)
   a. serious inherited disorders are more often due to dominant than to recessive genes.
   b. most inherited disorders are untreatable.
   c. even if we know the genetic makeup of the parents, it is difficult to predict the likelihood that children in a family will display a disorder.
   d. changes in the environment can alter the extent to which an inherited disorder influences a person's well-being.

7. Which disorder of the sex chromosomes, caused by abnormal repetition of a sequence of DNA bases on the X chromosome, results from genetic imprinting? (p. 49)
   a. PKU
   b. hemophilia
   c. Fragile X syndrome
   d. Turner syndrome

8. In which of the following patterns of inheritance are genes chemically marked in such a way that only one pair member is activated, regardless of its makeup? (p. 49)
   a. codominance
   b. homozygous inheritance
   c. polygenic inheritance
   d. genetic imprinting

41

9. Hazardous environmental agents, such as ionizing radiation, can lead to a sudden and permanent change in DNA called _____ . (p. 50)
   a. crossing over
   b. polygenic inheritance
   c. mutation
   d. genetic imprinting

10. The most common chromosomal abnormality is (p. 50)
    a. Klinefelter's syndrome.
    b. PKU.
    c. cystic fibrosis.
    d. Down syndrome.

11. Except for _____ and _____ , prenatal diagnosis should not be used routinely, since other methods have some chance of injuring the fetus. (p. 52)
    a. ultrasound; amniocentesis
    b. ultrasound; maternal blood analysis
    c. fetoscopy; chorionic villus sampling
    d. amniocentesis; maternal blood analysis

12. Which of the following statements about adoption is true? (pp. 56–57)
    a. Adopted children and adolescents fare as well as or better than children growing up with their biological parents.
    b. Children who are adopted later in life are better adjusted than children who are adopted in infancy and toddlerhood.
    c. Adopted children and adolescents have more learning and emotional difficulties than do other children.
    d. Adopted children are more similar in intelligence and personality to their adoptive parents than to their biological parents.

13. Jonah is 3-years-old and has been difficult to care for since birth. He cries often, throws tantrums, screams, and has unpredictable eating and sleeping habits. His mother often becomes upset with Jonah, responding to his behavior with anger and harshness, which causes Jonah to act out even more. Which of the following is being described in the example? (p. 58)
    a. third parties
    b. bidirectional influences
    c. dynamic influences
    d. extraneous variables

14. Nearly _____ percent of the population in the United States and Canada live in poverty. Which groups are hardest hit by poverty? (p. 60)
    a. 12; infants and teenagers
    b. 32; parents over age 40 with adolescent children and elderly who reside in nursing homes
    c. 12; parents under age 25 with young children and elderly people who live alone
    d. 32; infants and the elderly

15. Compared to large cities, small towns are more likely to foster (p. 62)
    a. feelings of loneliness.
    b. limited social contact.
    c. active involvement in the community.
    d. more visits to museums and concerts.

16. Which of the following statements about collectivism versus individualism best describes the United States and Canada? (p. 63)
    a. Both the United States and Canada are strongly individualistic.
    b. The United States is less individualistic than Canada.
    c. The United States is strongly individualistic and Canada falls somewhere between the United States and most Western European nations.
    d. Both the United States and Canada are becoming increasingly collectivist.

17. A concordance rate of 50 percent indicates that (p. 67)
    a. if one twin has the trait, the other twin will have it half the time.
    b. variation in the trait can be fully explained by genetic makeup.
    c. the probability that one's offspring will have the trait is 50 percent.
    d. variation in the trait can be fully explained by environmental factors.

18. Which of the following statements represents a limitation of heritability estimates? (p. 68)
    a. They are only useful in studying fraternal twins.
    b. They neglect the role of biology in explaining human development.
    c. They can easily be misapplied, such as when they are used to suggest that ethnic differences in intelligence have a genetic basis.
    d. They are only useful in explaining personality traits.

19. Identical twins reared apart, who nevertheless have many psychological traits and lifestyle characteristics in common, illustrate a form of genetic–environmental correlation commonly called (p. 69)
    a. range of reaction.
    b. canalization.
    c. niche-picking.
    d. evocative.

20. Maria provides her baby with plenty of age-appropriate stimulation, which increases brain growth and transforms gene expression. This series of interactions leads to new gene-environment exchanges, which further enhance brain growth and gene expression. This is an example of _____ . (p. 71)
    a. niche picking
    b. canalization
    c. epigenesis
    d. range of reaction

PRACTICE TEST #2

1. Chromosomes are made up of (p. 44)
    a. ribonucleic acid.
    b. sequences of potassium.
    c. deoxyribonucleic acid.
    d. genotypes.

2. The process of cell division, or _____, helps to explain why siblings differ from each other even though their genotypes come from the same pool of parental genes. (p. 46)
    a. autosomes
    b. mitosis
    c. meiosis
    d. dominance

3. Peter and Colin are twins. Genetically, they are no more alike than ordinary siblings. Peter and Colin are _____ twins. (p. 46)
   a. monozygotic
   b. dizygotic
   c. identical
   d. homozygous

4. In a heterozygous pairing in which only one gene affects the child's characteristics, the pattern of genetic inheritance is called (p. 46)
   a. dominant–recessive.
   b. codominant.
   c. polygenic.
   d. mutagenic.

5. The sickle cell trait, a heterozygous condition present in many black Africans, is an example of (p. 47)
   a. codominance.
   b. concordance.
   c. dominant–recessive inheritance.
   d. monogenic inheritance.

6. Which of the following explains why males are more likely than females to be affected by X-linked disorders? (p. 49)
   a. Males are more often homozygous for harmful recessive genes.
   b. Males are more likely than females to be born to women over the age of 35.
   c. Males' sex chromosomes do not match.
   d. Males tend to have fewer autosomes.

7. Continuous traits, such as height and intelligence, are due to _____, in which many genes determine the characteristic. (p. 50)
   a. multigenic inheritance
   b. polygenic inheritance
   c. heterozygous inheritance
   d. homozygous inheritance

8. Most chromosomal defects are the result of (p. 50)
   a. recessive disorders.
   b. mistakes during meiosis.
   c. X-linked disorders.
   d. mistakes during mitosis.

9. Mr. and Mrs. Chow would like to have a baby but are concerned about the presence of Down syndrome in their family. Which of the following would you recommend to help them determine their chances of giving birth to a baby with this disorder? (p. 52)
   a. chorionic villus sampling
   b. genetic counseling
   c. ultrasound
   d. amniocentesis

10. Researchers view the family as (p. 58)
   a. a self-contained unit that is impervious to third party effects.
   b. a network of unidirectional influences.
   c. a system of interdependent relationships.
   d. a stable system that is resistant to change.

11. Which of the following is true with regard to socioeconomic influences on child-rearing?
    a. lower-SES fathers tend to play a more supportive role in child-rearing, while higher-SES fathers focus more on their provider role.
    b. lower-SES parents tend to emphasize external characteristics, such as obedience, neatness, and cleanliness, whereas higher-SES parents emphasize psychologial traits, such as curiosity, happiness, and self-direction.
    c. lower-SES families use more warmth, explanation and verbal praise, while higher-SES parents use more commands, criticism, and physical punishment.
    d. education has little impact on SES differences in parenting.

12. _____ is more common in neighborhoods where residents feel socially isolated. (p. 61)
    a. Child abuse and neglect
    b. Contact with relatives
    c. Church attendance
    d. Family cohesiveness

13. Which of the following has helped to protect African-American children from the harmful effects of poverty? (p. 63)
    a. publicly sponsored child care
    b. excellent schools in American inner cities
    c. migration of African Americans to small towns
    d. extended family households

14. Laws and government programs designed to improve current conditions are called
    a. legal policies
    b. domestic policies
    c. public policies
    d. democratic policies

15. Which of the following is true with regard to public policies in the United States and Canada?
    a. Compared to other industrialized nations, the United States and Canada rank 1st and 2nd, respectively, on key measures of children's health and well-being.
    b. Both countries devote more resources to infants and young children than to the elderly.
    c. The United States devotes considerably more of its resources to improving the quality of child-care services than does Canada.
    d. Canada devotes considerably more of its resources to education and health care than does the United States.

16. A statistic that measures the extent to which complex traits, such as intelligence and personality, can be traced to heredity is called a (p. 67)
    a. heritability estimate.
    b. kinship estimate.
    c. concordance rate.
    d. canalization estimate.

17. The concept of range of reaction explains that children who are exposed to the same environmental conditions (p. 68)
    a. may respond to them differently because of their genetic makeup.
    b. will tend to show the same pattern of responses over time.
    c. tend to overcome their inheritance, so their genes have little effect.
    d. will become genetically more similar than other children are.

18. Phil and Desiree, who are both artists, have enrolled their children in painting, drawing, and sculpting classes. This is an example of a(n) _____ genetic–environmental correlation. (p. 69)
    a. passive
    b. dynamic
    c. evocative
    d. active

19. Since all normal human babies roll over, sit up, crawl, and walk, one can conclude that infant motor behavior is a strongly _____ trait. (p. 69)
    a. canalized
    b. imprinted
    c. instinctive
    d. encouraged

20. Which of the following terms refers to development resulting from ongoing, bidirectional exchanges between heredity and the environment? (p. 71)
    a. genetic imprinting
    b. sociocultural development
    c. epigenesis
    d. accommodation

CHAPTER 3
PRENATAL DEVELOPMENT, BIRTH,
AND THE NEWBORN BABY

BRIEF CHAPTER SUMMARY

At no other time in the lifespan is change as rapid as it is before birth. Prenatal development takes place in three phases: (1) the period of the zygote, (2) the period of the embryo, and (3) the period of the fetus. Various environmental agents and maternal conditions can damage the developing organism, making the prenatal period a vulnerable time. For this reason, prenatal health care is vitally important to ensure the health of mother and baby.

Childbirth takes place in three stages: (1) dilation and effacement of the cervix, (2) delivery of the baby; and (3) birth of the placenta. Production of stress hormones helps the infant withstand the trauma of childbirth, and the baby's physical condition is assessed immediately after birth using the Apgar Scale. Alternatives to traditional hospital childbirth include natural childbirth and delivery in a birth center or at home. Still, childbirth in the United States is often accompanied by a variety of medical interventions. Although they help save the lives of many babies, these procedures can cause problems of their own when used routinely. When birth complications occur, they most often involve preterm and low-birth-weight infants. Fortunately, many of these babies recover from difficulties with the help of supportive home environments.

Infants begin life with a remarkable set of skills for relating to the surrounding world. They display a wide variety of reflexes, and with the exception of vision, their senses are well developed. In the early weeks, babies move in and out of different states of arousal frequently. They first communicate by crying, and with experience, parents become better at interpreting and responding to infants' cries. Tests of newborn behavior allow the assessment of the baby's many capacities. The baby's arrival is exciting, but it brings with it profound changes. Husbands and wives who support each other's needs typically adjust well to the demands of parenthood.

LEARNING OBJECTIVES

After reading this chapter, you should be able to:

3.1   List the phases of prenatal development, and describe major milestones of each. (pp. 76–81)

3.2   Define the term *teratogen,* and summarize the four factors that affect the impact of teratogens on prenatal development. (p. 81)

3.3   List agents known or suspected of being teratogens, and discuss evidence supporting the harmful impact of each. (pp. 82–88)

3.4   Discuss maternal factors other than exposure to teratogens that can affect the developing embryo or fetus. (pp. 88–89)

3.5   Describe the three stages of childbirth. (p. 91)

3.6   Discuss the baby's adaptation to labor and delivery, and describe the appearance of the newborn baby. (pp. 91–93)

3.7   Explain the purpose and main features of the Apgar Scale. (p. 93)

3.8   Discuss the concept of natural childbirth, noting the typical features of a natural childbirth program, the benefits of the natural childbirth experience, and the role of social support in the natural childbirth process. (p. 94)

3.9   Discuss the benefits and concerns associated with home delivery. (pp. 94–95)

3.10 Describe circumstances that justify the use of fetal monitoring, labor and delivery medication, and cesarean delivery, and explain any risks associated with each. (pp. 95–96)

3.11 Describe the risks associated with preterm and small-for-date births, and review the developmental outlook for infants born under such circumstances. (pp. 96–97)

3.12 Describe several interventions for preterm infants, including infant stimulation and parent training. (pp. 97–99)

3.13 Summarize findings from the Kauai study relating to the long-term consequences of birth complications. (pp. 99–100)

3.14 Name and describe major newborn reflexes, noting the functions served by each, and discuss the importance of assessing newborn reflexes. (pp. 100–101)

3.15 Describe the five infant states of arousal, with particular attention to sleep and crying. (pp. 102–105)

3.16 Describe the newborn baby's responsiveness to taste, smell, touch, sound, and visual stimulation. (pp. 105–107)

3.17 Describe Brazelton's Neonatal Behavioral Assessment Scale (NBAS), and explain its usefulness. (p. 107)

3.18 Describe typical changes in the family unit after the birth of a new baby. (p. 108)

STUDY QUESTIONS

Prenatal Development

Conception

1. About once every 28 days, an ovum is released from one of a woman's two _____, and it is drawn into one of the two _____, which are long, thin structures that lead to the uterus. (p. 76)

Period of the Zygote

1. The period of the zygote lasts about _____ weeks. (p. 78)

2. Match the following terms with the appropriate descriptions. (p. 78)

_____ Will provide protective covering and nourishment to the new organism
_____ A hollow, fluid-filled ball that is formed by a tiny mass of cells four days after fertilization
_____ Will become the new organism

1. Blastocyst
2. Embryonic disk
3. Trophoblast

3. List two functions of the amniotic fluid. (p. 78)

A. _____

B. _____

4. True or False: As many as 30 percent of zygotes do not make it through the first two weeks after fertilization. (p. 78)

5. The _____ permits food and oxygen to reach the developing organism and waste products to be carried away. (p. 78)

6. The placenta is connected to the developing organism by the _____. (p. 78)

Period of the Embryo

1. True or False: The most rapid prenatal changes take place during the period of the embryo. (p. 79)

2. List the organs and structures that will be formed from each of the following layers of the embryonic disk. (p. 79)

   Mesoderm: _____

   _____

   Ectoderm: _____

   _____

   Endoderm: _____

   _____

3. Summarize prenatal growth during the second month of pregnancy. (p. 79)

   _____

   _____

   _____

Period of the Fetus

1. The period of the fetus is sometimes referred to as the _____ _____ phase. (p. 79)

2. Prenatal development is divided into _____, or three equal periods of time. (p. 79)

3. The white, cheese-like substance that completely covers the fetus to protect the skin from chapping in the amniotic fluid is called _____. (p. 80)

4. _____ is the white, downy hair that covers the entire body of the fetus. (p. 80)

5. What major milestone in brain development is reached at the end of the second trimester? (p. 80)

   _____

6. The age at which the baby can first survive if born early is called the *age of* _____. When does this typically occur?

   _____ (p. 80)

7. Describe research findings on the relationship between fetal activity patterns and infant temperament at 3 and 6 months of age. (p. 80)

   _____

   _____

   _____

8. True or False: Research shows that the fetus develops a preference for the tone and rhythm of the mother's voice during the last weeks of pregnancy. (p. 81)

Teratogens

1. Define the term *teratogen,* and describe four factors that affect the impact of teratogens on prenatal development. (p. 81)

    Definition: _____

    _____

    A. _____

    _____

    B. _____

    _____

    C. _____

    _____

    D. _____

    _____

2. A _____ *period* is a limited time span in which a part of the body or a behavior is biologically prepared to develop rapidly and is especially vulnerable to its surroundings. (p. 82)

3. True or False: The fetal period is the time when teratogens are most likely to cause serious defects. (p. 82)

4. True or False: The effects of teratogens are limited to physical damage. (p. 82)

5. When taken by mothers 4 to 6 weeks after conception, _____, a sedative widely available in some countries during the early 1960s, produced deformities of the embryo's developing arms and legs, and less frequently, caused damage to the ears, heart, kidneys, and genitals. (p. 82)

6. True or False: Heavy caffeine intake during pregnancy is associated with prematurity, miscarriage, and newborn withdrawal symptoms. (p. 83)

7. Describe the difficulties faced by babies who are prenatally exposed to heroin, cocaine, or methadone. (p. 83)

    _____

    _____

    _____

    _____

8. Explain why it is difficult to isolate the precise damage caused by prenatal exposure to cocaine. (pp. 83–84)

    _____

    _____

    _____

9. Summarize physical and behavioral effects of maternal smoking during the prenatal period. (pp. 84–85)

_____

_____

_____

_____

10. True or False: If the mother stops smoking at any time during the pregnancy, even during the last trimester, she reduces the chances that her baby will be negatively impacted. (p. 84)

11. Explain the mechanisms through which smoking harms the fetus. (p. 85)

_____

_____

_____

12. True or False: Passive smoking has not been linked with any adverse effects on the infant. (p. 85)

13. Infants who have a cluster of physical and behavioral abnormalities and whose mothers drank heavily throughout most or all of pregnancy are said to have _____; infants who show some, but not all, of these deficits and whose mothers drank in smaller quantities during pregnancy are said to suffer from _____. (p. 86)

14. List some common impairments evidenced by children with _Fetal Alcohol Syndrome_ (FAS). (p. 86)

_____

_____

_____

15. True or False: The physical and mental impairments seen in babies with FAS typically lessen by the time the individual reaches adolescence or early adulthood. (p. 86)

16. Describe two ways in which alcohol produces its devastating effects. (p. 86)

   A. _____

   _____

   B. _____

   _____

17. True or False: There is no precise dividing line between safe and dangerous drinking levels during pregnancy. (p. 86)

18. Match each of the following environmental pollutants with its effect on development. (p. 87)

_____ This teratogen, commonly found in paint chippings from old buildings and other industrial materials, is related to prematurity, low birth weight, brain damage, and physical defects

_____ In the 1950s, children prenatally exposed to this teratogen in a Japanese community displayed mental retardation, abnormal speech, and uncoordinated movements

_____ Women who ate fish contaminated with this substance gave birth to babies with slightly reduced birth weights, smaller heads, and later memory and intellectual deficits

1. Mercury
2. Lead
3. PCBs

19. German, or 3 day, measles is a teratogen that inflicts the greatest damage when it strikes during the (embryonic / fetal) period. (p. 87)

20. When women carrying the AIDS virus become pregnant, they pass the deadly virus to the developing organism approximately _____ to _____ percent of the time. (p. 87)

21. True or False: Most infants prenatally exposed to the AIDS virus survive 8 to 10 years after the appearance of symptoms. (p. 87)

22. Pregnant women may become infected with _____ from eating undercooked meat or from contact with the feces of infected cats. (p. 88)

Other Maternal Factors

1. Summarize the behavioral and health problems of prenatally malnourished infants. (p. 88)

_____

_____

_____

_____

2. _____ supplementation around the time of conception greatly reduces abnormalities of the neural tube, such as anencephaly and spina bifida. (p. 88)

3. Describe the mechanisms through which maternal stress affects the developing organism, and note outcomes associated with severe emotional stress during pregnancy. (p. 89)

Mechanisms: _____

_____

_____

Outcomes: _____

_____

_____

4. Under what conditions can the Rh factor cause problems for the developing fetus? (p. 89)

_____

_____

_____

5. True or False: First-born children are more likely than later-born children to be affected by Rh incompatibility. (p. 89)

6. True or False: Research shows that healthy women in their forties experience far more prenatal difficulties than do women in their twenties. (p. 89)

7. The physical immaturity of teenage mothers (does / does not) lead to pregnancy complications. (p. 89)

8. Describe some of the benefits of prenatal health care. (pp. 89–90)

_____

_____

_____

_____

9. List three demographic characteristics that are common to women who do not seek prenatal care until late in their pregnancies. (p.90)

A. _____   B. _____

C. _____

10. Discuss some of the barriers to obtaining prenatal health care mentioned by expectant mothers who delay or never seek such care. (p. 90)

_____

_____

_____

_____

A Lifespan Vista: The Prenatal Environment and Health in Later Life

1. Explain the relationship between low birth weight and adult health problems, such as heart disease, stroke, and diabetes, noting possible causes for these associations. (p. 84)

_____

_____

_____

_____

2. True or False: High birth weight is related to breast cancer in adulthood. Briefly explain your response. (pp. 84–85)

_____

_____

The Stages of Childbirth

1. Name and describe the three stages of labor. (p. 91)

    A. _____

    _____

    _____

    B. _____

    _____

    _____

    C. _____

    _____

    _____

The Baby's Adaptation to Labor and Delivery

1. Cite three ways in which stress hormones help the baby withstand the trauma of childbirth. (p. 92)

    A. _____

    B. _____

    C. _____

The Newborn Baby's Appearance

1. The average newborn is _____ inches long and _____ pounds in weight. (p. 92)

2. At birth, the head is very (small / large) in relation to the trunk and legs. (p. 92)

Assessing the Newborn's Physical Condition: The Apgar Scale

1. List the five characteristics assessed by the Apgar Scale, and note which is the least reliable of these measures. (p. 93)

    A. _____

    B. _____

    C. _____

    D. _____

    E. _____

    Least reliable: _____

2. On the Apgar Scale, a score of _____ or better indicates that the infant is in good physical condition; a score between _____ and _____ indicates that the baby requires special assistance; a score of _____ or below indicates a dire emergency. (p. 93)

Approaches to Childbirth

Natural, or Prepared, Childbirth

1. What is the theory behind the natural childbirth approach? (p. 94)

   _____

   _____

   _____

2. List and describe three components of a typical natural childbirth program. (p. 94)

   A. _____

   _____

   B. _____

   _____

   C. _____

   _____

3. Research suggests that social support (is / is not) an important part of the success of natural childbirth techniques. (p. 94)

Home Delivery

1. Home births are typically handled by certified _____, who have degrees in nursing and additional training in childbirth management. (p. 94)

2. True or False: For healthy women assisted by a trained professional, it is just as safe to give birth at home as in a hospital. (p. 95)

Medical Interventions

1. _____ refers to oxygen deprivation during the birth process. (p. 95)

2. Infants in the _____ position are turned in such a way that the buttocks or feet would be delivered first. (p. 95)

Fetal Monitoring

1. Explain the purpose of *fetal monitoring.* (p. 95)

   _____

   _____

2. Cite four reasons why fetal monitoring is a controversial procedure. (p. 95)

   A. _____

   B. _____

   C. _____

   D. _____

Labor and Delivery Medication

1. True or False: Some form of medication is used in 85 to 90 percent of births in the United States. (p. 95)

2. Discuss three problems with the routine use of labor and delivery medications. (p. 95)

   A. _____

   _____

   B. _____

   _____

   C. _____

   _____

Cesarean Delivery

1. What is a *cesarean delivery*? (p. 96)

   _____

   _____

2. In what circumstances is a cesarean delivery warranted? (p. 96)

   _____

   _____

3. How can cesarean delivery affect the adjustment of the newborn baby, and consequently, the early infant-mother relationship? (p. 96)

   _____

   _____

   _____

Preterm and Low-Birth-Weight Infants

1. Babies are considered premature if they are born _____ weeks before the end of a full 38-week pregnancy or if they weigh less than _____ pounds. (p. 96)

2. True or False: Birth weight is the best available predictor of infant survival and healthy development. (p. 96)

3. List the problems associated with low birth weight. (p. 96)

   _____

   _____

   _____

   _____

Preterm versus Small-for-Date

1. Distinguish between preterm and small-for-date babies. (p. 97)

   Preterm: _____

   _____

Small-for-date: _____

2. Of the two types of babies, (preterm / small-for-date) infants usually have more serious problems. (p. 97)

Consequences for Caregiving

1. Describe the characteristics of preterm infants and explain how those characteristics may influence the behavior of parents. (p. 97)

_____

_____

_____

_____

_____

Interventions for Preterm Infants

1. Discuss several methods of stimulation used to foster the successful development of preterm infants. (pp. 97–98)

_____

_____

_____

_____

_____

2. True or False: Research suggests that all preterm infants, regardless of family characteristics, require continuous, high-quality interventions well into the school years in order to maintain developmental gains. Elaborate on your response. (pp. 98–99)

_____

_____

_____

_____

Social Issues: A Cross-National Perspective on Health Care and Other Policies for Parents and Newborn Babies

1. _____ *mortality* refers to the number of deaths in the first year of life per 1,000 live births. (p. 98)

2. True or False: Black infants are more than twice as likely as white infants to die in the first year of life. (p. 98)

3. _____ *mortality,* the rate of death in the first month of life, accounts for 67 percent of the infant death rate in the United States and for 80 percent in Canada. (p. 98)

4. List the two leading causes of neonatal mortality. (p. 98)

   A. _____

   B. _____

5. Discuss the factors largely responsible for the relatively high rates of infant mortality in the United States. (p. 98)

_____

_____

_____

_____

6. Discuss factors linked to lower infant mortality rates. (pp. 98–99)

_____

_____

_____

_____

Understanding Birth Complications

1. Summarize important findings from the Kauai study regarding the development of infants who experienced birth complications. (pp. 99–100)

_____

_____

_____

_____

The Newborn Baby's Capacities

Newborn Reflexes

1. What is a *reflex*? (p. 100)

_____

_____

2. Match each reflex with the appropriate response or function descriptor. (p. 101)

_____ Spontaneous grasp of adult's finger
_____ When the sole of foot is stroked, the toes fan out and curl
_____ Helps infant find the nipple
_____ Prepares infant for voluntary walking
_____ Permits feeding
_____ Infant lies in a "fencing position"
_____ Protects infant from strong stimulation
_____ In our evolutionary past, may have helped infant cling to mother
_____ Helps infants survive if dropped in water

1. Eye blink
2. Tonic neck
3. Palmar grasp
4. Babinski
5. Rooting
6. Sucking
7. Swimming
8. Stepping
9. Moro

3. True or False: Some reflexes have survival value. (p. 100)

4. When do most newborn reflexes disappear? (p. 101)

_____

5. Explain the importance of assessing newborn reflexes. (p. 101)

_____

_____

_____

Newborn States

1. Name and describe the five infant *states of arousal.* (p. 102)

A. _____

_____

B. _____

_____

C. _____

_____

D. _____

_____

E. _____

_____

2. Describe the characteristics of *REM* and *NREM* sleep. (p. 102)

REM: _____

_____

NREM: _____

_____

3. Why do infants spend more time in REM sleep than do children, adolescents, and adults? (pp. 102–103)

_____

_____

4. True or False: Trends in infant crying behavior are likely due to normal readjustments of the central nervous system, rather than resulting from parental response patterns. (p. 104)

5. What is the most effective way to soothe a crying baby when feeding and diaper changing do not work? (p. 104)

_____

6. How do the cries of brain-damaged babies and those who have experienced prenatal and birth complications differ from those of healthy infants, and how does this difference affect parental responding? (p. 105)

_____

_____

_____

Sensory Capacities

1. True or False: Infants are born with a poorly developed sense of touch, and consequently, they are not sensitive to pain. (p. 105)

2. True or False: Infants not only have taste preferences, but they are also capable of communicating these preferences to adults through facial expressions. (p. 106)

3. True or False: Certain odor preferences are innate. (p. 106)

4. True or False: Newborn infants are attracted to the scent of a lactating woman, but they are unable to discriminate the smell of their own mother's breast from that of an unfamiliar lactating woman. (p. 106)

5. True or False: Infants prefer pure tones to complex sounds. (p. 106)

6. True or False: Infants can discriminate almost all of the speech sounds of any human language. (p. 106)

7. Cite the characteristics of human speech preferred by infants. (p. 106)

_____

_____

8. Vision is the (most / least) mature of the newborn baby's senses. (p. 106)

9. Describe the newborn baby's visual acuity. (p. 106)

_____

_____

10. True or False: Infants have well-developed color vision at birth, and they are immediately capable of discriminating colors. (p. 107)

Neonatal Behavioral Assessment

1. Which aspects of behavior does the _Neonatal Behavioral Assessment Scale_ (NBAS) evaluate? (p. 107)

_____

_____

2. Since the NBAS is given to infants all around the world, researchers have been able to learn a great deal about individual and cultural differences in newborn behavior and the ways in which various child-rearing practices affect infant behavior. Briefly discuss these findings. (p. 107)

_____

_____

_____

_____

3. Why is a single NBAS score not a good predictor of later development, and what should be used in place of a single score? (p. 107)

_____

_____

4. How are NBAS interventions beneficial for the early parent–infant relationship? (p. 107)

_____

_____

Biology & Environment: The Mysterious Tragedy of Sudden Infant Death Syndrome

1. What is *Sudden Infant Death Syndrome (SIDS)*? (p. 103)

_____

_____

2. True or False: In industrialized countries, SIDS is the leading cause of infant mortality between one week and twelve months of age. (p. 103)

3. True or False: Researchers have recently determined the precise cause of SIDS. (p. 103)

4. Describe some early physical problems that are common among SIDS victims. (p. 103)

_____

_____

_____

5. Describe three environmental factors associated with SIDS. (p. 103)

A. _____

_____

B. _____

_____

C. _____

_____

1. Discuss several changes in the family system following the birth of a new baby. (p. 108)

_____

_____

_____

_____

_____

ASK YOURSELF...

For *Ask Yourself* questions for this chapter, please log on to the Companion Website at www.ablongman.com/berk.

1. Select the Companion Website for *Development Through the Lifespan,* Third Edition.

2. Use the "Jump to" menu to go directly to this chapter.

3. From the menu on the left side of your screen, select *Ask Yourself.*

4. Complete questions and choose "Submit answers for grading" or "Clear answers" to start over.

SUGGESTED STUDENT READINGS

Barr, R.G., Hopkins, B., & Green, J. A. (Eds.). (2000). *Crying as a sign, symptom, and a signal.: Clinical, emotional, and developmental aspects of infant and toddler crying.* New York: Cambridge University Press. Examines infant crying from a multidisciplinary perspective, describes normative developmental patterns of crying, and discusses how they are manifested in various settings—emergency rooms, painful procedures, colic, temper tantrums, and nonverbal and mentally challenged infants.

Kleinfeld, J., Morse, B., & Wescott, S. (Eds). (2000). *Fantastic Antone grows up: adolescents and adults with fetal alcohol syndrome.* Fairbanks, AK: University of Alaska Press. Primarily written as a guide for parents and caregivers, this book presents real-life accounts of the unique experiences of adolescents and young adults living with fetal alcohol syndrome.

Tracey, N. (Ed). (2000). *Parents of premature infants: Their emotional world.* London: Whurr Publishers, Ltd. Presents a series of in-depth interviews and personal accounts of parents of premature babies, carefully focusing on their emotions, thoughts, and fantasies.

PUZZLE 3.1 TERM REVIEW

Across

3. Any environmental agent that causes damage during the prenatal period
8. Long cord connecting the prenatal organism to the placenta; delivers nutrients and removes waste products (2 words)
10. Outer membrane that forms a protective covering around the prenatal organism
11. Prenatal organism from 2 to 8 weeks after conception, during which time the foundation for all body structures and internal organs is laid down
12. White, downy hair that covers the entire body of the fetus
13. White, cheese-like substance covering the fetus and preventing the skin from chapping in the amniotic fluid
14. Prenatal organism from the beginning of the third month to the end of pregnancy, during which time completion of body structures and dramatic growth in size take place
15. Inner membrane that forms a protective covering around the prenatal organism and encloses it in amniotic fluid

Down

1. Position of the baby in the uterus such that the buttocks or feet would be delivered first
2. Primitive spinal cord that develops from the ectoderm, the top of which swells to form the brain (2 words)
4. Organ that separates the mother's bloodstream from that of the fetus or embryo but permits exchange of nutrients and waste products
5. Attachment of the blastocyst to the uterine lining 7 to 9 days after fertilization
6. Three equal time periods in the prenatal period, each of which lasts three months
7. Inadequate oxygen supply
9. Fetal _____: electronic instruments that track the baby's heart rate during labor

PUZZLE 3.2 TERM REVIEW

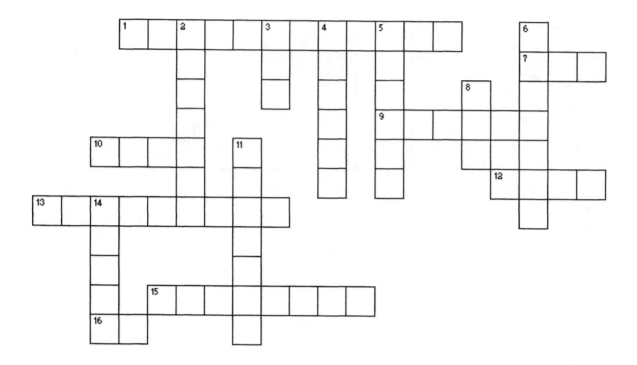

Across

1. Infants whose birth weight is below normal when the length of the pregnancy is taken into account (3 words)
7. An "irregular" sleep state in which brain wave activity is similar to that of the waking state (abbr.)
9. _____ mortality rate: the number of deaths in the first year of life per 1,000 live births
10. A test developed to assess the behavioral status of the infant during the newborn period (abbr.)
12. A "regular" sleep state in which the body is quiet and heart rate, breathing, and brain wave activity are slow and regular (abbr.)
13. Age of _____: age at which the fetus can survive if born early
15. _____ delivery: surgical delivery in which the doctor makes an incision in the mother's abdomen and lifts the baby out of the uterus
16. When present in the fetus's blood but not in the mother's, the _____ factor can cause the mother to build up antibodies that destroy the fetus's red blood cells

4. Inborn, automatic response to a particular form of stimulation
5. Visual _____: fineness of visual discrimination
6. Infants born several weeks or more before their due date
8. Set of defects that results when women consume large amounts of alcohol during most or all of their pregnancy (abbr.)
11. Childbirth approach designed to reduce pain and medical intervention
14. Scale used to assess the newborn's physical condition immediately after birth

Down

2. States of _____: different degrees of sleep and wakefulness
3. Condition of children who display some but not all of the defects of FAS (abbr.)

PRACTICE TEST #1

1. By the fourth day after conception, 60 to 70 cells form a hollow, fluid-filled ball called a(n) (p. 78)
   a. blastocyst.
   b. embryonic disc.
   c. trophoblast.
   d. zygote.

2. The organ that separates the mother's bloodstream from the embryonic or fetal bloodstream, but permits exchange of nutrients and waste, is called the (p. 78)
   a. amnion.
   b. chorion.
   c. placenta.
   d. umbilical cord.

3. The most rapid prenatal changes take place during the period of the _____, as the groundwork for all body structures and internal organs is laid down. (p. 79)
   a. zygote
   b. fetus
   c. neonate
   d. embryo

4. _____ covers the baby's skin and prevents it from chapping in the amniotic fluid. (p. 80)
   a. Lanugo
   b. The amnion
   c. Vernix
   d. The placenta

5 Exposure to teratogens during the period of _____ is associated with the most serious defects. (p. 82)
   a. the embryo
   b. the zygot
   c. the fetus
   d. labor and delivery

6. The most well-known effect of smoking during pregnancy is (p. 84)
   a. low birth weight.
   b. infant death.
   c. childhood behavioral problems.
   d. long-term respiratory difficulties.

7. Mental retardation, slow physical growth, and facial abnormalities are typical effects of which of the following teratogens? (p. 86)
   a. caffeine
   b. cocaine
   c. alcohol
   d. marijuana

8. The AIDS virus (p. 87)
   a. is transmitted from infected mothers to their fetus approximately 80% of the time.
   b. is now the leading cause of infant death in most Western nations.
   c. progresses especially rapidly in infants.
   d. progresses more slowly in infants than in older children and adults.

9. Prenatal malnutrition is known to cause (p. 88)
   a. damage to the central nervous system.
   b. Down syndrome.
   c. cleft palate.
   d. pyloric stenosis.

10. In cases where the *mother is negative* and the *baby is positive*, _____ can cause oxygen deprivation and may result in mental retardation, heart damage, and infant death. (p. 89)
   a. eclampsia
   b. Rh incompatibility
   c. antibody incompatibility
   d. the androgen factor

11. Which of the following takes place during Stage 1 of childbirth? (p. 91)
   a. delivery of the baby
   b. prelabor
   c. dilation and effacement of the cervix
   d. birth of the placenta

12. The _____ is used to assess the physical condition of the newborn at 1 and 5 minutes after birth. (p. 93)
   a. Brazelton Neonatal Behavioral Assessment Scale
   b. Apgar Scale
   c. Bayley Scales of Infant Development
   d. Neonatal Reflex Inventory

13. Natural, or prepared, childbirth (p. 94)
   a. tries to overcome the idea that birth is a painful ordeal that requires extensive medical intervention.
   b. is typically handled by a certified midwife.
   c. is not conducive to father presence in the delivery room.
   d. is associated with increased risk of birth complications.

14. Fetal monitors (p. 95)
   a. reduce the rate of infant brain damage and death in healthy pregnancies.
   b. save the lives of many babies in high-risk situations.
   c. reduce the rate of cesarean deliveries.
   d. are comfortable devices that ease the normal course of labor.

15. An infant born two months early but weighing an appropriate amount for the time spent in the uterus is called (p. 96)
   a. small-for-date.
   b. preterm.
   c. postterm.
   d. breech.

16. A careful assessment of newborn reflexes provides the pediatrician with important information about the infant's (p. 100)
    a. muscle tone.
    b. sensory capacities.
    c. responsiveness to physical stimulation.
    d. nervous system.

17. REM sleep (p. 102)
    a. accounts for a lower percentage of sleep time in infants than in children and adults.
    b. seems to fulfill young infants' need for stimulation since they spend so little time in an alert state.
    c. is a "regular" sleep state in which the body is almost motionless, and heart rate, breathing, and brain wave activity are slow and regular.
    d. is less frequent in the fetus and in preterm infants than in full-term infants.

18. Which of the following is true of infant crying? (p. 104)
    a. The "vocal signature" of the infant's cry is similar among babies.
    b. Newborns often cry at the sound of another crying baby.
    c. Crying typically declines around 6 weeks of age.
    d. A shrill, piercing cry is associated with normal infant development.

19. Newborn infants (p. 106)
    a. prefer pure tones to complex sounds.
    b. are most attentive to low-pitched, monotonous patterns of sound.
    c. can discriminate almost all sounds in human languages.
    d. can discriminate only the speech sounds of their native language.

20. Because the visual system is not yet well developed, _____, or fineness of discrimination, is limited in newborn infants. (p. 106)
    a. depth perception
    b. tunnel vision
    c. binocular vision
    d. visual acuity

PRACTICE TEST #2

1. The amniotic fluid (p. 78)
    a. produces blood cells until the developing liver, spleen, and bone marrow are mature enough to take over this function.
    b. permits oxygen and food to reach the developing organism.
    c. protects the fetus's skin from chapping.
    d. maintains a constant temperature in the womb and provides a cushion against jolts caused by the mother's movement.

2. The point at which the fetus can first survive if born early, called the age of viability, occurs sometime between (p. 80)
    a. 18 and 22 weeks.
    b. 22 and 26 weeks.
    c. 26 and 30 weeks.
    d. 30 and 34 weeks.

3. Which of the following is true about fetal behavior during the third trimester of pregnancy? (p. 80)
   a. Heart rate variability reveals that the fetus is rarely awake.
   b. Fetuses with long active periods are more likely to become fussy, active babies after birth.
   c. The fetus cannot yet feel pain.
   d. The fetus has little ability to discriminate sounds.

4. With respect to the impact of teratogens on the developing organism, (p. 82)
   a. the sensitive period applies.
   b. the fetus's genetic makeup plays little role.
   c. effects are limited to immediate physical damage.
   d. damage is usually greater during the fetal than embryonic period.

5. Infants who are prenatally exposed to cocaine (p. 83)
   a. rarely show addictions to the drug at birth.
   b. show few ill effects beyond the dangerous withdrawal period.
   c. typically have lasting difficulties.
   d. exhibit an easy temperament and are receptive to cuddling.

6. How much alcohol is required to produce Fetal Alcohol Effects (FAE)? (p. 86)
   a. maternal alcohol addiction
   b. more than two drinks per day
   c. as little as one ounce per day
   d. no amount is safe, so pregnant women should avoid alcohol entirely

7. Which of the following teratogenic effects of radiation followed the Chernobyl, Ukraine, nuclear power plant accident? (p. 86)
   a. increased rates of miscarriage but few brain and physical abnormalities
   b. no increase in miscarriage rates but a higher incidence of brain and physical abnormalities
   c. lower intelligence test scores and higher rates of language and emotional disorders in middle childhood, even in children who appeared normal
   d. higher cancer rates but few brain and physical abnormalities

8. Pregnant women should not eat undercooked meat or clean a cat's litter box due to the danger of acquiring (p. 88)
   a. toxoplasmosis.
   b. rubella.
   c. cytomegalovirus.
   d. tuberculosis.

9. Folic acid supplementation around the time of conception reduces the incidence of (p. 88)
   a. low birth weight.
   b. genetic disorders.
   c. neural tube defects.
   d. anoxia.

10. Severe emotional stress during pregnancy (p. 89)
    a. interferes with brain development, resulting in structural damage and abnormalities in brain functioning.
    b. causes the placenta to form abnormally, reducing the transfer of nutrients to the fetus.
    c. raises the concentration of carbon monoxide in the bloodstream in both mother and fetus, displacing oxygen from the red blood cells.
    d. reduces blood flow to the uterus, causing the fetus to receive less oxygen and nutrients.

11. An Apgar score of _____ indicates that the infant is in good physical condition. (p. 93)
    a. 4 to 6
    b. 7 or above
    c. 3 or below
    d. 5 or above

12. Home delivery (p. 94–95)
    a. is recommended for women who are at risk for birth complications.
    b. commonly leads to serious birth complications, and therefore, should not be considered a safe option under any circumstances.
    c. accounts for approximately 15 percent of all births.
    d. is a safe option for healthy, well-assisted women.

13. Cesarean delivery (p. 96)
    a. emphasizes relaxation and breathing techniques.
    b. is rarely used in the United States except in extreme medical emergencies.
    c. may cause the baby to be sleepy and unresponsive.
    d. makes future vaginal births impossible.

14. Which of the following is true about small-for-date babies? (p. 97)
    a. All are preterm babies, who usually fare well.
    b. They usually have fewer problems than preterm babies.
    c. Most probably experienced inadequate nutrition before birth.
    d. By middle childhood, they generally are doing as well as other children.

15. With respect to stimulation of preterm infants, massaging the baby several times a day in the hospital led to (pp. 97–98)
    a. increased irritability.
    b. better mental and motor development.
    c. poorer muscle tone.
    d. overly rapid weight gain.

16. Findings from the Kauai study revealed that (p. 100)
    a. postterm births are strongly associated with exposure to environmental pollution.
    b. newborn reflexes typically disappear in the first six months of life.
    c. biological risks far outweigh the impact of personal characteristics and social experiences on later development.
    d. in a supportive home environment, even children with serious birth problems can develop successfully.

17. The _____ reflex helps a breast-fed baby find the mother's nipple. (p. 101)
    a. rooting
    b. sucking
    c. tonic neck
    d. Moro

18. The most effective way to sooth a crying baby is to (p. 104)
    a. lift the baby to the shoulder.
    b. swaddle the baby.
    c. offer a pacifier.
    d. play rhythmic sounds.

19. The cries of brain-damaged infants and those who have experienced prenatal and birth complications are often (p. 105)
    a. more difficult for adults to interpret.
    b. weak and sporadic.
    c. shrill and piercing.
    d. easier to sooth than the cries of other infants.

20. Research on the sense of smell indicates that (p. 106)
    a. infants do not have a well-developed sense of smell until several months after birth.
    b. newborn infants recognize the smell of their own mother's breast and amniotic fluid.
    c. odor preferences are gradually developed through environmental exposure to a variety of scents.
    d. infants can distinguish pleasant and unpleasant odors but defend themselves from unpleasant odors by turnin away.

CHAPTER 4
PHYSICAL DEVELOPMENT IN INFANCY
AND TODDLERHOOD

BRIEF CHAPTER SUMMARY

Body size increases dramatically during the first 2 years of life, following organized patterns of growth called cephalocaudal and proximodistal trends. Fat increases much more rapidly than muscle during the first year. During the first 2 years, neurons form intricate connections, and their fibers myelinate, leading to a rapid increase in brain weight. Already, the two hemispheres of the cortex have begun to specialize, although the brain retains considerable plasticity during the first year of life. Researchers have identified key, sensitive periods of brain development when appropriate stimulation is key to acquiring skills.

A variety of factors affect early physical growth. While heredity contributes to height, weight, and rate of physical maturation, good nutrition is essential for rapidly growing babies, and breast milk is especially well-suited to meet their needs. Malnutrition during the early years can lead to serious dietary diseases, which are associated with permanent stunting of physical growth and brain development. Finally, affection and stimulation are also vital for healthy physical growth.

Infants are marvelously equipped to learn immediately after birth. Classical and operant conditioning, habituation-dishabituation, and imitation are important mechanisms through which infants learn about their physical and social worlds.

The rapid motor development that occurs during the first 2 years follows the same organized sequences as does physical growth. The mastery of motor skills involves acquiring increasingly complex, dynamic systems of action. In this way, maturation and experience combine to influence the development of motor skills.

Perception changes remarkably over the first year of life. Hearing and vision undergo major advances during the first 2 years as infants organize stimuli into complex patterns, improve their perception of depth and objects, and combine information across sensory modalities. The Gibsons' differentiation theory helps us understand the course of perceptual development.

LEARNING OBJECTIVES

After reading this chapter, you should be able to:

4.1   Describe changes in body size, body proportions, and muscle–fat makeup during the first 2 years of life. (pp. 114–115)

4.2   Describe the development and functions of neurons and glial cells. (p. 116)

4.3   Describe the development of the cerebral cortex, and explain the concepts of brain lateralization and brain plasticity. (pp. 117–119)

4.4   Describe research findings related to the existence of sensitive periods in brain development, and note the evidence of brain growth spurts and the need for appropriate stimulation. (pp. 119–120)

4.5   Discuss changes in the organization of sleep and wakefulness between birth and 2 years of age. (pp. 120–123)

4.6   Discuss the impact of heredity on early physical growth. (p. 123)

4.7   Discuss the nutritional needs of infants and toddlers, the advantages of breastfeeding, and the extent to which chubby babies are at risk for later overweight and obesity. (pp. 123–125)

4.8   Discuss the impact of severe malnutrition on the development of infants and toddlers, and cite two dietary diseases associated with this condition. (pp. 125–126)

4.9　Describe the growth disorder known as nonorganic failure to thrive, noting common symptoms and family circumstances surrounding the disorder. (p. 126)

4.10　Explain how infants learn through classical conditioning, operant conditioning, habituation, and imitation. (pp. 126–129)

4.11　Describe the sequence of motor development during the first 2 years of life. (p.129–130)

4.12　Explain the dynamic systems theory of motor development, and discuss support for this approach stemming from cross-cultural research. (pp. 130–132)

4.13　Describe the development of reaching and grasping, and explain how early experiences affect these skills. (p. 132)

4.14　Summarize the development of hearing in infancy, giving special attention to speech perception. (p. 133)

4.15　Summarize the development of vision in infancy, including depth perception, pattern perception, and face perception. (pp. 133–138)

4.16　Explain the concept of intermodal perception. (pp. 138–139)

4.17　Explain the differentiation theory of perceptual development. (p. 139)

STUDY QUESTIONS

Body Growth

Changes in Body Size and Muscle–Fat Makeup

1.　True or False: Infants and toddlers grow in spurts, wherein they may experience relatively long stretches without any growth and then add as much as half-an-inch in a 24-hour period. (p. 114)

2.　Why do infants experience an increase in body fat during the first year of life? (p. 114)

_____

_____

Individual and Group Differences

1.　True or False: Boys and girls have an equal muscle-to-fat ratio during infancy. (p. 114)

2.　True or False: Trends in body growth tend to be consistent cross-culturally. (p. 114)

3.　The best way to estimate a child's physical growth is to use _____, a measure of the development of the bones in the body. Explain how this estimate is obtained. (p. 115)

_____

_____

Changes in Body Proportions

1.　Briefly explain the *cephalocaudal* and *proximodistal* trends, which represent two growth patterns used to describe changes in body proportions. (p. 115)

Cephalocaudal: _____

_____

Proximodistal: _____

_____

Brain Development

Development of Neurons

1. What are *neurons* and what is their function? (p. 116)

    A. _____
    _____

    B. _____
    _____

2. Between neurons, there are tiny gaps, or _____, across which messages pass. (p. 116)

3. True or False: During the prenatal period, the neural tube produces more neurons than the brain will ever need. (p. 116)

4. Explain the process of *synaptic pruning.* (p. 116)

    _____
    _____
    _____

5. About half of the brain's volume is made up of _____ *cells,* whose most important function is _____, the coating of neural fibers with an insulating fatty sheath that improves the efficiency of message transfer. (p. 116)

Development of the Cerebral Cortex

1. True or False: The cerebral cortex is the largest, most complex brain structure, containing the greatest number of neurons and synapses. (p. 117)

2. Describe the different functions controlled by the left and right hemispheres of the brain. (p. 118)

    A. Left: _____

    B. Right: _____

3. Explain the concepts of *lateralization* and *brain plasticity,* noting how the two are related. (p. 118)

    Lateralization: _____
    _____
    _____

    Brain plasticity: _____
    _____
    _____

    Relationship: _____
    _____
    _____

4. During the early years of life, the brain is (more / less) plastic than at any time later in life. (p. 119)

1. Adults who suffered brain injuries in infancy and early childhood show (fewer / more) cognitive impairments than do adults with later occurring injuries. (p. 120)

2. Describe the impact of brain injury on childhood language development, noting how this relates to brain plasticity. (p. 120)

_____

_____

_____

3. (Language / Spatial) skills are less impaired after early brain injury. (p. 120)

4. True or False: Brain plasticity is restricted to childhood and is no longer evident by the time individuals reach adulthood. Provide research evident to support your response. (pp. 120–121)

_____

_____

_____

Sensitive Periods of Brain Development

1. Ethically, researchers cannot expose children to extreme sensory deprivation. However, less direct evidence closely parallels the animal evidence. Cite two examples of human evidence that support the existence of sensitive periods in the development of the cerebral cortex. (p. 119)

   A. _____

   _____

   B. _____

   _____

2. True or False: Overstimulation of infants and toddlers threatens their interest in learning and may create conditions similar to those of stimulus deprivation. (p. 120)

Changing States of Arousal

1. Describe major changes in the organization of sleep and wakefulness during the first 2 years of life, and discuss how the social environment impacts these changing arousal patterns. (p. 121)

   _____

   _____

   _____

   _____

   _____

Cultural Influences: Cultural Variation in Infant Sleeping Arrangements

1. True or False: Although rare in the United States, parent–infant cosleeping is common in many other countries around the world. (p. 122)

2. Explain the role of collectivist versus individualistic cultural values in determining infant sleeping arrangements. (p. 122)

_____

_____

_____

_____

Influences on Early Physical Growth

Heredity

1. True or False: When diet and health are adequate, height and rate of physical growth are largely determined by heredity. (p. 123)

2. Describe the phenomenon known as *catch-up growth*. (p. 123)

_____

_____

_____

Nutrition

1. Describe four nutritional and health benefits of breast milk. (p. 124)

   A. _____

   _____

   B. _____

   _____

   C. _____

   _____

   D. _____

   _____

2. Discuss the benefits of breastfeeding as they relate to mothers and infants in poverty-stricken regions of the world. (p. 123)

_____

_____

_____

_____

3. True or False: Chubbiness in infancy typically leads to obesity at older ages. (p. 125)

4. Cite two ways in which parents can prevent infants and toddlers from becoming overweight at later ages. (p. 125)

   A. _____

   B. _____

Malnutrition

1. Describe the causes of *marasmus* and *kwashiorkor,* two dietary diseases associated with severe malnutrition, and summarize the developmental outcomes associated with these extreme forms of malnutrition. (pp. 125–126)

    Marasmus: _____

    _____

    Kwashiorkor: _____

    _____

    Outcomes: _____

    _____

    _____

    _____

    _____

Emotional Well-Being

1. What is *nonorganic failure to thrive,* and what are some common symptoms? (p. 126)

    _____

    _____

    _____

    _____

2. Describe family circumstances surrounding nonorganic failure to thrive. (p. 126)

    _____

    _____

    _____

    _____

Learning Capacities

1. Define *learning.* (p. 126)

    _____

Classical Conditioning

1. Briefly explain how learning takes place through *classical conditioning.* (p. 126)

    _____

    _____

    _____

2. Why is classical conditioning of great value to infants? (p. 126)

    _____

    _____

3. Match the following terms to the appropriate definition. (pp. 126–127)

    _____ A neutral stimulus that leads to a reflexive response (if
    learning occurs)
    _____ A learned response exhibited toward a previously neutral
    stimulus
    _____ A reflexive response
    _____ A stimulus that automatically leads to a reflexive response

    1. Unconditioned stimulus (UCS)
    2. Conditioned stimulus (CS)
    3. Unconditioned response (UCR)
    4. Conditioned response (CR)

4. Using the above definitions as a guide (see question 3), outline the three steps involved in classical conditioning. (pp. 126–127)

    A. _____

    _____

    B. _____

    _____

    C. _____

    _____

5. In classical conditioning, if the CS is presented alone enough times, without being paired with the UCS, the CR will no longer occur. This is referred to as _____. (p. 127)

Operant Conditioning

1. Briefly explain how learning takes place through *operant conditioning*. (p. 127)

    _____

    _____

    _____

2. Define the terms *reinforcer* and *punishment* as they relate to operant conditioning. (p. 127)

    Reinforcer: _____

    _____

    Punishment: _____

    _____

3. Describe how operant conditioning plays a role in the development of infant–caregiver attachment. (p. 128)

    _____

    _____

    _____

Habituation

1. Define the terms *habituation* and *recovery*. (p. 128)

    Habituation: _____

    _____

Recovery: _____

_____

2. Explain how studying infants' habituation and recovery allows researchers to understand infant perception and cognition. (p. 128)

_____

_____

_____

Imitation

1. Describe what infants are able to learn through the process of imitation. (p. 128)

_____

_____

_____

Motor Development

The Sequence of Motor Development

1. Distinguish between *gross* and *fine motor development,* and provide examples of each. (p. 130)

Gross: _____

_____

Examples: _____

Fine: _____

_____

Examples: _____

2. True or False: Although the *sequence* of motor development is fairly uniform, large individual differences exist in the *rate* of development. (p. 130)

3. Discuss the organization and direction of motor development in relation to the cephalocaudal and proximodistal trends. (p. 130)

_____

_____

_____

4. True or False: Motor development follows a fixed maturational timetable. (p. 130)

Motor Skills as Dynamic Systems

1. According to the *dynamic systems theory of motor development,* mastery of motor skills involves acquisition of increasingly complex *systems of action.* Explain what this term means. (p. 130)

    _____

    _____

    _____

    _____

2. List four factors that contribute to the development of each new motor skill. (p. 130)

    A. _____

    B. _____

    C. _____

    D. _____

3. True or False: Dynamic systems theory regards motor development as a genetically determined process. Briefly explain your response. (p. 131)

    _____

    _____

    _____

Cultural Variations in Motor Development

1. True or False: When infants are denied early movement opportunities and a stimulating environment, their motor development is delayed. (p. 131)

2. Explain how cultural variations in infant-rearing practices affect motor development. (pp. 131–132)

    _____

    _____

    _____

    _____

Fine Motor Development: Reaching and Grasping

1. Match the following terms to the appropriate definition. (p. 132)

    _____ Well-coordinated movement in which infants use the thumb and   1. Prereaching
    forefinger opposably   2. Ulnar grasp
    _____ Poorly coordinated swipes or swings toward an object   3. Pincer grasp
    _____ Clumsy motion in which the fingers close against the palm

2. Voluntary reaching (is / is not) affected by early experience. (p. 132)

Hearing

1. Describe changes in auditory perception over the first year of life that prepare infants for language acquisition. (p. 133)

    By 6 months: _____

    _____

    _____

    6–12 months: _____

    _____

    _____

    _____

Vision

1. What is *depth perception,* and why is it important in infant development? (p. 134)

    A. _____

    _____

    B. _____

    _____

2. Describe Gibson and Walk's studies using the visual cliff, and cite the limitations of this approach for the study of infant depth perception. (p. 134)

    A. _____

    _____

    _____

    _____

    B. _____

    _____

    _____

3. Name and describe the three cues for depth. (p. 134)

    A. _____

    _____

    B. _____

    _____

    C. _____

    _____

4. Summarize research on the relationship between crawling and depth perception. (pp. 134–135)

_____

_____

_____

_____

5. Provide an example from adult experience which helps to explain why crawling plays such an important role in the infant's knowledge and understanding of the three-dimensional world. (p. 135)

_____

_____

6. The principle of _____, which accounts for early pattern preferences, states that if infants are sensitive to the contrast between two or more patterns, they will prefer the one with more contrast. (p. 135)

7. Summarize the development of pattern perception during the first year of life. (pp. 135–138)

Birth–1 month: _____

_____

2–4 months: _____

_____

5–12 months: _____

_____

8. True or False: By 2 months of age, infants recognize aspects of their mother's facial features, and they look longer at her face than at an unfamiliar woman's face. (p. 138)

Biology & Environment: Development of Infants with Severe Visual Impairments

1. True or False: Children with severe visual impairments show delays in motor, cognitive, language, and social development. (p. 136)

2. Discuss how severe visual impairments impact motor exploration and spatial understanding. (p. 136)

_____

_____

_____

_____

3. Explain how severe visual impairments affect the caregiver–infant relationship. (p. 136)

_____

_____

_____

4. List three techniques that can help infants with severe visual impairments become aware of their physical and social surroundings. (p. 136)

A. _____

_____

B. _____

_____

C. _____

_____

Intermodal Perception

1. What is *intermodal perception*? (p. 138)

_____

_____

2. True or False: From birth, infants are capable of combining information from multiple sensory systems. Cite research evidence supporting your response. (pp. 138–139)

_____

_____

_____

_____

Understanding Perceptual Development

1. Explain the *differentiation theory* of perceptual development. (p. 139)

_____

_____

_____

_____

2. True or False: According to differentiation theory, opportunities to act on the environment play a vital role in perceptual development. (p. 139)

ASK YOURSELF . . .

For *Ask Yourself* questions for this chapter, please log on to the Companion Website at www.ablongman.com/berk.

SUGGESTED STUDENT READINGS

Bremner, G., & Fogel, A. (Eds.). (2002). Blackwell handbook of infant development. Malden, MA: Blackwell. Written primarily for students and instructors of psychology, this book presents current research in infant development, including health and nutrition, perceptual development, risk factors that interfere with normal development, and public policies pertaining to infants and toddlers.

Bruer, J. T. (1999). *The myth of the first three years.* New York: Free Press. Challenges the widely accepted belief that the first three years of life determine whether or not a child will develop into a successful, thinking person. Drawing on research on brain development, this book shows that learning and cognitive development occur not just in infancy and toddlerhood, but also throughout childhood and adulthood.

Lacerda, F., von Hofsten, C., & Heimann, M. (Eds.). (2001). *Emerging cognitive abilities in early infancy.* Mahwah, NJ: Erlbaum. An interdisciplinary approach to infant development, this book presents up-to-date research on evolving infant capacities. Although research focuses primarily on the cognitive milestones of infancy, the authors integrate various other achievements, such as the importance of perceptual development and imitation.

PUZZLE 4.1 TERM REVIEW

Across

4. _____ trend: pattern of growth that proceeds from head to tail
6. A disease appearing between 1 and 3 years of age that is caused by a diet low in protein
8. Process in which neural fibers are coated with an insulating fatty sheath that improves the efficiency of message transfer
9. Brain _____ refers to the ability of other parts of the brain to take over the functions of damaged regions.
10. _____ trend: pattern of growth that proceeds from the center of the body outward
12. _____ failure to thrive: growth disorder caused by lack of affection and stimulation

Down

1. _____ cells are responsible for myelinization of neural fibers
2. A disease usually appearing in the first year of life; caused by a diet low in all essential nutrients.
3. Nerve cells that store and transmit information to the brain
5. Specialization of functions of the two hemispheres of the cortex
7. The largest structure of the human brain is the _____ cortex.
10. Synaptic _____ is the loss of connective fibers by seldom-stimulated neurons.
11. The gaps between neurons, across which messages are sent

PUZZLE 4.2 TERM REVIEW

Across

3. _____ conditioning: form of learning in which a spontaneous behavior is followed by a stimulus that changes the probability that the behavior will occur again
6. In classical conditioning, a reflexive response that is produced by an UCS (abbr.)
7. _____ perception combines information from more than one sensory system.
10. In operant conditioning, removing a desirable stimulus or presenting an unpleasant one to decrease the occurrence of a response
12. In operating conditioning, a stimulus that increases the occurrence of a response
13. _____ conditioning: form of learning that involves associating a neutral stimulus with a stimulus that leads to a reflexive response
14. A gradual reduction in the strength of a response due to repetitive stimulation
15. Learning by copying the behavior of another person

Down

1. _____ sensitivity: the ability to detect contrast or differences in light levels between adjacent regions in a pattern
2. In the differentiation theory of perceptual development, _____ features are those that remain stable in a constantly changing perceptual world
4. Following habituation, an increase in responsiveness to a new stimulus
5. The _____ systems theory of motor development views new motor skills as reorganizations of previously mastered skills that lead to more effective ways of exploring and conrolling the environment.
6. In classical conditioning, a stimulus that leads to a reflexive response (abbr.)
8. _____ theory: view that perceptual development involves detection of increasingly fine-grained, invariant features in the environment
9. In classical conditioning, a neutral stimulus that through pairing with an UCS leads to a new response (abbr.)
11. In classical conditioning, a new response produced by a CS that resembles the UCR (abbr.)

PRACTICE TEST #1

1. During the first 2 years of life, physical growth is (p. 114)
   a. more rapid than it was during the prenatal period.
   b. slow and steady.
   c. rapid only for bottle-fed babies.
   d. faster than it will be at any other time after birth.

2. Which of the following provides the best estimate of a child's physical maturity? (p. 115)
   a. comparison of the child's physical growth to universal growth norms for his/her age
   b. measures of the child's muscle-fat makeup
   c. measures of the development of the bones of the body
   d. examination of the child's gross motor skills

3. The _____ trend refers to a pattern of physical growth which proceeds from head to tail. (p. 115)
   a. intermodal
   b. cephalocaudal
   c. proximodistal
   d. invariant

4. The process in which neural fibers are coated with an insulating fatty sheath that improves the efficiency of message transfer is called (p. 116)
   a. myelination.
   b. synaptic pruning.
   c. neural sheathing.
   d. brain plasticity.

5. Brain plasticity refers to (p. 118)
   a. the specialization of functions of the two hemispheres of the brain.
   b. the ability of other parts of the brain to take over the functions of damaged regions.
   c. the extent of neural development at a particular period of development.
   d. the loss of neural connections resulting from inadequate stimulation.

6. Which of the following is true of breastfeeding during infancy? (p. 124)
   a. Breastfeeding is not recommended for women in developing countries because breast milk does not contain sufficient nutrients to protect against malnutrition and infection.
   b. Breastfeeding is rare among American mothers, and rates of breastfeeding have declined over the last two decades.
   c. Breastfeeding is essential for children's healthy psychological development.
   d. Breast milk provides infants with nutrients that are ideally suited for early rapid brain development.

7. Marasmus is caused by (p. 125)
   a. overeating during the first year of life.
   b. a severe iron deficiency.
   c. a diet low in protein.
   d. a diet low in all essential nutrients.

8. A longitudinal study of marasmic children revealed that (p. 125)
   a. early malnutrition did not have a long-term impact on learning and behavior.
   b. improved diet led to gains in motor development but not cognitive development.
   c. improved diet led to some catch-up growth in height but little improvement in head size.
   d. nutritional intervention failed to produce gains in physical, motor, or cognitive development.

9. Nonorganic failure to thrive (p. 126)
    a. is associated with a known biological cause.
    b. is caused by a lack of stimulation and affection.
    c. results from an inadequate diet in early infancy.
    d. is associated with long-term deficits, even when treated early.

10. In classical conditioning, the _____ must consistently produce a reflexive reaction before learning can take place. (p. 126)
    a. unconditioned stimulus (UCS)
    b. conditioned stimulus (CS)
    c. unconditioned response (UCR)
    d. conditioned response (CR)

11. In classical conditioning, if the conditioned stimulus (CS) is presented alone enough times, without being paired with the unconditioned stimulus (UCS), the conditioned response (CR) will no longer occur. This is known as (p. 127)
    a. dishabituation.
    b. termination.
    c. extinction.
    d. disassociation.

12. In operant conditioning, a stimulus that increases the likelihood of a response is a (p. 127)
    a. punishment.
    b. reward.
    c. reinforcer.
    d. conditioned stimulus.

13. After continually looking at the same pattern for a period of time, an infant shows a gradual reduction in responding to this stimulus. This phenomenon is known as (p. 128)
    a. imitation.
    b. habituation.
    c. classical conditioning.
    d. operant conditioning.

14. Crawling, standing, and walking are examples of (p. 130)
    a. fine motor development.
    b. gross motor development.
    c. coordinated motor development.
    d. dynamic motor development.

15. According to the dynamic systems theory of motor development (p. 130)
    a. new skills are acquired by revising and combining earlier accomplishments.
    b. new skills are acquired independently of previously learned skills.
    c. motor development is a genetically determined process.
    d. the pathways to motor skill acquisition are universal.

16. Cross-cultural research on motor development indicates that (p. 131)
    a. the rate and sequence of motor development are universal in all nations throughout the world.
    b. cultural variations in infant-rearing practices have little effect on motor development.
    c. infants in Western industrialized nations attain motor milestones at an earlier age than do their peers in less developed regions of the world.
    d. early movement opportunities and a stimulating environment contribute significantly to motor development.

17. Over the first year of life, the greatest change in hearing that takes place is the ability to (p. 133)
    a. hear a wider range of tones.
    b. analyze complex sound patterns.
    c. turn the eyes and head in the direction of a sound.
    d. increasingly attend to the sounds of all human languages.

18. _____ depth cues arise because our two eyes have slightly different views of the visual field. (p. 134)
   a. Kinetic
   b. Pictorial
   c. Binocular
   d. Inverse

19. From the start, infants expect sight, sound, and touch to go together, a capacity called (p. 138)
   a. intermodal perception.
   b. sensory perception.
   c. systematic perception.
   d. integrative perception.

20. According to the differentiation theory of perceptual development (p. 139)
   a. infants seek out variant, or ever-changing, features of the environment.
   b. infants seek out invariant, or stable, features of the environment.
   c. infants have an innate capacity to give order to their environment.
   d. infants impose meaning on their perceptions, thereby constructing categories of objects and events in the environment.

PRACTICE TEST #2

1. Skeletal age is estimated by (p. 115)
   a. using the child's weight to estimate bone density.
   b. x-raying the child's bones and determining the extent to which soft cartilage has hardened into bone.
   c. determining bone density through the use of ultrasound.
   d. examining the fontanels, or soft spots that separate the bones of the skull.

2. _____ are nerve cells in the brain that store and transmit information. (p. 116)
   a. Glial cells
   b. Neurons
   c. Synapses
   d. Epiphyses

3. The process through which seldom stimulated neurons lose their synapses is known as (p. 116)
   a. cortical specialization.
   b. lateralization.
   c. synaptic pruning.
   d. myelination.

4. Which is the largest, most complex brain structure, containing the greatest number of neurons and synapses? (p. 117)
   a. frontal lobe
   b. cerebellum
   c. corpus callosum
   d. cerebral cortex

5. The left hemisphere of the brain is largely responsible for (p. 118)
   a. regulation of negative emotion.
   b. attention and complex thought.
   c. spatial abilities.
   d. verbal abilities.

6. The greatest change in the organization of sleep and wakefulness during the first 2 years of life is that (p. 121)
   a. with age, infants require more naps.
   b. periods of sleep and wakefulness become fewer but longer.
   c. there is a dramatic decrease in total sleep time.
   d. by the end of the first year, infants no longer have night wakings.

7. Kwashiorkor results from (p. 125)
   a. a diet low in calcium.
   b. a diet lacking in vitamins A and D.
   c. a diet low in protein.
   d. a diet high in fat.

8. Which of the following is true with regard to classical conditioning? (p. 126)
   a. Infants are easily conditioned by pairing any two stimuli.
   b. Infants are conditioned most easily to fear responses.
   c. Classical conditioning is most effective when the neutral stimulus is presented several minutes after the unconditioned stimulus (UCS).
   d. Classical conditioning is valuable to infants because it makes the environment more orderly and predictable.

9. Which of the following best reflects the views of infant behavior suggested by classical conditioning and operant conditioning perspectives? (p. 127)
   a. In classical conditioning, infants are viewed as passive learners, whereas in operant conditioning, infants are viewed as active learners.
   b. In operant conditioning, infants are viewed as passive learners, whereas in classical conditioning, infants are viewed as active learners.
   c. Both classical and operant conditioning perspectives view infants as active learners.
   d. Both classical and operant conditioning perspectives view infants as passive learners.

10. When baby Sam sees his mother, he gazes at her and smiles. Sam's mother looks and smiles back, and then Sam looks and smiles again. This is an example of (p. 128)
    a. extinction.
    b. habituation.
    c. operant conditioning.
    d. classical conditioning.

11. After repeatedly listening to a particular tone for a period of time, an infant shows a gradual reduction in responding to this tone. When a new tone is introduced, the infant returns to a high level of responding. This increase in responsiveness to the new stimulus is known as (p. 128)
    a. habituation.
    b. recovery.
    c. differentiation.
    d. extinction.

12. Research on infants' habituation and recovery allows researchers to explore early (p. 128)
    a. motor development.
    b. imitation skills.
    c. perception and cognition.
    d. extinction responses.

13. Infants gain motor control of the head, trunk, and arms before coordination of the hands and fingers. This is an example of the _____ trend. (p. 130)
    a. anterior-posterior
    b. proximodistal
    c. cephalocaudal
    d. medialateral

14. Kicking, rocking on all fours, and reaching are gradually put together into crawling. This example illustrates that motor development is a matter of acquiring increasingly complex (p. 130)
    a. fine motor development.
    b. gross motor development.
    c. systems of action.
    d. coordinated action.

15. In which sequence do infants develop voluntary reaching and grasping behaviors? (p. 132)
    a. pincer grasp, ulnar grasp, prereaching
    b. ulnar grasp, pincer grasp, prereaching
    c. prereaching, ulnar grasp, pincer grasp
    d. prereaching, pincer grasp, ulnar grasp

16. Newborns' uncoordinated swipes or swings toward an object in front of them are called (p. 132)
    a. prereaching.
    b. proprioceptive reactions.
    c. arm reflexes.
    d. ulnar grasps.

17. Visual acuity reaches a near-adult level at approximately (p. 133)
    a. 3 months of age.
    b. 6 months of age.
    c. 11 months of age.
    d. 18 months of age.

18. Infant depth perception, as assessed by refusal to cross the deep side of the visual cliff, is promoted by (p. 134)
    a. a regimen of physical exercise.
    b. independent movement.
    c. opportunities to look at photographs and picture books.
    d. holding babies over drop-offs.

19. Which of the following best reflects the view of infant behavior suggested by operant conditioning? (p. 135)
    a. Infants are passive learners.
    b. Infants are inattentive learners.
    c. Infants are active learners.
    d. Infants prefer others to exert control over their environment.

20. Research suggests that intermodal perception (pp. 138–139)
    a. is a biologically primed capacity that is present at birth.
    b. emerges as a direct result of experience with the environment.
    c. develops as a result of independent locomotion.
    d. appears gradually over the first year of life.

CHAPTER 5
COGNITIVE DEVELOPMENT
IN INFANCY AND TODDLERHOOD

BRIEF CHAPTER SUMMARY

According to Piaget, by acting directly on the environment, children move through four stages of cognitive development in which psychological structures, or schemes, achieve a better fit with external reality. The first stage, or the sensorimotor stage, spans the first 2 years of life, and is divided into six substages. During the sensorimotor stage, infants make strides in intentional behavior and understanding of object permanence. By Substage 6, toddlers become capable of mental representation, as shown by sudden solutions to sensorimotor problems, mastery of object permanence problems involving hidden displacement, deferred imitation, and make-believe play. However, recent research suggests that some sensorimotor capacities emerge earlier than Piaget believed, raising questions about the accuracy of his account of sensorimotor development.

Information-processing theorists focus on many aspects of thinking, from attention, memory, and categorization skills to complex problem solving. With age, infants attend to more aspects of the environment and take information in more quickly. In the second year, attention to novelty declines, and sustained attention improves, especially during play with toys. In addition, as infants get older, they remember experiences longer and group stimuli into increasingly complex categories. Also, categorization shifts from a perceptual to conceptual basis. Information processing has contributed greatly to our view of young babies as sophisticated cognitive beings. However, its greatest drawback stems from its central strength—by analyzing cognition into its components, information processing has had difficulty putting them back together into a broad, comprehensive theory. Vygotsky believed that complex mental activities have their origins in social interaction. Through joint activities with more mature members of their society, children come to master activities and think in ways that have meaning in their culture.

Infant intelligence tests consist largely of perceptual and motor responses and predict later intelligence poorly. Speed of habituation and recovery to visual stimuli, which tap basic cognitive processes, are better predictors of future performance. Home and child care environments, as well as early intervention for at-risk infants and toddlers, exert powerful influences on mental development.

As perception and cognition improve during infancy, they pave the way for an extraordinary human achievement— language. Three theories provide different accounts of how young children develop language. The behaviorist perspective regards language development as entirely due to environmental influences; nativism assumes that children are prewired to master the intricate rules of their language; and the interactionist perspective maintains that language development results from interactions between inner capacities and environmental influences, such as social exchanges. First words appear around 12 months; two-word utterances between 18 months and 24 months. However, substantial individual differences exist in rate and style of early language progress. Adults in many cultures speak to young children in child-directed speech, a simplified form of language that is well suited to their learning needs. Conversational give-and-take between adults and toddlers is one of the best predictors of early language development and academic competence during the school years.

LEARNING OBJECTIVES

After reading this chapter, you should be able to:

5.1   Describe how schemes change over the course of development. (p. 144)

5.2   Identify Piaget's six sensorimotor substages, and describe the major cognitive achievements in each. (pp. 145–147)

5.3 Discuss recent research on sensorimotor development, noting its implications for the accuracy of Piaget's sensorimotor stage (pp. 147–151)

5.4 Describe the information-processing view of cognitive development and the general structure of the information-processing system. (p. 153)

5.5 Summarize the strengths and limitations of the information-processing approach. (p. 157)

5.6 Cite changes in attention, memory, and categorization during the first 2 years. (pp. 153–157)

5.7 Explain how Vygotsky's concept of the zone of proximal development expands our understanding of early cognitive development. (pp. 158–159)

5.8 Describe the mental testing approach, the meaning of intelligence test scores, and the extent to which infant tests predict later performance. (pp. 160–161)

5.9 Discuss environmental influences on early mental development, including home, child care, and early intervention for at-risk infants and toddlers. (pp. 161–163)

5.10 Summarize three theories of language development, and indicate the emphasis each places on innate abilities and environmental influences. (pp. 164–165)

5.11 Describe major milestones of language development in the first 2 years, noting individual and cultural differences, and discuss ways in which adults can support infants' and toddlers' emerging capacities. (pp. 165–169)

STUDY QUESTIONS

Piaget's Cognitive-Developmental Theory

1. During Piaget's _____ stage, which spans the first 2 years of life, infants and toddlers "think" with their eyes, ears, and hands. (p. 144)

Piaget's Ideas About Cognitive Change

1. According to Piaget, specific psychological structures, or organized ways of making sense of experience called _____, change with age. (p. 144)

2. Match the following terms with the appropriate description. (p. 144)

_____ Creating new schemes or adjusting old ones to produce a better fit with the environment	1. Adaptation
_____ Taking new schemes, rearranging them and linking them with other schemes to create an interconnected cognitive system	2. Accommodation
_____ Using current schemes to interpret the external world	3. Assimilation
_____ Building schemes through direct interaction with the environment	4. Organization

The Sensorimotor Stage

1. True or False: According to Piaget, at birth babies already know a great deal about the world. (p. 145)

2. Explain the differences between primary, secondary, and tertiary circular reactions. (p. 146)

Primary: _____

_____

Secondary: _____

_____

Tertiary: _____

_____

3. Match each of the following sensorimotor substages with the appropriate description. (p. 145)

_____ Infants' primary means of adapting to the environment is through reflexes.	1. Substage 1
_____ Infants engage in goal-directed behavior and begin to attain object permanence.	2. Substage 2
	3. Substage 3
_____ Toddlers repeat behaviors with variation, producing new effects.	4. Substage 4
_____ Infants' adaptations are oriented toward their own bodies.	5. Substage 5
_____ Infants' attention begins to turn outward toward the environment.	6. Substage 6
_____ Toddlers gain the ability to create mental representations.	

4. The understanding that objects continue to exist when out of sight is called _____
   _____. (p. 146)

5. Describe the A-not-B search error. (p. 146)

   _____

6. List three new capacities that result from the ability to create mental representations. (p. 147)

   A. _____

   B. _____

   C. _____

Follow-Up Research on Sensorimotor Development

1. Explain the *violation-of-expectation method,* which is often used by researchers to examine infants' grasp of object permanence and other aspects of physical reasoning. (p. 147)

   _____

   _____

   _____

2. Explain why the violation-of-expectation method is controversial. (p. 147)

   _____

   _____

   _____

3. True or False: Recent research findings by Renée Baillargeon and colleagues indicate that infants as young as 2 to 3 months of age show an understanding of object permanence. (p. 148)

4. Explain why young infants (who appear to grasp the notion of object permanence) do not try to search for hidden objects. (p. 148)

   _____

   _____

5. According to Piaget, infants cannot represent experience until about _____ months of age. However, laboratory research reveals that infants exhibit _____, a form of mental representation, as early as 6 weeks of age. (p. 149)

6. Provide an example of how toddlers use *deferred imitation* to enrich their range of sensorimotor schemes. (p. 149)

    _____

    _____

7. By 10 to 12 months, infants can solve problems by _____, meaning that they take a strategy from one problem and apply it to other relevant problems. (p. 149)

Evaluation of the Sensorimotor Stage

1. True or False: Recent research indicates that the cognitive attainments of infancy do in fact follow the neat, stepwise fashion that Piaget assumed. (p. 150)

2. According to the _____ perspective, babies are born with a set of innate knowledge systems, or core domains of thought. (p. 150)

3. Core knowledge theorists look at four domains of thought when assessing infants' cognitive knowledge. List these domains or types of knowledge. (pp. 150–151)

    A. _____ B. _____

    C. _____ D. _____

4. Cite Piaget's contributions to our knowledge of infant cognition. (p. 151)

    _____

    _____

    _____

Biology & Environment: Do Infants Have Built-In Numerical Knowledge?

1. What do research findings on infants' knowledge of numbers reveal? Why are these findings controversial? (p. 152)

    A. _____

    _____

    B. _____

    _____

Information Processing

Structure of the Information-Processing System

1. Describe the three basic parts of the information-processing system, including ways in which mental processes can facilitate the storage and retrieval of information at each level. (p. 153)

    Sensory Register: _____

    _____

Working Memory: _____

_____

Long-term Memory: _____

_____

2. True or False: Information-processing researchers believe that the basic structure of the mental system is similar throughout life. (p. 153)

Attention

1. List two ways in which attention improves between 1 and 5 months of age. (p. 154)

    A. _____

    B. _____

2. Summarize changes in attention from infancy to toddlerhood. (p. 154)

    _____

    _____

    _____

Memory

1. Habituation research greatly (underestimates/overestimates) infants' memory when compared with methods that rely on their active exploration of objects. (p. 154)

2. _____, the simplest form of memory, involves a simple indication as to whether a new experience is identical or similar to a previous one. _____, on the other hand, is much more challenging because it involves remembering something in the absence of perceptual support. (p. 155)

Categorization

1. The earliest categories are _____, or based on similar overall appearance or prominent object part. By the end of the first year, more categories are _____, or based on common function and behavior. (p. 155)

2. Briefly explain how the perceptual-to-conceptual change takes place. (p. 157)

    _____

    _____

    _____

Evaluation of Information-Processing Findings

1. Information-processing research underscores the (continuity/discontinuity) of human thinking from infancy into adult life. (p. 157)

2. In what way does information-processing research challenge Piaget's view of early cognitive development? (p. 157)

    _____

    _____

    _____

3. What is the greatest drawback of the information-processing approach to cognitive development? (p. 157)

_____

_____

_____

A Lifespan Vista: Infantile Amnesia

1. What is *infantile amnesia?* (p. 156)

_____

_____

2. Cite and briefly explain two explanations of *infantile amnesia.* (p. 156)

A. _____

_____

B. _____

_____

3. _____ memory refers to representations of special, one-time events that are long-lasting because they are imbued with personal meaning. (p. 156)

4. For memories to become autobiographical, at least two developments are necessary. List them. (p. 156)

A. _____

B. _____

The Social Context of Early Cognitive Development

1. According to Vygotsky's sociocultural theory, how do children come to master activities and think in culturally meaningful ways? (pp. 157–158)

_____

_____

2. Explain Vygotsky's concept of the *zone of proximal development,* emphasizing the role of adults in fostering children's cognitive devlopment. (p. 158)

_____

_____

_____

_____

3. True or False: As early as the first 2 years, cultural variations in social experiences affect mental strategies. (p. 158)

4. Using an example, explain how culture influences mental strategies. (p. 159)

_____

_____

_____

_____

Cultural Influences: Caregiver–Toddler Interaction and Early Make-Believe Play

1. Briefly summarize Vygotsky's view of make-believe play. (p. 158)

_____

_____

_____

2. Explain why adults' participation in toddlers' make-believe play is so important. (p. 159)

_____

_____

_____

Individual Differences in Early Mental Development

1. How does the mental testing approach differ from the cognitive theories discussed earlier in this chapter? (p. 160)

_____

_____

Infant Intelligence Tests

1. What types of respones are tapped by most infant tests of intelligence? (p. 160)

_____

_____

_____

2. One commonly used infant test is the _____ *of Infant Development*, designed for children between one month and 3½ years. (p. 160)

3. Describe how intelligence scores are computed. (p. 160)

_____

_____

4. Explain the difference between an *intelligence quotient,* or *IQ,* and a *developmental quotient,* or *DQ.* (p. 160)

_____

_____

_____

5. True or False: Scores on infant intelligence tests are excellent predictors of later intelligence. Why or why not? (pp. 161–162)

_____

_____

6. For what purpose are infant intelligence tests largely used? (p. 161)

_____

_____

7. Why does habituation and recovery predict later IQ more effectively than traditional infant tests? (p. 161)

_____

_____

Early Environment and Mental Development

1. What is the *Home Observation for Measurement of the Environment (HOME)*? What factors does HOME measure? (p. 161)

   A. _____

   _____

   B. _____

   _____

2. Cite ways in which both heredity and home environment contribute to mental test scores. (pp. 161–162)

   Heredity: _____

   _____

   Environment: _____

   _____

3. Today, more than _____ of North American mothers with children under age 2 are employed. (p. 162)

4. Discuss the impact of low versus high quality child care on mental development. (p. 162)

   Low quality: _____

   _____

   High quality: _____

   _____

5. Describe the overall quality of child care for infants and toddlers in the United States and Canada. (p. 162)

   _____

   _____

   _____

   _____

6. List and describe at least four signs of developmentally appropriate infant and toddler child care. (p. 163)

   A. _____
   _____
   B. _____
   _____
   C. _____
   _____
   D. _____
   _____

Early Intervention for At-Risk Infants and Toddlers

1. Describe the nature of center-based and home-based interventions for infants and toddlers (p. 162)
   _____
   _____

2. Discuss the effectiveness of early intervention programs with relation to infant and toddler mental development. (pp. 162–163)
   _____
   _____

3. Briefly describe the Carolina Abecedarian Project. What were the outcomes of the program? (p. 163)

   A. _____
   _____
   B. _____
   _____

Language Development

1. On average, children say their first word at _____ months of age. (p. 164)

Three Theories of Language Development

1. Match the following terms with the appropriate description. (pp. 164–165)

   _____ A theory stating that children acquire language through operant conditioning, imitation, and reinforcement
   _____ A theory arguing that children are biologically primed to acquire language
   _____ A theory stating that language development reflects interactions between the child's inner capacities and environmental influences

   1. Interactionist perspective
   2. Behaviorist perspective
   3. Nativist perspective

2. True or False: Research supports the idea that there is a sensitive period for language acquisition. (p. 165)

Getting Ready to Talk

1. Around 2 months, babies begin to make vowel-like noises, called _____. Around 4 months, _____ appears, in which infants repeat consonant-vowel combinations in long strings. (p. 165)

2. What evidence indicates that maturation cannot fully account for the development of babbling? (p. 165)

   _____

   _____

3. Describe joint attention and indicate how it impacts early language development. (p. 166)

   _____

   _____

   _____

4. True or False: Turn-taking games such as pat-a-cake and peekaboo contribute to infants' acquisition of language skills. (p. 166)

First Words

1. List the three subjects to which toddlers' first words typically refer. (p. 167)

   A. _____ B. _____

   C. _____

2. Some early words are linked to specific cognitive achievements. Provide an example to illustrate this relationship. (p. 167)

   _____

   _____

   _____

3. When young children learn new words, they tend to make two errors. List and provide an example of each type of error. (p. 167)

   A. _____

   B. _____

4. True or False: Children overextend many more words in comprehension than they do in production. (p. 167)

The Two-Word Utterance Phase

1. Explain the nature of telegraphic speech. (p. 167)

   _____

   _____

   _____

Individual and Cultural Differences

1. True or False: Early language development of boys and girls proceeds at about the same rate. (p. 168)

2. Distinguish between *referential* and *expressive styles* of early language learning. Indicate which style is associated with faster vocabulary development. (p. 168)

Referential: _____

_____

Expressive: _____

_____

3. Cite factors that influence the development of referential and expressive styles. (p. 168)

_____

_____

Supporting Early Language Development

1. Describe three ways caregivers can support early language learning. (p. 169)

    A. _____

    B. _____

    C. _____

2. Describe the characteristics of *child-directed speech (CDS)*, noting how it promotes language development. (p. 168)

_____

_____

_____

3. Conversational _____ between parent and toddler is one of the best predictors of early language development and academic competence during the school years. (p. 169)

4. Explain how CDS and parent–child conversation create a zone of proximal development. (p. 169)

_____

_____

ASK YOURSELF . . .

For *Ask Yourself* questions for this chapter, please log on to the Companion Website at www.ablongman.com/berk.

SUGGESTED STUDENT READINGS

Bjorklund, D. F. (2000). *Children's thinking (3rd ed.)*. Belmont, CA: Wadsworth. Offers an overview of major research findings in areas such as development of perception, memory, conceptual understanding, language, and problem solving. The author also discusses major theories of cognitive development, including Piagetian, information processing, and sociocultural approaches.

Bloom, P. (2000). *How children learn the meaning of words.* Cambridge, MA: The MIT Press. Examines the dynamic cognitive processes involved in the acquisition of word meaning. The author argues that learning new words, even simple nouns, requires complex interactions between the child's conceptual, social, and linguistic capacities.

Reynolds, A. J. (2000). *Success in early intervention: The Chicago child-parent centers.* Lincoln, NE: University of Nebraska Press. Presents an overview of the Child-Parent Center (CPC) program in Chicago, the second oldest federally funded early intervention program in the United States. The author emphasizes the unique features of this program, including mandatory parental involvement and a single, sustained educational system that extends from preschool to third grade. Also includes follow-up data from a study on the long-term benefits of the CPC.

PUZZLE 5.1 TERM REVIEW

Across

1. Zone of _____ development: a range of tasks that the child cannot yet handle independently but can do with the help of more skilled partners
5. Object _____: understanding that objects continue to exist when they are out of sight
7. _____ register: first part of the mental system where sights and sounds are represented directly but held only briefly
8. Type of memory that involves noticing whether a stimulus is identical or similar to one previously experienced
12. _____ memory: representations of special, one-time events that are long-lasting and particularly meaninful in terms of the life story that each of us creates
14. Type of memory that involves generating a mental representation of an absent stimulus
15. Central _____: part of working memory that directs the flow of information by coordinating information coming from the environment with information already in the system
16. Process of building schemas through direct interaction with the environment
17. _____-_____ memory: the part of the mental system that contains our permanent knowledge base
18. _____ memory: conscious part of the mental system where we work on a limited amount of information to ensure that it will be retained

Down

2. Internal rearrangement and linking together of schemas so that they form a strongly interconnected cognitive system
3. _____ behavior: sequence of actions in which schemas are deliberately combined to solve a problem
4. Piaget's first stage, during which infants and toddlers "think" with their eyes, ears, and hands
6. _____ reaction: infants try to repeat a chance event caused by their own motor activity
9. _____-of-expectation method: use of habituation procedures to examine infants' understanding of physical experience
10. A specific structure, or organized way of making sense of experience, that changes with age
11. Creation of new schemas or adjustment of old ones to produce a better fit with the environment
13. Use of current schemas to interpret the external world

103

PUZZLE 5.2 TERM REVIEW

Across

2. Repetition of consonant-vowel combinations in long strings, beginning around 4 months of age
4. Mental _____: learned procedures that operate on and transform information
11. In Chomsky's theory, an innate system that permits children to speak in a rule-oriented fashion as soon as they learn enough words (abbr.)
12. _____ speech: children's two-word utterances that leave out smaller and less important words
16. _____ style of language learning: toddlers use language mainly to talk about people's feelings and needs
18. _____ appropriate practice: set of standards devised by NAEYC that specify program characteristics that meet the development and individual needs of young children varying in age

Down

1. _____ - _____ play: type of play in which children pretend, acting out everyday and imaginary activities
3. _____ imitation: ability to remember and copy the behavior of models who are not immediately present
5. Early vocabulary error in which a word is applied too narrowly, to a wider collection of objects and events than is appropriate
6. Early vocabulary error in which a word is applied too broadly, to a wider collection of objects and events than is appropriate
7. _____ - _____ speech: form of speech marked by high-pitched, exaggerated expression, clear pronunciations, distinct pauses between speech segments, and repetition of new words
8. Perspective emphasizing that babies are born with innate knowledge systems (2 words)
9. Mental _____: an internal image of an absent object or past event
10. _____ quotient: a score on an infant intelligence test that is based primarily on perceptual and motor responses
13. Pleasant vowel-like noises made by infants beginning around 2 months of age
14. _____ style of language learning: toddlers use language mainly to label objects
15. _____ quotient: a score that permits an individual's performance on an intelligence test to be compared to the typical performance of same-age individuals
17. Checklist for gathering information about the quality of children's home lives (abbr.)

PRACTICE TEST #1

1. In Piaget's theory, _____ are organized ways of making sense of experience that change with age. (p. 144)
   a. representations
   b. concepts
   c. schemes
   d. stages

2. According to Piaget, during _____, children interpret experiences in terms of existing schemes. (p. 144)
   a. assimilation
   b. equilibration
   c. referential learning
   d. make-believe play

3. Primary circular reactions are oriented toward _____, whereas secondary circular reactions are aimed toward _____. (p. 146)
   a. involuntary actions; voluntary actions
   b. the infant's own body; the environment
   c. external actions; internal representations
   d. concrete thought; abstract thought

4. According to Piaget, which of the following provides evidence that 18-to-24-month-olds can mentally represent their experiences? (p. 147)
   a. they begin arriving at solutions suddenly instead of relying on trial-and-error
   b. they reach Substage 4 of sensorimotor development
   c. they use circular reactions to build schemes
   d. they begin to engage in intentional behavior

5. To study infants' grasp of physical reasoning, researchers often use a violation-of-expectation method in which (p. 147)
   a. infants are habituated to a physical event and then researchers determine whether they recover faster to a possible or impossible event.
   b. infants are asked to seek an object after it has been moved from one hiding place to another.
   c. infants are instructed to perform a response after seeing it modeled by an adult.
   d. infants are asked to retrieve an object that has been hidden from their view.

6. Recent research on object permanence suggests that (p. 148)
   a. babies search for hidden objects only when those objects are toys.
   b. before 12 months, infants have difficulty translating what they know about object location into a successful search strategy.
   c. infants as young as 2 to 3 months of age can search for hidden objects.
   d. sensorimotor children lack the attention needed to remember where hidden objects have been placed.

7. Raegon's mother showed her how to obtain an out-of-reach toy by pulling a string. When encouraged to imitate her mother with a different-looking toy, Raegon successfully retrieved the toy. Raegon's behavior demonstrates that she (p. 149)
   a. can solve problems by analogy.
   b. has attained hypothetical thought.
   c. no longer exhibits the A-not-B error.
   d. can engage in make-believe play.

8. Recent studies on infant cognitive development suggest that Piaget (p. 150)
   a. greatly exaggerated the abilities of young infants.
   b. correctly predicted the neat, stepwise fashion in which cognitive attainments develop.
   c. overlooked many important areas of cognitive development.
   d. underestimated young infant's cognitive abilities.

9. The three parts of the information-processing system are (p. 153)
   a. sensation, perception, and interpretation.
   b. assimilation, accommodation, and equilibration.
   c. stimulus input, input manipulation, and response output.
   d. the sensory register, working memory, and long-term memory.

10. Information-processing theorists believe that _____ is / are responsible for gains in children's thinking. (p. 153)
    a. social interaction
    b. brain development and improvements in mental strategies
    c. language development
    d. improvements in sensory capacities

11. Which type of memory involves noticing whether a new experience is identical or similar to one previously experienced? (p. 155)
    a. recall
    b. recognition
    c. autobiographical
    d. retrospective

12. Two-year-old Kirkland was given a Lego block set for his birthday. Noticing that Kirkland seemed unsure of what to do with the blocks, his father sat on the floor and showed him how to put them together. Once Kirkland figured out how to put the blocks together independently, his father slowly withdrew his support and let Kirkland continue building on his own. This example demonstrates Vygotsky's concept of _____. (p. 158)
    a. reciprocal teaching
    b. zone of proximal development
    c. developmentally appropriate practice
    d. adaptation

13. While cognitive theories try to explain the _____ of development, designers of mental tests are interested in the _____ of development. (p. 160)
    a. products; process
    b. continuity; discontinuity
    c. process; products
    d. relevance; products

14. Which of the following statements accurately describes the stability of IQ? (p. 160)
    a. IQ scores are relatively stable throughout the lifespan.
    b. IQ scores obtained in infancy accurately predict IQ in early childhood.
    c. The majority of children show substantial IQ fluctuations between toddlerhood and adolescence.
    d. The younger the child at the time of the first testing, the better the prediction of later IQ.

15. Today, most infant intelligence tests are used for (p. 161)
    a. making long-term predictions about intelligence.
    b. identifying babies who may be at risk for developmental problems in the future.
    c. determining cognitive strengths.
    d. determining language delays.

16. Which of the following provides evidence that children are biologically primed to acquire language? (p. 165)
    a. Children's first word combinations do not appear to follow grammatical rules.
    b. Parental reinforcement results in rapid vocabulary acquisition.
    c. Children all over the world reach major language development milestones in a similar sequence.
    d. Children's progress in mastering many sentence constructions is steady and gradual.

17. Kaleb runs into the kitchen and points to the cabinet where his mother keeps a box of animal crackers. Kaleb is using _____ to tell his mother that he wants the animal crackers. (pp. 166–167)
    a. preverbal gestures
    b. mental strategies
    c. coercion
    d. telegraphic speech

18. One-year-old Fiona uses the word *doggie* to refer only to her family's pet dog and not to other dogs. Fiona's error is known as an (p. 167)
    a. underextension.
    b. overextension.
    c. underregularization.
    d. overregularization.

19. When first learning to talk, Alex used words mostly to label objects, such as "doggie," ball," "car," and "book." Alex's style of language learning is best categorized as (p. 168)
    a. expressive.
    b. referential.
    c. concrete.
    d. attributional.

20. Child-directed speech (pp. 168–169).
    a. is calming to infants because of its low-pitched, monotonous tone.
    b. fails to build on effective communication strategies and inhibits young children's ability to join in conversation.
    c. Is effective for keeping children's attention and easing their task of understanding.
    d. Is appealing to infants but has little impact on their later development of language comprehension.

PRACTICE TEST #2

1. On a trip to a farm, 2-year-old Liam sees a horse for the first time. Noticing the horse's four legs, tail, and fur, Liam integrates it into his "dog" scheme. This is an example of (p. 144)
    a. accommodation.
    b. assimilation.
    c. organization.
    d. equilibrium.

2. According to Piaget, when children create new schemes or adjust old ones to produce a better fit with the environment, they are using (p. 144)
    a. overextension.
    b. recognition.
    c. accommodation.
    d. intentional behavior.

3. Baby Antonio accidentally kicks his rattle with his foot. Later, he tries to repeat this behavior again and again. In Piaget's theory, this is an example of a _____ circular reaction. (p. 146)
    a. reflexive
    b. primary
    c. secondary
    d. tertiary

4. Tertiary circular reactions differ from primary and secondary circular reactions in that they are (pp. 146–147)
    a. rich in mental representation.
    b. directed toward the environment.
    c. centered around the infant's own body.
    d. deliberately exploratory.

5. Some research suggests that 8-to-12-month-olds make the A-not-B search error (p. 149)
    a. when the hidden object is unfamiliar.
    b. because they have lost interest in the object-hiding task.
    c. because they have trouble inhibiting a previously rewarded response.
    d. because they lack the skills to problem solve.

6. Baby Gary's father playfully sticks his tongue out when changing Gary's diaper. The next day, the father notices Gary sticking his tongue out while waiting to have his diaper changed. Baby Gary is demonstrating (p. 149)
    a. make-believe play.
    b. a circular reaction.
    c. a reflex.
    d. deferred imitation.

7. According to the _____ perspective, babies are born with a set of innate knowledge systems that allow them to grasp new, related information rapidly. (p. 150)
    a. sociocultural
    b. core knowledge
    c. cognitive-developmental
    d. information processing

8. Which of the following is the conscious part of our mental system, where we actively work on a limited amount of information? (p. 153)
    a. perceptual register
    b. sensory register
    c. working memory
    d. long-term memory

9. Which of the following best reflects changes in attention from infancy to toddlerhood? (pp. 153–154)
    a. During the second year of life, children shift from thorough exploration of objects and patterns to unitary focus on high contrast features.
    b. Toddlers have increasing difficulty disengaging their attention from interesting stimuli.
    c. With age, attraction to novelty declines and sustained attention improves.
    d. Because of their limited need for sustained attention, young children's efficiency at managing their attention changes very little from infancy to toddlerhood.

10. Babies' earliest categories are _____, whereas categories become increasingly _____ during toddlerhood. (p. 155)
    a. functional; conceptual
    b. conceptual; perceptual
    c. perceptual; functional
    d. perceptual; conceptual

11. The greatest drawback of information processing approach is that it (p. 157)
    a. fails to account for the continuity of human thinking from infancy into adulthood.
    b. regards infants and toddlers as passive beings who are acted on their environment rather than acknowledging them as active, inquiring beings.
    c. explains cognitive development in terms of discrete stages.
    d. analyses cognition in terms of its components but has difficulty putting the components back together into a comprehensive theory.

12. According to Vygotsky, children's cognition develops through (pp. 157–158)
    a. joint activities with more mature members of their society.
    b. learning to master tasks independently.
    c. direct instruction from more mature members of their society.
    d. the physical world acting on the child.

13. Vygotsky's theory emphasizes that individual differences in complex mental activities are mainly due to cultural differences in (pp. 158–159)
    a. genetic makeup.
    b. social experiences.
    c. nutrition.
    d. infant physical care practices.

14. Which of the following statements illustrates why infant and toddler IQ scores often do not reflect their true abilities? (p. 160)
    a. They are not compared to a normative sample.
    b. They are often biased.
    c. Infants and toddlers are likely to become distracted, fatigued, or bored during testing.
    d. infant tests focus on concepts that infants and toddlers have not yet developed.

15. Research indicates that _____ predict(s) children's IQ beyond the contribution of parental IQ and education. (p. 162)
    a. long-term memory capacity
    b. family living conditions
    c. child care quality
    d. language development

16. Which of the following statements about infant and toddler child care is true? (p. 162)
    a. Most research indicates that all child care is detrimental to children's mental development.
    b. High-quality child care can reduce the negative impact of a stressed, poverty-stricken home life.
    c. High-quality child care is related to cognitive competence but has no impact on emotional and social competence.
    d. Most studies on infant and toddler child care fail to identify characteristics of high-quality child care that support children's development.

17. Gains in IQ and academic achievement are greatest when early intervention (p. 163)
    a. begins in the primary grades.
    b. includes home visits.
    c. is intense and long lasting.
    d. is indirect, focusing on availability of community services rather than child and family functioning.

18. According to the nativist perspective, the early and rapid development of language in humans is due primarily to (p. 165)
    a. parental reinforcement of children's communication attempts.
    b. an innate system that contains a set of rules common to all languages.
    c. children's ability to imitate other people.
    d. parents' use of child-directed speech.

19. Research on babbling suggests that (pp. 165–166)
    a. babies in industrialized countries begin babbling a few months before babies in nonindustrialized countries.
    b. sounds of infants' native language are incorporated into their babbling even in the absence of exposure to human speech.
    c. hearing-impaired infants do not babble.
    d. early babbling is due to maturation, since babies everywhere started babbling at about the same age and produce a similar range of early sounds.

20. Children's knowledge of categorical relationghips would lead us to predict that they would be most likely to overextend the word *doggie* to (p. 167)
    a. other furry, four-legged animals.
    b. all other animals.
    c. any living thing.
    d. nearly anything—their errors are random.

CHAPTER 6
EMOTIONAL AND SOCIAL DEVELOPMENT IN INFANCY AND TODDLERHOOD

BRIEF CHAPTER SUMMARY

According to Erikson, warm, responsive caregiving leads infants to resolve the psychological conflict of basic trust versus mistrust on the positive side. During toddlerhood, the conflict of autonomy versus shame and doubt is resolved favorably when parents provide appropriate guidance and reasonable choices. If children emerge from the first few years without sufficient trust in caregivers, and without a healthy sense of individuality, the seeds are sown for adjustment problems.

Emotions play an important role in organizing the attainments that Erikson regarded as so important—social relationships, exploration of the environment, and discovery of the self. During the first year, basic emotions—happiness, interest, surprise, fear, anger, sadness, and disgust—become well-organized signals. Infants' emotional expressions are closely tied to their ability to interpret the emotional cues of others. As toddlers become more self-aware, self-conscious emotions—shame, embarrassment, guilt, envy, and pride—appear. Besides experiencing a wider range of emotions, infants and toddlers begin to manage their emotional experiences. Rapid development of the cerebral cortex, sensitive caregiving, and growth in representation and language contribute to the development of self-regulation.

Infants differ greatly in temperament, or quality and intensity of emotion, activity level, attention, and emotional self-regulation. Research findings have inspired a growing body of research on temperament, including its stability, biological roots, and interaction with child-rearing experiences. The goodness-of-fit model explains how temperament and environment can together produce favorable outcomes.

Attachment refers to the strong, affectional tie we have with special people in our lives that leads us to experience pleasure when we interact with them and to be comforted by their nearness during times of stress. By the second half of the first year, infants have become attached to familiar people who have responded to their needs. Today, ethological theory of attachment is the most widely accepted view of the infant's emotional tie to the caregiver, recognizing it as an evolved response that promotes survival. Opportunity to establish a close relationship, quality of caregiving, the baby's characteristics, and family context are four factors that influence attachment security. Babies form attachments to a variety of familiar people—not just mothers, but fathers, siblings, grandparents, and professional caregivers.

During the first 2 years, knowledge of the self as a separate, permanent identity emerges. The earliest aspect of the self to emerge is the I-self, followed by the me-self in the second year. Self-awareness also gives way to the development of empathy, social categories, self-control, and compliance.

LEARNING OBJECTIVES

After reading this chapter, you should be able to:

6.1 Discuss the first two stages of Erikson's psychosocial theory, noting the psychological conflict at each stage, as well as how each conflict can be positively resolved. (pp. 174–175)

6.2 Describe changes in the expression of happiness, sadness, and fear across infancy and toddlerhood. (pp. 177–178)

6.3 Summarize changes in infants' ability to understand and respond to the emotions of others, with particular attention to the emergence of social referencing. (p. 178)

6.4 Explain the nature of self-conscious emotions, noting why they emerge during the second year and indicating their role in development. (p. 179)

6.5 Trace the development of emotional self-regulation during the first two years. (pp. 179–180)

6.6 Discuss the four underlying components of temperament, and identify the three temperamental styles elaborated by Thomas and Chess. (pp. 180–181)

6.7 Compare and contrast Thomas and Chess's model of temperament with that of Rothbart. (p. 181)

6.8 Explain how temperament is measured, and discuss the stability of temperament over time. (pp. 181–183)

6.9 Summarize genetic and environmental influences on temperament, and describe the goodness-of-fit model. (pp. 183–185)

6.10 Describe and compare psychoanalytic, behavioral, and ethological theories of attachment. (pp. 185–187)

6.11 Describe the Strange Situation procedure for measuring attachment, and discuss the four patterns of attachment that have been identified using this technique. (pp. 187–188)

6.12 Discuss research on the stability of attachment, and summarize cultural variations in attachment patterns. (p. 188)

6.13 Discuss the factors that affect attachment security, including opportunity for attachment, quality of caregiving, and family circumstances. (pp. 188–191)

6.14 Discuss infants' attachment relationships with fathers and siblings, noting factors that impact these relationships. (pp. 192–193)

6.15 Describe the link between early attachment and later cognitive, emotional, and social development, and explain how continuity of caregiving affects this link. (pp. 193–194)

6.16 Trace the emergence of self-awareness, and explain how it influences early emotional and social development, categorization of the self, and development of self-control. (pp. 194–197)

STUDY QUESTIONS

Erikson's Theory of Infant and Toddler Personality

Basic Trust versus Mistrust

1. How did Erikson expand upon Freud's view of development during the oral stage? (p. 174)

_____

_____

2. Based on Erikson's theory, summarize the psychological conflict of the first year, *basic trust versus mistrust,* and explain how it can be positively resolved. (p. 174)

A. _____

_____

B. _____

_____

Autonomy versus Shame and Doubt

1. In what way did Erikson expand upon Freud's view of development during the anal stage? (pp. 174-175)

_____

_____

2. Explain how the psychological conflict of toddlerhood, *autonomy versus shame and doubt,* is resolved favorably. (p. 175)

_____

_____

Emotional Development

Development of Some Basic Emotions

1. Define the term *basic emotions,* and provide several examples. (p. 175)

   A. _____

   _____

   B. _____

   _____

2. True or False: At birth, infants are able to express all of the basic emotions. (p. 175)

3. What is a *social smile,* and when does it develop? (p. 177)

   _____

   _____

   _____

4. Laughter, which appears around _____ to _____ months, reflects (faster / slower) processing of information than does smiling. (p. 177)

5. How do expressions of happiness change between early infancy and the middle of the first year? (p. 177)

   _____

   _____

6. The frequency and intensity of infants' angry reactions (increases / decreases) with age. (p. 177)

7. Fear reactions (increase / decrease) during the second half of the first year. (p. 177)

8. The most frequent expression of fear in infancy is to unfamiliar adults, a response called _____ *anxiety.* (p. 177)

9. True or False: To minimize stranger anxiety, an unfamiliar adult should immediately pick up the infant and talk to him or her. (p. 177)

10. Explain how the rise in angry and fearful reactions with age has important survival value for infants. (p. 178)

    _____

    _____

11. Describe how cognitive development impacts infants' angry and fearful reactions. (p. 178)

    Anger: _____

    _____

    Fear: _____

    _____

12. True or False: Anger and fear are universal emotions that are unaffected by cultural variations in infant rearing practices. (p. 178)

A Lifespan Vista: Maternal Depression and Children's Development

1. Approximately _____ to _____ percent of women experience chronic depression—mild to severe feelings of sadness, distress, and withdrawal that continue for months or years. (p. 176)

2. Depression that emerges or strengthens after childbirth but fails to subside as the new mother adjusts to hormonal changes in her body and gains confidence in caring for her baby is called _____ *depression.* (p. 176)

3. Discuss how the experience of postpartum depression affects the mother's interactions with her infant. (p. 176)

_____

_____

_____

4. Explain the ways in which persistent maternal depression and associated parenting behaviors may impact the development of the child. (p. 176)

_____

_____

_____

_____

5. Explain the best way to prevent postpartum depression from interfering with the parent–child relationship. (p. 176)

_____

_____

Understanding and Responding to the Emotions of Others

1. Early on, babies detect others' emotions through the fairly automatic process of *emotional* _____. (p. 178)

2. Define *social referencing,* and explain its role in infant development. (p. 178)

    A. _____

    _____

    B. _____

    _____

3. True or False: By the middle of the second year, children appreciate that others' emotional reactions may differ from their own. (p. 178)

Emergence of Self-Conscious Emotions

1. What are *self-conscious emotions*? (p. 179)

_____

_____

2. Cite several examples of self-conscious emotions. (p. 179)

    _____

    _____

3. Besides self-awareness, what ingredient is required in order for children to experience self-conscious emotions? (p. 179)

    _____

4. True or False: The situations in which adults encourage children's expressions of self-conscious emotions are very similar from culture to culture. (p. 179)

Beginnings of Emotional Self-Regulation

1. Define *emotional self-regulation.* (p. 179)

    _____

    _____

2. Explain how a caregiver's responses to an infant's emotional cues impact the infant's development of self-regulation. (pp. 179–180)

    _____

    _____

3. By the end of the second year, gains in representation and language lead to new ways of regulating emotion. Explain how this occurs.(p. 180)

    _____

    _____

    _____

Temperament and Development

1. Define *temperament.* (p. 180)

    _____

    _____

2. Cite two important findings from the New York longitudinal study of temperament. (p. 180)

    A. _____

    B. _____

The Structure of Temperament

1. List and describe the three temperamental types that have emerged from the work of Thomas and Chess. (pp. 180–181)

    A. _____

    _____

    B. _____

    _____

C. _____

_____

2. True or False: All children fit into one of the three categories of temperament described above. (p. 181)

3. Of the three styles of temperament, the _____ pattern places children at highest risk for adjustment problems. (p. 181)

Measuring Temperament

1. Discuss the advantages and disadvantages of using parent reports to assess children's temperament. (p. 181)

   Advantages: _____

   _____

   _____

   Disadvantages: _____

   _____

   _____

2. Parental ratings are (strongly / moderately) related to observational measures of children's behavior. (p. 181)

3. Most physiological assessments of temperament have focused on _____ children, who react negatively to and withdraw from novel stimuli, and _____ children, who display positive emotion to and approach novel stimuli. (p. 182)

Biology & Environment: Biological Basis of Shyness and Sociability

1. Kagan, a researcher who studies shyness and sociability in children, believes that individual differences in arousal of the _____, an inner brain structure that controls avoidance reactions, contributes to these contrasting temperamental styles. (p. 182)

2. Discuss four physiological correlates of approach-withdrawal behavior. (pp. 182–183)

   A. _____

   B. _____

   C. _____

   D. _____

3. Heritability research indicates that genes contribute (modestly / substantially) to shyness and sociability. (p. 183)

4. Explain how child-rearing practices affect the chances that an emotionally reactive baby will become a fearful child. (p. 183)

   _____

   _____

   _____

Stability of Temperament

1. True or False: Temperamental stability from one age period to the next is generally low to moderate. (p. 182)

2. Long-term predictions about early temperament are best achieved after the _____ year of life, when styles of responding are better established. (p. 183)

3. True or False: Many children show little or no change in biologically-based temperamental traits, suggesting that such traits cannot be modified through environmental experiences. (p. 183)

Genetic Influences

1. Research shows that identical twins (are / are not) more similar than fraternal twins in temperament and personality. (p. 183)

2. True or False: Lack of consistent ethnic and sex differences in early temperament have called into question the role of heredity. (p. 183)

Environmental Influences

1. Describe how parental behaviors contribute to ethnic and sex differences in temperament. (p. 184)

   _____

   _____

   _____

2. Explain how children reared in the same family develop distinct temperament styles. (p. 184)

   _____

   _____

   _____

Temperament and Child Rearing: The Goodness-of-Fit Model

1. Describe the *goodness-of-fit* model. (p. 184)

   _____

   _____

   _____

2. The goodness-of-fit model helps to explain why Western middle-SES children with (easy / slow-to-warm-up / difficult) temperaments are at high risk for later behavior problems. Describe how this occurs. (p. 184)

   _____

   _____

   _____

3. Provide two examples of how the goodness-of-fit model is culturally dependent. (pp. 184–185)

   A. _____

   _____

B. _____

_____

Development of Attachment

1. Define *attachment*. (p. 185)

_____

_____

2. True or False: Both psychoanalytic and behaviorist theories emphasize feeding as the central context in which infants and caregivers build a close emotional bond. (p. 185)

3. How did Harlow's research on rhesus monkeys challenge the idea that attachment depends on hunger satisfaction? (p. 185)

_____

_____

Ethological Theory of Attachment

1. True or False: The ethological theory of attachment, which recognizes attachment as an evolved response that promotes survival, is the most widely accepted view of the infants' emotional tie to the caregiver. (p. 186)

2. According to Bowlby, the attachment bond has strong (biological / environmental) roots. It can best be understood within an evolutionary framework in which survival of the fittest is of utmost importance. (p. 186)

3. Match each phase of attachment with the appropriate description. (pp. 186–187)

_____ Attachment to the familiar caregiver is evident, and infants display separation anxiety
_____ Infants are not yet attached to their mother and do not mind being left with an unfamiliar adult
_____ Separation anxiety declines as children gain an understanding of the parent's comings and goings and can predict his/her return
_____ Infants start to respond differentially to a familiar caregiver than to a stranger

1. The preattachment phase
2. The attachment-in-the-making phase
3. The phase of "clear-cut" attachment
4. Formation of a reciprocal relationship

4. According to Bowlby, children develop an *internal working model* based on their experiences during the four phases of attachment. Define and explain this term. (p. 187)

_____

_____

_____

Measuring the Security of Attachment

1. The _____ technique, designed by Mary Ainsworth, is the most widely used technique for measuring the quality of attachment between 1 and 2 years of age. (p. 187)

2. Provide a brief description of the *Strange Situation* technique. (p. 187)

_____

_____

_____

_____

3. Match each of the following attachment classifications with the appropriate description. (p. 187)

_____ Before separation, these infants seek closeness to the parent and fail to explore. When she returns, they display angry behaviors, may continue to cry after being picked up, and cannot be easily comforted.

_____ Before separation, these infants use the parent as a base from which to explore. They are upset by the parent's absence, and they seek contact and are easily comforted when she returns.

_____ Before separation, these infants seem unresponsive to the parent. When she leaves, they react to the stranger in much the same way as to the parent. Upon the parent's return, they are slow to greet her.

_____ When the parent returns, these infants show confused, contradictory behaviors, such as looking away while being held.

1. Secure
2. Avoidant
3. Resistant
4. Disorganized/Disoriented

Stability of Attachment and Cultural Variations

1. True or False: Insecurely attached infants maintain their attachment status more often than do securely attached infants. (p. 188)

2. German infants show considerably more _____ attachment than American babies, while an unusually high number of Japanese infants display _____ attachment. (p. 188)

3. True or False: The secure pattern is the most common attachment classification in all societies studied to date. (p. 188)

Factors That Affect Attachment Security

1. List four important influences that affect attachment security. (p. 188)

A. _____

B. _____

C. _____

D. _____

2. True or False: Research on adopted children indicates that children can develop a first attachment bond as late as 4 to 6 years of age. (p. 189)

3. Describe several adjustment problems evidenced by children and adolescents who lacked the opportunity to develop attachment bonds during infancy and early childhood. (p. 189)

_____

_____

_____

4. Describe differences in the sensitivity of caregiving experienced by securely attached and insecurely attached infants. (p. 189)

Securely attached: _____

_____

Insecurely attached: _____

_____

5. A special form of communication known as *interactional* _____ appears to separate the experiences of securely and insecurely attached infants. Describe this pattern of communication. (p. 189)

_____

_____

_____

6. How does the child care experienced by securely attached infants differ from that experienced by avoidant and resistant infants? (p. 189)

_____

_____

_____

_____

7. Among maltreated infants, _____ attachment is especially high. (p. 189)

8. True or False: Research findings consistently show that infant temperament exerts an extremely powerful influence on attachment security. (p. 190)

9. A major reason that temperament and other child characteristics do not show strong relationships with attachment quality may be that their influence depends on _____. (p. 190)

10. Summarize the relationship between parents' childhood experiences and the quality of attachment with their own children. (p. 192)

_____

_____

_____

11. True or False: The way parents view their childhood experiences is more influential than the actual experiences themselves in determining how parents rear their own children. (p. 192)

Social Issues: Does Child Care in Infancy Threaten Attachment Security and Later Adjustment?

1. True or False: American infants placed in full-time child care before 12 months of age are more likely than home-reared infants to display insecure attachments. (p. 190)

2. Discuss several reasons why we must be cautious about concluding that child care is harmful to infants' attachment security. (pp. 190–191)

A. _____

_____

B. _____

_____

C. _____

_____

3. Based on findings from the NICHD Study of Early Child Care, cite two factors that influence the impact of child care experiences on attachment security. (p. 190)

A. _____

B. _____

4. True or False: Research suggests that early, extensive child care has a far stronger impact on preschoolers' problem behavior than does parenting. (p. 190)

Multiple Attachments

1. Describe how mothers and fathers differ in the way they relate to and interact with their infants, and discuss how these patterns are changing due to the revised work status of women. (p. 192)

_____

_____

_____

_____

2. List two conditions associated with increased paternal involvement with caregiving. (p. 192)

A. _____

B. _____

3. When a new baby arrives, how is a preschool-age sibling likely to respond? Include both negative and positive reactions in your answer. (pp. 192–193)

Negative: _____

_____

Positive: _____

_____

Attachment and Later Development

1. Discuss research findings on the link between infant-mother attachment and cognitive, emotional, and social development. (pp. 193–194)

_____

_____

_____

_____

2. _____ attachment is consistently related to high hostility and aggression in early and middle childhood. (p. 194)

3. Some researchers have suggested that *continuity of caregiving* determines whether attachment is linked to later development. Briefly explain this relationship. (p. 194)

_____

_____

_____

Self-Development During the First Two Years

Self-Awareness

1. The earliest aspect of the self to emerge is the _____-*self*, or sense of self as agent, which involves the awareness that the self is separate from the surrounding world and can control its own thoughts and actions. (p. 195)

2. A second aspect of the self, the _____-*self*, is a sense of self as an object of knowledge and evaluation. What qualities make up this component of the self? (p. 195)

_____

_____

3. True or False: The development of self is fostered by sensitive caregiving. (p. 195)

4. Describe two ways in which self-awareness is associated with early emotional and social development. (pp. 195–196)

A. _____

_____

B. _____

_____

Categorizing the Self

1. Describe categorizations of the self that appear in toddlerhood, and cite an example of how children use this knowledge to organize their behavior. (p. 196)

_____

_____

_____

_____

Emergence of Self-Control

1. Define *self-control*, and list three developmental milestones that are essential for the development of this capacity. (pp. 196–197)

Definition: _____

_____

Milestones:

A. _____

B. _____

C. _____

2. True or False: Among toddlers who experience warm, sensitive caregiving and reasonable expectations for mature behavior, compliance is more common than opposition. (p. 197)

3. List several ways of helping toddlers develop compliance and self-conrol. (pp. 196–197)

_____

_____

_____

ASK YOURSELF . . .

For *Ask Yourself* questions for this chapter, please log on to the Companion Website at www.ablongman.com/berk.

SUGGESTED STUDENT READINGS

Brandstaetter, H., & Elias, A. (Eds.). (2001). *Persons, situations, and emotions: An ecological approach.* New York: Oxford University Press. An edited book highlighting the dynamic interaction between temperament and personality traits and their contribution to social and emotional development.

Bronson, M. B. (2000). *Self-regulation in early childhood: Nature and nurture.* New York: The Guilford Press. A collection of chapters on the development of self-regulation through the first 8 years of life. Also includes practical advice to parents and educators for enhancing self-regulatory skills throughout infancy and early childhood.

Crittenden, P. M., & Claussen, A. H. (Eds.). (2000). *The organization of attachment relationships: Maturation, culture, and context.* New York: Cambridge University Press. Investigates the role of culture, maturation, and developmental context in relation to attachment theory. Topics include: variations in attachment styles, the influence of attachment style on adolescent behavior, risks to attachment security (such as maternal depression, child abuse, and institutionalization), and factors affecting attachment status in twins.

PUZZLE 6.1 TERM REVIEW

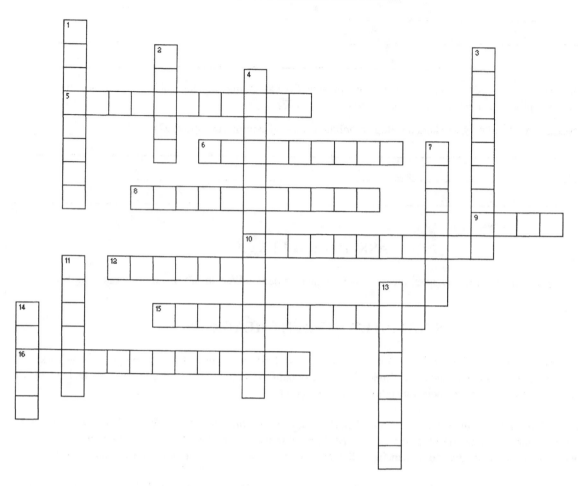

Across

5. Stable, individual differences in quality and intensity of emotional reaction, activity level, attention, and emotional self-regulation

6. Temperament style characterized by irregular daily routines, slow acceptance of new experiences, and negative, intense reactions

8. Social _____ involves reliance upon another's emotional reaction to appraise uncertain situations.

9. Temperament style characterized by establishment of regular routines in infancy, general cheerfulness, and easy adaptation to new experiences

10. A child who reacts positively to and approaches novel stimuli

12. Self-_____: capacity to resist an impulse to engage in socially disapproved behavior

15. Temperament style characterized by inactivity, mild, low-key reactions to envionmental stimuli, negative mood, and slow adjustment to new experiences (4 words, hyph.)

16. _____ - _____ emotions involve injury to or enhancement of the sense of self.

Down

1. Basic trust versus _____: Erikson's psychological conflict of the first year

2. Sense of self as agent (2 words, hyph.)

3. A child who reacts negatively to and withdraws from novel stimuli

4. Emotional _____ - _____: strategies for adjusting our emotional state to a comfortable level of intensity

7. Ability to understand another's emotional state and feel with that person

11. Sense of self as an object of knowledge and evaluation (2 words, hyph.)

13. _____ versus shame and doubt: Erikson's psychological conflict of toddlerhood

14. Emotions that can be directly inferred from facial expressions

PUZZLE 6.2 TERM REVIEW

Across

4. Interactional _____: sensitively-tuned emotional dance in which caregiver responds to infant signals in a well-timed, appropriate fashion and both partners match emotional states

6. The _____ smile is evoked by the stimulus of the human face

7. _____ caregiving involves prompt, consistent, and appropriate responding to infant signals.

12. _____ theory of attachment: views the infant's emotional tie to the caregiver as an evolved response that promotes survival

13. Infants use the caregiver as a secure _____ from which to explore, returning for emotional support.

14. Attachment style characterizing infants who respond in a confused, contradictory fashion when reunited with the parent (a.k.a. disoriented attachment)

15. Attachment style characterizing infants who are not distressed by parental separation and who avoid the parent when she returns

16. Procedure involving brief separations from and reunions with the parent that assesses the quality of the attachment bond (2 words)

Down

1. Attachment style characterizing infants who are distressed at parental separation and easily comforted upon parental return

2. _____ anxiety: infant's expressions of fear in response to unfamiliar adults

3. _____ working model: set of expectations derived from early caregiving experiences

5. Model of attachment which states that an effective match between child-rearing practices and a child's temperament leads to favorable adjustment (3 words, hyph.)

8. _____ anxiety refers to an infant's distressed reaction to the departure of a familiar caregiver

9. Voluntary obedience to requests and commands

10. The strong affectional ties that humans feel toward special people in their lives

11. Attachment style characterizing infants who remain close to the parent prior to separation and display angry behavior upon reunion

PRACTICE TEST #1

1. Erikson's stage of basic trust versus mistrust builds on Freud's _____ stage. (p. 174)
    a. oral
    b. anal
    c. phallic
    d. ego

2. According to Erikson, the great conflict of the autonomy versus shame and doubt stage is resolved favorably when (p. 175)
    a. parents are very controlling and set rigid limits.
    b. parents adopt a permissive attitude, allowing the child complete freedom to explore.
    c. parents provide children with suitable guidance and reasonable choices.
    d. the child is successfully toilet trained by the age of 2.

3. Emotions that can be directly inferred from facial expressions are referred to as (p. 175)
    a. social emotions.
    b. self-conscious emotions.
    c. basic emotions.
    d. referential emotions.

4. Stranger anxiety (p. 177)
    a. is a universal phenomenon demonstrated by children in all cultures.
    b. is lessened if the parent remains nearby.
    c. is diminished if the unfamiliar adult immediately picks up the infant.
    d. is a relatively uncommon fear among young children.

5. When an unfamiliar adult offers Heather a toy, she hesitates and looks at her mother, who smiles and nods. Heather then reaches out and takes the toy. This is an example of (p. 178)
    a. self-control.
    b. social referencing.
    c. emotional contagion.
    d. compliance.

6. Which of the following are characterized as self-conscious emotions? (p. 179)
    a. happiness and sadness
    b. fear and anger
    c. interest and surprise
    d. shame and embarrassment

7. The capacity to adjust one's emotional state to a comfortable level of intensity is known as (p. 179)
    a. affective monitoring.
    b. emotional self-regulation.
    c. emotional self-control.
    d. emotive self-referencing.

8. A child who has irregular daily routines, is slow to accept new experiences, and tends to react negatively and intensely would best fit into which of the following categories of temperament? (p. 181)
    a. easy
    b. difficult
    c. slow-to-warm-up
    d. apathetic

9. Research on the stability of temperament shows that (p. 182)
   a. temperament is highly stable from infancy to adulthood.
   b. temperament is moderately stable from one age period to the next.
   c. temperament is not at all stable from one age period to the next.
   d. temperament stabilizes in late childhood and is consistent after that time.

10. The notion that an effective match between child-rearing practices and a child's temperament will lead to favorable outcomes is known as (p. 184)
   a. secure base.
   b. goodness-of-fit.
   c. interactional synchrony.
   d. sensitive caregiving.

11. The _____ theory of attachment views the infant's emotional tie to the caregiver as an evolved response that promotes survival. (p. 186)
   a. psychoanalytic
   b. behaviorist
   c. ethological
   d. ecological

12. According to Bowlby, during which phase of attachment development do infants display separation anxiety, becoming upset when the caregiver leaves? (p. 186)
   a. the preattachment phase
   b. the attachment-in-the-making phase
   c. the phase of "clear-cut" attachment
   d. the formation of a reciprocal relationship phase

13. Based on their experiences during Bowlby's four phases of attachment development, children construct a(n) _____, or a set of expectations about the availability of attachment figures, their likelihood of providing support during times of stress, and the self's interactions with those figures. (p. 187)
   a. attachment schema
   b. secure attachment
   c. secure base
   d. internal working model

14. When placed in the Strange Situation, infants who seek closeness to their mother before separation but display angry behavior when she returns are classified as having which pattern of attachment? (p. 187)
   a. secure
   b. avoidant
   c. resistant
   d. disorganized / disoriented

15. A sensitively tuned interaction in which the mother responds to infant signals in a well-timed, appropriate fashion and both partners match emotional states is called (p. 189)
   a. interactional synchrony.
   b. sensitive caregiving.
   c. social reciprocity.
   d. social referencing.

16. Research on the relationship between caregiving and attachment style shows that (p. 189)
   a. sensitive caregiving distinguishes securely from insecurely attached infants.
   b. secure attachment is associated with almost 100 percent interactional synchrony between mother and infant.
   c. resistant infants tend to have mothers who are minimally involved in caregiving and unresponsive to infant signals.
   d. children who experience abuse and neglect are no more likely than other children to develop insecure attachments.

17. _____ determines whether attachment security is linked to later development. (p. 194)
    a. Continuity of caregiving
    b. Individual temperament
    c. Quality of caregiving during infancy
    d. Strength of the child's internal working model

18. Which term refers to one's sense of self as agent, involving awareness that the self is separate from the surrounding world and can control its own thoughts and actions? (p. 195)
    a. me-self
    b. I-self
    c. objective-self
    d. agentic-self

19. The beginnings of the I-self are grounded in (p. 195)
    a. gains in perspective-taking.
    b. children's continually developing theory of mind.
    c. infants' recognition that their actions cause objects and people to react in predictable ways.
    d. infants' conscious awareness of the self's physical features.

20. Self-awareness provides the foundation for _____, the capacity to resist an impulse to engage in socially disapproved behavior. (p. 196)
    a. self-regulation
    b. self-control
    c. compliance
    d. perspective taking

PRACTICE TEST #2

1. According to Erikson's theory, a mother who provides suitable guidance and reasonable choices is fostering her child's sense of (p. 175)
    a. attachment.
    b. autonomy.
    c. trust.
    d. self.

2. Research on happiness indicates that (p. 177)
    a. infants do not begin to smile until around 3 months of age.
    b. by 3 months of age, infants smile more often when they see a dynamic, eye-catching object than when they interact with people.
    c. smiling reflects faster processing of information than does laughing.
    d. infants smile and laugh when they achieve new skills.

3. The social smile typically appears (p. 177)
    a. at birth.
    b. between 6 and 10 weeks.
    c. at 3 to 4 months.
    d. between 12 and 18 months.

4. Angry expressions (p. 177)
    a. first emerge at 8 to 10 months of age.
    b. increase in frequency and intensity from 4 to 6 months into the second year.
    c. decrease in frequency and intensity after the middle of the first year.
    d. rarely occur during infancy and early childhood.

5. Infants' expression of fear toward unfamiliar adults during the second half of the first year is called (p. 177)
   a. separation anxiety.
   b. the strange situation.
   c. stranger anxiety.
   d. avoidant attachment.

6. Social referencing is (p. 178)
   a. the use of a familiar adult as a base from which the infant confidently explores the environment and to which the infant returns for emotional support.
   b. the process of continuously monitoring progress toward a goal, checking outcomes, and redirecting unsuccessful efforts.
   c. thinking about the self, other people, and social relationships.
   d. relying on another person's emotional reaction to appraise an uncertain situation.

7. Self-conscious emotions appear in the _____, as the sense of self emerges and toddlers can combine separate emotions. (p. 179)
   a. first year
   b. second year
   c. third year
   d. fourth year

8. Which of the following is true? (p. 180)
   a. As early as the first few months of life, parenting practices often promote the well-known sex difference in emotional expression (i.e., girls as more emotionally expressive than boys).
   b. Infants learn effective strategies for self-regulation more quickly when parents do not intervene to regulate stressful experiences for the child.
   c. Individualistic cultures place a greater emphasis on socially appropriate emotional behavior than do collectivist cultures.
   d. Emotional self-regulation is a direct result of biological maturation and is unaffected by environmental variables, such as parenting practices and cultural norms.

9. In the measurement of temperament (pp. 181–182)
   a. parent reports have been found to be the most unbiased source of information.
   b. behavior ratings by pediatricians and teachers are the measures most often used.
   c. direct observations by researchers have been emphasized because of their convenience.
   d. physiological assessments have been successful in differentiating shy children from sociable children.

10. Research on genetic and environmental influences on temperament shows that (p. 183)
    a. identical twins are no more alike than fraternal twins across a wide range of temperament traits.
    b. about half of the individual differences in temperament and personality can be traced to differences in genetic makeup.
    c. findings on ethnic and sex differences have failed to reveal distinct patterns, suggesting that temperament is entirely attributable to genetic foundations.
    d. environmental factors appear to be solely responsible for the development of temperament.

11. According to the _____ theory of attachment, feeding is a primary context in which caregivers and infants form a close emotional bond because this context allows the baby to pair the mother's smiles and tender words with tension relief. (p. 185)
    a. psychoanalytic
    b. sociocultural
    c. behaviorist
    d. ethological

12. The most widely accepted view of attachment is the _____ theory. (p. 186)
    a. behaviorist
    b. psychoanalytic
    c. ethological
    d. drive-reduction

13. Which of the following lists the stages of the ethological theory of attachment in the correct order? (p. 186)
    a. preattachment, formation of a reciprocal relationship, attachment-in-the-making, clear-cut attachment
    b. attachment-in-the-making, formation of a reciprocal relationship, preattachment, clear-cut attachment
    c. preattachment, attachment-in-the making, clear-cut attachment, formation of a reciprocal relationship
    d. formation of a reciprocal relationship, preattachment, attachment-in-the-making, clear-cut attachment

14. Which of the following patterns of attachment is linked to extremely negative caregiving and is highly stable over the second year? (p. 188)
    a. secure
    b. resistant
    c. avoidant
    d. disorganized / disoriented

15. Studies of institutionalized infants indicate that (pp. 188–189)
    a. infants fail to form close emotional bonds with caregivers when adopted after the first year of life.
    b. when infants are adopted in early childhood, they easily formed strong attachments to caregivers and cease to exhibit further social and emotional problems.
    c. children adopted as late as 4 to 6 years of age are able to form a first attachment bond, although they continue to display emotional and social problems.
    d. institutionalized children experience fully normal development, even in the absence of close attachment relationships.

16. During the Strange Situation, baby Emmanuel seeks closeness to his mother and fails to explore. When his mother returns, Emmanuel cries and displays angry, resistive behavior. Emmanuel most likely receives _____ care from his mother. (p. 189)
    a. overstimulating
    b. unresponsive
    c. inconsistent
    d. neglectful

17. Which attachment pattern is especially high among maltreated infants? (p. 189)
    a. avoidant
    b. resistant
    c. secure
    d. disorganized / disoriented

18. Which of the following is supported by research on mothers' and fathers' attachment relationships? (p. 192)
    a. Unemployed mothers engage in more playful stimulation of their babies than do employed mothers.
    b. Fathers who are the primary caregivers tend to be more gender stereotyped in their beliefs compared to fathers who are not the primary caregivers.
    c. Mothers', but not fathers', sensitive caregiving predicts attachment security.
    d. Mothers are more likely to engage their infants in conventional games, such as pat-a-cake and peekaboo, whereas fathers tend to engage in more exciting, highly physical games.

19. Which of the following terms refers to one's sense of self as an object of knowledge and evaluation? (p. 195)
    a. me-self
    b. I-self
    c. objective-self
    d. agentic-self

20. As soon as children develop the ability to categorize themselves, they exhibit a sharp increase in (p. 196)
    a. their capacity to resist an impulse to engage in socially disapproved behavior.
    b. their ability to understand another's emotional state.
    c. sociable play with peers
    d. gender-stereotyped responses.

CHAPTER 7
PHYSICAL AND COGNITIVE
DEVELOPMENT IN EARLY CHILDHOOD

BRIEF CHAPTER SUMMARY

While body growth slows during early childhood, the brain continues to grow faster than other parts of the body. Lateralization increases, and language development is supported by the more rapid growth of the left hemisphere. Myelination continues, and connections between parts of the brain increase, supporting motor and cognitive development. Heredity influences physical growth by controlling the release of hormones and, similar to earlier periods of development, environmental factors also play an important role. Emotional deprivation and malnutrition can interfere with physical development, and illness can interact with malnutrition to undermine children's growth. During early childhood, the leading cause of death is unintentional injury. As the child's center of gravity shifts toward the trunk and balance improves, gross motor skills enhance and become more refined. At the same time, increasing control of the hands and fingers leads to dramatic improvements in fine motor skills. Both gross and fine motor skills are influenced by a combination of heredity and environment.

Rapid advances in mental representation, notably language and make-believe play, mark the beginning of Piaget's preoperational stage. Although Piaget described children in terms of deficits rather than strengths, research indicates that preschoolers use logical, reflective thought on familiar tasks. Despite its criticisms, Piaget's theory has had a powerful influence on education, promoting discovery learning, sensitivity to children's readiness to learn, and acceptance of individual differences. In contrast to Piaget, Vygotsky regarded language as the foundation for all higher cognitive processes. As adults and skilled peers provide children with verbal guidance on challenging tasks, children incorporate these dialogues into their own self-directed, or private, speech. A Vygotskian approach to education emphasizes assisted discovery, including verbal support and peer collaboration.

A variety of information-processing skills improve during early childhood. Attention gradually becomes more sustained, and planning improves. Young children's recognition memory is very accurate but their recall for listlike information is much poorer than that of older children and adults, mostly because preschoolers use memory strategies less effectively. Like adults, young children remember everyday experiences in terms of scripts. Preschoolers develop a basic understanding of written symbols and arithmetic concepts through informal experiences.

Children growing up in warm, stimulating homes with parents who make reasonable demands for mature behavior score higher on mental tests. While at-risk children show long-term benefits from early intervention and high-quality child care, poor child care undermines the development of all children. Language development proceeds at a rapid pace in early childhood, supported by conversational give-and-take. By the end of the preschool years, children have an extensive vocabulary, use most grammatical constructions competently, and are effective conversationalists.

LEARNING OBJECTIVES

After reading this chapter, you should be able to:

7.1   Describe changes in body size, proportions, and skeletal maturity during early childhood, and discuss asynchronies in physical growth. (pp. 204–205)

7.2   Discuss brain development in early childhood, including lateralization and handedness, as well as myelination of the cerebellum, reticular formation, and corpus callosum. (pp. 206–207)

7.3 Explain how heredity and hormones, emotional well-being, nutrition, infectious disease, and malnutrition impact early childhood growth. (pp. 208–209)

7.4 Compare childhood immunization rates in the United States and Canada with those of other industrialized nations. (pp. 209–210)

7.5 Summarize factors related to childhood injuries, and cite preventive measures. (pp. 210–212)

7.6 Cite advances in gross and fine motor development in early childhood, including individual and sex differences. (pp. 213–215)

7.7 Describe advances in mental representation during the preschool years, including the changes in and benefits of make-believe play. (pp. 216–217)

7.8 Describe the limitations of Piaget's preoperational stage, and summarize recent research on preoperational thought. (pp. 217–222)

7.9 Describe three educational principles derived from Piaget's theory. (pp. 222–223)

7.10 Contrast Piaget's and Vygotsky's views on the development and significance of children's private speech. (p. 223)

7.11 Explain Vygotsky's position on the social origins of cognitive development. (pp. 223–224)

7.12 Discuss applications of Vygotsky's theory to education, and summarize challenges to his ideas. (pp. 224–225)

7.13 Describe the development of attention and memory during early childhood. (pp. 225–228)

7.14 Discuss preschoolers' awareness of an inner mental life, factors that support their early understanding, and limitations of theory of mind. (pp. 228–230)

7.15 Trace the development of preschoolers' literacy and mathematical reasoning. (pp. 230–231)

7.16 Cite individual differences in mental development. (pp. 232–235)

7.17 Describe the impact of home environment, preschool, kindergarten, child care, and educational television on mental development in early childhood. (pp. 232–235)

7.18 Trace the development of vocabulary, grammar, and conversational skills, and cite factors that support language learning in early childhood. (pp. 236–238)

STUDY QUESTIONS

Physical Development

Body Growth

1. On the average, children add _____ inches in height and about _____ pounds in weight each year. (p. 204)

Skeletal Growth

1. Between ages 2 and 6, approximately 45 new _____, or growth centers in which cartilage hardens into bone, emerge in various parts of the skeleton. (p. 204)

2. Explain how heredity and environment influence the age at which children lose their primary, or "baby," teeth. (p. 204)

_____

_____

Asynchronies in Physical Growth

1. Describe the *general growth curve,* which represents changes in body size from infancy to adolescence. (p. 205)

_____

_____

2. List two exceptions to the general growth curve. (p. 205)

A. _____

B. _____

Brain Development

1. Between 2 and 6 years, the brain increases from _____ to _____ percent of its adult weight. (p. 206)

2. The (right / left) hemisphere is especially active between 3 and 6 years of age and then levels off. In contrast, activity in the (right / left) hemisphere increases steadily throughout early and middle childhood. This helps explain the pattern of development of what two skills? (p. 206)

A. _____   B. _____

Handedness

1. By age 5, _____ percent of children prefer one hand over the other. (p. 207)

2. A strong hand preference reflects the greater capacity of one side of the brain, or the _____, to carry out skilled motor action. (p. 207)

3. True or False: The ambidextrous abilities displayed by many left-handers suggest that their brains tend to be more strongly lateralized than those of right-handers. (p. 207)

4. List three theories regarding the origins of handedness. (p. 207)

A. _____

_____

B. _____

_____

C. _____

_____

Other Advances in Brain Development

1. For each of the following brain structures, describe developmental changes in early childhood, and indicate their impact on children's physical and cognitive skills: (p. 207)

Cerebellum

Changes: _____

_____

Impact: _____

_____

Reticular Formation

Changes: _____

_____

Impact: _____

_____

Corpus Callosum

Changes: _____

_____

Impact: _____

_____

Influences on Physical Growth and Health

Heredity and Hormones

1. The _____, located at the base of the brain, plays a critical role by releasing two hormones that induce growth. (p. 208)

2. Without *growth hormone (GH)*, children reach an average mature height of only about _____ . (p. 208)

3. How does treatment with injections of GH influence growth in GH-deficient children? (p. 208)

_____

4. _____ stimulates the release of thyroxin, which is necessary for normal development of the nerve cells of the brain and for GH to have its full impact on body size. (p. 208)

Emotional Well-Being

1. True or False: Preschoolers with very stressful home lives suffer more respiratory and intestinal illnesses and unintentional injuries than their peers. (p. 208)

2. List the cause and characteristics of *psychosocial dwarfism.* (p. 208)

Cause: _____

Characteristics: _____

_____

Nutrition

1. True or False: During early childhood, many children become picky eaters. (p. 208)

2. Why does appetite decline in early childhood? What is the possible adaptive value of preschoolers' wariness of new foods? (p. 208)

A. _____

B. _____

135

3. Cite two factors that influence young children's food preferences. (p. 209)

A. _____

B. _____

4. List the five most common dietary deficiencies during the preschool years. (p. 209)

A. _____   B. _____

C. _____   D. _____

E. _____

Infectious Disease and Malnutrition

1. Describe the bi-directional relationship between infectious disease and malnutrition. (p. 209)

_____

_____

_____

2. Most growth retardation and deaths due to diarrhea can be prevented with a nearly cost-free
_____, a glucose, salt, and water solution that quickly replaces fluids the body loses. (p. 209)

Immunization

1. Overall, _____ percent of American preschoolers lack essential immunizations, a rate that rises to _____ percent for poverty-stricken preschoolers. Fewer than _____ percent of preschoolers lack immunizations in Canada, the Netherlands, and Sweden. (p. 209)

2. What are some causes of inadequate immunization in the United States? (pp. 209–210)

_____

_____

3. Childhood illness (rises / remains the same) with child-care attendance. (p. 210)

Childhood Injuries

1. What is the leading cause of childhood mortality? _____ List the three most common types during the early childhood years. (p. 210)

A. _____   B. _____

C. _____

2. Cite two child characteristics that increase the risk of injury. (p. 210)

A. _____   B. _____

3. Briefly describe family characteristics associated with injury. (p. 210)

_____

_____

_____

4. Why are injury rates in the United States and Canada higher than other developed nations? (p. 212)

_____

_____

_____

5. List three approaches used to prevent childhood injuries. (p. 212)

A. _____ B. _____

C. _____

Social Issues: Chronic Middle Ear Infection in Early Childhood: Consequences for Development

1. Discuss the impact of otitis media on language development and academic functioning. (p. 211)

_____

_____

_____

2. True or False: Children who attend child-care programs are at increased risk for developing otitis media. (p. 211)

3. List four ways in which negative outcomes of early otitis media can be prevented. (p. 211)

A. _____

B. _____

C. _____

D. _____

Motor Development

1. Which principle that governed motor development in the first 2 years continues to operate in early childhood? (p. 213)

_____

Gross Motor Development (p. 213)

1. As children's bodies become more streamlined and less top-heavy, their center of gravity shifts downward, and as a result, _____ improves greatly, paving the way for new motor skills involving the large muscles of the body. (p. 213)

2. Match the following sets of gross motor developments with the ages at which they are typically acquired. (p. 213)

_____ Walks up stairs with alternating feet; flexes upper body when jumping and hopping; throws with slight involvement of upper body, still catches against chest; pedals and steers tricycle

1. 2 to 3 years
2. 3 to 4 years
3. 4 to 5 years
4. 5 to 6 years

_____ Walks down stairs with alternating feet, gallops; throws ball with transfer of weight on feet, catches with hands; rides tricycle rapidly, steers smoothly.

_____ Hurried walk changes to true run; jumps, hops, throws, and catches with rigid upper body; little steering

_____ Engages in true skipping; displays mature throwing and catching style; rides bicycle with training wheels

Fine Motor Development

1. To parents, fine motor development is most apparent in what two areas? (p. 213)

   A. _____ B. _____

2. Match the following sets of fine motor developments with the ages at which they are typically acquired. (p. 213)

   _____ Draws first tadpole image of a person; copies vertical line and   1. 2 to 3 years
   circle; uses scissors; fastens and unfastens large buttons   2. 3 to 4 years
   _____ Draws a person with six parts; copies some numbers and words;   3. 4 to 5 years
   ties shoes; uses knife   4. 5 to 6 years
   _____ Copies triangle, cross, and some letters; cuts along line with
   scissors; uses fork effectively
   _____ Scribbles gradually become pictures; puts on and removes simple
   items of clothing; zips large zippers; uses spoon effectively

3. List and briefly describe the sequence in which drawing develops in early childhood. (p. 214)

   A. _____

   B. _____

   C. _____

4. How does culture influence children's drawing skills? (pp. 214–215)

   _____

Individual Differences in Motor Skills

1. Describe sex differences in motor development during early childhood. (p. 215)

   _____

   _____

   _____

2. Provide an example of how social pressures might exaggerate small, genetically-based sex differences in motor skills. (p. 215)

   _____

   _____

3. True or False: Preschoolers exposed to formal lessons in motor skills are generally ahead in motor development. (p. 215)

Cognitive Development

Piaget's Theory: The Preoperational Stage

1. As children move from the sensorimotor to the *preoperational stage,* the most obvious change is an extraordinary increase in _____. (p. 216)

Advances in Mental Representation

1. According to Piaget, _____ is the most flexible means of mental representation. (p. 216)

2. True or False: Piaget believed that language plays a major role in cognitive development. (p. 216)

Make-Believe Play

1. List and provide an example of three important changes in make-believe play that take place in early childhood. (pp. 216–217)

   A. _____

   Example: _____

   B. _____

   Example: _____

   C. _____

   Example: _____

2. Summarize contributions of make-believe play to children's cognitive and social development. (p. 217)

   _____

   _____

   _____

Limitations of Preoperational Thought

1. Piaget described preschoolers in terms of what they (can / cannot) understand. (p. 217)

2. According to Piaget, young children are not capable of _____, or mental actions that obey logical rules. (p. 217)

3. For Piaget, the most serious deficiency of preoperational thinking is _____, or failure to distinguish the symbolic viewpoints of others from one's own. (p. 217)

4. The belief that inanimate objects have lifelike qualities, such as thoughts, wishes, and intentions is called _____. (p. 218)

5. Explain the meaning of *conservation*. (p. 218)

   _____

   _____

6. Match each of the following features of preoperational thought with the appropriate description. (p. 218)

   _____ Focus on one aspect of a situation to the neglect of other features
   _____ Cannot mentally go through a series of steps and then reverse direction, returning to the starting point
   _____ Treat initial and final states as unrelated events, ignoring states in between them
   _____ Easily distracted by the appearance of objects

   1. Perception-based
   2. Centration
   3. Dynamic transformation
   4. Irreversibility

7. Preschoolers' performance on Piaget's class inclusion problem illustrates their difficulty with
_____. (p. 218)

Follow-Up Research on Preoperational Thought

1. True or False: Current research supports Piaget's account of a cognitively deficient preschooler. (p. 218)

2. Cite two examples of nonegocentric responses in preschoolers' everyday interactions. (p. 219)

   A. _____

   B. _____

3. Under what circumstances do children make errors in problems tapping animistic beliefs? (p. 219)

   _____

4. Between 4 and 8 years of age, as familiarity with physical events and principles increases, children's magical beliefs (increase / decline). (p. 220)

5. When preschoolers are given tasks that are simplified and relevant to their everyday lives, they do better than Piaget might have expected. Provide an example illustrating this point. (p. 220)

   _____

   _____

6. True or False: Preschoolers use logical, causal expressions, such as if-then and because, with the same degree of accuracy as adults do. (p. 220)

7. By the _____ year of life, children easily move back and forth between basic-level categories and general categories, such as "furniture." (p. 221)

8. How can adults help guide children's inferences about categories? (p. 221)

   _____

9. Explain how make-believe play helps children master appearance-reality distinctions. (p. 221)

   _____

   _____

Evaluation of the Preoperational Stage

1. Provide an example that illustrates preschoolers' gradual understanding of logical operations. (p. 222)

   _____

   _____

2. Some neo-Piagetian theorists combine Piaget's stage approach with the information-processing emphasis on task-specific change. Briefly describe this viewpoint. (p. 222)

   _____

   _____

Piaget and Education

1. List and briefly describe three educational principles derived from Piaget's theory. (pp. 222–223)

   A. _____

   _____

B. _____

_____

C. _____

_____

Vygotsky's Sociocultural Theory

1. Vygotsky's sociocultural theory stresses the _____ context of cognitive development. (p. 223)

Private Speech

1. Contrast Piaget's view of children's self-directed speech with that of Vygotsky. (p. 223)

Piaget: _____

_____

Vygotsky: _____

_____

2. Most research findings have supported (Piaget's / Vygotsky's) view of children's private speech. (p. 223)

3. Under what circumstances are children likely to use private speech? (p. 223)

_____

_____

Social Origins of Early Childhood Cognition

1. Vygotsky believed that children's learning takes place within a *zone of proximal development*. Explain what this means and provide an example. (pp. 223–224)

A. _____

B. _____

2. _____ involves adjusting the support offered during a teaching session to fit the child's current level of performance. (p. 224)

Vygotsky and Education

1. What features do Piagetian and Vygotskian classrooms have in common? In what ways do they differ? (p. 224)

A. _____

_____

B. _____

_____

141

2. Describe the techniques of *assisted discovery* and *peer collaboration* in the context of a Vygotskian classroom. (p. 224)

Assisted discovery: _____

Cooperative learning: _____

3. Vygotsky saw _____ as the ideal social context for fostering cognitive development in early childhood. (p. 224)

Evaluation of Vygotsky's Theory

1. Cite two criticisms of Vygotsky's theory. (p. 225)

   A. _____

   B. _____

Cultural Influences: Young Children's Daily Life in a Yucatec Mayan Village

1. How do the lives of Mayan children differ from the lives of children growing up in Western nations? (p. 226)

   _____

   _____

   _____

   _____

2. Explain how Mayan parents interact with their children. What skills do Mayan children have that are not common in Western children? (p. 226)

   A. _____

   _____

   B. _____

   _____

Information Processing

Attention

1. Describe preschoolers' ability to plan. When are they likely to plan well? What are some limitations in their planning? (p. 225)

   A. _____

   _____

   B. _____

   _____

Memory

1. Preschoolers' recognition memory is much (better / poorer) than their recall memory. (pp. 226–227)

2. What explains preschoolers' deficiency in recall? (p. 227)

   _____

3. True or False: It is not until middle childhood and adolescence that children begin to use and perfect memory strategies. (p. 227)

4. Like adults, preschoolers remember familiar experiences in terms of _____, general descriptions of what occurs and when it occurs in a particular situation. (p. 227)

5. What are two benefits of using scripts to aid in memory and recall? (p. 227)

   A. _____ B. _____

6. Adults use two styles for prompting children's autobiographical narratives. List and briefly describe them. (p. 227)

   A. _____

   B. _____

The Young Child's Theory of Mind

1. A theory of mind, also called _____, is a coherent set of ideas about mental activities. (p. 228)

2. Trace changes in children's awareness of mental life from the toddler years through the preschool years. (p. 228)

   _____

   _____

   _____

3. Describe three factors that contribute to preschoolers' theory of mind. (p. 228)

   A. _____

   B. _____

   C. _____

Limitations of the Young Child's Understanding of Mental Life

1. Briefly summarize two limitations of preschoolers' awareness of mental activities. (p. 230)

   A. _____

   B. _____

2. Young children view the mind as a(n) _____ container for information, while older children view it as a(n) _____ agent that selects and transforms information. (p. 230)

Early Childhood Literacy

1. True or False: Preschoolers understand a great deal about written language long before they are able to read and write. (p. 230)

2. Explain how preschoolers' ideas about written language differ from adults'. (p. 230)

   _____

   _____

3. List two ways in which adults can foster young children's literacy development. (p. 230)

A. _____

B. _____

Young Children's Mathematical Reasoning

1. List five steps in the development of preschoolers' mathematical reasoning that correspond with the following general age ranges: (p. 231)

Between 14 and 16 months: _____

Between 2 and 3 years: _____

Between 3 and 4 years: _____

Between 4 and 5 years: _____

2. True or False: Basic arithmetic knowledge emerges universally around the world, but at different rates. (p. 231)

Biology & Environment: "Mindblindness" and Autism

1. The term *autism* means _____. (p. 229)

2. Cite three common characteristics of children with autism. (p. 229)

A. _____

B. _____

C. _____

3. Describe two hypotheses about the cause of autism. (p. 229)

_____

_____

_____

Individual Differences in Mental Development

1. Why do minorities and children from low-SES homes sometimes do poorly on intelligence tests? What steps can be taken to help improve their performance? (p. 232)

A. _____

B. _____

2. Intelligence tests (do / do not) sample all human abilities and performance (is / is not) affected by cultural and situational factors. (p. 232)

3. Despite their flaws, intelligence tests are important. Explain why. (p. 232)

_____

_____

_____

Home Environment and Mental Development

1. Describe the characteristics of homes that foster young children's intellectual growth. (p. 232)

   _____

   _____

   _____

   _____

2. True or False: When low-SES parents manage, despite daily pressures, to obtain high HOME scores, their preschoolers perform substantially better on intelligence tests. (p. 232)

Preschool, Kindergarten, and Child Care

1. Currently, _____ percent of American and _____ percent of Canadian preschool-age children have mothers who are employed. (p. 233)

2. A _____ is a program with planned educational experiences aimed at enhancing the development of 2- to 5-year-olds. In contrast, _____ identifies a variety of arrangements for supervising children of employed parents. (p. 233)

3. Describe the difference between child-centered preschools and academic preschools. (p. 233)

   Child-centered: _____

   _____

   Academic: _____

   _____

4. True or False: Children in academic preschools demonstrate higher levels of achievement than those in child-centered preschools, including greater mastery of motor, academic, language, and social skills. (p. 233)

5. True or False: High quality preschool experiences have a larger impact on low-SES than middle-SES children. (p. 233)

Early Intervention for At-Risk Preschoolers

1. What is *Project Head Start*? How does Project Head Start compare to Canada's *Aboriginal Head Start*? (p. 233)

   A. _____

   _____

   B. _____

   _____

2. Describe the long-term benefits of preschool intervention. (p. 233)

   _____

   _____

   _____

   _____

   _____

3. True or False: Research suggests that gains in IQ and achievement scores from attending Head Start and other interventions are maintained across the school years. (pp. 233–234)

4. List four key ingredients of high-quality child care in early childhood, and describe their effects on caregiver behavior and children's development. (p. 234)

A. _____ B. _____

C. _____ D. _____

Effects: _____

Educational Television

1. The average 2- to 6-year-old watches TV for _____ hours a day. _____ children are more frequent viewers, possibly because their parents are less able to pay for other entertainment. (p. 234)

2. Describe the benefits of watching educational programs, such as *Sesame Street*. (p. 235)

_____

_____

_____

3. What does research reveal about the effects of heavy TV viewing on children's cognitive development? (p. 235)

_____

_____

Language Development

Vocabulary

1. True or False: Preschoolers learn an average of 5 new words each day, increasing their vocabulary from 200 words at age 2 to 10,000 at age 6. (p. 236)

2. Explain how children build their vocabularies so quickly over the preschool years. (p. 236)

_____

_____

3. How do Western children learn words in comparison to Asian-speaking children? (p. 236)

_____

_____

4. When children assume that words refer to entirely separate categories, they are applying the principle of _____. (p. 236)

5. Preschool children (are / are not) able to effectively use social cues to identify word meanings. (p. 236)

Grammar

1. True or False: All English-speaking children master grammatical markers in a regular sequence. (p. 236)

2. By age _____, children have acquired many grammatical rules, and they apply them so consistently that they occasionally overextend the rules to words that are exceptions, a type of error called _____. (p. 236)

3. Briefly describe the predictable errors preschoolers make in forming questions and demonstrating their understanding of the passive voice. (p. 237)

   Questions: _____

   _____

   Passive voice: _____

   _____

4. True or False: By the end of the preschool years, children have mastered most of the grammatical constructions of their language. (p. 237)

Conversation

1. The practical, social side of language is called _____. (p. 237)

2. Cite evidence that at the beginning of early childhood, children are already skilled conversationalists. (p. 237)

   _____

   _____

   _____

3. Preschoolers (do / do not) adjust their speech to fit the age, sex, and social status of the listener. (p. 237)

Supporting Language Learning in Early Childhood

1. Describe two techniques adults use to promote language skills when talking to preschoolers. (p. 238)

   A. _____

   B. _____

2. Adults provide subtle, indirect feedback about grammar using two strategies. List and briefly describe these strategies. (p. 238)

   A. _____

   B. _____

ASK YOURSELF . . .

For *Ask Yourself* questions for this chapter, please log on to the Companion Website at www.ablongman.com/berk.

SUGGESTED STUDENT READINGS

Berk, L.E. (2001). *Awakening children's minds: How parents and teachers can make a difference.* New York: Oxford University Press. Written for parents and teachers of young children, this book provides an overview of current theories of child development, straightforward advice for child rearing, and suggestions for concrete practice. Moreover, the author stresses the importance of parents and teachers in the development of competent, caring, and well-adjusted children.

Neuman, S. B., Copple, C., & Bredekamp, S. (2001). *Learning to read and write: Developmentally appropriate practice for young children.* Washington, DC: National Association of Young Children. Firmly grounded in empirical research, this book presents developmentally appropriate practice for fostering early literacy development in young children. Also included are guidelines and suggestions for ensuring that all children learn to read and write by the end of the third grade.

Roskos, K. A., & Christie, J. F. (Eds.). (2000). *Play and literacy in early childhood: Research for multiple perspectives.* Mahwah, NJ: Lawrence Erlbaum Associates. Explores the relationship between play and literacy by drawing on research from cognitive, ecological, and cultural perspectives. Also accompanying each chapter is a critical review of research by leading scholars in the field of child development.

PUZZLE 7.1 TERM REVIEW

Across

3. _____ hormone is a pituitary hormone that affects the development of almost all body tissues.
10. _____-stimulating hormone: pituitary hormone that stimulates the thyroid gland to produce thyroxine
11. Corpus _____: large bundle of fibers that connects the two hemispheres of the brain
14. _____ formation: structure in the brain stem that maintains alertness and consciousness
16. Oral _____ therapy: treatment for diarrhea in which sick children are given a glucose, salt, and water solution
17. Inability to mentally go through a series of steps in a problem and then reverse direction, returning to the starting point
18. _____ thinking: belief that inanimate objects have lifelike qualities

Down

1. Psychosocial _____: growth disorder caused by severe emotional deprivation
2. The _____ cerebral hemisphere is the hemisphere of the brain responsible for skilled motor action.
4. The understanding that certain physical properties of objects remain the same, even when their outward appearance changes
5. Piaget's second stage in which rapid development of representation takes place
6. The tendency to focus on one's own viewpoint and ignore other perspectives
7. The _____ gland, located near the base of the brain, releases hormones affecting physical growth.
8. The tendency to focus on one aspect of a situation to the exclusion of other important features.
9. _____ play: make-believe play with others
12. _____ classification: organization of objects into classes and subclasses based on similarities and differences
13. Brain structure that aids in balance and control of body movements
15. The _____ growth curve represents changes in overall body size—rapid growth during infancy, slower gains in early and middle childhood, and rapid growth again in adolescence.

PUZZLE 7.2 TERM REVIEW

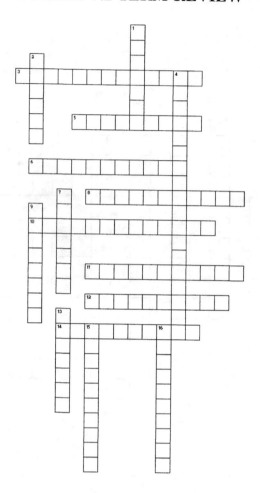

Across

3. Thinking about thought; awareness of mental activities
5. Project _____ is a federally funded program that provides low-income children with a year or two of preschool, as well as encouraging parent involvement in children's development. (2 words)
6. Connecting a new word with an underlying concept after only a brief encounter (2 words, hyph.)
8. Changing quality of support over a teaching session in which adults adjust the assistance they provide to fit the child's current level of performance
10. Preschools in which teachers provide a wide variety of activities from which the children select and most of the day is devoted to free play (2 words, hyph.)
11. Mathematical principle that the last number in a counting sequence indicates the quantity of items in the set
12. _____ Head Start: program initiated in Canada that provides low-income children with preschool education and nutritional and health services
14. Adult responses that elaborate on children's speech, increasing its complexity

Down

1. General descriptions of what occurs and when it occurs in a particular situation
2. _____ strategies: deliberate mental activities that improve the likelihood of remembering
4. Application of regular grammatical rules to words that are exceptions
7. _____ speech: self-directed speech that children use to plan and guide their own behavior
9. Preschools in which teachers structure the program, training children in academic skills through repetition and drill
13. Adult responses that restructure children's incorrect speech into a more mature form
15. The practical, social side of language that is concerned with how to engage in effective and appropriate communication with others
16. Principle specifying order relationships between quantities

PRACTICE TEST #1

1. Which of the following is most helpful in diagnosing growth disorders in early and middle childhood? (p. 204)
   a. universal growth norms
   b. chronological age
   c. skeletal age
   d. developmental quotient

2. Because different body systems have their own unique, carefully timed patterns of maturation, physical development is (p. 205)
   a. an asynchronous process.
   b. a synchronous process.
   c. governed only by genetic factors.
   d. governed only by environmental factors.

3. How is lateralization different for right-handers versus left-handers? (p. 207)
   a. Language skills are housed in the right hemisphere for right-handers and in the left hemisphere for left-handers.
   b. Language skills are shared between both hemispheres for right-handers.
   c. Language skills are shared between both hemispheres for left-handers.
   d. The research is inconclusive on hemispheric control related to handedness.

4. Which of the following brain structures supports integration of many aspects of thinking, such as perception, attention, memory, language, and problem solving? (p. 207)
   a. cerebellum
   b. reticular formation
   c. myelin
   d. corpus collosum

5. The pituitary gland plays a critical role in growth by releasing which two hormones? (p. 208)
   a. growth hormone and estrogen
   b. growth hormone and thyroid-stimulating hormone
   c. thyroid-stimulating hormone and testosterone
   d. thyroxine and thyroid-stimulating hormone

6. Shayla is 5 years old and recently experienced her parents' divorce. Her mother has been unemployed for months and they live in an extremely impoverished neighborhood. Shayla's mother leaves her alone in the apartment for long periods of time and when she's home, she often engages in harsh, punitive child rearing. Shayla is very short and frail. Which of the following disorders does Shayla likely have? (p. 208)
   a. GH deficiency
   b. a TSH deficiency
   c. psychosocial delay
   d. psychosocial dwarfism

7. Mario only eats carrots and turkey, and his parents are concerned that he may not be getting enough nutrients. What should they do to increase Mario's acceptance of new foods? (p. 209)
   a. Serve only one new food at each meal, and put a large amount on his plate.
   b. Continue to expose him to a variety of new foods without insisting that he eat them.
   c. Demand that he sit at the table until he eats everything on his plate.
   d. Bribe him with sweets to get him to eat new foods.

8. Which of the following statements is true? (p. 209)
   a. Ordinary childhood illnesses have an adverse effect on physical growth in many children.
   b. In industrialized nations, childhood diseases have continued to increase dramatically over the past 50 years.
   c. The United States and Canada have the highest immunization rates of all industrialized nations, with nearly 100 percent of all children receiving a full program of immunizations in the first two years.
   d. While childhood illnesses have no negative consequences on physical growth among well-nourished children, the consequences for growth among malnourished children may be severe.

9. The leading cause of death among children over 1 year of age is (p. 210)
    a. motor vehicle collisions.
    b. infectious diseases.
    c. drowning.
    d. choking.

10. Which of the following children is most at-risk for experiencing a serious injury? (p. 212)
    a. Keri, a 6-year-old girl who lives in a middle-class neighborhood
    b. Sam, a 3-year-old boy whose father is a teacher and mother is a stay-at-home mom
    c. Winston, a 5-year-old boy living in the inner city with his unemployed mother and five siblings
    d. Valencia, a 6-year-old girl who lives with her father and older sister in a small, rural town with most of her extended family living nearby

11. Gross motor development involves improvement in the child's ability to (p. 213)
    a. put puzzles together.
    b. build with small blocks.
    c. cut and paste.
    d. throw and catch a ball.

12. While throwing a ball, Mary Grace turns her body only slightly to help increase the distance, and when she catches the ball she usually traps it against her chest. Mary Grace is likely to be a (p. 213)
    a. 2-year-old.
    b. 3-year-old.
    c. 5-year-old.
    d. 6-year-old.

13. To parents, which of the following gains in fine motor development are most apparent during the preschool years? (p. 213)
    a. the ability to put together puzzles and grip pencils
    b. self-help and drawing skills
    c. self-help and athletic skills
    d. drawing and athletic skills

14. Children's drawings (p. 214)
    a. are random scribbling until approximately age 4.
    b. become more realistic as their fine motor skills improve.
    c. become more realistic only as a result of practice.
    d. do not appear to follow a developmental course.

15. Between the ages of 2 and 7, children are in Piaget's _____ stage of development. (p. 216)
    a. formal operational
    b. concrete operational
    c. preoperational
    d. sensorimotor

16. Dante's mother has recently noticed some significant changes in his play. For example, she saw him using the television remote as a telephone, holding it up to his ear and talking into it. Dante's play illustrates which of the following changes in symbolic mastery? (p. 216)
    a. Over time, play increasingly detaches from the real-life conditions associated with it.
    b. Play becomes less self-centered with age.
    c. Play gradually includes more complex scheme combinations.
    d. Play remains egocentric throughout early childhood.

17. _____, or a child's inability to go through a series of steps and then reverse direction, returning to the starting point, is the most important illogical feature of preoperational thought. (p. 218)
    a. Centration
    b. Irreversibility
    c. Reversibility
    d. Transformation

18. Vygotsky's theory states that the force that drives a child's cognitive development is (p. 223)
    a. joint activities with adults or more competent peers.
    b. interaction with the physical environment.
    c. the biological unfolding of genetic structures.
    d. the physical world acting on the child.

19. When asked the question, "Can you tell me what happens when you go to the doctor's office," Yvonne answers, "The nurse gives you a shot, the doctor checks your heart, you get a lollipop, and then you go home." This is an example of a(n) (p. 227)
    a. verbatim memory
    b. autobiographical memory
    c. script
    d. semantic memory

20. Which of the following is true? (p. 230)
    a. Preschoolers do not understand much about written language until they learn to read and write.
    b. Preschoolers have a great deal of understanding about written language long before they learn to read and write.
    c. Since written language lacks meaning for preschool-age children, they typically do not attend to it.
    d. Preschoolers demonstrate a simultaneous understanding of the names of letters and their corresponding sounds.

PRACTICE TEST #2

1. In addition to gains in height and weight during early childhood, parents and children are especially aware of another aspect of physical growth (p. 204)
    a. Preschoolers no longer have soft spots on their skulls.
    b. Children start to lose their primary, or "baby," teeth.
    c. Children's heads become much larger than they were in infancy and toddlerhood.
    d. Children have impressive athletic skills.

2. Which of the following statements about growth trends in early childhood is true? (p. 205)
    a. The lymph system grows very slowly during the preschool years.
    b. The brain grows faster than any other part of the body.
    c. The arms and legs become especially long and muscular.
    d. All body systems grow at virtually the same rate.

3. Which of the following suggests that the two hemispheres of the brain continue to latereralize throughout childhood and adolescence? (p. 206)
    a. Language skills increase at an astonishing pace in early childhood, whereas spatial skills develop gradually over childhood and adolescence.
    b. Children experiment with their right and left hands, eventually developing a strong hand preference in middle childhood.
    c. For most children, language is shared between the two hemispheres.
    d. Mathematical skills develop more slowly than language skills.

4. Dramatic gains in motor control at the end of the preschool years can be attributed to completed myelinization of the _____. (p. 207)
   a. reticular formation
   b. corpus callosum
   c. cerebellum
   d. cerebral cortex

5. Why must children born with a thyroxine deficiency receive it at once? (p. 208)
   a. Thyroxine is necessary for brain development and growth. Its absence results in mental retardation and stunted growth.
   b. Thyroxine controls heart rate. Its absence results in cardiac distress.
   c. Thyroxine is necessary for the air sacs in the lungs to function properly. Its absence causes anoxia.
   d. Children with thyroxine deficiencies are at-risk for developing psychosocial dwarfism.

6. Bailey's parents often eat rice and seafood. Research on nutrition in early childhood suggests that (p. 208)
   a. Bailey will reject these foods.
   b. Bailey will eat rice but not seafood.
   c. Bailey will likely develop an allergy to these foods.
   d. Bailey will also prefer rice and seafood.

7. Which of the following milestones permit children to draw their first person? (p. 214)
   a. the ability to hold a pencil or crayon
   b. the ability to see another's perspective
   c. the ability to use lines to represent the boundaries of objects
   d. the ability to draw three dimensional images

8. Although sex-related differences in muscle mass can explain certain skill advantages, _____ is / are the primary reason for differences in motor performance between boys and girls. (p. 215)
   a. growth spurts among boys
   b. disinterest in sports among girls
   c. cultural influence
   d. adult expectations and encouragement

9. As children move from the sensorimotor to the preoperational stage, the most obvious change is (p. 216)
   a. an increase in the child's use of senses and movements to explore the world.
   b. development of the capacity for abstract, scientific reasoning.
   c. an increase in representational, or symbolic, activity.
   d. more logical, flexible, and organized thought.

10. Research on the benefits of make-believe play indicates that (p. 217)
    a. play contributes to certain mental abilities, such as attention and memory, but does little to support children's social skills.
    b. children who spend more time in make-believe are rated as more socially competent by their teachers.
    c. the benefits only apply to children living in middle-income homes.
    d. children who spend a great deal of time playing are more intelligent than their peers but often interact with others in an immature, make-believe manner.

11. Three-year-old Grace, who explains that it rains when the clouds are sad and crying, is demonstrating (p. 219)
    a. egocentrism.
    b. animistic thinking.
    c. reversibility.
    d. centration.

12. Current research on preoperational thought indicates that when preschoolers are presented with familiar objects, they (p. 221)
    a. continue to give egocentric responses.
    b. show clear awareness of others' viewpoints.
    c. show the beginnings of logical operations.
    d. perform worse than when unfamiliar objects are used.

13. Tanya is a Piagetian first-grade teacher who wants all her students to excel in cognitive development. What will she do to encourage their development? (pp. 222–223)
    a. nothing at all; children will learn successfully in any environment
    b. arrange situations that allow self-paced discovery
    c. reinforce correct answers and ignore incorrect ones
    d. provide explicit verbal training in each subject area

14. According to Vygotsky, private speech during the preschool years (p. 223)
    a. reflects young children's egocentrism.
    b. helps young children guide their behavior during challenging tasks.
    c. is due to young children's poor communicative skills.
    d. does not play a major role in young children's cognitive development.

15. Virgil is in the first grade. In his classroom, students work in small groups throughout the day. Instead of creating groups out of children who are similar in ability and achievement, his teacher creates mixed ability groups and encourages all students to participate and help one another with projects and assignments. This classroom style is consistent with Vygotsky's concept of (p. 224)
    a. zone of proximal development
    b. intersubjectivity
    c. peer collaboration
    d. peer-teacher collaboration

16. Gyoung-Young is 4 years old. Her mother presented her with ten pictures of household items. The pictures were then mixed with eight unfamiliar pictures. Which of the following best represents Gyoung-Young's memory? (pp. 226–227)
    a. When the pictures were laid out in front of her, Gyoung-Young was able to point out all of the pictures from the original set, but when asked to recall those items from memory, she was only able to identify three pictures.
    b. When the pictures were laid out in front of her, Gyoung-Young selected all of the pictures, unable to determine which pictures belonged to the original set.
    c. Gyoung-Young was too distracted by the activity to identify or recall the pictures from the original set.
    d. Gyoung-Young could only identify the unfamiliar pictures but could recall all of the pictures accurately.

17. Research on planning indicates that (p. 225)
    a. the ability to generate and follow plans emerges during the elementary school years.
    b. even when young children design effective plans, they often forget to implement important steps.
    c. the development of planning is not directly related to changes in other cognitive processes.
    d. when children use rehearsal, it has little impact on performance.

18. Which of the following contribute to preschoolers' theory of mind? (p. 228)
    a. television viewing
    b. make-believe play and language development
    c. the ability to master conservation tasks
    d. grasp of ordinality

19. Alex spends much of his school day in learning and play centers, while Audrey spends a great deal of time writing her letters and numbers and listening to her teacher instruct the class. Which type of kindergarten does each child attend? (p. 233)
    a.   Alex attends an academic program; Audrey attends a child-centered program.
    b.   Both children attend an academic program.
    c.   Alex attends a child-centered program; Audrey attends an academic program.
    d.   Alex attends an academic program; Audrey attends an early intervention program.

20. Young Colleen says, "I go school, too." Her mother says, "Yes, you are going to school, too." Her mother's response would be classified as (p. 238)
    a.   repetition and correction.
    b.   correction and reflection.
    c.   rejection and restatement.
    d.   expansion and recast.

CHAPTER 8
EMOTIONAL AND SOCIAL
DEVELOPMENT IN EARLY CHILDHOOD

BRIEF CHAPTER SUMMARY

Preschoolers develop a new sense of purposefulness as they grapple with the psychological conflict of initiative versus guilt. In early childhood self-concept begins to take shape and children's self-esteem is high, contributing greatly to preschoolers' initiative during a period in which they must master many new skills. Preschoolers' understanding of emotion, emotional self-regulation, and capacity to experience self-conscious emotions improve, supported by gains in cognition and language as well as warm, sensitive parenting.

During the preschool years, peer interaction increases, cooperative play becomes common, and first friendships are formed, providing important contexts for the development of a wide range of social skills. Parents influence peer sociability both directly, through attempts to influence their child's peer relations, and indirectly, through their child-rearing practices. Secure attachment and emotionally positive parent-child conversations are linked to favorable peer interaction.

All theories of moral development recognize that conscience begins to take shape in early childhood. Psychoanalytic and social learning approaches to morality focus on how children acquire ready-made standards held by adults; the cognitive developmental perspective views children as active thinkers about social rules. When used frequently, punishment promotes only momentary compliance, not lasting changes in children's behavior, and harsh punishment has negative consequences for development. Ineffective discipline, a conflict-ridden family atmosphere, and televised violence promote and sustain aggression in children.

Gender typing develops rapidly over the preschool years. Through prenatal hormones, heredity contributes to boys' higher activity level and overt aggression and children's preference for same-sex playmates. At the same time, parents, teachers, peers, and the broader social environment encourage many gender-typed responses. Masculine and androgynous identities are linked to better psychological adjustment. Neither cognitive-developmental theory nor social learning theory provide a complete account of the development of gender identity. Gender schema theory is an information-processing approach to gender typing that combines social learning and cognitive developmental features. It emphasizes that both environmental pressures and children's cognition combine to affect gender-role development.

Three features differentiate an authoritative style of child rearing from authoritarian, permissive, and uninvolved parenting: acceptance and involvement, control, and autonomy granting. Compared to children of authoritarian and permissive parents, children whose parents use an authoritative style are especially well adjusted and socially mature. Warmth, explanations, and reasonable demands for mature behavior account for the effectiveness of the authoritative style. When child maltreatment occurs, it is the combined result of factors within the family, community, and larger culture. Interventions at all of these levels are essential for preventing it.

LEARNING OBJECTIVES

After reading this chapter, you should be able to:

8.1 Describe Erikson's initiative versus guilt stage, noting how this psychological conflict impacts children's emotional and social development. (pp. 244–245)

8.2 Discuss preschool children's self-development, including characteristics of self-concept and emergence of self-esteem. (pp. 245–246)

8.3 Describe changes in the understanding of emotion during early childhood, noting achievements and limitations. (pp. 247–248)

8.4 Explain how language and temperament contribute to the development of emotional self-regulation during the preschool years, and discuss ways in which adults can help young children manage common fears of early childhood. (p. 248)

8.5 Discuss the development of self-conscious emotions, empathy, and sympathy during early childhood, noting how various parenting styles affect emotional development in these areas. (pp. 248–249)

8.6 Describe advances in peer sociability over the preschool years, with particular attention to the types of play outlined by Mildred Parten, and discuss cultural variations in peer sociability. (pp. 249–250)

8.7 Describe the quality of preschoolers' friendships, and discuss parental influences on early peer relations. (pp. 251–252)

8.8 Compare psychoanalytic, social learning, and cognitive-developmental approaches to moral development, and trace milestones of morality during early childhood, noting child-rearing practices that support or undermine them. (pp. 252–256)

8.9 Describe the development of aggression in early childhood, noting the influences of family and television, and cite ways to control aggressive behavior. (pp. 257–259)

8.10 Describe preschoolers' gender-stereotyped beliefs and behaviors, and discuss genetic and environmental influences on gender-role development. (pp. 260–263)

8.11 Describe and evaluate the major theories of gender identity development, and cite ways to reduce gender stereotyping in young children. (pp. 263–264)

8.12 Describe the four styles of child rearing, indicating which is most effective, and discuss cultural variations in child-rearing beliefs and practices. (pp. 265–267)

8.13 Describe the five forms of child maltreatment, and discuss factors associated with child maltreatment, consequences of child maltreatment, and strategies for the prevention of child maltreatment. (pp. 267–269)

STUDY QUESTIONS

Erikson's Theory: Initiative versus Guilt

1. Define *initiative,* and describe how it is exhibited in preschoolers. (p. 244)

_____

_____

_____

2. Erikson regarded play as the central means through which children find out about themselves and their social world. Explain why this is the case. (p. 244)

_____

_____

_____

3. Compare Erikson's theory of development during the preschool years with that of Freud. (p. 244)

    _____

    _____

    _____

4. According to Erikson, what leads to a negative resolution of the initiative versus guilt stage? (p. 244)

    _____

    _____

    _____

Self-Understanding

1. Define *self-concept*. (p. 245)

    _____

    _____

    _____

Foundations of Self-Concept

1. Describe the quality of preschoolers' self-descriptions. (p. 245)

    _____

    _____

    _____

2. Explain the link between preschoolers' self-development and their possessiveness of objects. Given this information, how can adults promote friendly peer interaction? (p. 245)

    _____

    _____

    _____

Emergence of Self-Esteem

1. Define *self-esteem*. (p. 245)

    _____

    _____

    _____

2. True or False: When making self-evaluations, preschoolers tend to rate their own ability as extremely low and often overestimate task difficulty. (p. 246)

3. Discuss four ways to foster a healthy self-image in young children. (p. 247)

    A. _____

    B. _____

    C. _____

    D. _____

1. Based on the ethnographic research of Peggy Miller, discuss differences in storytelling practices between Chinese and Irish-American parents, and explain how these differences influence children's self-images. (p. 246)

_____

_____

_____

_____

Emotional Development

Understanding Emotions

1. By age _____ to _____, children can correctly judge the causes of many basic emotions. (p. 247)

2. Preschoolers (do / do not) realize that thoughts and feelings are interconnected. (p. 247)

3. True or False: In situations with conflicting cues about how a person is feeling, preschoolers can easily reconcile this differing information. (p. 247)

Emotional Self-Regulation

1. Explain how language contributes to preschoolers' improved emotional self-regulation, and note three strategies that children use to control their emotions during early childhood. (p. 248)

   Contribution of language to self-regulation: _____

   _____

   A. _____

   B. _____

   C. _____

2. Discuss the impact of parenting on children's development of emotional self-regulation. (p. 248)

   _____

   _____

   _____

Self-Conscious Emotions

1. Preschoolers experience self-conscious emotions (more / less) often than do toddlers. Briefly elaborate on your response. (p. 248)

   _____

   _____

   _____

2. Beginning in early childhood, (guilt / shame) is associated with feelings of personal inadequacy and is linked with maladjustment. In contrast, (guilt / shame), as long as it occurs in appropriate circumstances, is related to positive adjustment, perhaps because it helps children resist harmful impulses. (pp. 248–249)

Empathy

1. Distinguish between *empathy* and *sympathy*. (p. 249)

    Empathy: _____

    _____

    Sympathy: _____

    _____

2. Empathy serves as an important motivator of _____ behavior, or actions that benefit another person without any expected reward for the self. (p. 249)

3. True or False: In some children, empathizing with an upset peer or adult escalates into personal distress. (p. 249)

4. Discuss the impact of parenting on children's development of empathy and sympathy. (p. 249)

    _____

    _____

    _____

    _____

Peer Relations

Advances in Peer Sociability

1. Describe Parten's three-step sequence of social development. (p. 249)

    A. _____

    _____

    B. _____

    _____

    C.1. _____

    _____

    C.2. _____

    _____

2. True or False: Longitudinal research shows that Parten's play types emerge in a developmental sequence, with later-appearing ones replacing earlier ones. (p. 250)

3. True or False: It is the *type,* rather than the *amount,* of solitary and parallel play that changes during early childhood. (p. 250)

4. True or False: High rates of nonsocial activity during the preschool years is a sign of maladjustment. (p. 250)

5. True or False: Peer sociability takes essentially the same form in collectivist and individualistic cultures. (p. 250)

6. Provide an example of how cultural beliefs affect early peer associations. (p. 250)

    _____

    _____

    _____

First Friendships

1. Summarize children's understanding of friendship in early childhood. (p. 251)

_____

_____

_____

2. Describe the unique quality of preschoolers' interactions with friends. (p. 251)

_____

_____

_____

Parental Influences on Early Peer Relations

1. List three ways in which parents influence their children's peer relationships. (pp. 251–252)

   A. _____

   _____

   B. _____

   _____

   C. _____

   _____

2. Explain how parent-child attachment can promote children's peer interaction skills. (p. 252)

   _____

   _____

   _____

Foundations of Morality

1. Cite three points on which all major theories of moral development are in agreement. (pp. 252–253)

   A. _____

   _____

   B. _____

   _____

   C. _____

   _____

2. Match each of the following theories of moral development with the aspect of moral functioning that it emphasizes: (pp. 253–256)

   _____ Emotional side of conscience   1. Social learning theory
   _____ Ability to reason about justice and fairness   2. Psychoanalytic theory
   _____ Moral behavior   3. Cognitive-developmental theory

The Psychoanalytic Perspective

1. Summarize Freud's psychoanalytic theory of morality development. (p. 253)

    _____

    _____

    _____

2. True or False: Most researchers agree with Freud's assertion that fear of punishment and loss of parental love motivates children to behave morally. (p. 253)

3. A special type of discipline called _____ supports conscience development by pointing out the effects of the child's misbehavior on others. Cite three ways in which it does so. (p. 253)

    A. _____

    _____

    B. _____

    _____

    C. _____

    _____

4. Why is discipline that relies too heavily on threats of punishment less effective than induction? (p. 253)

    _____

    _____

5. True or False: Recent research shows that Freud was incorrect in his assertion that guilt is an important motivator of moral action. (p. 253)

Social Learning Theory

1. Why is operant conditioning insufficient for children to acquire moral responses? (p. 254)

    _____

    _____

2. Social learning theorists believe that children learn to behave morally largely through _____ —observing and imitating adults who demonstrate appropriate behavior. (p. 254)

3. List three characteristics of models that affect children's willingness to imitate them. (p. 254)

    A. _____

    B. _____

    C. _____

4. Models exert their strongest influence during the (preschool / elementary school) years. (p. 255)

5. True or False: Punishment promotes immediate compliance but does not produce long-lasting changes in children's behavior. (p. 255)

6. List three undesirable side effects of harsh punishment. (p. 255)

   A. _____

   B. _____

   C. _____

7. Describe two alternatives to harsh punishment. (p. 255)

   A. _____

   B. _____

8. Describe three ways that parents can increase the effectiveness of punishment when they decide to use it. (pp. 255–256)

   A. _____

   _____

   B. _____

   _____

   C. _____

   _____

9. Explain *positive discipline,* noting how it reduces the need for punishment. (p. 256)

   _____

   _____

   _____

   _____

The Cognitive-Developmental Perspective

1. In what major way does the cognitive-developmental perspective of morality differ from the psychoanalytic and behaviorist approaches? (p. 256)

   _____

   _____

   _____

   _____

2. Preschoolers are able to distinguish _____ *imperatives,* which protect people's rights and welfare, from two other forms of action: _____ *conventions,* or customs determined solely by consensus, such as table manners and dress style, and *matters of* _____, which do not violate rights or harm others, are not socially regulated, and therefore are up to the individual. (p. 256)

3. Explain how young children learn to make distinctions between moral rules and social-conventional transgressions. (p. 256)

   _____

   _____

The Other Side of Morality: Development of Aggression

1. By the early preschool years, two general types of aggression emerge. The most common is _____ aggression, aimed at obtaining an object, privilege, or space with no deliberate intent to harm. The other type is _____ aggression, which is intended to hurt another person. (p. 257)

2. Distinguish between *overt* and *relational aggression.* (p. 257)

   Overt: _____

   _____

   Relational: _____

   _____

3. For most preschoolers, instrumental aggression (declines / increases) with age. Why is this the case? (p. 257)

   _____

   _____

4. Hostile outbursts (decline / increase) over early and middle childhood. Why is this the case? (p. 257)

   _____

   _____

5. Summarize sex differences in aggression, noting factors that contribute to these differences. (p. 257)

   _____

   _____

   _____

6. Describe child-rearing practices associated with antisocial behavior from early childhood through adolescence. (p. 257)

   _____

   _____

   _____

7. (Boys / Girls) are more likely to be targets of angry, inconsistent discipline. (p. 257)

8. True or False: Of all TV programs, children's cartoons are the least violent. (p. 258)

9. Explain why young children are especially likely to be influenced by television. (p. 258)

   _____

   _____

   _____

10. Summarize the long-term effects of TV violence on children's behavior. (p. 258)

    _____

    _____

    _____

    _____

11. True or False: TV violence hardens children to aggression, making them more willing to tolerate it in others. (p. 258)

12. Why is the V-Chip an incomplete solution for regulating children's TV? (p. 258)

_____

_____

_____

13. List several strategies parents can use to monitor and control children's TV viewing. (pp. 258–259)

A. _____

B. _____

C. _____

14. List several ways to help parents and children break the cycle of hostilities between family members. (p. 259)

Parents:

A. _____

B. _____

C. _____

Children:

A. _____

B. _____

Biology & Environment: Temperament and Conscience Development in Young Children

1. Contrast parenting practices that best promote responsibility and concern for others among temperamentally inhibited children and fearless, impulsive children. (p. 254)

Inhibited children: _____

_____

Fearless, impulsive children: _____

_____

2. Explain why secure attachment is predictive of conscience development in non-anxious children. (p. 254)

_____

_____

_____

Gender Typing

1. Define *gender typing.* (p. 260)

_____

_____

_____

Gender Stereotyped Beliefs and Behavior

1. Preschoolers' gender stereotypes are (flexible / rigid). Elaborate on your response. (p. 260)

   _____

   _____

   _____

2. True or False: Most preschoolers believe that the characteristics associated with each sex (for example, clothes, hairstyles, and occupation) determine whether a person is male or female. (p. 260)

Genetic Influences on Gender Typing

1. Discuss Eleanor Maccoby's argument that hormonal differences between males and females have important consequences for gender typing, including play styles evidenced in early childhood. (p. 260)

   _____

   _____

   _____

   _____

Environmental Influences on Gender Typing

1. Describe ways in which parents encourage gender-stereotyped beliefs and behaviors in their children. (p. 260–262)

   _____

   _____

   _____

   _____

2. Of the two sexes, (boys / girls) are clearly more gender-stereotyped. Why might this be the case? (p. 262)

   _____

   _____

   _____

3. Discuss gender typing in the classroom setting, noting its impact on social behaviors. (p. 262)

   _____

   _____

   _____

   _____

4. Peer rejection is greater for (girls / boys) who frequently engage in "cross-gender" behavior. (p. 262)

5. Discuss the different styles of social influence promoted within gender-segregated peer groups. (p. 262)

   Boys: _____

   _____

   Girls: _____

   _____

Gender Identity

1. Define *gender identity* and indicate how it is measured. (p. 263)

   _____

   _____

2. _____ refers to a type of gender identity in which the person scores highly on both masculine and feminine personality characteristics. (p. 263)

3. How is gender identity related to psychological adjustment? (p. 263)

   _____

   _____

   _____

4. Contrast social learning and cognitive-developmental accounts of the emergence of gender identity. (p. 263)

   Social Learning: _____

   _____

   Cognitive-Developmental: _____

   _____

5. *Gender* _____ refers to the understanding that sex is biologically-based and remains the same even if clothing, hairstyles, and play activities change. (p. 263)

6. What Piagetian task is associated with the mastery of gender constancy? (p. 263)

   _____

7. Cite evidence supporting the notion that cognitive immaturity, not social experience, is largely responsible for preschoolers' difficulty grasping the permanence of sex. (p. 263)

   _____

   _____

   _____

8. Is gender constancy responsible for children's gender-typed behavior? Why or why not? (p. 263)

   _____

   _____

   _____

9. Explain *gender schema theory*. (p. 263)

   _____

   _____

   _____

10. What are *gender schemas*? (p. 263)

   _____

11. Explain how gender schemas influence gender-typed preferences and behavior. (p. 263)

_____

_____

_____

_____

Reducing Gender Stereotyping in Young Children

1. Cite several ways that parents can reduce gender stereotyping in young children. (p. 264)

_____

_____

_____

_____

A Lifespan Vista: David: A Boy Reared As A Girl

1. Explain how David Reimer's personal experience confirms the impact of genetic sex and prenatal hormones on a person's sense of self as male or female, as well as highlighting the importance of social experience. (p. 261)

Genetic sex and prenatal hormones: _____

_____

_____

Social experience: _____

_____

_____

Child Rearing and Emotional and Social Development

Child-Rearing Styles

1. Based on the research findings of Baumrind and others, cite three features that consistently differentiate a competent, authoritative parenting style from less effective authoritarian and permissive styles. (p. 265)

A. _____

B. _____

C. _____

2. Describe the four styles of child rearing, noting where each stands in relation to the characteristics listed above. (pp. 265–266)

Authoritative: _____

_____

_____

Authoritarian: _____

_____

_____

Permissive: _____

_____

_____

Uninvolved: _____

_____

_____

3. Summarize child outcomes associated with each of the following styles of parenting: (pp. 265–266)

Authoritative: _____

_____

_____

Authoritarian: _____

_____

_____

Permissive: _____

_____

_____

Uninvolved: _____

_____

_____

4. Which child-rearing approach is most effective? (p. 265)

_____

5. At its extreme, uninvolved parenting is a form of child maltreatment called _____
_____. (p. 266)

Cultural Variations

1. Describe how the parenting practices of the following cultural groups often differ from those of Caucasian Americans. (p. 266)

Chinese: _____

_____

_____

Hispanic and Asian Pacific Island: _____

_____

_____

African-American: _____

_____

_____

Child Maltreatment

2. List and describe four forms of child maltreatment. (p. 267)

A. _____

_____

_____

B. _____

_____

_____

C. _____

_____

_____

D. _____

_____

_____

2. Which form of abuse may be the most common, since it accompanies most other types? (p. 267)

_____

3. True or False: Researchers have identified a single "abusive" personality type. (p. 267)

4. List parent, child, and family environment characteristics associated with an increased likelihood of abuse. (p. 268)

Parent: _____

_____

_____

Child: _____

_____

_____

Family Environment: _____

_____

_____

5. List two reasons why most abusive parents are isolated from supportive ties to their communities. (p. 268)

A. _____

B. _____

6. Societies that view violence as an appropriate way to solve problems set the stage for child abuse. These conditions (do / do not) exist in the United States. (p. 268)

7. Summarize the consequences of child maltreatment for abused children. (p. 268)

_____

_____

_____

_____

8. True or False: Maltreated children evidence serious adjustment problems in the school setting. Elaborate on your response. (p. 268)

_____

_____

_____

_____

9. Discuss strategies for preventing child maltreatment. (pp. 268–269)

_____

_____

_____

_____

10. Providing social supports to families (is / is not) effective in reducing child maltreatment. (p. 269)

ASK YOURSELF . . .

For *Ask Yourself* questions for this chapter, please log on to the Companion Website at www.ablongman.com/berk.

SUGGESTED STUDENT READINGS

Hoffman, M. L. (2000). *Empathy and moral development: Implications for caring and justice.* New York: Cambridge University Press. Presents a comprehensive approach to studying and understanding moral development in young children. The author also examines the psychological process involved in the development of empathy and altruism in a variety of contexts.

Kinder, M. (Ed.) (2000). *Kids media culture.* Durham, NC: Duke University Press. Explores the effects of children's media on development. Also compares the books, cartoons, and television shows of the 1950s and 1960s with today's mass media. Finally, this book addresses concerns with television in schools and how various forms of mass media communicate messages about gender and socialization.

Straus, M. A. (2001). *Beating the devil out of them: Corporal punishment in American families and its effects on children.* Written primarily for parents, teachers, social workers, and other professionals who work with children, this book presents the negative effects of physical punishment on child development.

PUZZLE 8.1 TERM REVIEW

Across

3. _____ aggression is intended to harm another person.
6. Feelings of concern or sorrow for another's plight
7. _____, or altruistic, behavior: actions that benefit another without any expected reward for the self
8. _____ versus guilt: Erikson's psychological conflict of the preschool years
10. Type of discipline in which the effects of the child's behavior on others are communicated to the child
11. _____ aggression is a form of hostile aggression that damages another's peer relationships.

Down

1. Self-_____ refers to judgments that we make about our own worth and the feelings associated with those judgments.
2. Self-_____: set of attributes, abilities, attitudes, and values that an individual believes defines who he/she is
4. _____ aggression is aimed at obtaining an object, privilege, or space with no deliberate intent to harm another person
5. Form of punishment in which children are removed from the immediate setting until they are ready to act appropriately (2 words)
9. _____ aggression is a form of hostile aggression that harms others through physical injury or the threat of such injury.

PUZZLE 8.2 TERM REVIEW

Across

3. Type of gender identity in which a person scores high on both masculine and feminine characteristics
4. _____ style of child rearing: high in acceptance but overindulging and inattentive, low in conrol, lax rather than appropriate autonomy granting
5. _____ activity: unoccupied, onlooker behavior and solitary play
7. Gender _____ theory is an information processing approach to gender typing that combines social learning and cognitive-developmental features.
8. Gender _____: the perception of oneself as relatively masculine or feminine in characteristics
10. _____ style of child rearing: low acceptance and involvement, little control or effort to grant autonomy, minimal commitment to parenting
11. _____- _____ styles: constellations of parenting behaviors that occur over a wide range of situations
12. _____ style of child rearing: low in acceptance and involvement, high in coercive control, restricts rather than grants autonomy
13. _____ play: form of true social participation in which children engage in separate activities but interact by exchanging toys and commenting on one another's behavior
14. _____ play: form of true social participation in which children's actions are directed toward a common goal

Down

1. _____ play: the child plays near other children, with similar materials, but does not interact or try to influence their behavior
2. Gender _____: the process of developing gender-linked beliefs, gender roles, and a gender-role identity
6. _____ style of child rearing: high in acceptance and involvement, emphasizes firm control with explanations, includes gradual, appropriate autonomy granting
9. Gender _____: understanding that sex is biologically-based and remains the same even if clothing, hairstyle, and play activities change.

174

PRACTICE TEST #1

1. According to Erikson, the critical conflict of the preschool years is (p. 244)
   a. autonomy versus shame and doubt.
   b. trust versus mistrust.
   c. initiative versus guilt.
   d. industry versus inferiority.

2. Preschoolers' self-concepts are (p. 245)
   a. concrete, typically focused on observable characteristics.
   b. abstract, usually centered on their unique psychological characteristics.
   c. internalized, since they cannot yet talk about their own subjective experiences.
   d. based on stable personality traits.

3. Which of the following is true with regard to emotional understanding in preschoolers? (p. 247)
   a. Preschoolers emphasize internal states rather than external events when explaining another's emotions.
   b. Preschoolers are good at predicting what a playmate who is expressing a certain emotion might do next.
   c. Preschoolers are able to reconcile conflicting cues about how a person is feeling.
   d. Preschoolers recognize that people can experience more than one emotion at a time.

4. Empathy (p. 249)
   a. always promotes sympathetic, prosocial responding.
   b. is equally likely in all children, regardless of parental influence.
   c. leads to personal distress and self-focused responding in some children.
   d. is expressed more often by abused children than their nonabused agemates.

5. In _____ play, a child plays near another child, with similar materials, but they do not interact. (p. 249)
   a. nonsocial
   b. parallel
   c. associative
   d. cooperative

6. Recent research on peer interaction indicates that (p. 250)
   a. it is the *type,* rather than the *amount,* of play that changes during early childhood.
   b. Parten's play types emerge in a developmental sequence, with later-appearing ones replacing earlier ones.
   c. nonsocial activity among preschoolers is a sign of maladjustment.
   d. sociodramatic play declines during the preschool years.

7. The _____ theory of moral development emphasizes identification and guilt as motivators of good conduct. (p. 253)
   a. ecological
   b. behavioral
   c. cognitive-developmental
   d. psychoanalytic

8. A form of discipline known as _____ supports conscience formation by pointing out the effects of the child's misbehavior on others. (p. 253)
   a. positive discipline
   b. induction
   c. punishment
   d. time out

9. The most effective form of discipline is (p. 256)
    a. withdrawal of privileges.
    b. time out.
    c. encouraging good conduct.
    d. punishment.

10. The _____ view of morality regards children as active thinkers about social rules. (p. 256)
    a. psychoanalytic
    b. cognitive-developmental
    c. behaviorist
    d. social learning

11. _____ aggression, aimed at obtaining an object, privilege, or space with no deliberate intent to harm another person, is the most common form of aggression exhibited during the preschool years. (p. 257)
    a. Hostile
    b. Overt
    c. Instrumental
    d. Relational

12. TV violence (p. 258)
    a. hardens children to aggression, making them more willing to tolerate it in others.
    b. teaches children that violence is socially unacceptable and has harsh negative consequences.
    c. is unlikely to increase violent behavior, even among highly aggressive children.
    d. is uncommon in children's programming, particularly cartoons.

13. Research on gender stereotyping during the preschool years shows that (p. 260)
    a. preschoolers are not yet able to label their own and others' sex.
    b. preschoolers use gender stereotypes as flexible guidelines rather than blanket rules.
    c. preschoolers believe that the characteristics associated with one's sex, such as activities, toys, occupations, hairstyle, and clothing, determine whether a person is male or female.
    d. although preschoolers are capable of categorizing people by sex, they do not yet have the necessary cognitive capacities to form gender stereotypes.

14. Research on familial influences on gender typing shows that (p. 262)
    a. from birth, parents hold similar perceptions and expectations of their sons and daughters.
    b. parents espouse similar child-rearing values for sons and daughters.
    c. of the two sexes, boys are more gender-stereotyped than are girls.
    d. mothers are less tolerant of cross-gender behavior in their children than are fathers.

15. Individuals who are androgynous (p. 263)
    a. display highly gender-stereotyped behavior.
    b. demonstrate mostly cross-gender behaviors.
    c. score high in both masculine and feminine personality characteristics.
    d. have a poorly developed gender identity.

16. Gender schema theory (p. 263)
    a. stresses genetic influences on gender typing.
    b. emphasizes development of gender-stereotyped beliefs through identification with the same-sex parent.
    c. focuses on the role of modeling and reinforcement in gender identity development.
    d. emphasizes how environmental pressures and children's cognitions work together to shape gender-role development.

17. _____ child rearing is marked by high acceptance and involvement, use of firm control with explanations, and gradual, appropriate autonomy granting. (p. 265)
    a. Authoritative
    b. Authoritarian
    c. Permissive
    d. Uninvolved

18. Which of the following outcomes are typically associated with children exposed to permissive parenting? (p. 265)
    a. positive mood, high self-confidence and self-control, superior academic achievement
    b. anxiety, withdrawal, unhappiness
    c. impulsivity, disobedience, rebelliousness, dependence on adults, low persistence on tasks
    d. poor emotional self-regulation, low academic self-esteem and school performance, frequent anti-social behavior

19. Which form of abuse is likely to be the most common, since it also accompanies most other types? (p. 267)
    a. physical abuse
    b. psychological abuse
    c. emotional neglect
    d. physical neglect

20. Child maltreatment (p. 268)
    a. is rare in large, industrialized nations and has declined in recent years.
    b. is rooted in adult psychological disturbance, and therefore, abusers demonstrate an easily identifiable abusive personality type.
    c. is best understood from a social learning perspective.
    d. is associated with peer difficulties, academic failure, depression, substance abuse, and delinquency.

PRACTICE TEST #2

1. Erikson regarded _____ as the central means through which preschoolers find out about themselves and their social world. (p. 244)
    a. conflicts with peers
    b. interaction with adults
    c. play
    d. modeling

2. Preschoolers tend to (p. 246)
    a. overestimate the difficulty of tasks.
    b. appraise the difficulty of tasks accurately.
    c. underestimate their abilities.
    d. overestimate their abilities.

3. The high self-esteem characteristic of most preschoolers contributes to their developing sense of (p. 246)
    a. initiative.
    b. empathy.
    c. altruism.
    d. androgyny.

4. Children have the capacity to correctly judge the causes of many basic emotions by age (p. 247)
    a. 2 to 3.
    b. 4 to 5.
    c. 6 to 7.
    d. 8 to 9.

5. Which of the following is true of preschoolers' self-conscious emotions? (p. 248)
   a. By early childhood, children have a well-developed understanding of self-conscious emotions and are no longer reliant on adults' messages to know when they should feel them.
   b. Self-conscious emotions are clearly linked to self-evaluation in early childhood.
   c. Beginning in early childhood, guilt is associated with feelings of personal inadequacy and often leads to maladjustment.
   d. Intense shame, as long as it occurs in appropriate circumstances, is related to positive adjustment.

6. According to Parten, the first form of true social interaction to develop during early childhood is (p. 249)
   a. cooperative play.
   b. associative play.
   c. parallel play.
   d. onlooker behavior.

7. Which of the following is true of preschoolers' first friendships? (p. 251)
   a. Preschoolers do not yet understand the concept of friendship.
   b. Preschoolers' interactions with friends cannot be distinguished from their interactions with nonfriends.
   c. Preschoolers' first friendships have a long-term, enduring quality.
   d. Preschoolers' first friendships are based on pleasurable play and sharing of toys.

8. Modeling of prosocial behavior (p. 255)
   a. is less effective than reinforcement in helping children acquire moral responses.
   b. has no long-term effects on children's behavior.
   c. exerts the greatest influence on children's behavior during the preschool years.
   d. is equally effective regardless of the model's characteristics.

9. Harsh discipline, such as yelling at, slapping, or spanking children for misbehavior (p. 255)
   a. is never justified.
   b. promotes lasting changes in children's behavior.
   c. has been linked with increases in adaptive behavior and academic performance.
   d. often has undesirable side effects, including modeling of aggressive behavior.

10. While talking to a group of classmates, Alexis says, "Don't play with Maggie, she's a nerd." This is an example of _____ aggression. (p. 257)
    a. relational
    b. emotional
    c. overt
    d. instrumental

11. During the preschool years (p. 257)
    a. boys and girls display the same type and amount of aggression.
    b. girls are less aggressive than are boys.
    c. boys are more overtly aggressive, whereas girls are more relationally aggressive.
    d. aggressive behavior is highly atypical and is cause for great concern.

12. The process of developing gender-linked preferences and behaviors valued by the larger society is called (p. 260)
    a. gender typing.
    b. gender intensification.
    c. gender identification.
    d. gender constancy.

13. Eleanor Maccoby's research on hormonal influences on play indicates that (p. 260)
    a. preference for same-sex playmates is rarely found in cultures outside of the United States, suggesting that hormones exert little influence on play behavior.
    b. hormonal differences lead boys to prefer rough, noisy play and girls prefer calm, gentle actions.
    c. preference for same-sex playmates declines during the preschool years.
    d. hormonal differences lead girls to prefer large group activities, while boys prefer to play in pairs.

14. In the classroom setting (p. 262)
    a. teachers try to override gender stereotypes taught in the home by promoting gender equality.
    b. boys are more involved in adult-structured activities than are girls, thereby facilitating the development of assertiveness, leadership, and creative use of materials.
    c. girls get more encouragement to participate in adult-structured activities, which normally promote compliance and bids for help.
    d. boys and girls engage in similar social behaviors, even when teachers encourage gender-typed beliefs and behaviors.

15. At the end of the preschool years, when children understand that their sex is a permanent characteristic of the self, they have developed (p. 263)
    a. gender constancy.
    b. sexual stability.
    c. gender identity.
    d. gender neutrality.

16. Research on gender constancy shows that (p. 263)
    a. providing children with information about genital differences between males and females significantly improves their understanding of gender constancy.
    b. gender constancy is responsible for children's gender-typed behavior.
    c. understanding of gender constancy leads to a reduction in gender-stereotyped behaviors.
    d. cognitive immaturity, not social experience, is largely responsible for preschoolers' difficulty grasping the permanence of sex.

17. Four-year-old Gisele's mother often tells her that "cars and trucks are for boys." According to gender schema theory, Gisele is likely to (p. 263)
    a. avoid playing with cars and trucks.
    b. ask her father to play cars and trucks with her.
    c. be resentful when she sees other girls playing with cars and trucks.
    d. seek out opportunities to play with boys who are playing with cars and trucks.

18. Research on the child-rearing beliefs and practices of particular ethnic groups indicates that (p. 266)
    a. Chinese parents tend to emphasize control.
    b. Hispanic fathers show little parental warmth and low commitment to parenting.
    c. African-American mothers tend to be permissive.
    d. there are no distinct ethnic child-rearing practices and beliefs.

19. Which of the following is strongly associated with all forms of child abuse? (p. 268)
    a. the abuser having been abused as a child
    b. unmanageable stress in the abuser
    c. a personality disturbance on the part of the abuser
    d. a sick or premature baby

20. Parents Anonymous combats child maltreatment by providing (p. 269)
    a. access to health care.
    b. social supports.
    c. clean, uncrowded living conditions.
    d. low-cost, high-quality child care.

CHAPTER 9
PHYSICAL AND COGNITIVE DEVELOPMENT
IN MIDDLE CHILDHOOD

BRIEF CHAPTER SUMMARY

The rate of physical growth during the school years is an extension of the slow, regular pattern that characterized early childhood. Bones of the body lengthen and broaden, and primary teeth are replaced with permanent teeth. Although most children appear to be at their healthiest in middle childhood, a variety of health problems do occur. During the past several decades, a rise in overweight and obesity has occurred among children in many Western nations. Children experience a somewhat higher rate of illness during the first 2 years of elementary school than they will later, due to exposure to sick children and an immune system that is not yet mature. The frequency of injury fatalities increases from middle childhood into adolescence, with the rate for boys rising considerably above that for girls.

Gains in flexibility, balance, agility, and force contribute to school-age children's gross motor development, and steady gains in reaction time also occur. Fine motor development also improves over the school years. Sex differences in motor skills that appeared during the preschool years extend into middle childhood and, in some instances, become more pronounced. Although school-age boys' genetic advantage in muscle mass contributes to their gross motor superiority, the environment plays a larger role. Rule-oriented games become common in the school years, and high-quality physical education classes help ensure that all children have access to the benefits of regular exercise and play.

During Piaget's concrete operational stage, children's thought is far more logical, flexible, and organized than it was during early childhood. However, concrete operational thought is limited in that children have difficulty reasoning about abstract ideas. Specific cultural practices, especially those associated with schooling, affect children's mastery of Piagetian tasks. Some neo-Piagetian theorists argue that the development of operational thinking can best be understood in terms of gains in information-processing capacity rather than a sudden shift to a new stage.

In contrast to Piaget's focus on overall cognitive change, the information-processing perspective examines separate aspects of thinking. Brain development contributes to an increase in information-processing capacity and gains in cognitive inhibition. In addition, attention becomes more selective, adaptable, and planful. As attention improves, so do memory strategies. Although metacognition expands, school-age children are not yet good at cognitive self-regulation. Fundamental discoveries about the development of information processing have been applied to children's learning of reading and mathematics.

Around age 6, IQ becomes more stable than it was at earlier ages, and it correlates well with academic achievement. Intelligence tests provide an overall score (the IQ), which represents general intelligence and an array of specific mental abilities. Sternberg's triarchic theory of intelligence and Gardner's theory of multiple intelligences look at how information-processing skills underlie intelligent behavior. SES accounts for some, but not all, of the black-white IQ difference, and many experts acknowledge that IQ scores can underestimate the intelligence of culturally different children.

Vocabulary, grammar, and pragmatics continue to develop in middle childhood, although less obviously than at earlier ages. In addition, school-age children develop language awareness. Many children throughout the world grow up bilingual, and as with first-language development, a sensitive period for second-language development exists. Research shows that bilingualism has positive consequences for development, but the question of how to educate bilingual children continues to be hotly debated.

Class size, educational philosophies, teacher-interaction patterns, and larger cultural context exert a strong influence on student learning. Teaching children with learning disabilities and special intellectual strengths introduces unique challenges. A great many factors, both within and outside schools, affect children's learning. Social values, school resources, quality of teaching, and parental encouragement all play important roles.

LEARNING OBJECTIVES

After reading this chapter, you should be able to:

9.1 Describe changes in body size, proportions, and skeletal maturity during middle childhood. (pp. 276–277)

9.2 Identify common health problems in middle childhood, discuss their causes and consequences, and cite ways to treat them. (pp. 277–281)

9.3 Cite major milestones of gross and fine motor development in middle childhood, noting sex differences. (pp. 281–282)

9.4 Describe qualities of children's play during middle childhood, along with consequences for cognitive and social development. (pp. 282–283)

9.5 Discuss the benefits of high-quality physical education during the school years. (pp. 283–284)

9.6 Summarize the major achievements of Piaget's concrete operational stage. (pp. 285–286)

9.7 Cite limitations of concrete operational thought, noting challenges to Piaget's findings. (pp. 286–287)

9.8 Discuss the information-processing view of cognitive change. (pp. 287–288)

9.9 Cite two basic changes in information processing that occur during middle childhood. (p. 288)

9.10 List three ways attention changes in middle childhood. (pp. 288–289)

9.11 Describe the development of memory strategies in middle childhood. (pp. 289–290)

9.12 Explain how the school-age child's knowledge base, culture, and schooling contribute to memory performance. (pp. 290–291)

9.13 Describe the school-age child's theory of mind and capacity to engage in cognitive self-regulation. (p. 291)

9.14 Cite applications of information processing to academic learning, noting existing controversies in teaching reading and mathematics to elementary school children. (pp. 291–293)

9.15 Discuss major approaches to defining and measuring intelligence, including Sternberg's triarchic theory and Gardner's theory of multiple intelligences. (pp. 293–296)

9.16 Describe evidence indicating that both heredity and environment contribute to IQ, and discuss cultural influences on mental test scores of ethnic minority children. (pp. 296–299)

9.17 Discuss advances in vocabulary, grammar, and pragmatics during middle childhood, and discuss the advantages of bilingualism. (pp. 299–301)

9.18 Explain how class size, educational philosophies, teacher–student interaction patterns, and larger cultural context contribute to children's learning in school. (pp. 301–304)

9.19 Cite ways in which schools serve children with special learning needs. (pp. 305–307)

9.20 Compare the academic accomplishments of North American children with those of Asian children. (pp. 307–308)

Physical Development

Body Growth

1. During middle childhood, children add about _____ inches in height and _____ pounds in weight each year. (p. 277)

2. Describe sex differences in body growth and proportions during middle childhood. (p. 277)

   _____

   _____

3. List two factors that account for unusual flexibility of movement in middle childhood. (p. 277)

   A. _____ B. _____

4. Between the ages of _____ and _____, all primary teeth are replaced by permanent teeth. (p. 277)

Common Health Problems

1. List two factors that lead many children from advantaged homes to be at their healthiest in middle childhood. (p. 277)

   A. _____ B. _____

2. True or False: During the school years, poverty no longer acts as a predictor of ill health. (p. 277)

Vision and Hearing

1. The most common vision problem in middle childhood is _____, or nearsightedness. (p. 277)

2. Cite evidence indicating that both heredity and environment contribute to nearsightedness. (p. 277)

   Heredity: _____

   _____

   Environment: _____

   _____

3. True or False: Myopia is one of the few health conditions that increases with SES. (p. 277)

4. Briefly explain why middle ear infections become less frequent in middle childhood. (p. 277)

   _____

   _____

5. True or False: If left untreated, chronic ear infections can lead to permanent hearing loss. (p. 277)

Malnutrition

1. The percentage of children eating dinner with their families (rises / drops) sharply between 9 and 14 years. (p. 278)

2. List five ways in which the prolonged effects of malnutrition are apparent by middle childhood. (p. 278)

    A. _____ B. _____

    C. _____ D. _____

    E. _____

Obesity

1. About _____ percent of Canadian children and _____ percent of American children are obese. (p. 278)

2. Why is obesity becoming common in developing nations? (p. 278)

    _____

    _____

3. How is obesity in childhood related to health problems in adulthood? (p. 278)

    _____

    _____

4. Genetics (does / does not) account for a tendency to gain weight. (p. 278)

5. (Low-SES / Middle SES) children are more likely to be overweight. Cite three factors that contribute to this trend. (p. 278)

    A. _____

    B. _____

    C. _____

6. Describe parenting practices that contribute to obesity, along with their consequences for children's eating habits. (pp. 278–279)

    _____

    _____

    _____

7. Describe evidence of the relationship between TV viewing and obesity. (p. 279)

    _____

    _____

    _____

8. Summarize the effects of childhood obesity on emotional and social development. (p. 279)

    _____

    _____

    _____

9. Why is childhood obesity difficult to treat? (p. 279)

_____

_____

10. List characteristics of effective interventions for treating obesity. (p. 279)

_____

_____

_____

11. What can schools do to help reduce childhood obesity? (p. 279)

_____

_____

Illnesses

1. What accounts for the somewhat higher rate of illness during the first 2 years of elementary school than in the later school years? (p. 280)

_____

2. The most common chronic illness, representing the most frequent cause of school absence and childhood hospitalization, is _____. (p. 280)

3. Cite three categories of children who are at greatest risk for developing asthma. (p. 280)

    A. _____   B. _____

    C. _____

Unintentional Injuries

1. _____ is / are the leading cause of injury in middle childhood. (p. 280)

2. Cite three characteristics of effective safety education programs. (p. 280)

    A. _____

    B. _____

    C. _____

3. Describe characteristics of children who are most at-risk for injury in middle childhood. (p. 280–281)

_____

_____

_____

_____

Gross Motor Development

1. Improvements in motor skills over middle childhood reflect gains in what four capacities? (p. 281)

   A. _____ B. _____

   C. _____ D. _____

2. Body growth, as well as more efficient _____, contributes to improved motor performance in middle childhood. (p. 281)

Fine Motor Development

1. Describe typical gains in writing and drawing during middle childhood. (p. 281)

   Writing: _____

   _____

   Drawing: _____

   _____

Sex Differences

1. Summarize sex differences in motor skills and explain how environmental factors contribute to these differences. (p. 282)

   _____

   _____

   _____

2. True or False: School-age boys' genetic advantage in muscle mass is great enough to account for their superiority in most gross motor skills. (p. 282)

3. List two extra measures that can help raise girls' participation, self-confidence, and sense of fair treatment in athletics. (p. 282)

   A. _____ B. _____

Games with Rules

1. What cognitive capacity permits the transition to rule-oriented games in middle childhood? (p. 283)

   _____

2. Briefly describe how child-organized games contribute to development. (p. 283)

   _____

   _____

   _____

3. List two factors that have contributed to the recent decline in child-organized games. (p. 283)

   A. _____ B. _____

4. List four arguments against and four arguments in favor of adult-organized sports for children. (p. 283)

In favor:

A. _____

B. _____

C. _____

D. _____

Against:

A. _____

B. _____

C. _____

D. _____

Physical Education

1. The average American school-age child gets only _____ minutes of physical education a week, and the average Canadian child gets about _____ minutes a week. (p. 283)

2. What kinds of activities should physical education classes emphasize to help the largest number of children develop active and healthy life styles? (p. 283)

_____

_____

3. List at least three benefits of being physically fit in childhood. (pp. 283–284)

A. _____   B. _____

C. _____

Cognitive Development

Piaget's Theory: The Concrete Operational Stage

1. During Piaget's *concrete operational stage,* thought is far more _____, _____, and _____ than it was during early childhood. (p. 285)

2. Match the following terms with the appropriate descriptions and examples. (p. 285)

_____ The ability to order items along a quantitative dimension, such as length or weight

_____ Awareness of classification hierarchies and the ability to focus on relations between a general and two specific categories at the same time

_____ Focusing on several aspects of a problem and relating them rather than centering on just one

_____ Thinking through a series of steps and then mentally reversing direction, returning to the starting point

1. Seriation
2. Decentration
3. Reversibility
4. Classification

3. What evidence did Piaget use to conclude that school-age children have a more accurate understanding of space than younger children? (pp. 285–286)

_____

_____

_____

_____

Limitations of Concrete Operational Thought

1. Cite the major limitation of concrete operational thought. (p. 286)

_____

2. Explain what is meant by the term *horizontal décalage,* noting how it is related to concrete operational hought. (p. 286)

_____

_____

_____

Recent Research on Concrete Operational Thought

1. Cite two examples that illustrate how culture and schooling contribute to children's mastery of conservation and other Piagetian problems. (p. 286)

   A. _____

   _____

   B. _____

   _____

2. True or False: The forms of logic required by Piagetian tasks appear to emerge spontaneously during childhood and are not heavily influenced by training, context, or cultural conditions. (p. 286)

3. Some neo-Piagetian theorists argue that the development of operational thinking can best be understood in terms of gains in _____ rather than a sudden shift to a new stage. (p. 287)

4. Define and explain how *central conceptual structures* help school-age children master Piagetian tasks. (p. 287)

   _____

   _____

   _____

Evaluation of the Concrete Operational Stage

1. Many researchers believe that two types of change may be involved in the school-age child's approach to Piagetian problems. Cite them. (p. 287)

   A. _____

   B. _____

1. Summarize the two basic changes in information processing that facilitate diverse aspects of thinking. (p. 288)

    A. _____

    _____

    B. _____

    _____

Attention

1. Describe the three ways in which attention changes in middle childhood. (pp. 288–289)

    A. _____

    _____

    B. _____

    _____

    C. _____

    _____

2. True or False: The demands of school tasks, such as teachers' explanations for how to plan, contribute to gains in planning. (p. 289)

Memory Strategies

1. List and define three memory strategies that develop in middle childhood, in the order in which they typically appear. (pp. 289–290)

    A. _____

    B. _____

    C. _____

2. Explain why *elaboration* develops later than other memory strategies. (p. 290)

    _____

    _____

    _____

3. Because organization and elaboration combine items into _____, they permit children to hold on to much more information. (p. 290)

The Knowledge Base and Memory Performance

1. Explain how extensive knowledge and use of memory strategies are intimately related to and support one another. (p. 290)

    _____

    _____

    _____

188

Culture, Schooling, and Memory Strategies

1. True or False: People in non-Western cultures who have no formal schooling are likely to use and benefit from instruction in memory strategies. (p. 290)

2. Discuss how culture and schooling are related to the development of memory strategies. (pp. 290–291)

_____

_____

_____

The School-Age Child's Theory of Mind

1. Compared to preschoolers, how do school-age children view the mind? (p. 291)

_____

2. How does schooling contribute to the school-age child's theory of mind? (p. 291)

_____

_____

Cognitive Self-Regulation

1. Explain why cognitive self-regulation develops gradually. What can parents and teachers do to foster self-regulation? (p. 291)

A. _____

_____

B. _____

_____

Applications of Information Processing to Academic Learning

1. List the diverse information-processing skills that contribute to reading. (pp. 291–292)

_____

_____

_____

2. Summarize the two sides of the "great debate" over how to teach beginning reading. (p. 292)

A. _____

_____

B. _____

_____

_____

3. What research supports the use of both whole language and phonics instruction for teaching children to read? (p. 292)

_____

_____

_____

4. During the early elementary school years, children acquire basic math facts through a combination of _____, _____, and _____. (p. 292)

5. Arguments about how to teach mathematics resemble those in reading. Summarize those arguments. (p. 292)

_____

_____

_____

_____

6. List four factors that support the acquisition of mathematical knowledge in Asian countries. (p. 293)

A. _____

B. _____

C. _____

D. _____

Biology & Environment: Children with Attention-Deficit Hyperactivity Disorder

1. (Boys / Girls) are three to nine times more likely to be diagnosed with ADHD than are children of the opposite sex. (p. 288)

2. Describe the characteristics of children with ADHD. (p. 288)

_____

_____

_____

_____

3. True or False: All children with ADHD exhibit hyperactive symptoms. (p. 288)

4. Cite evidence that ADHD is influenced by both heredity and environmental factors. (p. 288)

_____

_____

_____

_____

5. The most common treatment for ADHD is _____. List two additional interventions that help children with ADHD. (p. 289)

    A. _____

    B. _____

6. List the areas in which adults with ADHD may need help. (p. 289)

    _____

    _____

Individual Differences in Mental Development

Defining and Measuring Intelligence

1. What does an IQ score actually measure? (p. 293)

    _____

2. Explain the difference between group administered and individually administered IQ tests. (p. 293)

    _____

    _____

    _____

    _____

3. The (Stanford-Binet Intelligence Scale / Wechsler Intelligence Scale for Children) is the first test to be standardized on children representing the total population of the United States, including ethnic minorities. It has also been adapted for and standardized in Canada. (p. 293)

Recent Efforts to Define Intelligence

1. What is *componential analyses,* and why is it used? (p. 294)

    _____

    _____

    _____

2. Cite evidence that speed of processing is related to IQ. (p. 294)

    _____

    _____

    _____

Sternberg's Triarchic Theory of Intelligence

1. List and briefly summarize the three interacting subtheories described by Sternberg's *triarchic theory of intelligence.* (pp. 294–295)

    A. _____

    _____

    B. _____

    _____

C. _____

_____

2. How does Sternberg's theory help explain cultural differences in IQ? (p. 295)

_____

_____

_____

Gardner's Theory of Multiple Intelligences

1. Howard Gardner's _____ defines intelligence in terms of distinct processing operations that permit individuals to engage in a wide range of culturally valued activities. (p. 295)

2. List Gardner's eight independent intelligences. (p. 296)

A. _____   B. _____

C. _____   D. _____

E. _____   F. _____

G. _____   H. _____

Explaining Individual and Group Differences in IQ

1. How does SES relate to IQ? What do these findings reveal about the black-white IQ gap? (p. 296)

A. _____

_____

B. _____

_____

2. What do kinship studies reveal about the role of heredity in IQ? (p. 296)

_____

_____

3. What do adoption studies reveal about the contribution of environmental factors in IQ? (p. 297)

_____

_____

4. Explain how ethnic minority families foster unique communication skills that do not fit with the expectations of most classrooms and testing situations. (p. 297)

_____

_____

_____

_____

5. Describe the difference between collaborative and hierarchical styles of communication. (p. 297)

   A. _____

   _____

   B. _____

   _____

6. True or False: Because low-income ethnic minority children grow up in "object oriented" homes, they often lack opportunities to use games and objects that promote certain intellectual skills. (p. 298)

7. Why is assessment of adaptive behavior especially important for minority children? (p. 298)

   _____

   _____

8. _____ is one culturally relevant testing procedure for enhancing minority children's test performance. This approach is consistent with Vygotsky's zone of proximal development. (p. 298)

Language Development

Vocabulary

1. On average, children learn about _____ new words each day. (p. 299)

2. Cite three changes in vocabulary that occur in middle childhood. (p. 299)

   A. _____

   B. _____

   C. _____

3. Provide an example that illustrates the school-age child's ability to appreciate the psychological and physical meanings of words. (p. 299)

   _____

Grammar

1. Cite two grammatical achievements that occur in middle childhood. (p. 299)

   A. _____

   B. _____

Pragmatics

1. Define pragmatics. How do the pragmatic skills of school-age children differ from those of preschool-age children? (pp. 299–300)

   A. _____

   _____

   B. _____

   _____

Learning Two Languages at a Time

1. Cite two ways that children can become bilingual. (p. 300)

   A. _____

   B. _____

2. True or False: Children of bilingual parents who teach them both languages in early childhood show no special problems with language development. (p. 300)

3. What research evidence suggests a sensitive period for second-language development? (p. 300)

   _____

   _____

4. List some positive consequences of bilingualism. (p. 300)

   _____

   _____

   _____

5. Describe Canada's language immersion programs. (p. 300)

   _____

   _____

6. Summarize the current debate regarding how American ethnic minority children with limited English proficiency should be educated. (p. 300)

   _____

   _____

   _____

Learning in School

Class Size

1. Cite research indicating that class size influences children's learning. (p. 301)

   _____

   _____

   _____

2. List two reasons why small class size is beneficial. (pp. 301–302)

   A. _____

   B. _____

Educational Philosophies

1. How is a *traditional classroom* different from an *open classroom*? (p. 302)

   _____

   _____

   _____

2. How do children benefit from open settings? (p. 302)

   _____

   _____

   _____

3. Cite three educational themes inspired by Vygotsky's sociocultural theory. (p. 304)

   A. _____

   B. _____

   C. _____

4. What is *reciprocal teaching*? List its characteristics. (p. 304)

   A. _____

   _____

   B. _____

   _____

Teacher–Student Interaction

1. List three characteristics of elementary school teachers that are positively associated with learning. (p. 304)

   A. _____   B. _____

   C. _____

2. How does teacher interaction with well-behaved, high-achieving students differ from teacher interaction with unruly students? (p. 304)

   _____

   _____

3. Define *educational self-fulfilling prophecies,* and explain what type of student is most likely to be affected by them. (p. 304)

   A. _____

   B. _____

Grouping Practices

1. What is homogenous grouping? How can it be a potent source of self-fulfilling prophecies? (p. 304)

   A. _____

   _____

B. _____

_____

2. List the benefits associated with multigrade classrooms. (p. 304)

_____

_____

Teaching Children with Special Needs

1. Explain the difference between *mainstreaming* and *full inclusion*. (p. 305)

_____

_____

2. Describe characteristics of students labeled *mildly mentally retarded*. (p. 305)

_____

_____

3. A large number of mainstreamed students have _____, or great difficulty with one or more aspects of learning, usually reading. As a result, their achievement is considerably behind what would be expected on the basis of their IQ. (p. 305)

4. Using research to support your answer, how effective are mainstreaming and full inclusion? (p. 305)

_____

_____

_____

_____

_____

5. What special steps can be taken to promote peer acceptance of students with special needs? (p. 305)

_____

_____

Gifted Children

1. List characteristics of *gifted* children. (p. 305)

_____

_____

2. Match the following terms with the appropriate descriptions. (p. 306)

_____ Outstanding performance in a specific field	1. Creativity
_____ The ability to produce work that is original yet appropriate	2. Divergent thinking
_____ Involves arriving at a single correct answer and is emphasized on intelligence tests	3. Convergent thinking
_____ The generation of multiple and unusual possibilities when faced with a task or problem	4. Talent

3. Cite environmental characteristics that help foster talent. (p. 306)

_____

_____

_____

4. Briefly summarize the debate regarding the effectiveness of programs for the gifted. (p. 307)

_____

_____

_____

How Well Educated Are North American Children?

1. Cite four factors, both within and outside schools, that affect children's learning. (p. 307)

   A. _____   B. _____

   C. _____   D. _____

2. Explain why American children fall behind in academic achievement. (pp. 307–308)

_____

_____

_____

Social Issues: School Readiness and Grade Retention

1. Cite some disadvantages of delaying kindergarten entry. (p. 303)

_____

_____

2. What are some negative consequences of grade retention? (p. 303)

_____

_____

_____

3. What are *transition* classes? What are some negative consequences of placing children in transition classes? (p. 303)

   A. _____

   _____

   B. _____

   _____

Cultural Influences: Education in Japan, Taiwan, and the United States

1. Briefly summarize five cultural conditions in Japan and Taiwan that support high academic achievement. (p. 308)

    A. _____

    B. _____

    C. _____

    D. _____

    E. _____

ASK YOURSELF . . .

For *Ask Yourself* questions for this chapter, please log on to the Companion Website at www.ablongman.com/berk.

SUGGESTED STUDENT READINGS

Barkley, R. A. (1998). *Attention-deficit hyperactivity disorder: A handbook for diagnosis and treatment (2nd ed)*. New York: The Guilford Press. For anyone interested in working with school-age children, this book presents current literature on the symptoms, diagnosis, assessment, and treatment of ADHD.

Champion, T. B. (2003). *Understanding storytelling among African American children: A journey from Africa to America*. Mahwah, NJ: Erlbaum. A useful resource for teachers, researchers, and professionals working with African-American children, this book explores the unique communication style of African-American children, including the structure of their story telling and its impact on learning and achievement.

Sternberg, R. J. (Ed.). (2000). *Handbook of Intelligence*. New York: Cambridge University Press. A collection of chapters examining the development and assessment of intelligence. Other topics include groups and cultural differences in intelligence, biological influences, and the relationship between intelligence and information processing.

Woolf, A. D., Howard, S. C., Kenna, M. A., & Allison, K. C. (Eds.). (2001). *The Children's Hospital guide to your child's health and development*. Boston, MA: Harvard Medical School. Written primarily for parents, teachers, and other professionals working with children, this book details physical development through the school years, common childhood illnesses, risk factors associated with obesity, and relevant health and safety information

PUZZLE 9.1 TERM REVIEW

Across

5. Memory strategy of repeating the information
9. _____-_____ approach to beginning reading: emphasizes training in phonics
11. Ability to focus on several aspects of a problem at once and relate them
12. Memory strategy of grouping related items together
13. Ability to mentally go through a series of steps and then reverse direction, returning to the starting point
14. _____-_____ approach to beginning reading: parallels natural language and keeps reading materials whole and meaningful

Down

1. _____ décalage: development within a Piagetian stage
2. Memory strategy of creating a relationship between two or more pieces of information that are not members of the same category
3. The ability to seriate mentally is known as transitive _____.
4. Ability to order items along a quantitative dimension
6. Cognitive _____-_____: process of continually monitoring progress toward a goal, checking outcomes, and redirecting unsuccessful efforts
7. A greater than 20 percent increase over average body weight, based on an individual's age, sex, and physical build
8. Cognitive _____: ability to conrol internal and external distracting stimuli
10. _____ operational stage: Piaget's third stage, during which thought becomes more logical, flexible, and organized than it was during early childhood

PUZZLE 9.2 TERM REVIEW

Across

1. Gardner's theory of _____ intelligences identifies eight independent intelligences.
4. Outstanding performance in a specific field
5. _____ thinking: generation of a single correct answer for a problem
6. _____ mental retardation is a condition that characterizes children whose IQs fall between 55 and 70 and who also show problems in adaptive behavior.
11. Childhood disorder involving inattentiveness, impulsivity, and excessive motor activity (abbr.)
12. Educational _____ - _____ prophecy: idea that students may adopt teachers' positive and negative attitudes toward them and start to live up to these views
14. _____ classroom: teachers share decision making with students
15. Sternberg's _____ theory of intelligence states that information-processing skills, prior experience with tasks, and contextual factors combine to influence intelligent behavior.
16. _____ testing: individualized teaching is introduced into the testing situation to see what the child can attain with social support
17. _____ thinking: generation of multiple and unusual possibilities when faced with a task or problem

Down

2. _____ classroom: children are regarded as passive learners who acquire information presented by teachers
3. _____ teaching: a teacher and 2–4 students form a cooperative group and take turns leading dialogues on the content of a text passage
7. Full _____ refers to placement of students with learning difficulties in regular classrooms for the entire school day.
8. Ability to produce work that is original yet appropriate
9. Placement of students with learning difficulties in regular classrooms for part of the school day
10. Displaying exceptional intellectual strengths
13. _____ disabilities: great difficulty with one or more aspects of learning that results in poor school achievement, despite average to above-average IQ

PRACTICE TEST #1

1. Which of the following statements best characterizes body growth in middle childhood? (p. 277)
   a. After age 8, boys begin accumulating fat at a faster rate than girls.
   b. Children's growth during the school years tends to be fast and irregular.
   c. Children's legs grow faster than their arms and torsos.
   d. Children lack the flexibility of movement they had during the preschool years.

2. Retarded physical growth, low intelligence scores, poor motor coordination, inattention, and distractibility are associated with (p. 278)
   a. otis media.
   b. obesity.
   c. malnutrition.
   d. rapid development of the immune system.

3. Chronically ill children (p. 280)
   a. often show improved health in middle childhood.
   b. are at-risk for academic, emotional, and social difficulties.
   c. get a great deal of sympathy from parents and peers.
   d. often perform as well in school as their healthy agemates.

4. During middle childhood, body growth and more efficient information processing contribute to (p. 281)
   a. sex differences in motor skills.
   b. improved motor performance.
   c. children's desire to play sports.
   d. gradual improvements in writing and drawing.

5. With the exception of skipping, jumping, and hopping, school-age boys (p. 282)
   a. continue to lag behind girls in other gross motor skills, such as throwing and kicking.
   b. have less confidence in their athletic abilities than school-age girls.
   c. have a genetic advantage in muscle mass that fully accounts for their gross-motor superiority.
   d. outperform girls in gross motor skills and in throwing and kicking.

6. Gains in perspective-taking permit the transition to (p. 283)
   a. training in competitive sports.
   b. gender-stereotyped games.
   c. rule-oriented games.
   d. participation and self-confidence in sports.

7. Nine-year-old Albert easily solves Piaget's transitive inference problem with sticks. However, Albert has difficulty solving the following problem: "Jim is taller than Frank, and Frank is taller than Joe. Who is the tallest?" Piaget would attribute Albert's failure on the latter task to (p. 286)
   a. egocentrism.
   b. centration.
   c. analogical problem solving.
   d. horizontal décalage.

8. According to some neo-Piagetian theorists, the development of operational thinking (p. 287)
   a. results from a sudden shift to a new stage.
   b. emerges spontaneously.
   c. reflects gains in information-processing capacity.
   d. cannot explain how children come to master Piagetian tasks.

9. Gains in cognitive inhibition help school-age children (p. 288)
   a. prevent their minds from straying to irrelevant thoughts.
   b. retrieve information from long-term memory.
   c. retrieve information from short-term memory.
   d. understand their own mental processes.

10. Quentin needs to remember the words *tree* and *toaster*. If he uses the memory strategy of elaboration, he will (p. 290)
    a. think of words that rhyme with both.
    b. imagine a tree with toasters growing out of it.
    c. write the words several times on a piece of paper.
    d. say the words over and over to himself.

11. The basic skills approach to reading stresses (p. 292)
    a. an appreciation of written language as communication.
    b. the basic rules for translating written symbols into sounds.
    c. an appreciation for word concepts in a story context.
    d. children's exposure to a text in its complete form.

12. In Sternberg's triarchic theory of intelligence, which subtheory states that intelligent individuals skillfully adapt their thinking to fit with their personal desires and the demands of their everyday worlds? (p. 295)
    a. componential
    b. experiential
    c. contextual
    d. pragmatic

13. When black and white children are matched on family income, the black-white IQ gap (p. 296)
    a. is unaffected.
    b. disappears.
    c. is reduced by a third.
    d. is exaggerated.

14. _____ is / are a strong predictor of IQ. (p. 298)
    a. Sociability
    b. Amount of time spent in school
    c. Interest in novelty
    d. Race

15. When asked which shirt he wanted to wear, 9-year-old Vaughn said, "the blue shirt with the baseball on the sleeve." Vaughn's description illustrates which of the following language developments in middle childhood? (pp. 299–300)
    a. vocabulary
    b. grammar
    c. a reflective approach to language
    d. pragmatics

16. Which of the following statements is true of bilingual development? (p. 300)
    a. When bilingual parents try to teach their children both languages during early childhood, the children often experience severe problems in language development.
    b. Parents and teachers should not be concerned if children learning two languages display semilingualism, or inadequate proficiency in both languages.
    c. Recent research refutes the notion of a sensitive period for second language learning.
    d. Bilingual children are advanced in cognitive development.

17. Katrina has just been placed in a "low-ability" reading group. Which is a probable outcome of this placement? (p. 304)
    a. Katrina will exhibit a drop in self-esteem.
    b. She will view herself as intelligent.
    c. Her reading skills will improve.
    d. She will exhibit the same level of achievement as her peers in higher-ability reading groups.

18. Which of the following statements about multigrade classrooms is true? (p. 304)
    a. Self-esteem and attitudes toward school are more positive.
    b. There are no differences in academic performance between same-age and multigrade classrooms.
    c. Multigrade grouping seems to increase student competition.
    d. Pupils get more drill on basic facts and skills, a slower learning pace, and less time on academic work.

19. Louisa has an above average IQ but is failing math. Louisa may have (p. 305)
    a. mild mental retardation.
    b. a learning disability.
    c. difficulty with divergent thinking.
    d. a lack of talent.

20. Which of the following statements about gifted and creative children is accurate? (pp. 305–306)
    a. Although gifted and creative children have high IQs, they usually struggle with academic tasks.
    b. Gifted and creative children are better at convergent thinking than divergent thinking.
    c. Gifted and creative children often show uneven ability across academic subjects.
    d. Gifted and creative children often show high ability across all academic subjects.

PRACTICE TEST #2

1. The most common vision problem in middle childhood is (p. 277)
   a. myopia, or nearsightedness.
   b. hyperopia, or farsightedness.
   c. astigmatism.
   d. lack of eye muscle control.

2. Which of the following statements about obesity is true? (p. 278)
   a. Obesity is declining in developing nations.
   b. Parental feeding practices have little impact on childhood obesity.
   c. Using high-fat, sugary foods to reward children reduces their tendency to overeat during mealtime.
   d. Research indicates a consistent relationship between low SES and obesity.

3. Obese children (p. 279)
   a. rarely become obese adults.
   b. eat more than their normal-weight peers but maintain a high level of physical activity.
   c. are more responsive to external stimuli associated with food—taste, sight, smell, and time of day—and less responsible to internal hunger cues than are normal weight individuals.
   d. are no more likely to become depressed than their normal-weight peers.

4. Sage lives in a low-income housing unit with his mother who frequently smokes. Which of the following is Sage at risk for? (p. 280)
   a. asthma
   b. diabetes
   c. sickle cell anemia
   d. arthritis

5. By middle childhood, the greatest risk-takers tend to be (p. 280)
    a. highly active girls.
    b. children who live near busy highways.
    c. children whose parents do not act as safety-conscious models.
    d. children who live in rural areas.

6. Jillian and Justin are in the third grade. Which of the following statements best illustrates their motor skills? (p. 281)
    a. Both Jillian and Justin do well at skills requiring balance and agility, such as skipping and jumping.
    b. Jillian is ahead of Justin in drawing skills but lags behind in skipping, jumping, and hopping.
    c. Justin is able to throw and kick a ball farther than Jillian but is unable to write and draw as well as Jillian.
    d. Both Jillian and Justin do well on fine and gross motor tasks. Sex differences in motor skills don't become evident until adolescence.

7. In a study of elementary school students, girls (p. 282)
    a. saw themselves as having less talent at sports than their male classmates.
    b. saw themselves as having more talent at sports than their male classmates.
    c. often refused to participate in athletics.
    d. saw themselves as having equal talent at sports as their male classmates.

8. In first grade, Caleb began collecting baseball cards. Now that he's older, Caleb spends a great deal of time sorting his cards, arranging them by team, and putting them into albums. Which of Piaget's concepts is Caleb demonstrating? (p. 285)
    a. conservation
    b. centration
    c. classification
    d. spatial reasoning

9. Recent research indicates that _____ seems to promote mastery of Piagetian tasks. (p. 286)
    a. practice with conservation problems
    b. going to school
    c. stern parenting
    d. interacting with peers

10. Children learn a great deal about planning by (p. 289)
    a. watching adults engage in planning activities.
    b. making frequent lists of everyday activities.
    c. collaborating on tasks with more expert planners.
    d. mentally rehearsing information.

11. Compared to Western children, children in non-Western cultures who have no formal schooling (p. 290)
    a. do not use or benefit from instruction in memory strategies.
    b. benefit from instruction in memory strategies.
    c. are more motivated to use memory strategies.
    d. develop memory strategies at the same rate as Western children.

12. Parents and teachers can foster self-regulation by (p. 291)
    a. allowing children to figure out task demands independently.
    b. encouraging children to use ineffective strategies first and then providing them with more effective strategies.
    c. pointing out the special demands of tasks, suggesting effective strategies, and emphasizing the value of self-correction.
    d. forcing children to use strategies until they effectively apply them across settings.

13. In first grade, teaching that includes phonics (p. 292)
    a. is overwhelming for young children and can result in low reading achievement scores.
    b. only boosts reading achievement scores for children coming from high-SES backgrounds at risk for reading difficulties.
    c. boosts reading achievement scores, especially for children from low-SES backgrounds at risk for reading difficulties.
    d. has no empirical benefits over the whole-language approach.

14. Sternberg's experiential subtheory states that compared to less intelligent individuals, highly intelligent ones (p. 295)
    a. process information more skillfully in novel situations.
    b. apply strategies more adaptively in all types of experiences.
    c. process information more quickly in familiar settings.
    d. exhibit a rapid reaction time on a wide range of complex tasks.

15. Gardner defines intelligence in terms of (p. 295)
    a. three interacting subtheories.
    b. 180 unique intellectual factors organized along three dimensions.
    c. a pyramid with "g" at the top.
    d. eight independent intelligences that are based on distinct sets of processing operations.

16. Adoption studies reveal that (p. 297)
    a. children of low-IQ biological mothers rarely benefit from being adopted by higher income families.
    b. children of low-IQ biological mothers show a steady decline in IQ over middle childhood.
    c. heredity is a more powerful predictor of IQ test performance than environmental factors.
    d. IQ test performance can be greatly improved by an advantaged home life.

17. From an early age, white parents ask _____ questions that resemble the questioning style of tests and classrooms. In contrast, black parents ask _____ questions—ones that they themselves cannot answer. (p. 297)
    a. knowledge-training; real
    b. real; knowledge-training
    c. analogy; story-starter
    d. complex; simple

18. Dynamic testing (p. 298)
    a. shows no transfer effects to new test items.
    b. often underestimates the IQs of ethnic minority children.
    c. presents challenges that are easier than those faced in traditional assessments.
    d. introduces purposeful teaching to find out what the child can attain with social support.

19. As he walked out of the movie theater, Jamal exclaimed, "What a *cool* movie!" Jamal's comment illustrates that he understands that many words can have _____ (p. 299)
    a. a unitary meaning
    b. metaphorical meaning
    c. psychological as well as physical meaning
    d. phonological meaning

20. In the Tennessee study of the effects of class size, students in small classes (p. 301)
    a. got twice as much adult attention.
    b. maintained higher academic achievement all year long.
    c. were more emotionally well adjusted.
    d. maintained higher academic achievement, even years later

CHAPTER 10
EMOTIONAL AND SOCIAL DEVELOPMENT
IN MIDDLE CHILDHOOD

BRIEF CHAPTER SUMMARY

According to Erikson, the combination of adult expectations and children's drive toward mastery sets the stage for the psychosocial conflict of middle childhood—industry versus inferiority—which is resolved positively when experiences lead children to develop a sense of competence at useful skills and tasks. Psychological traits and social comparisons appear in children's self-concepts, and a hierarchically organized self-esteem emerges. Greater self-awareness and social sensitivity support emotional development in middle childhood. Gains take place in experience of self-conscious emotions, understanding of emotional states, and emotional self-regulation. Cognitive maturity and experiences in which adults and peers encourage children to take note of another's viewpoint support gains in perspective-taking skill. An expanding social world, the capacity to consider more information when reasoning, and perspective-taking lead moral understanding to improve greatly in middle childhood.

By the end of middle childhood, children form peer groups. Whereas peer groups provide children with insight into larger social structures, one-to-one friendships contribute to the development of trust and sensitivity. During the school years, friendship becomes more complex and psychologically based. Peer acceptance becomes a powerful predictor of current and future psychological adjustment. School-age children extend the gender-stereotyped beliefs they acquired in early childhood. Boys' masculine gender identities strengthen, whereas girls' identities become more flexible. Cultural values and parental attitudes influence these trends.

In middle childhood, the amount of time children spend with parents declines dramatically. Child rearing shifts toward coregulation as parents grant children more decision making power. Sibling rivalry tends to increase in middle childhood, and siblings strive to be different from one another. When children experience divorce or entry into blended families through remarriage, child, parent, and family characteristics influence how well they fare. Maternal employment can lead to many benefits for school-age children, particularly when mothers enjoy their work, when work settings and communities support their child-rearing responsibilities, and when high-quality child care is available.

Fears and anxieties in middle childhood are directed toward new concerns, including physical safety, media events, academic performance, parents' health, and peer relations. Child sexual abuse has devastating consequences for children and is especially difficult to treat. Personal characteristics of children, a warm, well-organized family life, and social supports outside the immediate family are related to children's ability to cope with stressful life conditions.

LEARNING OBJECTIVES

After reading this chapter, you should be able to:

10.1 Explain Erikson's stage of industry versus inferiority, noting major personality changes. (pp. 314–315)

10.2 Describe the development of the self during middle childhood, noting changes in self-concept and self-esteem, as well as factors that influence children's self-evaluations. (pp. 315–318)

10.3 Describe changes in self-conscious emotions, understanding of emotional states, and emotional self-regulation in middle childhood. (pp. 319–320)

10.4 Trace the development of perspective taking, and discuss the relationship between perspective taking and social skills. (pp. 320–321)

10.5 Describe changes in moral understanding during middle childhood. (pp. 321–322)

10.6 Describe changes in peer relations during middle childhood, including characteristics of peer groups and friendships, and explain how these relationships contribute to children's social development. (pp. 322–324)

10.7 Describe the four categories of peer acceptance, noting how each is related to social behavior, and discuss ways to help rejected children. (pp. 324–326)

10.8 Describe changes in gender-stereotyped beliefs and gender identity during middle childhood, noting sex differences and cultural influences. (pp. 326–327)

10.9 Discuss changes in the parent–child relationship during middle childhood, including new issues confronting parents and changes in parent–child communication. (pp. 327–328)

10.10 Describe changes in sibling relationships during middle childhood, and compare the experiences and developmental outcomes of only children with those of children who have siblings. (pp. 328–329)

10.11 Discuss children's adjustment to divorce and blended families, noting the influence of parent and child characteristics, as well as social supports within the family and surrounding community. (pp. 329–333)

10.12 Discuss the impact of maternal employment and dual-earner families on school-age children's development, noting the influence of social supports within the family and surrounding community, and explain issues regarding child care for school-age children. (pp. 333–334)

10.13 Discuss common fears and anxieties in middle childhood, with particular attention to school phobia. (p. 334)

10.14 Discuss factors related to child sexual abuse, its consequences for children's development, and ways to prevent and treat it. (pp. 334–336)

10.15 Cite factors that foster resilience in middle childhood. (pp. 336–338)

STUDY QUESTIONS

Erikson's Theory: Industry versus Inferiority

1. Erikson's theory of personality change during the school years builds upon Freud's _____ stage. (p. 314)

2. According to Erikson, what two factors set the stage for the psychological conflict of middle childhood, *industry versus inferiority*? (p. 314)

    A. _____

    B. _____

3. Discuss factors that lead to a positive resolution of the industry versus inferiority stage. (pp. 314–315)

_____

_____

_____

4. List two ways that children can develop a sense of inferiority during middle childhood. (p. 315)

   A. _____

   B. _____

Self-Understanding

Changes in Self-Concept

1. List three ways in which self-concept changes during middle childhood. (p. 315)

   A. _____

   B. _____

   C. _____

2. Discuss how the capacity to make social comparisons impacts children's self-concept during middle childhood. (p. 315)

   _____

   _____

   _____

   _____

3. Discuss the relationship between perspective-taking skills and self-concept development. (p. 315)

   _____

   _____

   _____

   _____

4. True or False: Beginning in middle childhood, peers become more important than parents in children's self-definitions. (p. 315)

Development of Self-Esteem

1. List four self-esteems that children form by the age of 6 to 7. (p. 315)

   A. _____
   B. _____
   C. _____
   D. _____

2. True or False: Separate self-evaluations contribute equally to general self-esteem. Briefly explain your response. (p. 316)

_____

_____

_____

3. For most children, self-esteem (drops / rises) during the first few years of elementary school and then (drops / rises) from fourth to sixth grade. (p. 316)

Influences on Self-Esteem

1. Chinese and Japanese children score (lower / higher) in self-esteem than do American children. Briefly explain why this is the case. (p. 316)

_____

_____

_____

2. Describe the child-rearing practices associated with high self-esteem in middle childhood. (p. 317)

_____

_____

_____

_____

3. _____ are common, everyday explanations for the causes of behavior. (p. 317)

4. Distinguish between mastery-oriented attributions and learned helplessness, noting the differences between children who possess these types of attributional styles. (p. 317)

Mastery-oriented attributions:

_____

_____

_____

Learned-helplessness:

_____

_____

_____

5. True or False: Over time, the ability of learned-helpless children no longer predicts their performance. Explain your response. (p. 317)

_____

_____

_____

6. Discuss the role of parent communication in accounting for children's development of learned-helpless attributions. (pp. 317–318)

_____

_____

_____

_____

7. Differentiate teacher behaviors that lead students to develop mastery-oriented attributions from those that lead students to develop learned-helpless attributions. (p. 318)

Mastery-oriented:

_____

_____

_____

Learned-helpless:

_____

_____

_____

8. True or False: Girls and low-income ethnic minority children are especially vulnerable to learned helplessness. (p. 318)

9. _____ is an intervention that encourages learned-helpless children to believe that they can overcome failure by exerting more effort. Describe this technique. (p. 318)

_____

_____

_____

_____

Emotional Development

Self-Conscious Emotions

1. Discuss changes in how children experience the self-conscious emotions of pride and guilt during middle childhood. (p. 319)

Pride:

_____

_____

_____

Guilt:

_____

_____

_____

Emotional Understanding

1. List three changes in children's understanding of emotion during middle childhood. (p. 319)

   A. _____

   B. _____

   C. _____

Emotional Self-Regulation

1. By age 10, most children have an adaptive set of strategies for regulating emotion. Distinguish the strategies that they endorse in situations where they have some control over the outcome versus those in which outcomes are beyond their control. (p. 320)

   Control over outcome:

   _____

   _____

   _____

   No control over outcome:

   _____

   _____

   _____

2. When the development of emotional self-regulation has gone well, young people acquire a sense of *emotional* _____ — a feeling of being in control of their emotional experience. (p. 320)

3. Distinguish characteristics of emotionally well-regulated children versus children with poor emotional regulation. (p. 320)

   Well-regulated:

   _____

   _____

   _____

   Poorly-regulated:

   _____

   _____

   _____

1. Match each of Selman's stages of perspective taking with the appropriate description. (p. 321)

   _____ Understand that third-party perspective taking can be influenced by larger societal values

   _____ Recognize that self and others can have different perspectives, but confuse the two

   _____ Understand that different perspectives may be due to access to different information

   _____ Can imagine how the self and others are viewed from the perspective of an impartial third person

   _____ Can view own thoughts, feelings, and behavior from other's perspective

1. Undifferentiated
2. Social-informational
3. Self-reflective
4. Third-party
5. Societal

2. What factors contribute to individual differences in perspective-taking skill? (p. 320)

_____

_____

_____

_____

Moral Development

Learning About Justice Through Sharing

1. Define *distributive justice.* (p. 321)

_____

_____

2. Using Damon's three-step sequence, trace the development of children's conception of distributive justice during middle childhood. (pp. 321–322)

A. _____

_____

B. _____

_____

C. _____

_____

3. True or False: Peer interaction is particularly important in the development of standards of justice. (p. 322)

Changes in Moral and Social-Conventional Understanding

1. Describe two changes in moral and social-conventional understanding during middle childhood. (p. 322)

A. _____

_____

B. _____

_____

2. True or False: Children in Western and non-Western cultures use the same criteria to distinguish moral and social-conventional concerns. (p. 322)

Peer Relations

Peer Groups

1. Describe the characteristics of a peer group. (p. 322)

_____

_____

_____

_____

2. Describe the positive functions of children's peer groups. (pp. 322–323)

_____

_____

_____

3. How do school-age boys and girls express hostility toward the "outgroup" differently? (p. 323)

Boys: _____

_____

Girls: _____

_____

Friendships

1. Describe changes in children's conception of friendship during middle childhood. (pp. 323–324)

_____

_____

_____

_____

2. True or False: New ideas about the meaning of friendship lead school-age children to be less selective in their choice of friends than they were at younger ages. (p. 324)

3. Friendships (do / do not) tend to remain stable over middle childhood. (p. 324)

4. Discuss the qualities of aggressive children's friendships. (p. 324)

Aggressive girls:

_____

_____

_____

Aggressive boys:

_____

_____

_____

Peer Acceptance

1. Define *peer acceptance,* noting how it is different from friendship. (p. 324)

    _____

    _____

    _____

    _____

2. Name and describe four categories of peer acceptance. (p. 324)

    A. _____

    _____

    B. _____

    _____

    C. _____

    _____

    D. _____

    _____

3. True or False: All school-age children fit into one of the four categories of peer acceptance described above in Question 2. (p. 324)

4. Discuss emotional and social outcomes associated with peer rejection. (p. 324)

    _____

    _____

    _____

    _____

5. Identify and describe two subtypes of popular children. (p. 324)

    A. _____

    _____

    _____

    B. _____

    _____

    _____

6. Describe the social behavior of rejected-aggressive and rejected-withdrawn children. (pp. 324–325)

   Rejected-Aggressive:

   _____

   _____

   _____

   Rejected-Withdrawn:

   _____

   _____

   _____

7. True or False: Controversial children are hostile and disruptive but also engage in high rates of positive, prosocial acts. (p. 326)

8. True or False: Neglected children are more poorly adjusted and display less socially competent behavior than do their "average" counterparts. (p. 326)

9. Describe three interventions designed to help rejected children. (p. 326)

   A. _____

   _____

   _____

   B. _____

   _____

   _____

   C. _____

   _____

   _____

Biology & Environment: Bullies and Their Victims

1. What is *peer victimization*? (p. 325)

   _____

   _____

2. Describe biological and familial characteristics common to victimized children. (p. 325)

   Biological:

   _____

   _____

   _____

Familial:

_____

_____

_____

3. List adjustment difficulties associated with peer victimization. (p. 325)

_____

_____

_____

_____

4. True or False: Passive victims of bullying are more despised by peers than are aggressive bully/victims. (p. 325)

5. Discuss individual and school-based interventions for peer victimization. (p. 325)

_____

_____

_____

_____

Gender Typing

Gender-Stereotyped Beliefs

1. Describe ways in which children extend their gender-stereotyped beliefs during middle childhood. (p. 326)

_____

_____

_____

_____

2. Differentiate academic subjects and skills that children regard as either masculine or feminine. (p. 326)

    Masculine:

_____

_____

_____

    Feminine:

_____

_____

_____

3. True or False: As school-age children extend their knowledge of gender stereotypes, they become more closed-minded about what males and females can do. (p. 326)

Gender Identity and Behavior

1. Contrast the gender identity development of girls and boys during middle childhood, and note implications for behavior. (pp. 326–327)

    Girls:

    _____

    _____

    _____

    Boys:

    _____

    _____

    _____

Cultural Influences on Gender Typing

1. Using cross-cultural evidence, show how assignment of "cross-gender" tasks can influence gender-typed behavior. (p. 327)

    _____

    _____

    _____

    _____

2. True or False: Research overwhelmingly shows that all boys benefit from assignment of "cross-gender" tasks. (p. 327)

Family Influences

Parent–Child Relationships

1. True or False: In middle childhood, the amount of time that children spend with their parents declines dramatically. (p. 328)

2. During the school years, child-rearing becomes easier for those parents who established a(n) _____ parenting style during the early years. (p. 328)

3. What is *coregulation,* and how does it foster a cooperative relationship between parent and child? (p. 328)

    A. _____

    _____

    B. _____

    _____

Siblings

1. During middle childhood, sibling rivalry tends to (increase / decrease). Why is this the case? (p. 328)

    _____

    _____

    _____

    _____

2. Cite sibling characteristics associated with frequent parental comparisons, noting the impact of parental comparisons on development. (p. 328)

    Sibling characteristics:

    _____

    _____

    _____

    Impact:

    _____

    _____

    _____

Only Children

1. True or False: Research indicates that sibling relationships are essential for healthy development. (p. 329)

2. True or False: Research supports the commonly held belief that only children are spoiled and selfish. (p. 329)

3. Discuss the adjustment of children in one-child families. (p. 329)

    _____

    _____

    _____

    _____

Divorce

1. True or False: The United States has the highest divorce rate in the world. (p. 329)

2. Summarize ways in which divorce has an immediate impact on the home environment. (p. 330)

    _____

    _____

    _____

    _____

3. Explain how children's ages affect their reactions to divorce, noting differences between younger and older children. (p. 330)

Younger:

_____

_____

_____

Older:

_____

_____

_____

4. Summarize sex differences in children's reactions to divorce. (p. 330)

Boys:

_____

_____

_____

Girls:

_____

_____

_____

5. In mother-custody families, (girls / boys) typically experience more serious adjustment problems. (p. 330)

6. True or False: Boys of divorcing parents receive more emotional support from mothers, teachers, and peers than do girls of divorcing parents. (p. 330)

7. Most children show improved adjustment by _____ years after their parents' divorce. (p. 330)

8. (Boys / Girls) and children with _____ temperaments are especially likely to drop out of school and display antisocial behavior in adolescence following a parental divorce. (pp. 330–331)

9. True or False: For both sexes, divorce is linked to problems with adolescent sexuality and development of intimate ties. (p. 331)

10. What is the overriding factor in children's positive adjustment following a parental divorce? (p. 331)

_____

11. Explain why a good father–child relationship is important for both boys and girls following a parental divorce. (p. 331)

Boys:

_____

_____

_____

Girls:

_____

_____

_____

12. True or False: Making the transition to a low-conflict, single-parent household is better for children than staying in a high-conflict intact family. (p. 331)

13. Describe *divorce mediation,* and explain why it is likely to have benefits for children. (p. 331)

_____

_____

_____

_____

14. In _____, the court grants the mother and father equal say in important decisions regarding the child's upbringing. (p. 331)

Blended Families

1. List two reasons why blended families present adjustment difficulties for most children. (pp. 331–332)

A. _____

_____

B. _____

_____

2. (Older / Younger) children and (girls / boys) have the hardest time adjusting to a parent's divorce. (p. 332)

3. The most frequent form of blended family is a (father-stepmother / mother-stepfather) arrangement. Contrast boys' and girls' adjustment in this type of family arrangement. (p. 332)

Boys:

_____

_____

Girls:

_____

_____

4. Explain why older children and adolescents of both sexes living in mother-stepfather families display more irresponsible, acting out, and antisocial behavior than do their agemates in nonstepfamilies. (p. 332)

_____

_____

_____

_____

5. Remarriage of noncustodial fathers often leads to (reduced / increased) contact with children, particularly if they have daughters. (p. 332)

6. Cite two alternative reasons why children tend to react negatively to the remarriage of custodial fathers. (p. 332)

   A. _____

   _____

   _____

   B. _____

   _____

   _____

7. (Girls / Boys) have an especially hard time getting along with stepmothers. Briefly explain your response. (p. 332)

   _____

   _____

   _____

8. Explain how family life education and therapy can help parents and children in blended families adapt to the complexities of their new circumstances. (p. 333)

   _____

   _____

   _____

   _____

   _____

Maternal Employment and Dual-Earner Families

1. True or False: Single mothers are far more likely than their married counterparts to enter the workforce. (p. 333)

2. Describe potential benefits of maternal employment for school-age children, and note the circumstances under which such outcomes are achieved. (p. 333)

   _____

   _____

   _____

3. True or False: Maternal employment results in children spending more time with fathers, who take on greater responsibility with child care. (p. 333)

4. List four supports which help parents juggle the demands of work and child rearing. (p. 333)

   A. _____

   _____

   B. _____

   _____

C. _____

_____

D. _____

_____

5. Differentiate self-care children who fare well from those who fare poorly. (pp. 333–334)

Children who fare well:

_____

_____

Children who fare poorly:

_____

_____

6. Before age _____ or _____, children should not be left unsupervised because most are not yet competent to handle emergencies. (p. 334)

Some Common Problems of Development

Fears and Anxieties

1. Summarize new fears and anxieties that emerge in middle childhood. (p. 334)

_____

_____

_____

_____

2. Describe the symptoms associated with *school phobia.* (p. 334)

_____

_____

_____

_____

3. Distinguish common causes of school phobia in early childhood from those in later childhood and adolescence, noting implications for treatment. (p. 334)

Early childhood:

_____

_____

_____

Later childhood and adolescence:

_____

_____

_____

Child Sexual Abuse

1. Sexual abuse is committed against children of both sexes, but more often against (girls / boys). (p. 335)

2. Describe typical characteristics of sexual abusers. (p. 336)

_____

_____

_____

_____

3. What type of children are abusers likely to select as targets? (p. 336)

_____

_____

4. Discuss the adjustment problems of sexually abused children, noting differences between younger children and adolescents. (p. 336)

    Younger children:

_____

_____

_____

    Adolescents:

_____

_____

_____

5. Describe common behavioral characteristics of sexually abused girls as they move into young adulthood. (p. 336)

_____

_____

_____

6. Why is it difficult to treat victims of child sexual abuse? (p. 336)

_____

_____

_____

_____

7. Discuss the role of educational programs in preventing child sexual abuse. (p. 336)

_____

_____

_____

_____

Fostering Resiliency in Middle Childhood

1. List three broad factors that help children cope with stress and protect against maladjustment. (pp. 336–337)

   A. _____

   _____

   B. _____

   _____

   C. _____

   _____

A Lifespan Vista: Children of War

1. Discuss children's adjustment to war and social crises, noting differences between situations involving temporary crises and those involving chronic danger. (p. 335)

   _____

   _____

   _____

   _____

2. What is the best safeguard against lasting problems? (p. 335)

   _____

   _____

   _____

3. Discuss some interventions used to help children from Public School 31 in Brooklyn, New York, in the wake of the September 11 attack on the World Trade Center. (p. 335)

   _____

   _____

   _____

   _____

1. True or False: Children as young as age 3 are frequently asked to provide testimony in court cases involving child abuse and neglect. (p. 337)

2. Summarize how age differences affect children's ability to provide accurate testimony. (p. 337)

_____

_____

_____

_____

3. True or False: When adults lead children by suggesting incorrect information, they increase the likelihood of incorrect reporting among preschool and school-age children alike. (p. 337)

4. True or False: Special interviewing methods involving the use of anatomically correct dolls have been successful in prompting more accurate recall of sexual abuse experiences, particularly among preschoolers. (p. 337)

5. Summarize interventions that can be used to assist child witnesses. (p. 337)

_____

_____

_____

_____

ASK YOURSELF . . .

For *Ask Yourself* questions for this chapter, please log on to the Companion Website at www.ablongman.com/berk.

SUGGESTED STUDENT READINGS

Bohart, A. C., & Stipek, D. J. (Eds.). (2001). *Constructive and destructive behavior: Implications for family, school, and society.* Washington: The American Psychological Association. An interdisciplinary collection of research, this book explores the influence of constructivist and prosocial behavior on children's destructive and antisocial tendencies. Other topics include the effects of media violence on children's behavior, how self-control in childhood predicts adult behavior, how age and sex influence bullying, and whether early intervention can successfully prevent delinquency.

Hetherington, E. M. (Ed.). (1999). *Coping with divorce, single parenting, and remarriage: A risk and resiliency perspective.* Mahwah, NJ: Erlbaum. Examines family functioning and child adjustment in different kinds of families. Discusses individual, familial, and extra familial interactions and risk and protective factors associated with marriage, divorce, single parenting, and remarriage.

Violato, C., Oddone-Paolucci, E., & Genius, M. (Eds.). (2000). *The changing family and child development.* Aldershot, England: Ashgate Publishing. An interdisciplinary approach to understanding the modern family, this book explores the causal impact of early childhood experiences, factors contributing to resiliency, changing roles for girls and women, and the long-term consequences of maternal employment and nonmaternal care.

PUZZLE 10.1 TERM REVIEW

Across

4. Social _____ : judging one's appearance, abilities, and behavior in relation to those of others
6. Divorce _____ attempts to settle disputes of divorcing couples while avoiding legal battles that intensify family conflict.
7. _____ versus inferiority: Erikson's psychological crisis of middle childhood
8. Supervision in which parents exercise general oversight but permit children to manage moment-to-moment decisions
9. Children who develop learned _____ attribute failures, but not successes, to ability.
10. _____ taking: the capacity to imagine what other people may be thinking and feeling

Down

1. _____ - _____ children regularly look after themselves during after-school hours.
2. Distributive _____ refers to beliefs about how to divide material goods fairly.
3. In _____ custody, the court grants both parents equal say in important decisions about the child's upbrining.
5. Children with _____ - _____ attributions credit their successes to ability and their failures to insufficient effort or the difficulty of the task.

PUZZLE 10.2 TERM REVIEW

Across

2. A child with school _____ feels severe apprehension about attending school, often accompanied by physical complaints that disappear once he is allowed to stay home.
8. _____ children get many positive votes on sociometric measures of peer acceptance.
9. _____ children are actively disliked and get many negative votes on sociometric measures of peer acceptance
10. Peer _____: destructive form of peer interaction in which certain children become frequent targets of verbal and physical attacks or other forms of abuse
11. _____ children are seldom chosen, either positively or negatively, on sociometric measures of peer acceptance
12. Rejected-_____ children: subgroup of rejected children who are passive and socially awkward

Down

1. Peer _____: peers who form a social unit by generating unique values and standards of behavior and a social structure of leaders and followers
3. Rejected- _____ children: subgroup of rejected children who engage in high rates of conflict, hostility, and hyperactive, inattentive, and impulsive behavior
4. Popular-_____ children: subgroup of popular children largely made up of "tough" boys who are athletically skilled, highly aggressive, defiant of adult authority, and poor students
5. Popular-_____ children: subgroup of popular children who combine academic and social competence
6. Peer _____ refers to likability, or the extent to which a child is viewed by agemates as a worthy social partner.
7. _____ children get a large number of positive and negative votes on sociometric measures of peer acceptance

PRACTICE TEST #1

1. By developing competencies at useful skills and tasks, elementary school children show evidence of
   _____ in the fourth stage of Erikson's theory. (p. 314)
   a. initiative
   b. autonomy
   c. identity
   d. industry

2. Based on George Herbert Mead's concept of self, the ability to _____ is critical to the development of
   self-concept during middle childhood. (p. 315)
   a. become introspective
   b. compare one's own abilities and behaviors to those of others
   c. infer what other people are thinking
   d. resolve the Oedipal and Electra conflicts

3. During middle childhood (p. 315)
   a. children form at least four separate self-esteems.
   b. self-evaluations across multiple domains contribute equally to general self-esteem.
   c. children's overall sense of self-esteem (i.e., general self-esteem) is replaced by their separate self-evaluations
      regarding academic, social, and athletic competence and physical appearance.
   d. most children experience a steady increase in self-esteem.

4. Children who develop mastery-oriented attributions (p. 317)
   a. persist on tasks when they succeed but experience an anxious loss of control when they are given a difficult task.
   b. attribute failures to lack of ability, which they regard as a fixed trait.
   c. believe they can succeed at challenging tasks by increasing their effort.
   d. tend to have parents who use an authoritarian style of child rearing.

5. Attribution retraining (p. 318)
   a. works best when begun in late childhood or early adolescence.
   b. provides children with easy tasks in order to prevent failure and negative attributions.
   c. teaches low-effort children to focus less on learning and more on grades.
   d. encourages children to view their successes as due to both ability and effort rather than chance factors.

6. During which of Selman's stages of perspective taking can children "step into another person's shoes" and view their
   feelings and behavior from the other person's perspective? (p. 321)
   a. self-reflective perspective taking
   b. third-party perspective taking
   c. societal perspective taking
   d. undifferentiated perspective taking

7. By around 8 years of age, children view morality in terms of _____. They recognize that
   special consideration should be given to those at a disadvantage, such as the needy or the disabled. (p. 322)
   a. equality
   b. merit
   c. benevolence
   d. empathy

8. Which of the following is true of school-age children's peer groups? (p. 323)
   a. Peer groups organize on the basis of shared values and morals.
   b. Once children begin to form peer groups, relational and overt aggression toward "outgroup" members declines
      dramatically.
   c. Peer groups often direct their hostilities toward no-longer "respected" children within their own group.
   d. Formal group ties (e.g., scouting, 4-H) are ineffective for meeting school-age children's desire for group
      belonging.

9. Research on peer acceptance indicates that (p. 325)
   a. all children fit into one of the four categories of peer acceptance—popular, rejected, neglected, or controversial.
   b. rejected children, in particular, are at risk for poor school performance, absenteeism, dropping out, and antisocial behavior.
   c. peer status during the school years is unrelated to later adjustment.
   d. controversial children have few friends and are typically unhappy with their peer relationships.

10. Research on social behavior indicates that (p. 326)
   a. neglected children are usually well adjusted.
   b. rejected-withdrawn children display a blend of positive and negative social behaviors.
   c. controversial children are at high risk for social exclusion.
   d. popular-prosocial children are often "tough" boys who are athletically skilled but poor students.

11. Which of the following is true of gender-typing in middle childhood? (p. 326)
   a. From third to sixth grades, boys strengthen their identification with "masculine" personality traits, while girls strengthen their identification with "feminine" traits.
   b. Children and adults are fairly tolerant of boys' violations of gender roles, but they judge girls' violations harshly—as severely as a moral transgression.
   c. The sex differences typical in Western nations are also found in nearly all other cultures throughout the world.
   d. Although school-age children are aware of many gender stereotypes, they have a more open-minded view of what males and females can do.

12. A transitional form of supervision in which parents exercise general oversight while permitting children to be in charge of moment-by-moment decision making is called (p. 328)
   a. permissive parenting.
   b. cooperative parenting.
   c. coregulation.
   d. self-regulation.

13. During middle childhood, sibling rivalry (p. 328)
   a. tends to decrease.
   b. tends to increase.
   c. is very rare.
   d. is most common when siblings are far apart in age.

14. Compared with agemates who have siblings, only children (p. 329)
   a. exhibit higher rates of hyperactive, inattentive, and impulsive behavior.
   b. tend to be less popular with peers.
   c. are less socially competent.
   d. do better in school and attain higher levels of education.

15. The overriding factor in positive adjustment following divorce is (p. 331)
   a. child temperament.
   b. child age at the time of the divorce.
   c. effective parenting.
   d. economic stability.

16. Research suggests that, in the long run, divorce (p. 331)
   a. is better for children than remaining in a high-conflict intact family.
   b. has no impact on children's behavior and adjustment.
   c. is often associated with serious difficulties which persist into adulthood.
   d. is linked with more detrimental effects for girls than for boys.

17. Which of the following is true of blended families? (p. 332)
    a. Girls are especially likely to experience positive adjustment in mother–stepfather families.
    b. Older school-age children and adolescents of both sexes display more irresponsible and antisocial behavior than do their agemates in nonblended families.
    c. Remarriage of a noncustodial father often leads to increased contact with children.
    d. Both boys and girls react more positively to the remarriage of a custodial father than a custodial mother.

18. Maternal employment (p. 333)
    a. is linked with more positive outcomes for sons than for daughters.
    b. results in a decline in the amount of time that children spend on homework and household chores.
    c. results in a decline in the amount of time that fathers devote to child care and household duties.
    d. is associated with positive adjustment for children as long as the mother remains committed to her role as a parent.

19. School phobia (p. 334)
    a. is most commonly evidenced by low-SES children with below-average achievement.
    b. most often results from a troubled parent-child relationship.
    c. is common among elementary-age children but is rarely exhibited by older children and adolescents.
    d. is often accompanied by physical complaints.

20. Research on child sexual abuse indicates that (p. 336)
    a. both boys and girls are equally likely to be sexually abused.
    b. reported cases are highest in early childhood and adolescence.
    c. the abuser is most often a parent or someone the parent knows well.
    d. most sexually abused children experience only a single incident of abuse.

PRACTICE TEST #2

1. According to Erikson, children are at risk for developing a sense of _____ during middle childhood when their teachers and peers are so negative that they destroy the child's feelings of competency and mastery. (p. 314)
    a. guilt
    b. shame
    c. mistrust
    d. inferiority

2. Self-esteem (p. 316)
    a. rises steadily across middle childhood.
    b. declines sharply during middle childhood.
    c. increases when children first enter school, then declines throughout the remainder of the elementary school years.
    d. declines during the first few years of elementary school, then rises from fourth to sixth grade.

3. Which of the following is true of the cultural and familial influences on self-esteem? (p. 317)
    a. Because of their higher academic achievement, Chinese and Japanese children have higher self-esteem than North American children.
    b. Girls tend to have higher self-esteem than boys.
    c. Caucasian children typically have higher self-esteem than African-American children.
    d. Children whose parents adopt an authoritative style of child-rearing have especially high self-esteem.

4. Children who develop learned helplessness (p. 317)
    a. think that ability can be changed through increased effort.
    b. tend to attribute their failures, but not their successes, to ability.
    c. often perseverate on difficult tasks in an effort to gain a sense of mastery and competence.
    d. have parents who set unusually low standards.

5. In middle childhood (p. 319)
    a. the self-conscious emotions of pride and guilt become clearly governed by personal responsibility.
    b. children report guilt for any mishap, regardless of whether it was intentional or unintentional.
    c. feelings of shame become adaptive for modifying children's undesirable behavior.
    d. guilt is particularly destructive for children's developing self-esteem.

6. Children ages 4 to 9 engage in _____ perspective taking. (p. 321)
    a. undifferentiated
    b. social-informational
    c. third-party
    d. societal

7. Damon's sequence of distributive justice reasoning is as follows (pp. 321–322)
    a. merit, equality, and benevolence.
    b. equality, merit, and benevolence.
    c. benevolence, equality, and merit.
    d. merit, benevolence, and equality.

8. During middle childhood (pp. 323–324)
    a. children view a friend as someone who likes you, with whom you spend a lot of time playing, and with whom you share toys.
    b. children regard trust as the defining feature of friendships.
    c. children stress intimacy and loyalty as the most significant features of friendship.
    d. children regard friendship as a consensual relationship involving companionship, sharing, understanding of thoughts and feelings, and caring for one another in times of need.

9. Which of the following is true of school-age children's friendships? (p. 324)
    a. School-age children's friendships become less selective, and consequently, they often form close relationships with others who vary in age, sex, race, ethnicity, and SES.
    b. Friendships are usually unstable over middle childhood, lasting only a year or less.
    c. Friendship provides an important context in which children learn to tolerate criticism and resolve disputes.
    d. Aggressive children's closest peer ties are marked by kindness and compassion, suggesting that they may be a powerful context for strengthening these children's prosocial tendencies.

10. Rejected-aggressive children (pp. 324–325)
    a. make up the smallest subgroup of rejected children.
    b. are deficient in perspective-taking and regulation of negative emotion.
    c. are passive and socially awkward.
    d. are hostile and disruptive but also engage in positive, prosocial acts.

11. Cross-cultural research in Kenya suggests that Nyansongo girls score higher than girls of other village and tribal cultures in dominance, assertiveness, and playful roughhousing because (p. 327)
    a. the entire Nyansongo family engages in "masculine" activities such as hunting and fishing.
    b. traits such as freedom and independence are directly taught to and reinforced in Nyansongo girls.
    c. children of both sexes perform "feminine" activities such as tending to the cooking fire and care of young children, thereby relieving girls of total responsibility for "feminine" tasks and allowing them more time to interact with peers.
    d. Nyansongo boys take on the entire responsibility of caregiving and preparing meals.

12. Sibling rivalry tends to be especially strong (p. 328)
    a. among siblings who are close in age.
    b. when siblings strive to be different from one another.
    c. among different-sex siblings.
    d. when mothers prefer one child.

13. Immediately following a divorce (p. 330)
    a. family conflict declines.
    b. discipline becomes more consistent and reasonable.
    c. children have frequent contact with noncustodial fathers.
    d. mothers experience high rates of stress, depression, and anxiety, which typically leads to a disorganized family situation.

14. Which of the following is true with regard to age and sex differences in children's adjustment to divorce? (p. 330)
    a. Preschool and early school-age children are too cognitively immature to understand the circumstances of parental divorce, and consequently, they show few, if any, adverse effects.
    b. School-age children and adolescents are more likely than are preschool children to fantasize that their parents will get back together.
    c. In mother-custody families, girls experience more serious adjustment problems than do boys.
    d. Boys of divorcing parents receive less emotional support from mothers, teachers, and peers than do girls.

15. Most children show improved adjustment by _____ after a parental divorce. (p. 330)
    a. 4 to 6 weeks
    b. 6 months
    c. 2 years
    d. 5 years

16. Divorce mediation (p. 331)
    a. involves a series of meetings between divorcing adults and a trained professional aimed at reducing family conflict.
    b. encourages both parents to remain involved by granting the mother and father equal say in important decisions about the child's upbringing.
    c. involves court mandated counseling to help divorcing couples resolve their differences.
    d. has been shown to increase out-of-court settlements, although compliance with these agreements and cooperation between parents is low.

17. Which of the following reconstituted family arrangements is most likely to work out well? (p. 332)
    a. a boy in a mother / stepfather family
    b. a girl in a mother / stepfather family
    c. a boy in a father / stepmother family
    d. a girl in a father / stepmother family

18. Childhood self-care (p. 334)
    a. is consistently linked with adjustment problems, including low self-esteem, anti-social behavior, and poor academic achievement.
    b. is associated with worse outcomes for older children than for younger children.
    c. is inappropriate for children under the age of 9.
    d. is associated with positive outcomes for children who have a history of permissive parenting.

19. Approximately _____ percent of school age children develop an intense, unmanageable anxiety of some kind. (p. 334)
    a. 1–2
    b. 10–20
    c. 25–50
    d. 80–90

20. Sexual offenders tend to select child victims who are (p. 336)
    a. physically attractive.
    b. popular and outgoing.
    c. hostile and aggressive.
    d. physically weak, emotionally deprived, and socially isolated.

CHAPTER 11
PHYSICAL AND COGNITIVE DEVELOPMENT
IN ADOLESCENCE

BRIEF CHAPTER SUMMARY

Adolescence, initiated by puberty, is the period of transition between childhood and adulthood, leading to physical and sexual maturity. Although early theories described puberty as a period of storm and stress or entirely influenced by the social environment, modern research shows that adolescence is a product of both biological and social forces. Genetically influenced hormonal processes regulate puberty growth and on average, girls reach puberty 2 years earlier than boys. As the body enlarges, girls' hips and boys' shoulders broaden, girls add more fat, and boys add more muscle. Puberty is accompanied by steady improvement in gross motor performance, but the pattern of change differs for boys and girls. While girls' gains are slow and gradual, leveling off by age 14, boys show a dramatic spurt in strength, speed, and endurance that continues through the teenage years.

Menarche occurs late in the girl's sequence of pubertal events, following the rapid increase in body size. Among boys, as the sex organs and body enlarge and pubic and underarm hair appear, spermarche takes place. Heredity, nutrition, and overall health contribute to the timing of puberty. Reactions to pubertal changes are influenced by prior knowledge and support from family members and cultural attitudes toward puberty and sexuality. Puberty is related to increased moodiness and a mild rise in parent–child conflict. Early maturing boys and late maturing girls, whose appearance closely matches cultural standards of physical attractiveness, have a more positive body image and usually adjust well in adolescence. In contrast, early maturing girls and late maturing boys experience emotional and social difficulties.

The arrival of puberty is accompanied by new health issues related to the young person's striving to meet physical and psychological needs. As the body grows, nutritional requirements increase but because of poor eating habits, many adolescents suffer from vitamin and mineral deficiencies. Eating disorders, sexually transmitted disease, adolescent pregnancy and parenthood, and substance abuse are some of the most serious health concerns of the teenage years.

During Piaget's formal operational stage, abstract thinking appears. Recent research indicates that adolescents are capable of a much deeper grasp of scientific principles than are school-age children. However, even well-educated adults have difficulty with abstract reasoning, indicating that Piaget's highest stage is affected by specific, school-learning opportunities. Information-processing theorists agree with the broad outlines of Piaget's description of adolescent cognition. But they refer to a variety of specific mechanisms for cognitive change with metacognition regarded as central to the development of abstract thought. By coordinating theories with evidence, adolescents develop advanced scientific reasoning skills.

The development of formal operations leads to dramatic revisions in the way adolescents see themselves, others, and the world in general. Using their new cognitive powers, teenagers become more argumentative, idealistic, and critical. Although they show gains in self-regulation, adolescents often have difficulty making decisions in everyday life.

Boys and girls do not differ in general intelligence, but they do vary in specific mental abilities. The female advantage in verbal ability is slight and boys do better in mathematical reasoning. Although heredity is involved in these differences, the gender gap is affected by environmental factors.

School transitions create adjustment problems for adolescents. Girls experience a greater drop in self-esteem with each school change. Teenagers who must cope with added stresses are at greatest risk for adjustment problems following school transition. Enhanced support from parents, teachers, and peers and eases the strain of school transition.

Adolescent achievement is the result of a long history of cumulative effects. Early on, positive educational environments, both family and school, lead to personal traits that support achievement. Students who work more than 15 hours per week have poorer school attendance, lower grades, and less time for extracurricular activities. However, when work experiences are specially designed to meet educational and vocational goals, teenagers experience positive school and work attitudes and improved achievement. The dropout rate in the United States and Canada is particularly high among low-SES ethnic minority youths and is affected by family and school experiences.

LEARNING OBJECTIVES

After reading this chapter, you should be able to:

11.1 Discuss changing conceptions of adolescence over the twentieth century. (pp. 344–345)

11.2 Describe pubertal changes in body growth, body proportions, states of arousal, motor performance, and physical activity. (pp. 345–347)

11.3 Summarize changes in sexual maturity over the teenage years, including individual and group differences. (pp. 347–349)

11.4 Cite factors that influence the timing of puberty. (pp. 348–349)

11.5 Discuss adolescents' reactions to the physical changes of puberty, noting factors that influence their feelings and behavior. (pp. 349–351)

11.6 Discuss the impact of maturational timing on adolescent adjustment, noting sex differences and immediate and long-term outcomes. (pp. 351–352)

11.7 Describe the nutritional needs of adolescents, and cite factors related to serious eating disturbances during the teenage years. (pp. 352–353)

11.8 Explain how factors within the individual, family, and larger culture contribute to serious eating disorders. (pp. 353–354)

11.9 Discuss social and cultural influences on adolescent sexual attitudes and behavior. (pp. 354–355)

11.10 Describe factors related to the development of homosexuality, and discuss the unique adjustment problems of gay and lesbian adolescents. (pp. 356–357)

11.11 Discuss the risk of sexually transmitted disease in adolescence, particularly AIDS, and cite strategies for STD prevention. (pp. 356, 358)

11.12 Discuss factors related to teenage pregnancy, the consequences of early childbearing for adolescent parents and their children and strategies for preventing adolescent pregnancy. (pp. 358–361)

11.13 Distinguish between substance use and abuse, describe personal and social factors related to each, and cite prevention strategies. (pp. 361–362)

11.14 Describe the major characteristics of formal operational thought. (pp. 363–364)

11.15 Discuss recent research on formal operational thought and its implications for the accuracy of Piaget's formal operational stage. (pp. 364–365)

11.16 Explain how information-processing researchers account for the development of scientific reasoning during adolescence. (pp. 365–366)

11.17 Describe cognitive and behavioral consequences of adolescents' newfound capacity for abstract reasoning. (pp. 367–369)

11.18 Note sex differences in mental abilities at adolescence, along with biological and environmental factors that influence them. (pp. 369–370)

11.19 Discuss the impact of school transitions on adolescent adjustment, and cite ways to ease the strain of these changes. (pp. 371–372)

11.20 Discuss family, peer, school, and employment influences on academic achievement during adolescence. (pp. 372–374)

11.21 Describe personal, family, and school factors related to dropping out, and cite ways to prevent early school leaving. (pp. 374–377)

STUDY QUESTIONS

Physical Development

Conceptions of Adolescence

1. Contrast the biological and social perspectives of adolescence. What evidence suggests that adolescent development is the product of both biological and social forces? (pp. 344–345)

   A. _____

   _____

   B. _____

   _____

   C. _____

   _____

2. True or False: Rates of psychological disturbance increase dramatically during adolescence, supporting the conclusion that this is a period of storm and stress. (p. 344)

3. True or False: Adolescence, as an intervening phase between childhood and full assumption of adult roles, can be found in almost all societies. (p. 345)

Puberty: The Physical Transition to Adulthood

Hormonal Changes

1. Secretions of _____ and _____ increase during puberty, leading to tremendous gains in body size and attainment of skeletal maturity. (p. 345)

2. Cite ways in which estrogens and androgens contribute to pubertal growth in both sexes. (pp. 345–346)

   Estrogens: _____

   _____

   Androgens: _____

   _____

3. Pubertal changes can be divided into two broad types: (p. 346)

    A. _____ B. _____

Body Growth

1. The first outward sign of puberty is the rapid gain in height and weight known as the
   _____. (p. 346)

2. On average, the adolescent *growth spurt* is underway for North American girls shortly after age _____ and for boys around age _____. (p. 346)

3. True or False: During adolescence, the cephalocaudal growth trend of infancy and childhood reverses. (p. 346)

4. Briefly describe sex differences in body proportions and muscle-fat makeup that appear during adolescence. (pp. 346–347)

    Boys: _____

    _____

    Girls: _____

    _____

5. Explain changes in sleep and wakefulness during adolescence. What contributes to these changing states of arousal? (p. 347)

    A. _____

    _____

    B. _____

    _____

6. List three consequences of sleep-deprivation during adolescence. (p. 347)

    A. _____ B. _____

    C. _____

Motor Development and Physical Activity

1. Describe the motor development of adolescent girls and boys. How do differences in motor development influence physical education? (p. 347)

    Adolescent girls: _____

    _____

    Adolescent boys: _____

    _____

    Influence on physical education: _____

    _____

2. Physical activity rates (rise / decline) in adolescence. (p. 347)

3.   Cite the benefits of sports and exercise during adolescence. (p. 347)

_____

_____

_____

Sexual Maturation

1.   Distinguish between *primary* and *secondary sexual characteristics*. (p. 347)

Primary: _____

Secondary: _____

2.   _____, or first menstruation, typically happens around age _____ for North American girls and _____ for European girls. Around age _____ boys experience _____, or first ejaculation. (p. 348)

Individual and Group Differences

1.   Cite evidence that heredity contributes to the timing of puberty. What roles do nutrition and exercise play? (p. 348)

A. _____

B. _____

2.   How is pubertal growth influenced by SES and ethnicity? (p. 349)

_____

_____

_____

3.   Threats to emotional health (accelerate / delay) puberty, whereas threats to physical health (accelerate / delay) it. (p. 349)

4.   Describe the secular trend in age of menarche in industrialized nations, noting factors believed to be responsible for it. (p. 349)

_____

_____

_____

The Psychological Impact of Pubertal Events

Reactions to Pubertal Changes

1.   Cite three factors that contribute to girls' and boys' reactions to puberty. (pp. 349–350)

Girls:

A. _____

B. _____

C. _____

Boys:

A. _____

B. _____

C. _____

2. How does culture influence the experience of puberty? (p. 350)

_____

_____

_____

Pubertal Change, Emotion, and Social Behavior

1. Research shows that adolescents report (more / less) favorable moods than do school-age children and adults (p. 350)

2. Cite factors associated with high and low points in mood during adolescence. (p. 350)

High points: _____

_____

Low points: _____

_____

3. How might parent–child conflict during adolescence serve an adaptive function? (pp. 350–351)

_____

_____

4. True or False: Parent–child disputes are often severe in adolescence. (p. 351)

Early versus Late Maturation

1. Discuss research findings on the effects of maturational timing for the following groups of adolescents: (pp. 351–352)

Early maturing boys: _____

_____

Late maturing boys: _____

_____

Early maturing girls: _____

_____

Late maturing girls: _____

_____

2. Two factors influence how boys and girls adjust to the changes of puberty. List and briefly describe them. (p. 351)

A. _____

_____

B. _____

_____

3. True or False: Among boys, early maturation is linked to a positive body image. (p. 351)

4. Explain how school contexts can modify maturational timing effects. (p. 352)

_____

_____

_____

5. How does early maturation affect well-being in adulthood? How about late maturation? (p. 352)

Early Maturation: _____

Late Maturation: _____

Health Issues

Nutritional Needs

1. True or False: Of all age groups, adolescents have the worst eating habits. (p. 352)

2. The most common nutritional problem of adolescence is _____. List three other common nutritional deficiencies of the teenage years. (p. 353)

A. _____ B. _____ C. _____

Eating Disorders

1. What is the strongest predictor of the onset of an eating disorder in adolescence? (p. 353)

_____

2. Describe characteristics of *anorexia nervosa*. (p. 353)

_____

_____

_____

3. Explain how forces within the person, the family, and the larger culture give rise to anorexia nervosa. (p. 353)

Individual: _____

_____

Family: _____

_____

Culture: _____

_____

4. Why is treating anorexia nervosa so difficult? (pp. 353–354)

_____

_____

_____

5. Describe characteristics of *bulimia nervosa.* (p. 354)

_____

_____

_____

6. True or False: Bulimia is far less common than anorexia nervosa. (p. 354)

7. How are bulimics similar to anorexics? How are they different? (p. 354)

Similar: _____

Different: _____

Sexual Activity

1. Explain how hormonal changes contribute to an increased sex drive in adolescence. (p. 354)

_____

_____

_____

2. True or False: Exposure to sex, education about it, and efforts to limit the sexual curiosity of children and adolescents are very similar around the world. (p. 354)

3. Contrast the messages that adolescents receive from parents and the media regarding sexual activity, and note the impact of such contradictory messages on adolescents' understanding of sex. (p. 354)

Parents: _____

_____

Media: _____

_____

Impact: _____

_____

4. The sexual attitudes of American adolescents and adults have become (more / less) liberal over the past 30 years. (p. 354)

5. Describe trends in the sexual behavior of adolescents in the United States and Canada. (pp. 354–355)

_____

_____

_____

6. (Males / females) tend to have their first intercourse earlier than members of the opposite sex. (p. 355)

7. Cite personal, familial, peer, and educational variables linked to early and frequent teenage sexual activity. (p. 355)

Personal: _____

_____

Familial: _____

_____

Peer: _____

_____

Educational: _____

_____

8. Why do many sexually active adolescents fail to use contraception consistently? (p. 355)

_____

_____

_____

9. Explain how both heredity and environment might contribute to homosexuality. (p. 356)

Heredity: _____

_____

Environment: _____

_____

10. Cite one misconception about homosexuality. (p. 356)

_____

Sexually Transmitted Disease

1. True or False: Adolescents have the highest rates of sexually transmitted disease (STD) of any age group. (p. 356)

2. By far the most serious STD is _____. (p. 356)

3. True or False: Birth control pills provide some protection against AIDS. (p. 358)

Adolescent Pregnancy and Parenthood

1. True or False: The adolescent pregnancy rate in Canada is nearly double that of the United States. (pp. 358–359)

2. List three factors that heighten the incidence of adolescent pregnancy. (p. 359)

A. _____

B. _____

C. _____

3. Why is teenage pregnancy a much greater problem today than it was 30 years ago? (p. 359)

_____

_____

4. Summarize the consequences of adolescent parenthood in relation to the following areas: (p. 360)

Educational attainment: _____

_____

Marital patterns: _____

_____

Economic circumstances: _____

_____

5. Cite a birth complication that is common among babies of teenage mothers. (p. 360)

_____

6. List three common characteristics of children born to adolescent mothers. (p. 360)

A. _____ B. _____

C. _____

7. What factors protect teenage mothers and their children from long-term difficulties? (p. 360)

_____

_____

_____

8. List three components of effective sex education programs. (p. 360)

A. _____

B. _____

C. _____

9. Cite the most controversial aspect of adolescent pregnancy prevention. (p. 360)

_____

10. Why is building social competence important for preventing adolescent pregnancy and parenthood? (p. 360)

_____

_____

11. Describe interventions that are necessary to help adolescent parents and their babies. (p. 360–361)

_____

_____

_____

_____

Substance Use and Abuse

1. By age 14, _____ percent of American young people have tried cigarette smoking, _____ percent drinking, and _____ percent at least one illegal drug. Canadian rates of teenage alcohol and drug use are (similar / much) lower. (p. 361)

2. Cite factors that may explain recent trends in adolescent drug taking. (p. 361)

_____

_____

_____

3. True or False: Teenagers who experiment with alcohol, tobacco, and marijuana are headed for a life of addiction. (p. 361)

4. How do experimenters differ from drug abusers? (p. 362)

_____

5. What environmental factors are associated with adolescent drug abuse? (p. 362)

_____

_____

_____

6. List three life-long consequences of adolescent substance abuse. (p. 362)

   A. _____ B. _____

   C. _____

7. What are some characteristics of successful drug prevention programs? (p. 362)

_____

_____

_____

Social Issues: Homosexuality: Coming Out to Oneself and Others

1. Describe the three-phase sequence adolescents go through in coming out to themselves and others. (p. 357)

   A. _____

   _____

   B. _____

   _____

   C. _____

   _____

2. For most homosexual individuals, a first sense of their sexual orientation appears beween the ages of _____ and _____. In what context does this commonly occur? (p. 357)

_____

_____

3. Discuss the process of disclosure, or coming out, noting factors that are important for reaching this phase of acceptance. (p. 357)

_____

_____

4. Explain how coming out has the potential to foster development in homosexual adolescents. (p. 357)

_____

_____

Cognitive Development

Piaget's Theory: The Formal Operational Stage

1. Summarize the basic differences between concrete and formal operational reasoning. (p. 363)

_____

_____

_____

2. Describe two major features of the *formal operational stage.* (p. 363)

A. _____

_____

B. _____

_____

3. True or False: Piaget maintained that language plays a more central role in children's cognitive development than in adolescents' cognitive development. (p. 364)

Recent Research on Formal Operational Thought

1. Cite examples illustrating that school-age children show signs of *hypothetico-deductive reasoning* and *propositional thought,* but are not as competent at it as adolescents. (pp. 364–365)

Hypothetico-deductive reasoning: _____

_____

Propositional thought: _____

_____

2. True or False: Nearly 80 percent of college students fail Piaget's formal operational problems. (p. 365)

3. Describe two reasons why so many college students, and adults in general, are not formal operational. (p. 365)

A. _____

_____

B. _____

_____

An Information-Processing View of Adolescent Cognitive Development

1. Compared to early and middle childhood, how do information-processing theorists view each of the following cognitive mechanisms of change in adolescence? (p. 365)

Attention: _____

Strategies: _____

Knowledge: _____

Metacognition: _____

Cognitive Self-Regulation: _____

Processing Capacity: _____

Which mechanism do researchers regard as central to the development of abstract thought?

_____

Scientific Reasoning: Coordinating Theory with Evidence

1. Cite major changes in scientific reasoning from childhood into adolescence and adulthood (p. 366)

_____

_____

How Scientific Reasoning Develops

1. Identify three factors that support adolescents' skill at coordinating theory with evidence. (p. 366)

   A. _____

   B. _____

   C. _____

2. True or False: Like Piaget, information-processing theorists maintain that scientific reasoning develops from an abrupt, stagewise change. (p. 366)

Consequences of Abstract Thought

1. Explain how the development of abstract thought influences adolescents' argumentativeness. (p. 367)

_____

_____

_____

2. Describe two distorted images of the relation between self and others that appear at adolescence. (pp. 367–368)

   Imaginary audience: _____

_____

   Personal fable: _____

_____

3. When are the imaginary audience and personal fable the strongest? (p. 368)

_____

4. How are *idealism* and *criticism* advantageous to teenagers? (p. 368)

_____

_____

5. What accounts for improvements in study skills from middle childhood into adolescence? (p. 368)

_____

Sex Differences in Mental Abilities

1. Explain differences between boys and girls in specific mental abilities. (p. 369)

2. Summarize how heredity and social pressures contribute to the gender gap in mathematics. (p. 369)

   Heredity: _____

   Social Pressures: _____

3. True or False: Sex differences in cognitive abilities of all kinds have increased steadily over the past several decades. (p. 369)

4. Cite three steps used to promote girls' interest in and confidence at math and science. (p. 369)

   A. _____

   B. _____

   C. _____

Biology & Environment: Sex Differences in Spatial Abilities

1. List two sex differences in spatial skills. (p. 370)

   A. _____

   B. _____

2. True or False: Males score much higher than females on spatial visualization tasks. (p. 370)

3. What evidence suggests a biological explanation for sex differences in spatial abilities? (p. 370)

4. What environmental experiences enhance childrens' spatial performance? (p. 370)

School Transitions

1. Cite two adjustment problems that can occur with school transitions. How does the timing of school transition contribute to adjustment outcomes? (p. 371)

    A. _____

    B. _____

    C. _____

2. The (earlier / later) the school transition occurs, the more negative the impact. (p. 371)

3. List three ways parents, teachers, and peers can ease the strain of school transitions. (p. 372)

    A. _____

    B. _____

    C. _____

Academic Achievement

1. How do authoritative, authoritarian, permissive, and uninvolved parenting styles contribute to academic achievement? Which is the most effective, and why? (p. 372)

    Authoritative: _____

    Authoritarian: _____

    Permissive: _____

    Uninvolved: _____

    Most effective: _____

2. How do parent-school partnerships foster academic achievement? (p. 373)

    _____

    _____

3. What role do peers play in academic achievement? Why do low-SES minority adolescents often react against working hard at school? (p. 373)

    A. _____

    B. _____

4. Cite and briefly describe school characteristics that foster abstract thought. (p. 373)

    _____

    _____

    _____

    _____

248

5. True or False: Mixed-ability rather than tracked classes are desirable into the early years of secondary school. (p. 374)

6. How does a heavy commitment to part-time work affect adolescents' academic achievement? Under what circumstances are work experiences beneficial? (p. 374)

   A. _____

   _____

   B. _____

   _____

7. List two consequences of dropping out of school. (p. 375)

   A. _____ B. _____

8. Cite characteristics of students who are at-risk for dropping out of high school. (p. 375)

   _____

   _____

   _____

9. List four strategies for helping teenagers at-risk for dropping out of high school. (pp. 375–376)

   A. _____

   B. _____

   C. _____

   D. _____

10. Over the last half of the twentieth century, the percentage of American and Canadian adolescents completing high school has (increased / decreased) steadily. (p. 377)

A Lifespan Vista:
Extracurricular Activities: Contexts for Positive Youth Development

1. What types of extracurricular activities promote diverse academic and social skills and have a lasting positive impact on adjustment? (p. 376)

   _____

   _____

2. Cite ways in which extracurricular involvement shows benefits in adult life. (p. 376)

   _____

   _____

3. True or False: Adolescents who spend many afternoons and evenings engaged in unstructured activities show similar adjustment outcomes as adolescents who engage in structured, goal-oriented activities. (p. 376)

4. Who is especially likely to benefit from extracurricular participation? (p. 376)

ASK YOURSELF . . .

For *Ask Yourself* questions for this chapter, please log on to the Companion Website at www.ablongman.com/berk.

SUGGESTED STUDENT READINGS

Carskadon, M. A. (2003). *Adolescent sleep patterns: Biological, social, and psychological influences.* New York: Cambridge University Press. A collection of chapters focusing on adolescent wake and sleep patterns, including the role of sleep deprivation in risky driving behavior; the effects of school and work on sleep habits; severe disturbances in adolescent sleep cycles; and benefits of starting school later in the day.

D'Augelli, A. R., & Patterson, C. J. (Eds.). (2001). *Lesbian, gay, and bisexual identities and youth: Psychological perspectives.* Based on current theory and research, this book presents biological, social, psychological, and cultural forces impacting the lives of lesbian, gay, and bisexual youth. The authors also address unique challenges faced by homosexual teenagers and community interventions designed to deal with these challenges.

Johnson, N. G, Roberts, M. C., & Worell, J. P. (Eds.). (1999). *Beyond appearance: A new look at adolescent girls.* Washington, DC: American Psychological Association. An edited volume that explores key topics to understanding girls' adolescent development, including gender-role behaviors, body image issues, relationships with family and friends, sexual decision making, and school- and community-based experiences.

Merrick, E. (2001). *Reconceiving black adolescent child bearing.* New York: Barunch College. Based on the personal accounts of six African-American teenage girls, this book explores the effects of childbearing and adolescent development among lower-income minority youths.

Miller, M. A., Alberts, J. K., Hecht, M. L., Trost, M. R., & Krizek, R. L. (2000). *Adolescent relationships and drug use.* Mahwah, NJ: Lawrence Erlbaum Associates. A collection of chapters exploring the relational features of adolescent drug use, with particular emphasis on risk and protective factors. Other topics include: personality characteristics of drug users and dealers, the role of family and peers, and research-based recommendations for implementing drug prevention programs.

PUZZLE 11.1 TERM REVIEW

Across

3. _____ sexual characteristics: physical features that involve the reproductive organs
4. In Piaget's _____ operational stage, adolescents develop the capacity for abstract, scientific thinking.
7. _____ trend: change in body size and rate of growth from one generation to the next
8. Personal _____: adolescents' belief that they are special and unique and that others cannot understand their thoughts and feelings
10. _____ nervosa: eating disorder in which individuals starve themselves because of a compulsive fear of getting fat
12. _____ thought: type of formal operational reasoning in which adolescents evaluate the logic of verbal statements without referring to real-world circumstances
13. Biological changes at adolescence that lead to an adult-sized body and sexual maturity
14. _____ sexual characteristics: features visible on the outside of the body that serve as signs of sexual maturity but do not involve reproductive organs
15. First menstruation

Down

1. _____ nervosa: eating disorder in which individuals go on eating binges followed by deliberate vomiting, other purging techniques, and strict dieting
2. _____-deductive reasoning: formal operational problem-solving strategy in which adolescents begin with a general theory of all possible factors that could affect an outcome and deduce specific hypotheses, which they test systematically
5. Body _____: conception of and attitude toward one's physical appearance
6. Period of development in which the individual crosses the dividing line between childhood and adulthood
7. First ejaculation of seminal fluid
9. _____ audience: adolescents' belief that they are the focus of everyone else's attention and concern
11. Growth _____: rapid gain in height and weight during adolescence

PRACTICE TEST #1

1. Physical growth in adolescence (p. 346)
   a. occurs at a slow, steady pace.
   b. follows the cephalocaudal trend that is also characteristic of infancy and childhood.
   c. leads to large differences in the body proportions of boys and girls.
   d. causes boys to add more fat, while girls add more muscle.

2. The appearance of underarm hair is an example of _____ and serves as an indicator of sexual maturity. (p. 347)
   a. a secondary sexual characteristic
   b. a primary sexual characteristic
   c. menarche
   d. spermarche

3. Audrey is obese. You would expect her to reach menarche (p. 348)
   a. earlier than other girls.
   b. at the same time as other girls.
   c. slightly later than other girls.
   d. much later than other girls.

4. Boys' and girls' reactions to puberty are (p. 349)
   a. overwhelmingly positive.
   b. similar in all cultures around the world.
   c. dependent on the age of pubertal onset.
   d. dependent upon prior knowledge of such changes.

5. Boys usually (p. 350)
   a. get less social support for the physical changes of puberty than do girls.
   b. learn about spermarche from parents.
   c. are well prepared for their first spermarche.
   d. tell several friends about spermarche.

6. Adolescents experience the most emotional highs (p. 350)
   a. on days when they can sleep in.
   b. at school.
   c. on weekend evenings.
   d. when they get a chance to be alone.

7. Compared to anorexics, adolescents with bulimia nervosa (p. 354)
   a. do not have a pathological fear of getting fat.
   b. feel guilty about their eating habits.
   c. are afraid of becoming too thin.
   d. do not want help for their problem.

8. Which of the following factors is linked with increased contraceptive use among sexually active adolescents? (p. 356)
   a. sexual contact with multiple partners
   b. imitation of the sexually-responsible role-models seen in many prime-time TV shows
   c. having a good relationship with parents and being able to talk openly with them about sex and contraceptives
   d. participation in sex education courses

9. Homosexuality (p. 356)
   a. results entirely from hereditary causes, most notably the level and impact of prenatal sex hormones.
   b. is caused by growing up with a same-sex parent who is cold, rejecting, or distant.
   c. likely results from a variety of biological and environmental combinations.
   d. has a prevalence rate of approximately 15 to 20 percent in the adolescent population.

10. Adolescent mothers: (p. 360)
    a. are as likely as other adolescent girls to finish high school.
    b. usually have a good understanding of child development.
    c. tend to have children who achieve poorly in school and who engage in disruptive social behavior.
    d. rarely experience pregnancy and birth complications.

11. Research on adolescent drug use and abuse shows that (p. 361)
    a. the majority of adolescents completely abstain from using drugs and alcohol.
    b. adolescents who experiment with drugs and alcohol are psychologically healthy, sociable, and curious individuals.
    c. experimentation with drugs often leads to long-term abuse and dependency.
    d. drug experimentation should be taken lightly by parents and teachers because it is a normal part of adolescent development.

12. When faced with a problem, adolescents begin with a general theory, deduce from it specific predictions about outcomes, and then test the predictions—a process Piaget called (p. 363)
    a. hypothetico-deductive reasoning.
    b. horizonal décalage.
    c. transitive inference.
    d. inductive reasoning.

13. An experimenter hides a poker chip in her hand and asks participants to indicate whether the following statement is true, false, or uncertain: "Either the chip in my hand is green or is not green." A concrete operational child will indicate uncertainty, whereas a formal operational adolescent will respond "true." This response reflects the formal operational child's understanding of (p. 364)
    a. causal reasoning.
    b. concrete thought.
    c. propositional thought.
    d. relativistic reasoning.

14. After being rejected for a date, Jasmine's father tries to comfort her. Jasmine responds, "Leave me alone, Dad! You'll never understand what I'm going through!" This common adolescent distortion is known as (p. 368)
    a. logical necessity.
    b. hypothetico-deductive reasoning.
    c. the imaginary audience.
    d. the personal fable.

15. Adolescent idealism often leads teenagers to be (p. 368)
    a. more cooperative at home.
    b. more critical of parents and siblings.
    c. better students at school.
    d. more realistic in their evaluations of others.

16. In adolescence, boys (p. 369)
    a. perform similarly to girls in math.
    b. lack encouragement from teachers to excel at math.
    c. do better than girls in math, especially on tests of abstract reasoning.
    d. attain higher scores on reading and writing achievement tests.

17. Students are at especially great risk for academic and social difficulties after a school transition if they (p. 371)
    a. move from a larger school to a smaller one.
    b. had higher grades before the move.
    c. have to cope with added life transitions.
    d. come from a K–8 school.

18. One factor that supports high academic achievement during adolescence is: (p. 372)
    a. authoritative parenting.
    b. a strict, rule-oriented classroom structure.
    c. departmentalized school organization whereby students are placed in separate classes for each subject so that they can be taught by experts in each area.
    d. a strong commitment to a part-time job, which fosters a sense of responsibility.

19. Research on ability grouping shows that (p. 374)
    a. students in low-ability groups evidence gains in academic achievement since instruction is adapted to meet their needs.
    b. mixed-ability classes are preferable, at least into the early years of secondary school.
    c. good students from low-SES families are just as likely to be placed in academically oriented, college-bound tracks as are students from middle-SES homes.
    d. mixed-ability groups stifle high-achieving students and provide few, if any, intellectual or social benefits to low-achieving students.

20. Compared with many Western European nations, the United States and Canada (p. 374)
    a. have a much lower dropout rate.
    b. less often sort students into college or vocational tracks.
    c. have a higher percentage of high school students who regard themselves as educational failures.
    d. allocate a great many resources to the education of low-income minority students.

PRACTICE TEST #2

1. Recent research indicates that the image of adolescence as a period of storm and stress is (p. 344)
    a. accurate, just as described by Freud and Hall.
    b. the result of hormonal changes.
    c. inaccurate, since depression, law breaking, and eating disorders are uncommon.
    d. greatly exaggerated.

2. Sexual maturation in males results from the release of large quantities of _____ from the testes. (p. 345)
    a. estrogen
    b. adrenal androgens
    c. testosterone
    d. thyroxine

3. Compared to school-age children and adults, adolescents (p. 350)
    a. experience decreased moodiness.
    b. report less favorable moods.
    c. have more stable moods.
    d. are more likely to report negative mood during times of day spent with friends.

4. Studies indicate that _____ girls and _____ boys are popular in school and viewed as relaxed, independent, self-confident, and physically attractive. (p. 351)
    a. early maturing; early maturing
    b. late maturing; late maturing
    c. early maturing; late maturing
    d. late maturing; early maturing

5. Parent-adolescent conflicts typically focus on (p. 351)
   a. mundane, day-to-day matters such as driving or curfews.
   b. substance abuse.
   c. early sexual activity.
   d. long-term goals such as college or vocational training.

6. Mothers of anorexic girls tend to be (p. 353)
   a. obese.
   b. overprotective and controlling.
   c. uninvolved.
   d. indifferent about physical appearance.

7. Which of the following is true of sexually transmitted disease (STD) during adolescence? (p. 356)
   a. Adolescents have the highest incidence of STD of any age group.
   b. Homosexual adolescents are at a greater risk for STD than are heterosexual adolescents.
   c. The United States has the lowest rate of STD of all industrialized nations.
   d. Over 90 percent of high school students are not aware of the basic facts about AIDS.

8. Which of the following statements best represents the lives of teenage parents? (p. 360)
   a. Giving birth before the age of 18 rarely influences the likelihood of finishing high school.
   b. Teenager mothers often seek vocational training and transition to satisfying, high-paid jobs.
   c. Teenage motherhood reduces the chances of marriage.
   d. Similar to adult mothers, teenage mothers have realistic expectations about their babies.

9. The most controversial aspect of sex education programs is (p. 360)
   a. provision of access to contraceptives.
   b. teaching skills for handling sexual situations through discussion and role play.
   c. promoting the value of abstinence.
   d. participation in community service outreach programs.

10. Metacognition (p. 365)
    a. has little influence on adolescent cognitive development.
    b. is central to the development of abstract thought.
    c. interferes with the development of scientific reasoning.
    d. is largely affected by speed of processing.

11. Many college students and adults are not fully formal operational because (p. 365)
    a. they lack experiences necessary for solving formal operational tasks.
    b. they are not motivated to solve formal operational tasks.
    c. only the most intelligent people become formal operational.
    d. they are more interested in socializing than thinking.

12. The heart of scientific reasoning is (p. 365)
    a. coordinating theories with evidence.
    b. designing experiments.
    c. developing hypotheses.
    d. conducting statistical analyses of data.

13. Teenagers' argumentativeness and self-focus are consequences of (p. 367)
    a. egocentrism.
    b. abstract thought.
    c. anxiety.
    d. puberty.

14. Which of the following statements reflects the imaginary audience? (p. 367)
    a. "I don't care if my new haircut is bad. I'm going to the party anyway."
    b. "My parents don't understand how hard school is for me!"
    c. "I can't go to the party with a huge pimple on my cheek! Everyone will make fun of me!"
    d. "No one will care if I can't afford a new dress to wear to the prom. I will just wear the one I wore last year."

15. Over the past several decades, sex differences in cognitive abilities have (p. 369)
    a. increased.
    b. declined.
    c. remained stable.
    d. declined and then recently increased.

16. Research on school transitions shows that (p. 371)
    a. the earlier the transition occurs, the more dramatic and long-lasting its negative impact on psychological well-being, especially for girls.
    b. earlier transitions are associated with negative outcomes for boys, whereas later transitions are associated with negative outcomes for girls.
    c. the transition from junior high to high school is relatively problem-free for most adolescents and rarely has an effect on academic achievement.
    d. adolescents with multiple life strains, such as the onset of puberty and family disruption, tend to show improved adjustment following the transition to high school.

17. Which of the following is an effective way to ease the strain of school transition in adolescence? (p. 371)
    a. reorganizing schools into 6-3-3 arrangements
    b. making sure that academic expectations in junior high are tougher than those in elementary school
    c. creating smaller social units within larger schools
    d. reducing the number of extracurricular activities available in high school

18. Which of the following supports academic achievement in adolescence? (p. 372)
    a. authoritarian parenting
    b. reduced parental involvement in school-related issues
    c. having close friends who value school achievement
    d. heavy commitment to a part-time job

19. Typically, parents of students who drop out of school (p. 375)
    a. encourage achievement but just aren't successful.
    b. completed high school themselves.
    c. show little involvement in their teenager's education.
    d. have serious emotional problems.

20. High school students who work more than 15 hours per week (p. 374)
    a. develop a sense of responsibility which often leads to improved academic performance.
    b. develop many job skills that help them gain employment after high school.
    c. have poor school attendance and lower grades.
    d. develop positive attitudes about work life.

CHAPTER 12
EMOTIONAL AND SOCIAL DEVELOPMENT
IN ADOLESCENCE

BRIEF CHAPTER SUMMARY

Erikson was the first to recognize identity as the major personality achievement of adolescence and as a crucial step toward becoming a productive, happy adult. Young people who successfully resolve the psychological conflict of identity versus identity confusion construct a solid self-definition consisting of self-chosen values and goals. During adolescence, cognitive changes transform the young person's vision of the self into a more complex, well-organized, and consistent picture. For most young people, self-esteem rises over the teenage years and is affected by family, school, and the larger social environment. Adolescents' well-organized self-descriptions and differential sense of self-esteem provide the cognitive foundation for developing an identity. Adolescents vary in their degree of progress toward developing a mature identity. Identity achievement and moratorium are adaptive statuses associated with positive personality characteristics. Teenagers who remain in identity foreclosure or identity diffusion tend to have adjustment difficulties.

The most influential approach to moral development is Kohlberg's cognitive-developmental perspective, which was inspired by Piaget's early work on the moral judgment of the child. According to Kohlberg, moral development is a gradual process that extends into adulthood and consists of (1) actively grappling with moral issues and noticing weaknesses in one's current reasoning, and (2) gains in perspective taking, which permit individuals to resolve moral conflicts in more effective ways. Child-rearing practices, schooling, peer interaction, and culture contribute to moral development. As individuals advance through Kohlberg's stages, moral reasoning becomes more closely related to behavior.

Physical, social, and cognitive forces combine to make early adolescence a period of gender intensification. Development at adolescence involves striving for autonomy—a sense of oneself as a separate, self-governing individual. Over the adolescent years, relationships with parents and siblings change as teenagers strive to establish a healthy balance between connection to and separation from the family. As adolescents spend more time with peers, intimacy and loyalty become central features of friendship. Adolescent peer groups are organized into tightly knit groups called cliques, and as teenagers become interested in dating, several cliques come together to form a crowd. Although peer pressure rises in adolescence, most teenagers do not blindly conform to the dictates of agemates.

Although most young people move through adolescence with little difficulty, some encounter major disruptions, such as premature parenthood, substance abuse, and school failure. Depression is the most common psychological problem of the teenage years, influenced by a diverse combination of biological and environmental factors. The suicide rate increases dramatically at adolescence. Many teenagers become involved in some delinquent activity, but only a few are serious or repeat offenders. Family, school, peer, and neighborhood factors are related to delinquency.

LEARNING OBJECTIVES

After reading this chapter, you should be able to:

12.1 Discuss Erikson's theory of identity development. (pp. 382–383)

12.2 Describe changes in self-concept and self-esteem during adolescence. (pp. 383–384)

12.3 Describe the four identity statuses, noting how each is related to psychological adjustment, and discuss factors that influence identity development. (pp. 384–386)

12.4 Describe Piaget's theory of moral development and Kohlberg's extension of it, noting research that evaluates the accuracy of each. (pp. 387–390)

12.5 Discuss sex differences in moral reasoning, with particular attention to Gilligan's argument. (pp. 390–391)

12.6 Describe the factors that influence moral reasoning, and discuss the relationship between moral reasoning and behavior. (pp. 391–393)

12.7 Explain why early adolescence is a period of gender intensification, and cite factors that promote the development of an androgynous gender identity. (p. 394)

12.8 Discuss familial influences on adolescent development, including the impact of the parent–child relationship, family circumstances, and sibling interaction. (pp. 394–396)

12.9 Describe the characteristics of adolescent friendships and peer groups, and discuss the contributions of each to emotional and social development. (pp. 396–399)

12.10 Describe adolescent dating relationships. (p. 399)

12.11 Discuss the influence of peer pressure during adolescence, noting how parental behavior is related to adolescent conformity. (pp. 399–400)

12.12 Discuss factors related to adolescent depression and suicide, along with approaches for prevention and treatment. (pp. 400–403)

12.13 Discuss factors related to delinquency, and cite strategies for prevention and treatment. (pp. 403–405)

STUDY QUESTIONS

Erikson's Theory: Identity versus Identity Diffusion

1. Summarize what is involved in constructing an identity. (p. 382)

   _____

   _____

   _____

2. Discuss Erikson's notion of an *identity crisis*. (p. 382)

   _____

   _____

   _____

   _____

3. Current theorists (do / do not) agree with Erikson that the process of identity development constitutes a "crisis." (p. 383)

Self-Understanding

Changes in Self-Concept

1. True or False: Young adolescents often provide contradictory self-descriptions, for example, describing themselves as both shy and outgoing. (p. 383)

2. Compared to school-age children, teenagers place (more / less) emphasis on social virtues, such as being friendly, considerate, kind, and cooperative. Why is this the case? (p. 383)

_____

_____

Changes in Self-Esteem

1. Cite three new dimensions of self-esteem that are added during adolescence. (p. 383)

    A. _____

    B. _____

    C. _____

2. Except for temporary declines associated with_____, self-esteem rises among most adolescents. (p. 383)

3. Differentiate factors associated with high versus low self-esteem in adolescence. (pp. 383–384)

    High: _____

    _____

    Low: _____

    _____

Paths to Identity

1. Match each of the following identity statuses with the appropriate description. (p. 384)

    _____ Committed to values and goals without taking time
    to explore alternatives
    _____ Have not yet made definite commitments and are still exploring
    alternatives
    _____ Committed to self-chosen values and goals after having already
    explored alternatives
    _____ Lack clear direction; are not committed to values and goals and are
    not actively seeking them

    1. Identity achievement
    2. Moratorium
    3. Identity foreclosure
    4. Identity diffusion

2. Most adolescents start out at "lower" statuses, such as _____ and
_____, but by the time they reach their twenties, they have moved toward "higher" statuses, including _____ and _____. (p. 384)

3. True or False: Most adolescent girls follow a different path to identity formation than do boys: They postpone the task of establishing an identity, focusing instead on intimacy development. (p. 385)

Identity Status and Psychological Well-Being

1. True or False: Research supports the conclusion that identity achievement and moratorium are healthy routes to a mature self-definition, whereas identity foreclosure and identity diffusion are maladaptive. Elaborate on your answer. (p. 385)

_____

_____

_____

_____

Factors That Affect Identity Development

1. Match the following identity statuses with the appropriate description of associated personality, familial, school, community, and larger cultural factors. Descriptions may apply to more than one identity status. (pp. 384–386)

_____ Assume that absolute truth is always attainable
_____ Lack confidence in the prospect of ever knowing anything with certainty
_____ Appreciate that they can use rational criteria to choose among alternatives
_____ Feel attached to parents but are also free to voice their own opinions
_____ Have close bonds with parents but lack healthy separation
_____ Report the lowest levels of warm, open communication at home
_____ Fostered by classrooms that promote high-level thinking, as well as extracurricular and community activities that permit teens to take on responsible roles

1. Identity achievement
2. Moratorium
3. Identity foreclosure
4. Identity diffusion

Cultural Influences: Identity Development Among Ethnic Minority Adolescents

1. What is an ethnic identity? (p. 386)

_____

_____

_____

2. Explain why ethnic minority adolescents often experience unique problems in developing a sense of identity. (p. 386)

_____

_____

_____

_____

3. True or False: Many minority high school students are diffused or foreclosed on ethnic identity issues. (p. 386)

4. List three ways in which minority adolescents can be helped to resolve identity conflicts constructively. (p. 386)

A. _____

B. _____

C. _____

5. What is a *bicultural identity,* and how does it benefit minority adolescents? (p. 386)

_____

_____

_____

Moral Development

Piaget's Theory of Moral Development

1. Describe the main characteristics of Piaget's heteronomous and autonomous stages of moral development, noting the age at which children display each type of moral understanding. (pp. 387–388)

   Heteronomous: _____

   _____

   _____

   Age: _____

   Autonomnous: _____

   _____

   _____

   Age: _____

2. Explain the concept of *ideal reciprocity.* (p. 388)

   _____

   _____

   _____

3. True or False: Piaget's theory accurately describes the general direction of change in moral judgment. (p. 388)

4. Piaget (underestimated / overestimated) young children's ability to make moral judgments. (p. 388)

Kohlberg's Extension of Piaget's Theory

1. Explain Kohlberg's approach to the study of moral development. (p). 388

   _____

   _____

   _____

2. True or False: Kohlberg emphasized that it is *the way an individual reasons* about a dilemma, not *the content of the response,* which determines moral maturity. (p. 388)

3. List two factors that Kohlberg believed to promote moral understanding. (pp. 388–389)

   A. _____

   B. _____

4. Explain the basic characteristics of moral reasoning at each of Kohlberg's three levels: (pp. 389–390)

    Preconventional: _____

    _____

    Conventional: _____

    _____

    Postconventional: _____

    _____

5. Match each of the following moral orientations with the appropriate description. (pp. 389–390)

    _____ Laws must be obeyed under all circumstances;
    rules must be enforced in the same even-handed manner for
    everyone, and each member of society has a personal duty to
    uphold them

    _____ Right action is defined by self-chosen ethical principals of
    conscience that are valid for all humanity, regardless of law and
    social agreement

    _____ Ignore people's intentions and focus on fear of authority and
    avoidance of punishment as reasons for behaving morally

    _____ Desire to obey rules because they promote social harmony

    _____ Regard rules and laws as flexible and emphasize fair procedures
    for interpreting and changing the law in order to protect individual
    rights and the interests of the majority

    _____ View right action as flowing from self-interest;
    reciprocity is understood as equal exchange of favors

    1. Punishment and obedience
       orientation
    2. Instrumental purpose orientation
    3. "Good boy-good girl"
       orientation
    4. Social-order-maintaining
       orientation
    5. Social contract orientation
    6. Universal ethical principal
       orientation

6. True or False: Longitudinal research suggests that individuals do not move through the stages of moral development
    in the order in which Kohlberg suggested. (p. 390)

7. True or False: The development of moral understanding is very slow and gradual. (p. 390)

8. Moral reasoning for real-life problems tends to fall at a (lower / higher) stage than does reasoning related to
    hypothetical dilemmas. Explain why this is the case. (p. 390)

    _____

    _____

    _____

9. True or False: Kohlberg's stages develop in a neat, stepwise fashion. (p. 390)

Are There Sex Differences in Moral Reasoning?

1. Carol Gilligan believes that feminine morality emphasizes an ethic of care that is devalued in Kohlberg's model.
    Explain what she meant by this. (pp. 390–391)

    _____

    _____

    _____

2. True or False: Research supports Gilligan's claim that Kohlberg's approach underestimates females' moral maturity. (p. 391)

Environmental Influences on Moral Reasoning

1. Describe child-rearing practices that promote gains in moral development. (p. 391)

_____

_____

_____

_____

2. True or False: Years of schooling is one of the most powerful predictors of moral maturity. (p. 391)

3. True or False: Conflict with peers promotes moral understanding in adolescence. (p. 391)

4. Cite two aspects of peer discussions that stimulate moral development. (p. 391)

   A. _____

   B. _____

5. True or False: Cross-cultural research shows that individuals in industrialized nations move through Kohlberg's stages more quickly and advance to higher levels of moral reasoning than do individuals in village societies. Based on your response, provide some possible explanations. (p. 392)

_____

_____

_____

Moral Reasoning and Behavior

1. There is a (weak / moderate/ strong) relationship between moral thought and action. Elaborate on your response by citing research findings on the relationship between moral reasoning and behavior. (p. 393)

_____

_____

_____

_____

Social Issues: Development of Civic Responsibility

1. Civic responsibility involves _____ of political issues and the means through which citizens can resolve differing views fairly; _____ of attachment to the community, of wanting to make a difference in its welfare, and of trust in others' fairness and helpfulness; and _____ for achieving civic goals. (p. 394)

2. Summarize family, school, and community influences that contribute to adolescents' civic responsibility. (p. 394)

   Family: _____

_____

_____

School: _____

_____

_____

Community: _____

_____

_____

3. Cite two aspects of involvement in extracurricular activities and youth organizations that account for their lasting impact. (p.394)

A. _____

B. _____

Gender Typing

1. What is *gender intensification?* (p. 394)

_____

_____

2. Although it occurs in both sexes, gender intensification is stronger for (boys / girls). (p. 394)

3. Discuss biological, social, and cognitive factors associated with gender intensification. (p. 394)

Biological: _____

_____

_____

Social: _____

_____

_____

Cognitive: _____

_____

_____

4. (Androgynous / Gender-typed) adolescents tend to be psychologically healthier. (p. 394)

The Family

1. During adolescence, _____—establishing oneself as a separate, self-governing individual— becomes a salient task. (p. 394)

Parent–Child Relationships

1. Describe parenting practices that foster adolescent autonomy. (p. 395)

_____

_____

_____

2. Discuss the life transition that parents may be experiencing as their adolescent children are undergoing their own life transitions, and note how this impacts the parent-child relationship. (p. 395)

Parent transition: _____

Impact: _____

_____

_____

3. True or False: The quality of the parent–child relationship is the most consistent predictor of mental health throughout adolescence. (p. 395)

4. Explain how mild parent-child conflict is beneficial during adolescence. (p. 395)

_____

_____

_____

Family Circumstances

1. True or False: Maternal employment reduces the amount of time that parents spend with their teenagers and is harmful to adolescent development. (p. 396)

Siblings

1. During adolescence, teenagers invest (more / less) time and energy in siblings. Why is this the case? (p. 396)

_____

_____

_____

2. Sibling relationships become (more / less) intense during adolescence, in both positive and negative feelings. (p. 396)

Peer Relations

Friendships

1. Cite the two charactersitics of friendship stressed by teenagers. (pp. 396–397)

A. _____

B. _____

2. Summarize the ways in which friends are likely to resemble each other during adolescence. (p. 397)

_____

_____

_____

3. Summarize sex differences in the nature of adolescents' close friendships. (p. 397)

_____

_____

_____

4. True or False: Androgynous boys are just as likely as girls to form intimate same-sex ties, whereas boys who identify strongly with the traditional masculine role are less likely to do so. (p. 397)

5. Cite four reasons why gratifying childhood and adolescent friendships are related to psychological health and competence during early adulthood. (pp. 397–398)

A. _____

_____

B. _____

_____

C. _____

_____

D. _____

_____

Cliques and Crowds

1. Differentiate between cliques and crowds, noting the characteristics of each. (p. 398)

Cliques: _____

_____

Crowds: _____

_____

2. Provide some examples of typical high school crowds. (p. 398)

_____

_____

_____

_____

3. True or False: Peer group values are often an extension of values learned in the home. Elaborate on your response. (p. 398)

_____

_____

_____

_____

4. Describe the function of mixed-sex cliques in early adolescence. (pp. 398–399)

_____

_____

_____

5. True or False: Crowds increase in importance from early to late adolescence. (p. 399)

Dating

1. Differentiate younger and older adolescents' reasons for dating. (p. 399)

Younger: _____

_____

Older: _____

_____

2. True or False: Early dating is positively associated with social maturity. (p. 399)

3. Describe the unique challenges faced by homosexual adolescents in initiating and maintaining romances. (p. 399)

_____

_____

_____

Peer Conformity

1. True or False: Conformity to peer pressure is great er during adolescence than during childhood or young adulthood. (p. 399)

2. Describe the differing spheres of influence of parents and peers during the adolescent years. (pp. 399–400)

Parents: _____

_____

Peers: _____

_____

3. Summarize the link between parenting behavior and adolescents' conformity to peer pressure. (p. 400)

_____

_____

_____

Depression

1. About _____ to _____ percent of American teenagers have experienced one or more depressive episodes, and _____ to _____ percent are chronically depressed. (p. 400)

2. Summarize the consequences of adolescent depression. (p. 401)

    _____

    _____

    _____

3. Explain why adolescents' depressive symptoms tend to be overlooked by parents and teachers. (p. 401)

    _____

    _____

    _____

4. Kinship studies of identical and fraternal twins reveal that heredity (does / does not) play an important role in depression. (p. 401)

5. Explain how experience combines with biology to activate depression among youths. (p. 401)

    _____

    _____

    _____

6. Biological changes associated with puberty (can / cannot) account for sex differences in depression. Elaborate on your response. (p. 401)

    _____

    _____

    _____

    _____

7. Describe how stressful life events and gender-typed coping styles account for girls' higher rates of depression. (p. 401)

    _____

    _____

    _____

Suicide

1. True or False: Suicide is currently the leading cause of death among young people in the United States and Canada. (p. 401)

2. True or False: Adolescent suicide rates are roughly equivalent in all industrialized countries. (pp. 401–402)

3. Discuss sex differences in suicidal behavior, noting whether boys or girls are more likely to kill themselves. (p. 402)

   _____

   _____

   _____

4. Compared with the white majority, ethnic minority adolescents have (lower / higher) suicide rates. (p. 402)

5. True or False: Gay, lesbian, and bisexual youth are three times more likely to attempt suicide than are other adolescents. (p. 402)

6. List five warning signs of suicide. (p. 403)

   A. _____

   B. _____

   C. _____

   D. _____

   E. _____

7. Describe two types of young people who tend to commit suicide. (p. 402)

   A. _____

   _____

   B. _____

   _____

8. Discuss cognitive changes that contribute to the rise in suicide among adolescents. (p). 402)

   _____

   _____

   _____

9. What types of treatments are available for depressed and suicidal adolescents? (pp. 402–403)

   _____

   _____

   _____

10. True or False: Teenage suicides often take place in clusters. Elaborate on your response. (p. 403)

_____

_____

_____

Delinquency

1. Explain why delinquency rises during early adolescence, remains high in middle adolescence, and then declines into young adulthood. (p. 403)

_____

_____

_____

2. Describe personal, familial, neighborhood, and school factors associated with delinquency. (pp. 403–405)

Personal: _____

_____

Familial: _____

_____

Neighborhood: _____

_____

School: _____

_____

3. Describe characteristics of the most effective treatment programs for adolescent delinquency. (p. 405)

_____

_____

_____

A Lifespan Vista: Two Routes to Adolescent Delinquency

1. Persistent adolescent delinquency follows two paths of development, one with an onset of _____ problems in childhood, the second with an onset in _____. Longitudinal research reveals that the (early / late) onset type is far more likely to lead to a life course pattern of aggression and criminality. (p. 404)

2. True or False: Adolescent-onset delinquent youth show significantly higher levels of serious offenses, involvement with deviant peers, substance abuse, unsafe sex, dangerous driving, and time spent in correctional facilities than do childhood-onset delinquent youth. (p. 404)

3. Describe characteristics that distinguish early-onset from late-onset delinquent youth. (p. 404)

Early-onset: _____

_____

Late-onset: _____

_____

ASK YOURSELF . . .

For *Ask Yourself* questions for this chapter, please log on to the Companion Website at www.ablongman.com/berk.

SUGGESTED STUDENT READINGS

Kroger, J. (1999). *Identity development: Adolescence through adulthood.* Thousand Oaks, CA: Sage Publications. Presents the course of identity development throughout the lifespan by drawing on current theory and research. In addition, the author highlights the interactions between biological, social, and cultural forces that contribute to the identity-formation process.

Moeller, T. G. (2001). *Youth aggression and violence: A psychological approach.* Mahwah, NJ: Lawrence Erlbaum Associates. Explores theory and research in the study of adolescent aggression and violence. Other topics include: genetic and environmental contributions to the development of aggression, media violence, firearm accessibility, and the relationship between self-esteem and aggression.

Nangle, D. W., & Erdley, C. A. (Eds.). (2001). *The role of friendship in psychological adjustment: New directions for child and adolescent development.* San Francisco, CA: Jossey-Bass. A collection of chapters exploring the role of children and adolescents' peer relations in socioemotional development. Topics include: popularity, peer acceptance, the complex interactions that take place between friends, and historical and conceptual issues that have contributed to our understanding of childhood friendship.

PUZZLE 12.1 TERM REVIEW

Across

2. Kohlberg's second level of moral development; moral understanding is based on conforming to social rules to ensure positive relationships and social order
4. Identity _____: identity status of individuals who have explored and committed themselves to self-chosen values and goals
6. _____ morality: Piaget's first stage of moral development in which children view rules as permanent and unchangeable
9. Identity _____: identity status of individuals who have accepted ready-made values and goals that authority figures have chosen for them
10. _____ morality: Piaget's second stage of moral development in which children view rules as flexible, socially-agreed-upon principles that can be revised to suit the will of the majority
12. Gender _____: increased stereotyping of attitudes and behavior; movement toward a more traditional gender identity
13. A sense of oneself as a separate, self-governing individual
14. Kohlberg's first level of moral development; moral understanding is based on rewards, punishment, and the power of authority figures

_____

17. _____ identity: identity constructed by adolescents who explore and adopt values from both their subculture and the dominant culture

Down

1. Kohlberg's highest level of moral development; individuals define morality in terms of abstract principles and values that apply to all situations and societies
3. Identity status of individuals who are exploring alternatives in an effort to find values and goals to guide their life
5. Identity _____: identity status of individuals who do not have firm commitments to values and goals and are not actively trying to reach them
7. Identity versus identity_____: Erikson's psychological conflict of adolescence
8. A small group of about five to seven peers who are friends
11. A large, loosely organized peer group in which membership is based on reputation and stereotype
15. _____ identity: sense of ethnic group membership and the attitudes and feelings associated with that membership
16. A well-organized conception of the self made up of values, beliefs, and goals to which the individual is solidly committed

PRACTICE TEST #1

1. Erikson was the first to recognize the formation of a(n) _____ as the major personality achievement in adolescence. (p. 382)
   a. self-concept
   b. identity
   c. moral understanding
   d. gender schema

2. Compared to school-age children, adolescents place more emphasis on _____ in their self-descriptions. (p. 383)
   a. physical appearance
   b. favorite activities
   c. social virtues
   d. school performance

3. Research on identity construction indicates that (p. 385)
   a. most adolescents experience a serious identity crisis.
   b. adolescents typically retain the same identity status across adolescence and early adulthood.
   c. girls often postpone the task of identity development to focus instead on intimacy development.
   d. adolescents who go to work after high school settle on an identity status earlier than do college-bound youths.

4. Kieran has followed the religious path of his family without exploring alternatives and tends to be defensive when his teenage friends bring up the subject. Kieran is (p. 384)
   a. identity foreclosed.
   b. identity diffused.
   c. in moratorium.
   d. identity achieved.

5. In Piaget's heteronomous stage (p. 388)
   a. the wrongness of an act is judged on the basis of intent to do harm.
   b. moral rules are viewed as permanent, unchangeable features of the external world.
   c. rules are regarded as socially-agreed-upon principles that can be revised.
   d. a standard of fairness called reciprocity is used in making moral judgments.

6. Research evaluating the accuracy of Piaget's theory shows that (p. 388)
   a. Piaget underestimated young children's moral capacities.
   b. Piaget was inaccurate in his description of the general direction of change in moral judgment.
   c. Piaget placed unwarranted emphasis on the role of cognitive development and peer interaction in the development of moral understanding.
   d. Piaget accurately described the age-dependent, stepwise sequence in which children develop moral reasoning capacities.

7. During Kohlberg's _____ level of moral develpment, moral understanding is based on conforming to social rules to ensure positive human relatinships and societal order. (pp. 389–390)
   a. heteronomous
   b. preconventional
   c. conventional
   d. postconventional

8. When individuals are faced with real-life, as opposed to hypothetical, moral dilemmas, their moral reasoning tends to (p. 390)
   a. become more mature.
   b. become less mature.
   c. remain at the same level of maturity.
   d. follow no predictable pattern.

9. Research shows that (pp. 390–391)
   a. females show less mature moral reasoning than do males.
   b. females show more mature moral reasoning than do males.
   c. females and males reason about moral issues differently, with females emphasizing care, while males either emphasize justice or use justice and care equally.
   d. males and females do not differ in the level or content of their moral reasoning.

10. During early adolescence, gender intensification is (p. 394)
    a. stronger for boys.
    b. stronger for girls.
    c. equally strong for both boys and girls.
    d. not yet an important issue.

11. Throughout adolescence, the most consistent predictor of mental health is (p. 395)
    a. the quality of the parent–child relationship.
    b. development of positive peer relationships.
    c. attainment of identity achievement.
    d. success in academic efforts.

12. Which of the following is true of the parent-child relationship during adolescence? (p. 395)
    a. Parents and adolescents need to focus less on their attachment relationship and should begin to focus entirely on issues of separation.
    b. Adolescents tend to idealize their parents and are more compliant with parental authority than they were at younger ages.
    c. Both adolescents and parents are undergoing major life transitions, and the pressures of each generation often oppose the other.
    d. Positive parent–child interaction declines from early adolescence into late adolescence as teenagers start to drive, hold part-time jobs, and stay out late.

13. During adolescence, siblings (p. 396)
    a. have a more unequal relationship, with younger siblings showing greater willingness to accept direction from older siblings.
    b. devote more time to each other.
    c. have less intense interactions.
    d. experience a decline in the quality of their relationship.

14. Adolescent crowds (p. 398)
    a. are more intimate than cliques.
    b. become increasingly important across adolescence.
    c. are typically small groups of about five to seven members who are close friends.
    d. are based on reputation and stereotype.

15. In early adolescence, dating (p. 399)
    a. is done for recreational purposes, as well as to achieve status among agemates.
    b. is focused on psychological intimacy, shared interests, and the search for a good permanent partner.
    c. fosters social maturity.
    d. protects teens against drug use, delinquency, and poor school performance.

16. Peers would be most likely to influence one another's (pp. 399–400)
    a. religious values.
    b. choice of college.
    c. choice of clothes.
    d. career plans.

17. Adolescent depression (p. 401)
    a. occurs more often in boys than in girls.
    b. is usually recognized quickly by parents and teachers.
    c. can be entirely attributed to biological causes, namely hormonal changes during puberty.
    d. can seriously impair social, academic, and vocational functioning if left untreated.

18. Which of the following is true? (p. 402)
    a. Suicide rates have been steadily declining over the past 30 years.
    b. Boys are 4 to 5 times more likely to kill themselves than are girls.
    c. Ethnic minority adolescents have higher suicide rates than Caucasian-American adolescents.
    d. Adolescent suicide rates are similar in all industrialized nations.

19. Youth crime (p. 403)
    a. has declined over the past decade.
    b. accounts for a minimal proportion of police arrests—less than 5 percent.
    c. is most often serious in nature.
    d. forecasts a long-term pattern of anti-social behavior for most adolescents.

20. Treatment for serious juvenile offenders is most effective when interventions are (p. 405)
    a. carried out in a residential facility so that the adolescent is removed from his/her home and community during treatment.
    b. intense but brief so as not to interfere with family and occupational functioning.
    c. lengthy and use problem-focused strategies to teach cognitive and social skills for addressing social and academic difficulties.
    d. focused on improving ineffective parenting practices instead of directly addressing the adolescent's aggressive behavior.

PRACTICE TEST #2

1. Leslie is unable to select a vocation that matches her interests and skills. According to Erikson's theory, which earlier stage has she negatively resolved? (p. 382)
    a. trust versus mistrust
    b. autonomy versus shame and doubt
    c. initiative versus guilt
    d. industry versus inferiority

2. During adolescence (p. 383)
    a. self-esteem shows a steady decline for the majority of young people.
    b. several new dimensions are added to self-esteem, including close friendships, romantic appeal, and job competence.
    c. self-esteem rises as long as support from adults and peers is conditional.
    d. a profile of all highly favorable self-evaluations is associated with better adjustment than is a profile that is generally positive.

3. When asked about his career plans, Simon says, "Haven't thought about it. Doesn't make too much difference what I do." Simon's identity status is best characterized as (p. 384)
   a. identity achievement.
   b. identity diffusion.
   c. moratorium.
   d. identity foreclosure.

4. Adolescents who lack confidence in the prospect of ever knowing anything with certainty and who report low levels of warm, open communication in the home are likely to have which identity status? (p. 384)
   a. identity achievement
   b. moratorium
   c. identity foreclosure
   d. identity diffusion

5. In Piaget's autonomous stage of morality, children typically (p. 388)
   a. express the same concern for the welfare of others as they do for themselves.
   b. view moral rules as unchangeable and requiring strict obedience.
   c. base their judgments on outcomes rather than intentions.
   d. believe that others hold the same moral views as they do.

6. According to Kohlberg, which is more important in determining the maturity of responses to moral dilemmas? (p. 388)
   a. reasoning rather than content
   b. content rather than reasoning
   c. reasoning rather than emotion
   d. emotion rather than reasoning

7. When an individual's moral reasoning stems from self-interest, which stage of Kohlberg's theory would best characterize his or her level of moral understanding? (p. 389)
   a. Stage 2: The instrumental purpose orientation
   b. Stage 3: The "good boy-good girl" orientation
   c. Stage 4: The social-order-maintaining orientation
   d. Stage 6: The universal ethical principle orientation

8. In response to the Heinz dilemma, Maria says, "He should steal it. Heinz has a duty to protect his wife's life; it's a vow that he took in marriage. But it's wrong to steal, so he would have to take the drug with the intention of paying the pharmacist for it and accepting his penalty for breaking the law later." Which of Kohlberg's stages of moral development best characterizes Maria's response? (p. 390)
   a. Stage 3: The "good boy-good girl" orientation
   b. Stage 4: The social-order-maintaining orientation
   c. Stage 5: The social contract orientation
   d. Stage 6: The universal ethical principal orientation

9. Research on Kohlberg's stages indicates that (p. 390)
   a. progress through the stages is not related to age.
   b. individuals rarely move through the six stages in the predicted order.
   c. most individuals move through all six stages by early adulthood.
   d. development of moral reasoning is slow and gradual.

10. Which of the following is true with regard to the influences on moral reasoning? (p. 391)
    a. A rigid, closed-minded approach to new information and experiences is linked to gains in moral reasoning.
    b. Peer conflict facilitates moral reasoning by making children aware of others' perspectives.
    c. Strict, authoritarian parenting is associated with more mature moral reasoning.
    d. Movement through Kohlberg's stages is the same in all cultures throughout the world.

11. Which adolescent is most likely to be psychologically healthy? (p. 394)
    a. Jasmine, who has a strong feminine gender identity
    b. Luis, who has a strong masculine gender identity
    c. Gabriella, who has an androgynous gender identity
    d. Gordon, who has a feminine gender identity

12. Which of the following parenting styles is linked with positive outcomes in adolescence, including high self-esteem, self-reliance, academic achievement, and work orientation? (p. 395)
    a. authoritarian
    b. authoritative
    c. permissive
    d. uninvolved

13. Teenagers in the United States spend more time together outside the classroom than do teenagers in Asian countries. The difference is primarily due to (p. 396)
    a. less demanding academic standards in the United States.
    b. higher rates of maternal employment in the United States.
    c. differences in peer group structures between the countries.
    d. differences in parenting styles between the countries.

14. Research on adolescent friendships shows that: (pp. 396–397)
    a. teenagers define friendship in terms of intimacy and loyalty.
    b. cooperation and mutual affiliation between friends declines during adolescence as teens become immersed in forming their personal identity.
    c. the friendships of boys and girls are equally characterized by emotional closeness and exploration of achievement and status concerns.
    d. adolescent boys rarely form close friendship ties.

15. The first dating relationships of homosexual youths tend to be short-lived and involve little emotional commitment. This is largely because (p. 399)
    a. they are not emotionally ready for more mature, emotionally intense relationships.
    b. they are still questioning their sexual identity.
    c. they fear peer harassment and rejection.
    d. they are looking for relationships that are fun and recreational, with little interest in forming close, long-lasting relational ties.

16. Research on peer conformity indicates that (p. 399)
    a. individuals are less likely to conform to peer pressure during adolescence than during childhood and early adulthood.
    b. pressures from peers and parents tend to be extremely divergent.
    c. adolescents feel the greatest pressure to conform to obvious aspects of the peer culture, such as style of dress and participation in social activities.
    d. adolescents who experience authoritative parenting tend to be highly peer-oriented and are more likely to rely on advice from friends in making decisions about their personal lives and futures.

17. About _____ to _____ percent of adolescents have had one or more depressive episodes. (p. 400)
    a. 2–8
    b. 15–20
    c. 30–50
    d. 75–80

18. Research examining why girls are more prone to depression than are boys shows that (p. 401)
    a. the biological changes associated with puberty are primarily responsible for the gender gap.
    b. rates of depression for males and females are similar in all developing and industrialized countries around the world.
    c. stressful life events and gender-typed coping styles account for girls' higher rates of depression.
    d. girls with an androgynous or masculine gender identity are as likely as girls with a strong feminine identity to show signs of depression.

19. Which of the following factors contributes to the sharp rise in suicide from childhood to adolescence? (p. 402)
    a. adolescent impulsiveness
    b. belief in the personal fable
    c. increased emotional distance between parent and child
    d. impersonal school environments

20. Boys' greater likelihood of committing violent offenses in adolescence can be directly traced to (p. 403)
    a. angry, inconsistent discipline during childhood.
    b. gender discrimination by teachers.
    c. ostracism from peers during preschool.
    d. difficult temperament in infancy.

CHAPTER 13
PHYSICAL AND COGNITIVE DEVELOPMENT
IN EARLY ADULTHOOD

BRIEF CHAPTER SUMMARY

Current explanations of biological aging at the level of DNA and body cells are of two types: those that emphasize the programmed effects of specific genes, and those that emphasize the cumulative effects of random events. Support for both views exists, and a combination may eventually prove to be correct. The cross-linkage theory of aging suggests that over time, protein fibers form links and become less elastic, producing negative changes in many organs.

During the twenties and thirties, changes in physical appearance and declines in body functioning are so gradual that many are hardly noticeable. Heart disease rises with age and is a leading cause of death throughout adulthood. Declines in heart and lung functioning under conditions of exertion, combined with gradual muscle loss, lead to changes in motor performance. The capacity of the immune system to offer protection against disease increases through adolescence and declines after age 20. Finally, reproductive capacity decreases for both men and women beginning in early adulthood.

Income, education, and occupational status show a strong and continuous relationship with almost every disease and health indicator. Overweight and obesity and a high-fat diet are widespread nutritional problems with long-term consequences for health in adulthood. Regular exercise reduces body fat, builds muscle, helps prevent illness, and enhances psychological well-being. Despite an overall decrease in use of both legal and illegal substances in recent years, alcohol and drug dependency remain serious problems in early adulthood. Compared with earlier generations, adults today display a wider range of sexual choices and lifestyles, including cohabitation, marriage, extramarital experiences, and orientation toward a heterosexual or homosexual partner. Sexually transmitted disease, rape, premenstrual syndrome, and psychological stress are important concerns of early adulthood.

Adult cognition changes to reflect an awareness of multiple truths, integrates logic with reality, and tolerates the gap between the ideal and the real. Gains in expertise enhance problem solving as well as creativity. Although creativity tends to rise in early adulthood and peak in the late thirties and early forties, its development varies across disciplines and individuals. Longitudinal studies reveal that intellectual performance improves steadily into middle adulthood and declines only late in life.

Many people view the college years as formative, or more influential than any other period of adulthood. Through involvement in academic programs and campus life, college students engage in exploration that produces gains in knowledge and reasoning ability, revised attitudes and values, enhanced self-esteem and self-knowledge, and preparation for a high-status career. In societies with an abundance of career possibilities, occupational choice is a gradual process, beginning long before adolescence. Vocational choices are influenced by personality, family, teachers, and gender stereotypes, and many young people could profit from greater access to career information. High school graduates who do not continue their education are at risk for unemployment and when they do find work, most are limited to temporary, low-paid, unskilled jobs.

LEARNING OBJECTIVES

After reading this chapter, you should be able to:

13.1 Describe current theories of biological aging, including those at the level of DNA and body cells and those at the level of organs and tissues. (pp. 412–414)

13.2   Describe the physical changes of aging, paying special attention to the cardiovascular and respiratory systems, motor performance, the immune system, and reproductive capacity. (pp. 414–418)

13.3   Discuss the prevalence, causes, consequences, and treatment of overweight and obesity in adulthood. (pp. 420–423)

13.4   Describe the health benefits of regular, moderate-intensity exercise. (pp. 423–424)

13.5   Name the two most common substance disorders in early adulthood, and discuss the health risks of each. (pp. 424–426)

13.6   Summarize young adults' sexual attitudes and behaviors, including perspectives on both heterosexuality and homosexuality. (pp. 426–428)

13.7   Discuss prevalence rates and risk factors associated with sexually transmitted disease in early adulthood. (p. 428)

13.8   Describe individual and cultural correlates of sexually coercive behavior, and discuss the consequences, prevention, and treatment of rape. (pp. 428–430)

13.9   Describe the symptoms, possible causes, and treatment of premenstrual syndrome. (p. 430)

13.10 Explain the health outcomes associated with psychological stress.(pp. 430–431)

13.11 Summarize prominent theories on the restructuring of thought in adulthood, including those of Perry, Schaie, and Labouvie-Vief. (pp. 432–433)

13.12 Discuss the development of expertise and creativity in adulthood. (pp. 433–434)

13.13 Discuss changes in mental abilities during the adult years. (pp. 434–435)

13.14 Describe the psychological impact of attending college, and discuss factors associated with dropping out. (pp. 435–436)

13.15 Trace the phases of vocational development, and review factors that influence vocational choice. (pp. 436–439)

13.16 Discuss the vocational preparation and employment opportunities of non-college-bound youth in the United States and Canada. (pp. 439–441)

STUDY QUESTIONS

Physical Development

Biological Aging Begins in Early Adulthood

1.   Define *biological aging,* or *senescence.* (p. 412)

_____

_____

2. Briefly explain and evaluate the *wear-and-tear* theory of biological aging. (p. 413)

_____

_____

_____

_____

Aging at the Level of DNA and Body Cells

1. List two explanations of biological aging at the level of DNA and body cells that are supported by research. (p. 413)

   A. _____

   B. _____

2. Discuss evidence supporting the "genetic programming" theory, which proposes the existence of "aging genes" that control certain biological changes. Be sure to include the word *telomeres* in your response. (p. 413)

   _____

   _____

   _____

   _____

3. Briefly summarize the "random events" theory of biological aging. (p. 413)

   _____

   _____

   _____

4. One probable cause of age-related DNA and cellular abnormalities, implicated in more than 60 disorders of aging, is the release of _____—naturally occurring, highly reactive chemicals that form in the presence of oxygen. (p. 413)

Aging at the Level of Organs and Tissues

1. According to the _____ *theory of aging,* protein fibers that make up the body's connective tissue form bonds with one another over time. When these normally separate fibers link, tissue becomes less elastic, leading to many negative outcomes. (p. 414)

2. Gradual failure of the _____ *system,* which produces and regulates hormones, is another route to aging. List two examples of decreased hormone production, and explain how they contribute to aging. (p. 414)

   A. _____

   B. _____

3. Declines in _____ system functioning, which results in increased susceptibility to infectious disease, is related to many conditions of aging. (p. 414)

Cardiovascular and Respiratory Systems

1. True or False: In healthy individuals, the heart's ability to meet the body's oxygen needs under typical conditions does not change during adulthood. (p. 414)

2. Describe the heart condition known as *atherosclerosis*. (p. 414)

   _____

   _____

3. Explain why rates of heart disease have declined considerably over the past 15 years. (p. 416)

   _____

   _____

4. Cite two ways in which lung functioning changes with age. (p. 416)

   A. _____

      _____

   B. _____

      _____

Motor Performance

1. Research shows that athletic skill peaks between the ages of _____ and _____ and then declines. (p. 416)

2. True or False: Age related declines in athletic skill are almost entirely attributable to biological aging. (p. 417)

Immune System

1. Describe two types of white blood cells that play vital roles in immune system functioning. (p. 417)

   A. _____

      _____

   B. _____

      _____

2. One factor that contributes to age-related declines in immune response is shrinkage of the _____, which results in decreased production of certain hormones. (p. 417)

3. True or False: Stress can weaken immune response. Briefly explain your answer. (p. 418)

   _____

   _____

   _____

Reproductive Capacity

1. Explain why many women experience a decline in fertility across early and middle adulthood. (p. 418)

   _____

   _____

   _____

2. True or False: Male reproductive capacity is unaffected by age. (p. 418)

Health and Fitness

1. Summarize SES variations in health during adulthood, noting factors responsible for these differences. (p. 419)

    Variations: _____

    _____

    Factors responsible: _____

    _____

Nutrition

1. Today, _____ percent of American adults and _____ percent of Canadian adults are affected by obesity. (p. 420)

2. True or False: Obesity is especially high among middle-class Caucasian Americans relative to their lower-SES ethnic minority counterparts. (p. 420)

3. What factors contribute to the rising rates of obesity in the United States and other industrialized countries? (p. 420)

    _____

    _____

    _____

4. List several health problems associated with being overweight and with obesity. (p. 420)

    _____

    _____

5. Describe five elements of treatment for obesity that promote lasting behavioral change. (pp. 420–421)

    A. _____

    B. _____

    C. _____

    D. _____

    E. _____

6. Summarize the detrimental effects of excess dietary fat consumption. (pp. 421–422)

    _____

    _____

Exercise

1. True or False: About 75 percent of North Americans engage in at least moderate physical activity for 20 minutes or more at least five times per week. (p. 424)

2. True or False: Exercise helps prevent serious illnesses, such as cancer, adult-onset diabetes, and cardiovascular disease. (p. 424)

3. List five ways in which exercise helps prevent serious illnesses. (p. 424)

   A. _____

   B. _____

   C. _____

   D. _____

   E. _____

4. How much exercise is recommended for a healthier and longer life? (p. 424)

   _____

Substance Abuse

1. What are the two most common substance disorders in early adulthood? (p. 425)

   A. _____

   B. _____

2. Smoking rates have declined very (slowly / rapidly) over the past 35 years. (p. 425)

3. List several health consequences of smoking. (p. 425)

   A. _____

   B. _____

   C. _____

4. True or False: One out of every three young people who become regular smokers will die from a smoking-related disease. (p. 425)

5. Explain why treatment programs for smoking are often unsuccessful. (p. 425)

   _____

   _____

6. Twin studies (do / do not) support a genetic contribution to alcoholism. (p. 425)

7. List the personal and cultural characteristics associated with alcoholism. (p. 425)

   Personal: _____

   _____

   Cultural: _____

   _____

8. List some of the health problems associated with chronic alcohol use. (p. 426)

   _____

   _____

9. Describe components of the most successful treatment programs for alcoholism. (p. 426)

   _____

   _____

Sexuality

1. True or False: Sexual partners tend to be alike in age, education, ethnicity, and religion. (p. 426)

2. True or False: Consistent with popular belief, Americans today have more sexual partners than they did a generation ago. Briefly explain your response. (p. 426)

   _____

   _____

3. List three factors that affect frequency of sexual activity. (pp. 426–427)

   A. _____

   B. _____

   C. _____

4. True or False: As the number of sexual partners increases, satisfaction with one's sex life also increases. (p. 427)

5. List the two sexual difficulties most frequently reported by men and by women. (p. 427)

   Men: _____

   Women: _____

6. The majority of Americans (do / do not) support civil liberties and equal employment opportunities for gay men, lesbians, and bisexuals. (p. 428)

7. (Women / Men) judge homosexuals more harshly. (p. 428)

8. Explain the ways in which homosexual sex follows many of the same rules as heterosexual sex. (p. 428)

   _____

   _____

9. Why is the incidence of sexually transmitted disease (STD) especially high during adolescence and early adulthood? (p. 428)

   _____

   _____

10. The overall rate of STD is higher among (men / women). Why is this the case? (p. 428)

    _____

    _____

11. True or False: The incidence of HIV-positive adults is higher in the United States than in any other industrialized nation. (p. 428)

12. Cite several ways in which AIDS can be contained or reduced. (p. 428)

    _____

    _____

    _____

13. Approximately _____ percent of women have been raped—legally defined as intercourse by force, by threat of harm, or when the victim is incapable of giving consent. (p. 429)

14. Women are most often raped by (strangers / men they know well). (p. 429)

15. Describe the personal characteristics of men who engage in sexual assault. (p. 429)

_____

_____

_____

16. Describe two cultural forces that contribute to sexual coercion. (p. 429)

    A. _____

       _____

    B. _____

       _____

17. Summarize the immediate and long-term consequences of rape. (p. 429)

    Immediate: _____

    _____

    Long-term: _____

    _____

18. Cite three critical features in the treatment of rape victims that help to foster recovery. (p. 430)

    A. _____

    B. _____

    C. _____

19. Describe three ways of preventing sexual coercion. (p. 430)

    A. _____

    B. _____

    C. _____

20. List the common symptoms of premenstrual syndrome (PMS). (p. 430)

_____

_____

21. About _____ women worldwide experience some form of PMS, but only _____ percent of women experience symptoms severe enough to interfere with academic, occupational, or social functioning. (p. 430)

22. List common treatments for PMS. (p. 430)

_____

_____

Psychological Stress

1. Describe several physical consequences of psychological stress. (pp. 430–431)

_____

_____

_____

2. Explain why early adulthood is a particularly stressful time of life. (p. 431)

_____

_____

A Lifespan Vista: The Obesity Epidemic: How Americans Became the Heaviest People in the World

1. Today, _____ percent of Americans are either overweight or obese. (p. 422)

2. Summarize five environmental and lifestyle factors that have encouraged widespread, rapid weight gain. (pp. 422–423)

   A. _____

   B. _____

   C. _____

   D. _____

   E. _____

3. List five societal efforts needed to combat obesity. (p. 423)

   A. _____

   B. _____

   C. _____

   D. _____

   E. _____

Social Issues: Sex Differences in Attitudes toward Sexuality

1. Summarize psychoanalytic, evolutionary, and social learning perspectives on sex differences in sexual attitudes and behavior. (p. 427)

   Psychoanalytic: _____

   _____

   Evolutionary: _____

   _____

   Social Learning: _____

2. True or False: Women are more opposed to casual sex than are men and are only half as likely to engage in it. (p. 427)

3. True or False: Young women's complaints that many men are not interested in long-term commitments are generally unfounded. (p. 427)

Cognitive Development

Changes in the Structure of Thought

1. Cognitive development beyond Piaget's formal operational stage is known as _____ *thought*. (p. 432)

Perry's Theory

1. Based on Perry's research, describe differences in the structure of thought between younger college students and older college students. Be sure to refer to *dualistic* and *relativistic thinking* in your response. (p. 432)

Younger college students: _____

_____

Older college students: _____

_____

Schaie's Theory

1. Summarize Schaie's four stage sequence of cognitive development. (pp. 432–433)

A. _____

_____

B. _____

_____

C. _____

_____

D. _____

_____

Labouvie-Vief's Theory

1. According to Labouvie-Vief, adulthood marks a shift from hypothetical to _____ *thought*—a structural advance in which logic becomes a tool for solving real-world problems. What life changes motivate this shift in the structure of thought? (p. 433)

_____

_____

Information Processing: Expertise and Creativity

1. Define *expertise*. (p. 433)

   _____

   _____

2. Summarize differences in the problem-solving approaches used by experts and novices. (p. 434)

   Experts: _____

   _____

   Novices: _____

   _____

3. How does creativity differ in adulthood relative to childhood? (p. 434)

   _____

   _____

4. Trace general trends in the development of creativity across adulthood. (p. 434)

   _____

   _____

5. In addition to expertise, what other personal qualities foster the development of creativity? (p. 434)

   _____

   _____

Changes in Mental Abilities

1. Summarize Schaie's cross-sectional and longitudinal findings on intellectual ability in adulthood. (p. 435)

   _____

   _____

   _____

   _____

The College Experience

Psychological Impact of Attending College

1. List four psychological changes that take place during the college years. (p. 436)

   A. _____

   B. _____

   C. _____

   D. _____

2. Cite two factors that jointly determine the impact of college. (p. 436)

A. _____

B. _____

Dropping Out

1. Summarize personal and institutional characteristics that contribute to young people's decision to drop out of college. (p. 436)

Personal: _____

_____

Institutional: _____

_____

2. True or False: Usually typical problems of early adulthood, rather than a catastrophic event, lead individuals to withdraw from college. (p. 436)

Vocational Choice

Selecting a Vocation

1. Describe the three phases of vocational development, noting the developmental period at which each occurs. (p. 437)

Fantasy Period: _____

_____

Tentative Period: _____

_____

Realistic Period: _____

_____

Factors Influencing Vocational Choice

1. Match each of the following personality types that affect vocational choice with the appropriate description. (p. 437)

_____ Likes well-structured tasks and values social status; tends to choose business occupations		1. Investigative
_____ Prefers real-world problems and work with objects; tends toward mechanical occupations		2. Social
_____ Adventurous, persuasive, and a strong leader; drawn toward sales and supervisory positions		3. Realistic
_____ Enjoys working with ideas; drawn toward scientific occupations		4. Artistic
_____ Has a high need for emotional and individual expression; drawn to artistic fields		5. Conventional
_____ Likes interacting with people; drawn toward human services		6. Enterprising

2. The relationship between personality and vocational choice is (weak / moderate / strong). (p. 437)

3. Identify two reasons, other than educational attainment, why young people's vocational aspirations correlate strongly with the jobs of their parents. (p. 437)

A. _____

_____

B. _____

_____

4. Teachers (do / do not) play a powerful role in young adults' career decisions. (p. 438)

5. True or False: Over the past 20 years, young women's career preferences have remained strongly gender stereotyped, whereas young men have shown increasing interest in careers largely held by women. (p. 438)

6. Women's progress in entering and excelling at male-dominated professions has been (slow / rapid). (p. 438)

7. True or False: Sex differences in vocational achievement can be directly attributed to differences in ability. Elaborate on your response. (p. 438)

_____

_____

8. True or False: The educational and career aspirations of academically talented females often decline during the college years. (p. 438)

9. List four experiences common to young women who show high achievement during college. (p. 438)

A. _____

B. _____

C. _____

D. _____

10. What type of student is at-risk for becoming a "drifting dreamer," and how can schools better help these students to learn about the work that they are interested in? (p. 439)

_____

_____

_____

_____

Vocational Preparation of Non-College-Bound Young Adults

1. Non-college-bound high school graduates have (more / fewer) work opportunities than they did several decades ago. (p. 439)

2. Summarize the challenges faced by non-college-bound young adults in trying to gain employment, and describe the type of jobs they are likely to find. (p. 439)

Challenges: _____

_____

Type of jobs: _____

_____

Cultural Influences: Work / Study Apprenticeships in Germany

1. True or False: Two-thirds of adolescents participate in Germany's apprenticeship system, making it the most common form of secondary education. (p. 440)

2. Summarize the features of Germany's work–study apprenticeship system, and explain how it creates a smooth transition from school to work. (p. 440)

_____

_____

_____

_____

3. Identify three major challenges to the implementation of a national apprenticeship program in the United States and Canada. (p. 440)

A. _____

_____

B. _____

_____

C. _____

_____

ASK YOURSELF . . .

For *Ask Yourself* questions for this chapter, please log on to the Companion Website at www.ablongman.com/berk.

SUGGESTED STUDENT READINGS

Critser, G. (2003). *Fat land: How Americans became the fattest people in the world.* Boston: Houghton Mifflin. In this book, the author explores how multiple aspects of American life—class, politics, culture, and economics—have contributed to the obesity epidemic. In addition, the author presents up-to-date research on childhood obesity, marketing tactics of fast-food chains, adult-onset diseases resulting from poor eating habits, and suggestions for how American society should go about tackling this growing epidemic.

Massey, D. S., Lundy, G., Charles, C. Z., & Fischer, M. J. (2003). *The source of the river: The social origins of freshman at America's selective colleges and universities.* Princeton University Press. Drawing on the recently released National Longitudinal Survey of Freshman, the authors explore racial and ethnic differences in academic success; how experiences within the family, peer group, and community contribute to college performance; and how racial stereotypes of intellectual inferiority influence the life chances of many ethnic minority college students.

Sinnott, J. D. (1998). *Development of logic in adulthood: Postformal thought and its applications.* Perseus Publishing. A collection of chapters highlighting advances in adult thinking, refinements in decision making skills, and how postformal thought influences family and romantic relationships, adult education, social roles, and workplace functioning.

Smith, M. D. (Ed.). (2002). *Sex without consent: Rape and sexual coercion in America.* New York: New York University Press. A historical look at the experience, prosecution, and meaning of rape in America and how it relates to our understanding of crime and punishment, gender relations, gender roles, and sexual politics.

PUZZLE 13.1 TERM REVIEW

Across

4. During the ____ period of vocational development, adolescents weigh vocational options against their interests, abilities, and values.
5. During the ____ period of vocational development, individuals focus on a general career category and eventually settle on a single occupation.
6. Cognitive development beyond Piaget's formal operational stage is referred to as _____ thought.
8. In Schaie's ____ stage, the goal of mental activity is knowledge acquisition.
10. ____ aging: genetically-influenced, age-related declines in the functioning of organs and systems that are universal in all members of our species
14. ____ thinking: viewing all knowledge as imbedded in a framework of thought; favoring multiple truths relative to the context of evaluation
16. In Schaie's ____ stage, people re-examine and reintegrate their interests, attitudes, and values, using them as a guide for what knowledge to acquire and apply.
17. ___-___ theory: the formation of bonds between normally separate protein fibers causes the body's connective tissue to become less elastic

18. During the ____ period of vocational development, children fantasize about career options through make-believe play.

Down

1. Free ____: naturally occurring, highly reactive chemicals that form in the presence of oxygen and destroy cellular material
2. Acquisition of extensive knowledge in a field or endeavor
3. Array of physical and psychological symptoms that usually appear 6 to 10 days prior to menstruation (abbr.).
7. In Schaie's ____ stage, people adapt their cognitive skills to the expansion of responsibilities to others that take place on the job, in the community, and at home
9. ____ thinking: dividing information, values, and authority into right and wrong, good and bad, we and they
11. In Schaie's ____ stage, responsibilities are highly complex, requiring a more advanced form of responsibility.
12. In Schaie's ____ stage, people adapt their cognitive skills to situations that have implications for achieving long-term goals.
13. ____ thought: logic becomes a tool for solving real-world problems
15. The amount of energy the body uses at complete rest (abbr.)

PRACTICE TEST #1

1. Biological aging (p. 412)
    a. is an asynchronous process, meaning that change varies widely across different body parts.
    b. shows few individual differences because of its genetic origins.
    c. typically begins in late adulthood, as the body wears out from use.
    d. cannot be modified through behavioral or environmental interventions.

2. Which of the following is true of aging at the level of DNA and body cells? (pp. 413–414)
    a. Longevity is a strongly heritable trait, with environmental factors playing only a small role.
    b. Researchers have isolated specific "aging genes" that are responsible for the biological changes associated with aging, such as menopause and gray hair.
    c. The release of free radicals is one probable cause of age-related DNA and cellular abnormalities and has been linked with many disorders of aging, including heart disease and cancer.
    d. Research shows that it is the cumulative effects of random events, not the programmed effects of specific genes, that cause aging at the level of DNA and body cells.

3. Which of the following is true of cardiovascular and respiratory functioning in early adulthood? (p. 414)
    a. In healthy individuals, the heart's ability to meet the body's oxygen requirements under typical conditions does not change with age.
    b. Many individuals are at-risk for developing atherosclerosis in early adulthood, even when they exercise regularly and eat a low-fat diet.
    c. Rates of heart disease have increased over the last 15 years, placing young and middle-aged adults at high risk for developing this condition.
    d. Lung functioning actually improves during early and middle adulthood, especially during physical exertion, and then begins to decline in late adulthood.

4. Research on health and fitness indicates that (p. 419)
    a. heart disease is the leading cause of death among individuals age 25–44.
    b. death rates for all causes are essentially equivalent in industrialized nations throughout the world.
    c. income, education, and occupational status show a strong relationship with almost every disease and health indicator.
    d. SES differences in chronic illness are largest during childhood and adolescence and then decline throughout adulthood.

5. What underlies the rising rates of obesity in industrialized nations? (p. 420)
    a. hereditary vulnerability to weight gain
    b. reduced basal metabolic rate among individuals age 25–50
    c. reduced physical labor and increased fat intake
    d. low quality health care and lack of universal health insurance

6. Exercise (p. 424)
    a. occurs most regularly among women and low-SES adults.
    b. fosters resistance to disease.
    c. has many physical benefits but does not impact mental health.
    d. reduces individuals' ability to cope with stress and is associated with decreased life satisfaction.

7. Which of the following is true of cigarette smoking? (p. 425)
    a. Smoking rates have increased among North American adults over the last several decades.
    b. Most people who smoke start after the age of 25.
    c. One out of every three individuals who becomes a regular smoker will die from a smoking-related disease.
    d. Despite some improvement in health, those who quit smoking will never return to nonsmoker levels of disease risk.

8. Research on sexual behavior shows that (p. 426)
   a. sexual partners tend to be alike in age, education, ethnicity, and religion.
   b. almost 50 percent of adults who eventually marry meet at bars, through personal ads, or on vacation.
   c. Americans today have fewer sexual partners than they did a generation ago.
   d. the majority of Americans report having five or more sexual partners in a single year.

9. Homosexuals (p. 428)
   a. tend to live in small communities rather than large cities.
   b. are usually less well-educated than others, often failing to graduate high school.
   c. follow the same rules for sexual behavior as do heterosexuals.
   d. prefer to have sex outside the context of a committed relationship.

10. AIDS is spreading most rapidly among (p. 428)
    a. homosexual men.
    b. heterosexual men with a history of many sexual partners.
    c. heterosexual women.
    d. heterosexual individuals in poverty-stricken minority groups.

11. Men who engage in sexual assault (p. 429)
    a. are less likely to endorse traditional gender roles.
    b. have difficulty accurately interpreting women's social behavior.
    c. usually acknowledge their own responsibility.
    d. are most likely to be from low-SES, ethnic minority groups.

12. Which of the following is true of psychological stress during early adulthood? (p. 431)
    a. Psychological stress has not been shown to have negative health consequences for young adults, who are often in peak physical condition.
    b. Young adults report less stress and more effective coping strategies than middle-aged individuals.
    c. Research has failed to reveal any SES or age-related differences in response to stress.
    d. Establishing and maintaining satisfying social ties serves as a buffer against the negative health outcomes associated with stress.

13. William Perry's theory suggests that young adults make a transition from dividing information into absolutes, such as right and wrong, to _____, in which they favor multiple truths. (p. 432)
    a. dualistic thinking
    b. relativistic thinking
    c. adaptive cognition
    d. inquisitive thought

14. According to Labouvie-Vief, adulthood involves a shift from hypothetical to _____ thought, in which logic is used as a tool for solving real-world problems. (p. 433)
    a. pragmatic
    b. concrete
    c. abstract
    d. dualistic

15. Longitudinal findings from Schaie's Seattle Longitudinal Study show that (p. 435)
    a. intelligence test performance peaks at age 25 and then shows a steep decline into old age.
    b. intelligence test performance improves from early to middle adulthood in verbal skills and other abilities that depend on accumulated knowledge and then shows a decline late in life.
    c. all mental abilities, reflecting both acquired knowledge and skills that tap the capacity to detect relationships, continue to improve well into late adulthood.
    d. performance on intelligence tests in early and middle adulthood is closely linked to job achievement.

16. Which of the following is true with regard to dropping out of college? (p. 436)
    a. Most students who drop out of college do so during their sophomore or junior year because they are unable to decide on a major.
    b. Most students who withdraw from college do not have the ability to succeed at the institution to which they were admitted.
    c. Colleges typically have many supports in place to provide encouragement and assistance to students at high risk for dropping out.
    d. The problems that lead students to withdraw from college are usually typical rather than catastrophic in nature.

17. Twenty-year-old Dominic explored the possibility of becoming a teacher by tutoring in an after-school program and interviewing several of his previous teachers about their career choice. He then decided to major in education. Dominic is in the _____ period of vocational development. (p. 437)
    a. fantasy
    b. tentative
    c. realistic
    d. acquisition

18. The relationship between personality and vocational choice is (p. 437)
    a. weak, since people rarely choose occupations that compliment their personality.
    b. moderate, since most people are a blend of personality types and could do well at more than one kind of occupation.
    c. strong, since career choice, success, and satisfaction are almost entirely attributable to personality factors.
    d. inconclusive, with research findings varying widely on this topic.

19. Which of the following is true with regard to gender stereotyping in young adults' vocational choice? (p. 438)
    a. Young women's career preferences have remained strongly gender stereotyped over the last 20 years, whereas young men have expressed greater interest in occupations traditionally held by women.
    b. Women's progress in entering and excelling at male-dominated fields has been extremely rapid, and few women now remain in the less well-paid, traditionally female professions.
    c. Sex differences in ability account for the fact that women's achievements lag behind those of men in virtually all fields.
    d. The career aspirations of academically talented females tend to decline during the college years.

20. The term "dreaming drifters" is used to refer to young adults who (p. 439)
    a. are at high risk for dropping out of college.
    b. opt to enter the work force after high school rather than pursuing a college education.
    c. remain stuck in the fantasy phase of vocational development.
    d. are highly ambitious with regard to vocational development but lack knowledge about their preferred vocation and the requirements for entering their chosen field.

PRACTICE TEST #2

1. Which of the following provides support for the "programmed" effects of "aging genes"? (p. 413)
    a. the increase in DNA breaks and cellular deletions and damage with age
    b. the release of free radicals by the cells of the body
    c. human cells allowed to divide in the laboratory have a lifespan of 50 divisions plus or minus 10
    d. biological aging does not appear to be affected by environmental factors

2. According to the cross-linkage theory of aging (p. 414)
    a. shortening of telomeres eventually inhibits cell duplication and results in cell death.
    b. protein fibers that make up the body's connective tissue form bonds over time, making the tissue less elastic.
    c. biological aging results from gradual failure of the endocrine system, which produces and regulates hormones.
    d. declines in immune system functioning make people more susceptible to disease with age.

3. Studies of outstanding athletes show that (p. 416)
   a. even with intensive training, attainments fall short of what is biologically possible as athletes begin to age.
   b. athletic tasks that depend on endurance peak in the early twenties, while those involving speed, strength, and gross body coordination peak in the late twenties and early thirties.
   c. age-related decline in athletic skill is largely attributable to biological aging.
   d. athletic skill peaks between the ages of 20 and 30 and then declines.

4. What two types of blood cells play a role in the diminished functioning of the immune system with increasing age? (p. 417)
   a. axons and glial cells
   b. antigens and antibodies
   c. T cells and B cells
   d. red blood cells and white blood cells

5. Which of the following is true with regard to treatment of obesity? (pp. 420–421)
   a. The majority of obese American adults have been repeatedly advised by their doctors to control their eating and to exercise.
   b. For most obese individuals, substantial weight loss would be necessary in order to reduce health problems.
   c. Short-lived, highly stringent weight loss programs are most likely to result in sustained weight loss.
   d. Most individuals who start weight loss programs return to their original weight within five years.

6. Which of the following is true of fat consumption? (p. 421)
   a. U.S. and Canadian recommendations suggest that dietary fat should make up approximately 30 percent of total caloric intake.
   b. Unsaturated fats are more unhealthy than saturated fats.
   c. To maximize healthy body functioning, dietary fats should be avoided entirely.
   d. Behavioral interventions, such as regular exercise, are largely ineffective in reducing the harmful influence of dietary fats.

7. How much exercise is recommended to promote a healthier, happier, and longer life? (p. 424)
   a. 30 minutes of moderate physical activity on most days
   b. 15 minutes of high intensity physical activity every other day
   c. 90 minutes of low intensity physical activity every day
   d. 60 minutes of moderate physical activity once a week

8. Alcoholism (p. 426)
   a. typically has an earlier onset for women than for men.
   b. is almost entirely attributable to genetic factors.
   c. is more common in cultures where alcohol is a traditional part of religious and ceremonial activities.
   d. is difficult to treat, with about 50 percent of alcoholics relapsing within a few months.

9. Which group reports the highest rates of physical and emotional satisfaction in relation to their sex lives? (p. 427)
   a. individuals in committed relationships who are not yet married
   b. individuals with a large number of sexual partners
   c. young adults involved in casual dating relationships
   d. married couples

10. The majority of Americans (p. 428)
   a. believe that homosexuality is not wrong at all.
   b. disapprove of sexual relations between two adults of the same sex but support civil liberties and equal employment opportunities for gay men, lesbians, and bisexuals.
   c. disapprove of homosexual relations and contest the civil rights of gay men, lesbians, and bisexuals.
   d. do not take a strong stand on the issue of homosexuality.

11. Rates of STD (p. 428)
    a. are highest in early and middle adulthood.
    b. are higher among women than men.
    c. are higher in Canada than the United States.
    d. have decreased dramatically in recent years, particularly among those in their teens and twenties.

12. Victims of sexual coercion (p. 429)
    a. are usually over the age of 30.
    b. rarely know their abusers.
    c. show reactions similar to those of survivors of extreme trauma, including shock, withdrawal, and psychological numbing.
    d. are typically quick to confide in trusted family members and friends about the assault.

13. Premenstrual syndrome (p. 430)
    a. is only found among women in the United States and is not evident in other nations throughout the world.
    b. occurs in about 85 percent of women and usually involves moderate to severe intensity of symptoms.
    c. is more likely to co-occur in identical than fraternal twins, suggesting a genetic contribution.
    d. can be cured with hormone therapy.

14. During early adulthood, individuals reach Schaie's _____ stage, in which people focus less on acquiring knowledge and more on applying it in everyday life. (p. 432)
    a. acquisitive
    b. achieving
    c. responsibility
    d. reintegrative

15. Which of the following is true of expertise and creativity? (pp. 433–434)
    a. Experts and novices show remarkably similar reasoning and problem-solving skills.
    b. Creativity takes essentially the same form in childhood and adulthood.
    c. Creativity tends to peak in early adulthood, approximately five years after initial exposure to a field.
    d. Expertise is necessary for creativity, however, not all experts are creative.

16. Cognitive growth during the college years is promoted when (p. 436)
    a. students attend community colleges.
    b. students decide on a major during their freshman year.
    c. students live in the residence halls and become involved in campus life.
    d. students live at home in order to minimize distractions and promote a more high- quality study environment.

17. While 70–75 percent of high school graduates enroll in institutions of higher learning, approximately _____ percent of students at four-year institutions drop out during their freshman year. (p. 436)
    a. 2
    b. 10
    c. 25
    d. 45

18. According to Holland's personality classification, what type of person is adventurous, persuasive, and a strong leader and is drawn to sales and supervisory positions and politics? (p. 437)
    a. enterprising
    b. social
    c. investigative
    d. conventional

19. Which of the following is true of the influence of parents and teachers on young peoples' vocational choices? (pp. 437–438)
    a. Since children have considerable knowledge of the drawbacks of their parents' careers, they are likely to choose radically different occupations for themselves.
    b. Teachers are more influential than are parents in the career decisions of non-college-bound youths.
    c. Young adults tend to choose occupations that are consistent with their family values, yet teachers also play an important role in career decision making.
    d. Neither parents nor teachers are likely to influence young adults' career decisions since personality type is the strongest predictor of occupational choice.

20. Teenagers who do not plan to go to college after high school graduation (p. 439)
    a. have a much easier time finding employment than do many college graduates.
    b. are typically limited to temporary, low-paid, unskilled jobs.
    c. often have high-quality vocational preparation, which enables them to enter high-paying, high-skill occupations.
    d. do not have well-developed career aspirations.

CHAPTER 14
EMOTIONAL AND SOCIAL DEVELOPMENT
IN EARLY ADULTHOOD

BRIEF CHAPTER SUMMARY

In Erikson's theory, young adults must resolve the conflict of intimacy versus isolation. Erikson believed that successful resolution prepares the individual for the middle adulthood stage, which focuses on generativity.

Levinson suggested that the life course consists of a series of eras in which individuals revise their life structure to meet changing needs. Vaillant refined Erikson's stages, portraying the twenties as devoted to intimacy, the thirties to career consolidation, the fifties to cultural and philosophical values. Although societal expectations have become less rigid, conformity to or departure from the social clock can be a major source of personality change in adulthood. Following a social clock grants confidence to young adults, whereas deviating can bring psychological distress.

Although young adults are especially concerned with romantic love, the need for intimacy is also satisfied though other relationships that involve mutual commitment—friends, siblings, and co-workers. Romantic partners tend to resemble one another in age, ethnicity, SES, religion, and various personal and physical attributes.

Evolutionary and social learning theories provide perspectives on how biology and gender roles influence criteria for mate selection. Romantic love is the basis for relationships in Western cultures, but the balance among passion, intimacy, and commitment changes as relationships progress. Friendships continue to be based on trust, with women's friendships remaining more intimate than men's. Sibling relationships often become stronger. Through other-sex friendships, young people learn a great deal about masculine and feminine styles of intimacy. Young adults, who expect to form intimate ties at this time in their life, are at risk for loneliness. However, as long as it is not too intense, loneliness can encourage young people to reach out to others and better understand themselves.

Wide variation exists in the sequence and timing of phases of family life cycle. Departure from the parental home is a major step toward assuming adult responsibilities, although nearly half of young adults return home for a brief time after initial leaving. Young adults delay marriage more today than a half-century ago. Women's workplace participation affects both traditional and egalitarian marriages in defining marital roles, most couples attain a form of marriage in between traditional and egalitarian. Modern couples are having fewer children and postponing parenthood longer than in past generations. The transition to parenthood profoundly alters the lives of husbands and wives. But marriages that are gratifying and supportive tend to remain so after childbirth, whereas troubled marriages usually become more distressed. Parent education programs can help parents clarify their child-rearing values and use more effective strategies.

Today, more adults are single than in the past. Also, cohabitation has increased dramatically, and number of couples who choose to remain childless has risen as well. Voluntarily childless adults tend to be well educated and career-oriented and are just as satisfied with their lives as are parents who have good relationships with their children. Nearly half of all marriages end in divorce, and many divorcees remarry, resulting in blended families with unique challenges. Never-married parenthood has increased and, for low-SES women, often increases financial hardship. Families headed by homosexuals fare well, except for difficulties related to living in an unsupportive society.

Men's career paths are usually continuous, whereas women's are often discontinuous due to child rearing and other family needs. Although women and ethnic minorities have entered nearly all professions, they tend to be concentrated in occupations that are less well-paid and that offer little opportunity for advancement. Dual-earner marriages, now the norm, often face complex career decisions and challenges in meeting both work and family responsibilities. When dual-earner couples cooperate to surmount difficulties, they benefit from higher earnings, a better standard of living, and women's self-fulfillment and improved well-being.

LEARNING OBJECTIVES

After reading this chapter, you should be able to:

14.1 Describe Erikson's stage of intimacy versus isolation, noting related research findings. (pp. 446–447)

14.2 Summarize Levinson's and Vaillant's psychosocial theories of adult personality development, including how they apply to both men and women's lives and their limitations. (pp. 447–449)

14.3 Describe the social clock and how it relates to personality in adulthood. (p. 449)

14.4 Discuss factors that affect mate selection and the role of romantic love in the young adult's quest for intimacy. (pp. 450–452)

14.5 Explain how culture influences the experience of love. (pp. 452–453)

14.6 Cite characteristics of adult friendships, including differences between same-sex, other-sex, and sibling friendships. (pp. 453–455)

14.7 Cite factors that influence loneliness, and explain its role in early adult development. (p. 455)

14.8 Trace phases of the family life cycle that are prominent in early adulthood, and cite factors that influence these phases today. (pp. 456–465)

14.9 Discuss the diversity of adult lifestyles, focusing on singlehood, cohabitation, and childlessness. (pp. 466–468)

14.10 Discuss today's high rates of divorce and remarriage, and cite factors that contribute to them. (pp. 468–469)

14.11 Summarize the challenges associated with variant styles of parenthood, including stepparents, never-married parents, and gay and lesbian parents. (pp. 469–471)

14.12 Describe patterns of career development, and cite difficulties faced by women, ethnic minorities, and couples seeking to combine work and family. (pp. 471–474)

STUDY QUESTIONS

Erikson's Theory: Intimacy versus Isolation

1. According to Erikson, what is the psychological conflict of early adulthood? (p. 446)

_____

2. Describe the characteristics of individuals who have achieved a sense of intimacy and those who have a sense of isolation. (pp. 446–447)

Intimacy: _____

_____

Isolation: _____

_____

3. Erikson believed that successful resolution of intimacy versus isolation prepares the individual for the middle adulthood stage, which focuses on _____—caring for next generation and helping to improve society. (p. 447)

Levinson's Seasons of Life

1. True or False: Like Erikson, Levinson conceived of development as a sequence of qualitatively distinct eras (stages or seasons). (p. 447)

2. Each era begins with a _____, lasting about 5 years, which concludes the previous era and prepares the person for the next. (p. 447)

3. According to Levinson, what is the *life structure*? (p. 447)

   _____

   _____

4. Describe differences in the life dreams of men and women. (pp. 447–448)

   Men: _____

   _____

   Women: _____

   _____

5. How do mentors facilitate realization of young adults' dreams? Who are mentors likely to be? (p. 448)

   A. _____

   _____

   B. _____

   _____

6. How does career development differ for men and women? (p. 448)

   _____

   _____

7. Explain how young people reevaluate their life structure during the age-30 transition. (p. 448)

   _____

   _____

   _____

8. True or False: For men and women without satisfying relational or occupational accomplishments, the age-30 transition can be a relief. (p. 448)

9. Describe women's experiences with "settling down" during their thirties. How do their experiences compare to those of men? (pp. 448–449)

Women's Experiences: _____

_____

Men's Experiences: _____

_____

Vaillant's Adaptation to Life

1. Using Vaillant's theory, explain how men alter themselves and their social world to adapt to life at the following ages: (p. 449)

Twenties: _____

Thirties: _____

Forties: _____

Fifties: _____

Limitations of Levinson's and Vaillant's Theories

1. Identify three limitations of Levinson's and Vaillant's theories. (p. 449)

A. _____

B. _____

C. _____

The Social Clock

1. What is the *social clock,* and how does it influence adult development? (p. 449)

_____

_____

_____

2. Describe characteristics of college women born in the 1930s who followed a "feminine" social clock, a "masculine" social clock, or no social clock at all. (pp. 449–450)

Feminine: _____

Masculine: _____

No social clock: _____

3. How does following a social clock foster confidence during early adulthood? (p. 450)

_____

_____

Romantic Love

1. True or False: In selecting a mate, research suggests that "opposites attract." (pp. 450–451)

2. Men and women differ in the importance they place on certain characteristics when selecting a mate. How do the ethological and social learning perspectives explain this difference? (p. 451)

    Ethological: _____

    _____

    Social learning: _____

    _____

3. List the three components of Sternberg's *triangular theory of love.* (p. 451)

    A. _____   B. _____

    C. _____

4. Explain how intimacy, passion, and commitment shift in emphasis as a relationship develops. (p. 451)

    _____

    _____

    _____

5. What aspect of love probably determines whether a relationship survives? (p. 451)

    _____

6. What features define mature love in Western nations? (p. 452)

    _____

    _____

    _____

7. How does the Western perspective of love compare to the perspectives of Eastern cultures? (pp. 452–453)

    _____

    _____

    _____

Friendships

1. Cite three benefits of adult friendship. (p. 453)

    A. _____   B. _____

    C. _____

2. What features characterize adult friendships? (p. 454)

    _____

    _____

    _____

3. Compare characteristics of women's same-sex friendships with those of men. (p. 454)

Women: _____

_____

Men: _____

_____

4. True or False: Involvement in family roles affects reliance on friends. (p. 454)

5. What group of young adults has the largest number of other-sex friends? (p. 454)

_____

6. What are some benefits of other-sex friendships? (p. 454)

_____

7. True or False: Women are more likely than men to feel sexually attracted to an other-sex friend. (p. 455)

8. Explain why friend and sibling roles often merge in early adulthood. (p. 455)

9. In Vaillant's study of well-educated men, what was the best predictor of emotional health at age 65? (p. 455)

_____

Loneliness

1. What are some situations in which adults experience *loneliness*? (p. 455)

_____

_____

2. True or False: Loneliness is at its peak during the teens and early twenties, after which it declines steadily into the seventies. (p. 455)

3. When not involved in a romantic relationship, (men / women) feel lonelier, perhaps because they have fewer alternatives for satisfying intimacy needs. (p. 456)

4. Describe personal characteristics that contribute to loneliness. (p. 456)

_____

_____

_____

5. How can loneliness be motivating? (p. 456)

_____

_____

A Lifespan Vista: Childhood Attachment Patterns and Adult Romantic Relationships

1. Early attachment bonds lead to the construction of an _____, or set of expectations about attachment figures, that serve as a guide for close relationships. (p. 452)

2. Explain how attachment security in childhood influences adult experiences with romantic partners. (pp. 452–453)

_____

_____

_____

The Family Life Cycle

1. What is the *family life cycle*? What are some characteristics of individuals in the early adulthood phase? (p. 456)

   A. _____

   _____

   B. _____

   _____

Leaving Home

1. The average age of leaving the family home has (increased / decreased) in recent years. (p. 456)

2. What are some reasons young adults leave the family home? (pp. 456–457)

   _____

   _____

3. Nearly _____ percent of young adults return home for a brief time after initial leaving. Those who departed to marry are (most / least) likely to return. Those who left because of family conflict (usually / rarely) return. (p. 457)

4. How do SES and ethnicity contribute to early departure from the family home? (p. 457)

   _____

   _____

Joining of Families in Marriage

1. The number of first and second marriages in the United States and Canada has (increased / declined) over the last few decades. (p. 457)

2. Nearly _____ percent of North Americans marry at least once. (p. 457)

3. True or False: When their backgrounds differ greatly, married couples face extra challenges in achieving a successful transition to married life. (p. 458)

4. What is the most consistent predictor of marital stability? (p. 458)

   _____

5. Cite differences between *traditional* and *egalitarian marriages.* (p. 458)

   Traditional: _____

   Egalitarian: _____

6. Cite factors that differentiate troubled from gratifying marital relationships. (p. 459)

   Troubled: _____

   _____

   Gratifying: _____

   _____

7. Summarize sex differences in the relationship between marital satisfaction and mental health. (p. 459)

   Men: _____

   Women: _____

8. List three components in which marital happiness is grounded. (p. 459)

   A. _____

   B. _____

   C. _____

9. In a study of college students, more women than men said their partners should be (inferior / superior) to themselves and more men that women said their partners should be (inferior / superior) to themselves. How do these perceptions differentially influence the behavior of men and women? (p. 459)

   Men: _____

   Women: _____

10. Cite four myths that college students have about marital bliss. (p. 459)

   A. _____

   B. _____

   C. _____

   D. _____

11. Why are young people who hold a religious view of marriage as sacred less likely to enter it with unrealistic expectations? (p. 460)

   _____

   _____

12. True or False: Most couples spend little time reflecting on the decision to marry before their wedding day. (p. 460)

Parenthood

1. Family size in industrialized nations has (increased / declined). (p. 461)

2. List three factors which affect the decision to have children. (p. 461)

   A. _____ B. _____

   C. _____

3. True or False: Women with high-status, demanding careers less often choose parenthood and, when they do, more often delay it than women with less time-consuming jobs. (p. 461)

4. List two reasons for having children that are most important to parents across ethnic groups and geographic regions. (p. 462)

   A. _____ B. _____

5. Cite two disadvantages of parenthood mentioned most often by young adults. (p. 462)

   A. _____ B. _____

6. List some changes that occur in the early weeks after a baby enters the family. (p. 462)

_____

_____

_____

_____

7. After the arrival of a new baby, the roles of husbands and wives become (more / less) traditional. (p. 462)

8. List factors that contribute to marital satisfaction after childbirth. (p. 462)

_____

_____

_____

_____

9. True or False: In many non-Western cultures, childbirth has little or no impact on marital satisfaction. (p. 463)

10. How do interventions aimed at easing the transition to parenthood differ for couples who are not at high risk for problems and couples who are high risk? (p. 463)

Low Risk: _____

High Risk: _____

11. Besides more effective birth control, what is a major reason that couples in industrialized nations have fewer children today than in the past? (p. 463)

_____

12. Briefly describe benefits of maintaining a small family. (p. 463)

_____

_____

13. What are some characteristics that contribute to the negative relationship between family size and well-being? (p. 463)

_____

_____

14. True or False: In today's complex world, men and women are more certain about how to rear children than they were in previous generations. (p. 463)

15. Explain how the couple's relationship influences the quality of parenting. (p. 463)

_____

_____

16. Identify some benefits of child rearing for adult development. (p. 465)

_____

_____

17. Briefly describe how adolescence brings changes in parental roles. (p. 465)

_____

_____

18. List three advantages of parent education programs. (p. 465)

A. _____

B. _____

C. _____

Social Issues: Partner Abuse

1. True or False: Research shows that men are far more likely than women to abuse their spouse. Elaborate on your response. (p. 460)

2. List three reasons both husbands and wives give for abusing their spouse. (p. 460)

A. _____   B. _____

C. _____

3. Describe factors that contribute to spouse abuse. (p. 460)

Psychological: _____

_____

_____

Family: _____

_____

_____

Cultural: _____

_____

4. List five reasons why many people do not leave destructive relationships before abuse escalates. (p. 461)

A. _____

B. _____

C. _____

D. _____

E. _____

Cultural Influences: A Global Perspective on Family Planning

1. Explain how poverty and rapid population growth are intertwined. (p. 464)

_____

_____

2. Cite two interrelated strategies for intervening in the cycle of poverty and population growth. (p. 464)

A. _____

B. _____

3. What are some barriers to accessing family planning information? (p. 464)

_____

_____

The Diversity of Adult Lifestyles

Singlehood

1. Cite two factors that have contributed to the growing numbers of single adults. (p. 466)

A. _____ B. _____

2. Why are there more single adult men than women? (p. 466)

_____

3. According to the text, singlehood is a multifaceted experience with different meanings. Explain what this means. (p. 466)

_____

_____

_____

4. List the two most often mentioned advantages of singlehood, as well as five drawbacks of singlehood. (p. 466)

Advantages: _____

Drawbacks: _____

Cohabitation

1. Define *cohabitation,* and explain which group of young people has experienced an especially dramatic rise in this type of lifestyle. (pp. 466–467)

A. _____

B. _____

2. For some, cohabitation serves as _____ for marriage—a time to test the relationship and get used to living together. For others, it is an _____ to marriage—an arrangement that offers the rewards of sexual intimacy and companionship along with the possibility of easy departure if satisfaction declines. (p. 467)

3. American and Canadian couples who cohabit before marriage are (more / less) prone to divorce than married couples who did not cohabit. (p. 467)

4. How does the cohabitation experience contribute to the negative outcomes associated with living together before marriage? (p. 467)

_____

_____

_____

5. Cite advantages of cohabitation. (p. 468)

_____

_____

Childlessness

1. List reasons couples choose to remain childless. (p. 468)

_____

_____

2. True or False: Voluntarily childless adults are just as content with their lives as parents who have warm relationships with their children. (p. 468)

Divorce and Remarriage

1. Cite three factors related to divorce. (p. 468)

   A. _____

   B. _____

   C. _____

2. Why do women who were in traditional marriages have more difficulty adjusting to divorce than women in less traditional marriages? (p. 469)

_____

_____

3. True or False: On average, women remarry somewhat faster than men. (p. 469)

4. Summarize three reasons remarriages are especially vulnerable to breakup. (p. 469)

   A. _____

   B. _____

   C. _____

Variant Styles of Parenthood

1. Why are stepmothers especially likely to experience conflict? (p. 469)

_____

_____

2. What are three crucial ingredients for positive stepparent adjustment? (p. 470)

    A. _____

    B. _____

    C. _____

3. In the United States, the largest group of never-married parents are _____. (p. 470)

4. How do children of never-married parents usually fare? What factors determine their well-being? (p. 470)

    A. _____

    _____

    B. _____

    _____

5. True or False: Children of gay and lesbian parents are as committed to and effective at child rearing as heterosexual parents. (p. 470)

6. How are families headed by homosexuals distinguished from heterosexual families? (p. 471)

    _____

    _____

Career Development

Establishing a Career

1. Why can entry into the workforce be discouraging, even for those who enter their chosen field? (p. 471)

    _____

    _____

2. How do personal characteristics affect career progress? (p. 472)

    _____

3. Access to an effective mentor is jointly affected by _____ and _____.
   (p. 472)

Women and Ethnic Minorities

1. True of False: Women generally remain concentrated in occupations that offer little opportunity for advancement.
   (p. 472)

2. What three factors slow women's advancement even when they do enter high-status professions? (p. 472)

    A. _____

    B. _____

    C. _____

3. Cite examples of racial bias in the labor market. (p. 472)

_____

_____

_____

Combining Work and Family

1. Define *dual-earner marriage.* What are the main sources of strain in these families? (p. 473)

   A. _____

   _____

   B. _____

   _____

2. Role overload is greater for (men / women). (p. 474)

3. What factors determine how well dual-earner families function? (p. 474)

   _____

   _____

ASK YOURSELF . . .

For *Ask Yourself* questions for this chapter, please log on to the Companion Website at www.ablongman.com/berk.

SUGGESTED STUDENT READINGS

Cowan, C. P., & Cowan, P. A. (1999). *When partners become parents: The big life change for couples (2nd ed.).* Mahwah, NJ: Erlbaum. Explores the joys, challenges, and changes that couples face with the transition to parenthood.

Drucker, J. (1998). *Families of value: Gay and lesbian parents and their children speak out.* New York: Insight Books/Plenum Press. A collection of personal accounts by gay and lesbian families regarding the unique roles and challenges associated with raising children in a homophobic society. The author maintains that a nurturing environment contributes to healthy child development, regardless of the gender or sexual orientation of caregivers.

Hetherington, E. M. (Ed.). (1999). *Coping with divorce, single parenting, and remarriage: A risk and resiliency perspective.* Mahwah, NJ: Erlbaum. Explores individual, familial, and extrafamilial risk and protective factors in an attempt to explain parents' and children's responses to events associated with marriage, divorce, life in a single parent household, and remarriage.

Russell, A., Sobo, E. J., & Thompson, M. S. (Eds.). (2000). *Conception across cultures: Technologies, choices, constraints.* New York: Berg. A collection of chapters highlighting the social, economic, political, and cultural contexts of contraception use, family planning, and reproductive health.

PUZZLE 14.1 TERM REVIEW

Across

1. Social _____: age-graded expectations for life events, such as beginning a first job, getting married, birth of a first child, etc.
2. _____ versus isolation: Erikson's psychological conflict of young
4. According to Sternberg's _____ theory of love, love has three components—intimacy, passion, and commitment—that shift in emphasis as the romantic relationship develops
6. In Levinson's theory, the underlying pattern or design of a person's life at a given time is called the _____ structure
9. Lifestyle of unmarried individuals who have an intimate, sexual relationship and share a residence
10. Love based on intense sexual attraction
11. _____ life cycle: sequence of phases that characterizes the development of most families around the world

Down

1. Love based on warm, rusting affection and caretgiving
3. _____ marriage: form of marriage involving clear division of husband's and wife's roles
5. _____ marriage: form of marriage in which husband and wife share power and authority
7. In a _____-_____ marriage, both husband and wife are employed
8. Feelings of unhappiness that result from a gap between actual and desired social relationships

PRACTICE TEST #1

1. Intimacy versus isolation refers to (p. 446)
   a. the young person's thoughts and feelings about making a permanent commitment to an intimate partner.
   b. a feeling of hopelessness about the future.
   c. the age-30 transition.
   d. a period of instability for women and stability for men.

2. The life structure, a key concept of Levinson's theory, consists of (p. 447)
   a. feelings about the past.
   b. relationships with significant others.
   c. superficial relationships with people outside of one's immediate family.
   d. past events that influence how young adults cope with the age-30 transition.

3. Women's *dreams,* or images of the self in the adult world, are likely to (pp. 447–448)
   a. be split between marriage and career.
   b. be the same as men's.
   c. be more individualistic than men's.
   d. emphasize independence and career.

4. Vaillant's theory (p. 449)
   a. contradicts Levinson's theory.
   b. fills in gaps between Erikson's stages.
   c. included the study of women, unlike Levinson's.
   d. is based on experimental research.

5. According to the social learning perspective, gender roles (p. 449)
   a. profoundly influence criteria for mate selection among individuals of both sexes.
   b. influence men's criteria for mate selection but not women's.
   c. influence women's criteria for mate selection but not men's.
   d. have little influence on criteria for mate selection.

6. At the beginning of a relationship (p. 451)
   a. companionate love is especially strong.
   b. passionate love is especially strong.
   c. couples rarely experience love.
   d. couples who develop passionate love usually break up.

7. Couples who report having higher quality long-term relationships (p. 451)
   a. have sex much more often than the average couple.
   b. somehow keep the mystery in their relationship.
   c. credit their success to being very different, because opposites attract.
   d. consistently communicate their commitment to each other.

8. Which of the following statements about same-sex friendships is true? (p. 454)
   a. Like men, women report many barriers to intimacy with same-sex friends.
   b. When together, both male and female friends say they prefer to " do something," instead of "just talk."
   c. Men indicate that they sometimes feel as if they are in competition with male friends.
   d. Men have more intimate same-sex friendships than do women.

9. Young people from divorced, single-parent homes (p. 456)
   a. tend to leave the family home later than their peers.
   b. tend to leave the family home earlier than their peers.
   c. tend to leave the family home at approximately the same time as their peers.
   d. tend to live in the family home through early adulthood.

10. Which of the following statements about marital satisfaction is true? (p. 458)
    a. More women than men report being happily married.
    b. Both men and women report similar levels of satisfaction with their marriages.
    c. More men than women report being happily married.
    d. Most married couples report low levels of marital satisfaction during the early adult years.

11. When asked about the disadvantages of parenthood, young adults most often mention (p. 462)
    a. not receiving spousal support.
    b. not being able to save for their child's college education.
    c. loss of freedom.
    d. unwanted child-rearing advice from in-laws.

12. Compared to previous generations, men and women (p. 462)
    a. are more certain about how to rear children.
    b. have distinct and often oppositional viewpoints about how to rear children.
    c. are less certain about how to rear children.
    d. exhibit more punitive child-rearing styles.

13. When well-educated, high income parents have large families (p. 463)
    a. their financial situation often takes a turn for the worse.
    b. unfavorable outcomes, such as poorer physical health and lower IQ, are eliminated.
    c. marital satisfaction declines.
    d. older siblings are often ignored.

14. Which of the following statements about singlehood is true? (p. 466)
    a. Single women tend to have more physical and emotional health problems than single men, who usually come to terms with their lifestyle.
    b. The number of single adults in North American has declined in recent years.
    c. More young adult men than women are single.
    d. The percentage of never-married Caucasian Americans is nearly twice as great as that of African Americans.

15. American and Canadian couples who cohabit before marriage are (p. 467)
    a. more committed to each other and display more adaptive patterns of communication than couples who did not cohabit.
    b. more likely to divorce than married couples who did not cohabit.
    c. more prepared for the demands of marriage.
    d. more likely have conventional values.

16. For most divorced adults, negative reactions to divorce subside within (p. 469)
    a. 1 month.
    b. 6 months.
    c. 2 years.
    d. 5 to 7 years.

17. In the United States, the largest group of never-married parents are young (p. 470)
    a. Asian women.
    b. Mexican-American men.
    c. African-American women.
    d. Caucasian men.

18. Research on gay and lesbian parents indicates that (p. 470)
    a. their children are at-risk for maladjustment.
    b. they are as committed to and effective at child rearing as heterosexual parents.
    c. they are less committed to child rearing than heterosexual parents.
    d. they are often inconsistent and harsh with their children.

19. In general, women (p. 472)
    a. are overrepresented in executive and managerial jobs.
    b. earn nearly as much as men.
    c. remain concentrated in occupations that offer little opportunity for advancement.
    d. tend to feel confident about entering male-dominated fields.

20. Which of the following statements represents a major source of strain in dual-earner marriages? (p. 473)
    a. Women are often resentful toward their spouse, especially when he earns more money.
    b. Men often settle into unrewarding careers.
    c. Women are at-risk for role overload, or conflict between work and family responsibilities.
    d. Couples in more prestigious careers have less control over both work and family than couples in low-status work roles.

PRACTICE TEST #2

1. Like Erikson, Levinson conceived of development as (p. 447)
    a. a continuous sequence extending into late adulthood.
    b. especially turbulent for women.
    c. a. sequence of qualitatively distinct eras.
    d. biologically determined.

2. Levinson found that during the early adult transition, most individuals construct a(n) (p. 447)
    a. occupational identity.
    b. life structure.
    c. dream.
    d. social clock.

3. Mentors (p. 448)
    a. offer general advice about life but rarely have direct experience in the word that the person seeks to enter.
    b. are often assigned by large corporations but have little meaningful impact on young adults' occupational development.
    c. are only available to individuals entering high-status careers.
    d. are more readily available to men than to women.

4. In comparing her own life status to that of her same-age friends, Ellie noticed that she was significantly delayed in getting married and starting a family. As a consequence, Ellie was lonely, felt poorly about herself, and questioned her future. Which of the following is best illustrated by this example? (p. 449)
    a. the life structure
    b. the social clock
    c. the age-30 transition
    d. the family life cycle

5. When it comes to selecting a mate (p. 451)
    a. opposites attract.
    b. women prefer partners who are healthy and younger than themselves.
    c. men place more emphasis than women on physical attractiveness.
    d. both men and women place emphasis on intelligence, ambition, and moral character.

6. In the transformation of romantic involvements from passionate to companionate, commitment (p. 451)
   a. has little effect on the quality of the relationship.
   b. probably determines whether the relationship will survive.
   c. often declines as the relationship endures.
   d. is more important to men than women.

7. Compared to Eastern cultural perspectives, Western views of mature love are more likely to focus on (p. 452)
   a. lifelong dependence on your chosen partner.
   b. obligations to others, particularly parents.
   c. companionship and practical matters, such as similarity of background, career promise, and likelihood of being a good parent.
   d. autonomy, appreciation of the partner's unique qualities, and intense emotion.

8. Highly educated, employed women (p. 454)
   a. have the fewest number of other-sex friends.
   b. have the largest number of other-sex friends.
   c. rarely have time for either same-sex or other-sex friends.
   d. often look to other-sex friends for romantic involvement.

9. In a study of well-educated men, a close sibling tie in early adulthood (p. 455)
   a. was the single best predictor of emotional health at age 65.
   b. was the single best predictor of marital stability at age 65.
   c. was important for short-term emotional health but showed no long-term benefits.
   d. did little to alleviate feelings of loneliness.

10. Which of the following adults is likely to experience loneliness? (p. 455)
    a. Meg, a married mother of two, who has a small group of friends with whom she plays cards with twice a month.
    b. Joel, a recent college graduate, who just started a new job but continues to live with his college roommates.
    c. Denzel, a recently divorced father, who stays in contact with his ex-wife and child.
    d. Brenda, a college student, who still lives at home with her parents.

11. Which of the following beliefs is true? (p. 460)
    a. The best single predictor of marital satisfaction is the quality of the couple's sex life.
    b. If my spouse loves me, he or she should instinctively know what I want and need to be happy.
    c. No matter how I behave, my spouse should love me simply because he or she is my spouse.
    d. Young people who hold a religious view of marriage as sacred are less likely to enter it with unrealistic expectations.

12. The arrival of a baby results in little marital strain (p. 462)
    a. in marriages that are supportive.
    b. in troubled marriages.
    c. when women take primary responsibility for caregiving.
    d. in younger couples just launching their careers.

13. Which of the following are frequently cited advantages of singlehood? (p. 466)
    a. freedom and mobility
    b. exciting social and sex lives
    c. greater sense of financial security
    d. reduced loneliness

14. Voluntarily childless adults (p. 468)
    a. are just as content with their lives as parents who have warm relationships with their children.
    b. are less content with their lives than parents who have warm relationships with their children.
    c. generally have marriages that become increasingly unhappy over time.
    d. almost never change their minds about having children later in life.

15. Which of the following factors increases the chances of divorce? (p. 468)
    a. older age at marriage
    b. having parents who divorced
    c. high religious involvement
    d. high SES

16. Which of the following is true about adults' adjustment to divorce? (p. 469)
    a. Immediately after separation, women are more likely than men to become depressed and anxious and display impulsive behavior.
    b. Women who were in traditional marriages have the easiest time adjusting to divorce.
    c. Finding a new partner is more crucial for women, since they are better adjusted in the context of marriage than on their own.
    d. Although they are more lonely and have less income, most divorced women prefer their new life to an unhappy marriage.

17. Which of the following is true about remarriage? (p. 469)
    a. On average, women remarry sooner than men.
    b. Second marriages are less vulnerable to divorce than first marriages.
    c. People often transfer patterns of interaction from the first to the second marriage.
    d. Most remarriages take place within a year after divorce.

18. Which of the following is true of career development in early adulthood? (p. 472)
    a. Men have more discontinuous career paths than women.
    b. Most young people must revise their aspirations for promotion downward.
    c. The best mentors for career advancement are top executives.
    d. Individuals' beliefs about their ability to be successful have little impact on their actual career development.

19. In a study of racial bias in the labor market, researchers found that (p. 472)
    a. résumés with white-sounding names evoked more callbacks than résumés with black sounding names.
    b. as a result of Affirmative Action, individuals with black-sounding names received more callbacks than individuals with white-sounding names, regardless of the quality of their résumé.
    c. individuals with high-quality résumés received more callbacks than individuals with low-quality résumés, regardless of whether their names sounded white or black.
    d. Individuals with black-sounding names received more callbacks for low-paying jobs, while individuals with white-sounding names received more callbacks for skilled and managerial jobs.

20. Career-oriented, successful ethnic minority women (p. 473)
    a. often display unusually high self-efficacy.
    b. face racial but not gender discrimination.
    c. rarely receive support from other women.
    d. tend to have mothers who had low expectations for them.

CHAPTER 15
PHYSICAL AND COGNITIVE DEVELOPMENT
IN MIDDLE ADULTHOOD

BRIEF CHAPTER SUMMARY

Physical development in midlife is a continuation of the gradual changes under way in early adulthood. Age-related deterioration in visual abilities, hearing, and the condition of the skin become more apparent. Weight gain—referred to as "middle-age spread"—is a concern of both men and women. A common pattern of change is an increase in body fat and loss of lean body mass (muscle and bone). A low-fat diet and continued exercise offsets both excess weight and muscle loss. As new cells accumulate on their outer layers, the bones broaden, but their mineral content declines so they become more porous. This leads to a gradual loss in bone mass that begins in the late thirties and accelerates in the fifties, especially among women.

The climacteric, or decline in fertility, occurs gradually over a 10-year period for women. The climacteric concludes with menopause, the end of menstruation and reproductive capacity. Many doctors recommend hormone therapy to reduce the discomforts of menopause and to protect women from other impairments due to estrogen loss. The wide variation in physical symptoms and attitudes indicates that menopause is more than just a hormonal event; it is affected by societal beliefs and practices as well. Men also experience a climacteric, but the change is limited to a decrease in quantity of semen and sperm after age 40.

Frequency of sexual activity among married couples tends to decline in middle adulthood. Sexual activity in midlife, as in earlier periods, is the combined result of biological, psychological, and social forces. Cancer and cardiovascular disease are the leading causes of death in middle age. Unintentional injuries continue to be a major health threat, although they occur at a lower rate than in young adulthood, largely because motor vehicle collisions decline. When age-related bone loss is severe, a condition called osteoporosis develops. Hostility and anger predicts heart disease in both men and women.

Stress management in middle adulthood can limit the age-related rise in illness and, when disease strikes, reduce its severity. Heredity, diet, exercise, social support, coping strategies, and hardiness contribute to middle-aged adults' ability to cope with stress. Negative stereotypes of aging lead many middle-aged adults to fear physical changes. These unfavorable stereotypes are more likely to be applied to women than to men, yielding a double standard. However, new surveys suggest that the double standard of aging is declining.

Although declines in cognitive development occur in some areas, most people display cognitive competencies, especially in familiar contexts, and some attain outstanding accomplishment. Consistent with the lifespan perspective, cognitive change in middle adulthood is viewed as multidimensional, multidirectional, and plastic. Crystallized intelligence (which depends on accumulated knowledge and experience) increases steadily through middle adulthood, whereas fluid intelligence (which depends on basic information-processing skills) begins to decline in the 20s. Research shows that using intellectual skills seems to affect the degree to which they are maintained.

Speed of cognitive processing slows with age, a change explained by either the neural network view or the information-loss view. Slower processing speed makes it harder for middle-aged people to divide their attention, focus on relevant stimuli, and switch from one task to another as the situation demands. Memory is crucially important for all aspects of information processing. With age, the amount of information people can retain in working memory diminishes but general factual knowledge, procedural knowledge, and knowledge related to one's occupation either remain unchanged or increase into midlife. Middle-aged adults in all walks of life often become good at practical problem solving, largely due to development of expertise, and creativity becomes more deliberately thoughtful.

At all ages and in different cultures, the relationship between vocational life and cognitive development is reciprocal. Stimulating, complex work and flexible, abstract, autonomous thinking support one another. Often motivated by life transitions, adults are returning to undergraduate and graduate study in record numbers. Women are the majority of adult learners, and role demands outside the educational setting pull many women in several, often conflicting directions. Social supports for returning students can make the difference between continuing in school and dropping out.

LEARNING OBJECTIVES

After reading this chapter, you should be able to:

15.1 Describe physical changes of middle adulthood, including those related to vision, hearing, the skin and bones, and muscle–fat makeup. (pp. 483–484)

15.2 Summarize the reproductive changes experienced by middle-aged men and women, paying special attention to the symptoms of menopause, the benefits and risks of hormone therapy, and women's psychological reactions to menopause. (pp. 486–487)

15.3 Discuss sexuality in midlife, noting changes in frequency of sexual activity and intensity of sexual response. (p. 489)

15.4 Discuss the risks of illness and disability in middle adulthood, with particular attention to risk factors and interventions for cancer, cardiovascular disease, and osteoporosis. (pp. 489–493)

15.5 Discuss the association of hostility and anger with heart disease and other health problems. (p. 494)

15.6 Explain the benefits of stress management, exercise, and an optimistic outlook for dealing effectively with the physical challenges of midlife. (pp. 494–496)

15.7 Discuss the double standard of aging. (p. 497)

15.8 Describe changes in crystallized and fluid intelligence during middle adulthood, and discuss individual and group differences in intellectual development. (pp. 498–501)

15.9 Describe changes in information processing in midlife, paying special attention to speed of processing, attention, and memory. (pp. 501–503)

15.10 Summarize the cognitive changes of midlife that are associated with practical problem solving, expertise, and creativity. (pp. 503–505)

15.11 Discuss the relationship between vocational life and cognitive development. (p. 505)

15.12 Discuss challenges facing adults who return to college, ways of supporting returning students, and benefits of earning a degree in midlife. (pp. 506–507)

STUDY QUESTIONS

Physical Development

Physical Changes

Vision

1. Describe the condition known as *presbyopia*, and explain how changes in the structures of the eye cause many individuals to develop this condition during midlife. (p. 483)

_____

_____

_____

322

2. Cite two declines in visual functioning that are associated with yellowing of the lens, shrinking of the pupil, and increasing density of the vitreous. (p. 483)

   A. _____

   B. _____

3. After age 40, adults are at increased risk for _____ —a disease in which pressure builds up within the eye due to poor fluid drainage, causing damage to the optic nerve. (p. 484)

Hearing

1. True or False: Most adult-onset hearing impairments are age-related rather than hereditary. (p. 484)

2. Cite two physical changes which lead to age-related hearing loss. (p. 484)

   A. _____

   B. _____

3. (Men's / Women's) hearing tends to decline earlier. Why is this the case? (p. 484)

   _____
   _____

Skin

1. Name and describe the three layers that make up our skin, and describe how each changes with age. (p. 484)

   A. _____

   Changes: _____

   B. _____

   Changes: _____

   C. _____

   Changes: _____

Muscle–Fat Makeup

1. Summarize changes in body fat and muscle mass in middle adulthood. (p. 484)

   _____
   _____
   _____

2. Explain how weight gain and muscle loss can be prevented. (p. 484)

   _____
   _____
   _____

Skeleton

1. What change leads to substantial reduction in bone density during adulthood? (p. 486)

    _____

2. Cite one health problem associated with weakened bones. (p. 486)

    _____

3. Name several interventions that can slow bone loss in postmenopausal women. (p. 486)

    _____

    _____

Reproductive System

1. The midlife transition in which fertility declines is called the _____. (p. 486)

2. In women, the climacteric concludes with _____ —the end of menstruation and reproductive capacity. This occurs, on average, at _____ age among North American, European, and East Asian women. (p. 486)

3. Summarize the gradual changes which precede menopause, as well as the physical changes which occur subsequent to menopause. (p. 486)

    Changes preceding menopause: _____

    _____

    _____

    Changes subsequent to menopause: _____

    _____

    _____

4. Describe two types of hormone therapy. (p. 486)

    A. _____

    _____

    B. _____

    _____

5. Review the benefits and risks associated with hormone therapy. (p. 486)

    Benefits: _____

    _____

    Risks: _____

    _____

6. List several lifestyle changes that help to control the symptoms of menopause. (p. 486)

    _____

    _____

7. Describe women's psychological reactions to menopause, and explain what factors affect these reactions. (p. 487)

_____

_____

_____

8. True or False: Men lose their reproductive capacity during midlife and can no longer father children. (p. 487)

9. Summarize the reproductive changes experienced by middle-aged men. (p. 487)

_____

_____

_____

Biology & Environment: Anti-Aging Effects on Dietary Calorie Restriction: Relevant to Humans?

1. True or False: In nonhuman animals, reduction of daily caloric intake has been shown to slow aging while maintaining good health. (p. 485)

2. Summarize the physiological consequences of calorie restriction in monkeys. (p. 485)

_____

_____

_____

3. Describe two natural experiments that have provided some information about the effects of calorie restriction in humans. (p. 485)

    A. _____

        _____

    B. _____

        _____

4. Explain factors that make it difficult to study the impact of reduced caloric intake in humans. (p. 485)

_____

_____

_____

Cultural Influences: Menopause as a Biocultural Event

1. Summarize the differing views of menopause held by individuals in Western industrialized nations compared to their non-Western counterparts, noting how these disparate views impact reported symptoms of menopause. (p. 488)

    Western: _____

    _____

Non-Western: _____

_____

Impact on reported symptoms: _____

_____

2. True or False: Japanese women and doctors, like their North American counterparts, consider menopause to be a significant marker of female middle age. (p. 488)

3. Compare Mayan and Greek perspectives on menopause, noting similarities and differences. (p. 488)

Similarities: _____

_____

Differences: _____

_____

Health and Fitness

Sexuality

1. True or False: Frequency of sexual activity declines dramatically in middle adulthood, particularly after women go through menopause. (p. 489)

2. What is the best predictor of sexual frequency in midlife? (p. 489)

_____

3. How does the intensity of sexual response change during middle adulthood? (p. 489)

_____

_____

4. During middle adulthood, more (men / women) report having no sexual partners in the previous year. What factors are responsible for this gender difference in sexual activity? (p. 489)

Illness and Disability

1. List the two leading causes of death in midlife. (p. 489)

A. _____

B. _____

2. Middle-aged (men / women) are more vulnerable to most health problems. (p. 489)

3. Explain how cancer occurs, noting what happens when a cell's genetic program is disrupted. (p. 489)

_____

_____

_____

4. Describe three factors that contribute to the risk of cancer. (p. 489)

   A. _____
   _____

   B. _____
   _____

   C. _____
   _____

5. Name the most common types of cancer among men and women. (p. 490)

   Men: _____

   Women: _____

6. Cancer (is / is not) curable. (p. 491)

7. Describe at least five ways to reduce cancer illness and death rates. (p. 491)

   A. _____

   B. _____

   C. _____

   D. _____

   E. _____

8. Describe the relationship between SES and cancer, noting factors responsible for SES differences in cancer survival rates. (p. 491)

   _____
   _____
   _____

9. List three indicators of cardiovascular disease that are known as "silent killers" because they often have no symptoms. (p. 491)

   A. _____

   B. _____

   C. _____

10. Describe three symptoms of cardiovascular disease which are evident to the affected individual. (p. 492)

   A. _____
   _____

B. _____

_____

C. _____

_____

11. List eight ways to reduce the risk of having a heart attack. (p. 492)

A. _____

B. _____

C. _____

D. _____

E. _____

F. _____

G. _____

H. _____

12. Accurate diagnosis of cardiovascular disease is of special concern to (women / men), since doctors frequently overlook their symptoms. (p. 492)

13. When age-related bone loss is severe, a condition called _____ develops. (p. 493)

14. Summarize the symptoms of osteoporosis. (p. 493)

_____

_____

_____

15. List biological and environmental risk factors associated with osteoporosis. (p. 493)

Biological: _____

_____

Environmental: _____

_____

16. List several interventions for treating osteoporosis. (p. 493)

_____

_____

Hostility and Anger

1. Describe characteristics of the *Type A behavior pattern.* (p. 493)

   _____

   _____

   _____

2. What is the "toxic" ingredient of Type A, since isolating this characteristic from global Type A consistently predicts heart disease and other health problems in both men and women? (p. 493)

   _____

3. Explain the link between expressed hostility and health problems. (p. 494)

   _____

   _____

   _____

4. True or False: Suppressing anger is a healthier way of healing with negative feelings than is expressing anger. (p. 494)

Adapting to the Physical Challenges of Midlife

Stress Management

1. Identify at least five ways to manage stress. (p. 494)

   A. _____

   B. _____

   C. _____

   D. _____

   E. _____

2. Distinguish between *problem-centered* and *emotion-centered* coping. (p. 495)

   Problem-centered: _____

   _____

   Emotion-centered: _____

   _____

3. What approach to coping is most effective for reducing stress? (p. 495)

   _____

4. Cite several constructive approaches to anger reduction. (p. 495)

   _____

   _____

5. Summarize changes in coping with stress from early to middle adulthood. (p. 495)

_____

_____

_____

6. Communities provide (more / fewer) social supports to middle-aged individuals relative to young adults and senior citizens. (p. 495)

Exercise

1. Of those who begin an exercise program in midlife, _____ percent discontinue within the first six months. Among those who stay active, fewer than percent exercise at levels that lead to fewer health problems. (p. 496)

2. Define *self-efficacy,* and describe the link between self-efficacy and exercise. (p. 496)

   Definition: _____

   _____

   Link to exercise: _____

   _____

3. Identify characteristics of beginning exercisers that best fit group versus home-based exercise programs. (p. 496)

   Group: _____

   _____

   Home-based: _____

   _____

An Optimistic Outlook

1. _____ refers to a set of three personal qualities that help people cope with stress adaptively, thereby reducing its impact on illness and mortality. List and describe the three qualities that make up this trait. (p. 496)

   A. _____

   _____

   B. _____

   _____

   C. _____

   _____

2. Summarize differences in the coping strategies used by high-hardy and low-hardy individuals. (pp. 496–497)

   High-hardy: _____

   _____

   Low-hardy: _____

   _____

3. Describe the link between hardiness and physiological arousal. (p. 497)

_____

_____

_____

Gender and Aging: A Double Standard

1. Unfavorable stereotypes about aging are more often applied to (women / men), who are rated as less attractive and as having more negative characteristics. (p. 497)

2. What factor do researchers believe is at the heart of the double standard of aging? (p. 497)

_____

3. New evidence suggests that the double standard of aging is (increasing / declining). (p. 497)

Cognitive Development

Changes in Mental Abilities

1. Describe three core principles of the lifespan perspective which are exemplified by the cognitive changes of middle adulthood. (p. 498)

A. _____

_____

B. _____

_____

C. _____

_____

Crystallized and Fluid Intelligence

1. Differentiate between *crystallized* and *fluid intelligence.* (p. 498)

Crystallized: _____

_____

Fluid: _____

_____

2. (Crystallized / Fluid) intelligence increases steadily throughout middle adulthood, whereas (crystallized / fluid) intelligence begins to decline in the twenties. (p. 499)

3. Review findings from Schaie's Seattle Longitudinal Study, noting five crystallized and fluid skills that continue to show gains in midlife and one fluid skill that declines steadily from the twenties to the late eighties. (p. 499)

_____

_____

_____

4. Summarize findings from Kaufman's cross-sectional study of adult intelligence, with particular attention to changes in verbal and performance IQ during middle adulthood. (p. 499)

_____

_____

_____

5. List three reasons why middle-aged adults show stability in crystallized abilities despite a much earlier decline in fluid intelligence. (p. 500)

A. _____

B. _____

C. _____

Individual and Group Differences

1. List factors associated with the maintenance of intellectual skills in middle adulthood. (p. 500)

_____

_____

2. Describe sex differences in mental abilities during early and middle adulthood. (p. 500)

_____

_____

_____

3. Cite four factors that explain cohort differences between currently middle-aged adults and adults from the previous generation on measures of verbal memory, inductive reasoning, and spatial orientation. (p. 501)

A. _____

B. _____

C. _____

D. _____

Information Processing

Speed of Processing

1. True or False: Response time on both simple and complex reaction time tasks remains stable across early and middle adulthood. (p. 501)

2. Describe two explanations for age-related declines in cognitive processing. (p. 501)

A. _____

_____

B. _____

_____

3. True or False: Older adults are able to compensate for cognitive slowing on familiar tasks. (p. 502)

Attention

1. List four changes in attention during middle adulthood. (p. 502)

    A. _____

    B. _____

    C. _____

    D. _____

2. Explain how declines in attention might be related to slowed information processing during midlife. (p. 502)

    _____

    _____

    _____

3. True or False: Practice and experience with attentional skills can help middle-aged adults compensate for age-related declines in those abilities. (p. 502)

Memory

1. From early to middle adulthood, the amount of information people can retain in working memory (increases / diminishes). What explains these age-related changes? (p. 502)

    _____

    _____

2. True or False: Even when middle-aged adults are instructed to use memory strategies, such as organization and elaboration, their performance fails to improve. (p. 502)

3. Name and describe three types of knowledge that remain unchanged or show improvement during midlife. (p. 502)

    A. _____

    _____

    B. _____

    _____

    C. _____

    _____

4. What strategy do middle-aged adults often use to assist their recall of information? (p. 502)

    _____

    _____

Practical Problem Solving and Expertise

1. What is *practical problem solving*? (p. 503)

    _____

    _____

2. Expertise (peaks / declines) in midlife. (p. 503)

3. True or False: Advances in expertise are found only among highly educated individuals in administrative level occupations. (p. 503)

4. Briefly describe advances in practical problem solving during middle adulthood. (pp. 503–504)

_____

_____

Creativity

1. Summarize three ways in which the quality of creativity changes with advancing age. (p. 504)

   A. _____

   _____

   B. _____

   _____

   C. _____

   _____

Information Processing in Context

1. In what areas are middle-aged adults most likely to experience cognitive gains? (p. 505)

   _____

   _____

2. True or False: When given a challenging real-world problem related to their area of expertise, middle-aged adults outperform younger adults in both efficiency and quality of thinking. (p. 505)

Vocational Life and Cognitive Development

1. Summarize the relationship between vocational life and cognition. (p. 505)

   _____

   _____

   _____

2. Cross-cultural findings (support / refute) the notion that complex work leads to gains in cognitive flexibility. (p. 505)

3. True or False: The impact of challenging work on cognition is greater in early adulthood than in middle adulthood. (p. 505)

Adult Learners: Becoming a College Student in Midlife

1. List several reasons why middle-aged adults may decide to enroll in undergraduate and graduate programs. (p. 506)

   _____

   _____

   _____

Characteristics of Returning Students

1. (Men / Women) represent the majority of adult learners. (p. 506)

2. Discuss some of the challenges confronting middle-aged women who return to college. (p. 506)

_____

_____

_____

Supporting Returning Students

1. Describe social supports and institutional services which facilitate adult reentry into college. (pp. 506–507)

Social supports: _____

_____

Institutional services: _____

_____

2. Summarize the benefits of adult reentry to college. (p. 507)

_____

_____

_____

ASK YOURSELF . . .

For *Ask Yourself* questions for this chapter, please log on to the Companion Website at www.ablongman.com/berk.

SUGGESTED STUDENT READINGS

Blaikie, A. (1999). *Aging & popular culture.* New York: Cambridge University Press. Explores policy perceptions, media images, and social understanding of the aging process. Also presents research on the history and evolution of aging stereotypes.

McCabe, P.M., Schneiderman, N., Field, T. M., & Wellens, A. R. (Eds.). (1999). *Stress, coping, and cardiovascular disease.* Mahwah, NJ: Erlbaum. Discusses physiological, psychosocial, developmental, and mental health factors in the relationship between stress and heart disease.

Schindley, W. (2002). *A survival guide for nontraditional students.* Mt. Pleasant, TX: Dallas Publishing. Presents the unique experiences of nontraditional college students, including expectations, personal commitments, fears, and obstacles. In addition, the author provides suggestions for overcoming these obstacles with practical advice for success.

Tan, R. S. (2001). *Unraveling truths about the male menopause.* Houston, TX: Amred Publishing. Written for both men and women, the author examines the experience of male menopause. Like female menopause, male menopause is influenced by biology and environment and can affect physical and cognitive functioning.

PUZZLE 15.1 TERM REVIEW

Across

4. Behavior pattern consisting of competitiveness, ambition, impatience, angry outbursts, and time pressure
5. Midlife transition in which fertility declines
7. Treatment in which a woman takes daily doses of estrogen, sometimes combined with progesterone, during the climacteric and after menopause
8. Condition of aging in which the eye loses its capacity to accommodate entirely to nearby objects
9. Age-related hearing impairments that involve a sharp loss of hearing at high frequencies, gradually extending to all frequencies
11. _____ problem solving: requires people to size up real-world situations and analyze how best to achieve goals that have a high degree of uncertainty
12. _____ intelligence: skills that largely depend on basic information-processing skills
13. Condition associated with severre age-related bone loss
14. _____ network view: attributes age-related slowin of cognitive processing to breaks in neural networks as neurons die

Down

1. _____ intelligence: skills that depend largely on accumulated knowledge and experience, good judgment, and mastery of social conventions
2. Set of three personal qualities—commitment, conrol, and challenge—that help people cope with stress adaptively
3. The end of menstruation and, therefore, reproductive capacity in women
6. _____-_____ view: attributes age-related slowing of cognitive processing to greater loss of information as it moves through the system
10. A disease in which pressure builds up within the eye due to poor fluid drainage, damaging the optic nerve

PRACTICE TEST #1

1. Which of the following is true of visual changes during midlife? (p. 483)
   a. The lens of the eye begins to shrink, resulting in difficulties with nearsighted vision between ages 40 to 60.
   b. Enlargement of the pupils causes increasing problems with daylight vision.
   c. Risk of presbyopia and glaucoma begin to decline after age 40.
   d. Weakening of the eye muscles leads to difficulty adjusting focus to nearby objects.

2. Reduction in bone mass during midlife (p. 486)
   a. is caused by increased mineral content.
   b. is more substantial in men than in women.
   c. causes bones to fracture more easily and heal more slowly.
   d. cannot be slowed, even with lifestyle changes such as increased calcium intake.

3. Women's climacteric (p. 486)
   a. occurs suddenly and rapidly, usually over the course of 1 to 2 years.
   b. is associated with decreased production of estrogen and shortening of the menstrual cycle.
   c. does not change reproductive capacity.
   d. typically occurs by age 40 among North American, European, and East Asian women.

4. Which of the following is true of women's psychological reactions to menopause? (p. 487)
   a. Societal values offering greater respect, privilege, and responsibility to older women lead North American women to report favorable responses and few physical symptoms.
   b. Well-educated, career-oriented women usually report more positive attitudes than do women with less education.
   c. African-American and Mexican-American women report particularly negative attitudes toward menopause.
   d. Research shows no cultural or SES differences in psychological reactions to menopause.

5. Which of the following is true of sexuality in middle adulthood? (p. 489)
   a. Frequency of sexual activity declines dramatically in midlife.
   b. Among married couples, frequency of sexual activity is closely tied to the woman's menopausal status.
   c. The best predictor of sexual frequency is marital happiness.
   d. Intensity of sexual response increases in midlife.

6. Which indicator of cardiovascular disease is referred to as a "silent killer"? (p. 491)
   a. atherosclerosis—a buildup of plaque in the coronary arteries
   b. a heart attack—blockage of normal blood supply to an area of the heart
   c. arrhythmia—an irregular heartbeat
   d. angina pectoris—indigestion-like or crushing chest pains

7. Expressed hostility (p. 494)
   a. is the toxic ingredient in the Type A behavior pattern that predicts heart disease and other health problems.
   b. predicts health problems only among individuals with other risk factors, such as smoking, alcohol abuse, and obesity.
   c. poses fewer health risks than does suppressed hostility.
   d. is more common in women than men.

8. Sharon decided that she was unhappy at work. She realized that the primary cause was frustration with an irresponsible co-worker. She met with this individual, came up with strategies to help the young woman meet her responsibilities, and subsequently derived more enjoyment from her job. Sharon used (p. 495)
   a. avoidant coping.
   b. problem-centered coping.
   c. emotion-centered coping.
   d. behavior-focused coping.

9. When a person has a sense of control over life events, a commitment to important activities, and a tendency to view change as a challenge rather than a disappointment, this person is said to display (pp. 496–497)
   a. fluid intelligence.
   b. Type A behavior pattern.
   c. resilience.
   d. hardiness.

10. The double standard of aging refers to the notion that (p. 497)
    a. middle-aged men become less committed to occupational status and physical fitness, yet they are viewed by the larger culture as powerful and driven.
    b. middle-aged women often feel assertive and confident, yet they are viewed by the larger culture as being less attractive and as having more negative characteristics than men.
    c. middle-aged women gain in positive judgments of appearance, maturity, and power, whereas middle-aged men show a decline in such ratings.
    d. middle-aged adults of both sexes prefer younger sexual partners.

11. Crystallized intelligence (pp. 498–499)
    a. depends heavily on information processing skills.
    b. represents acquired abilities that are valued by the individual's culture.
    c. begins to decline during the twenties.
    d. is rarely useful in everyday life.

12. Fluid intelligence (p. 499)
    a. refers to skills that depend on accumulated knowledge and experience.
    b. is tapped by measures of vocabulary, verbal analogy, and general information.
    c. is influenced by conditions in the brain and learning unique to the individual.
    d. increases steadily throughout middle adulthood.

13. Kaufman's research on verbal and performance IQ shows that (p. 499)
    a. complex mental abilities decline throughout adulthood.
    b. cognitive processing improves from early to late adulthood.
    c. crystallized intelligence is extremely vulnerable to biological aging.
    d. crystallized intelligence is maintained into old age, while fluid intelligence declines across adulthood.

14. Reaction time (p. 501)
    a. shows a small but practically significant decline during midlife.
    b. remains stable across middle and late adulthood.
    c. improves from the twenties into the late eighties.
    d. declines more rapidly in men than in women.

15. Studies of attention during midlife indicate that (p. 502)
    a. cognitive inhibition–the ability to resist interference from irrelevant information–improves during middle adulthood.
    b. it becomes more difficult to engage in two activities at the same time.
    c. decrements in attention are caused by sensory impairments, such as diminished vision and hearing.
    d. practice with attention-related tasks does little to improve these skills.

16. Declines in working memory largely result from (p. 502)
    a. changes in the structure of the brain.
    b. declines in metacognitive knowledge.
    c. decreased motivation to learn and remember new information.
    d. infrequent and ineffective use of memory strategies.

17. Expertise (p. 503)
    a. starts to develop during midlife.
    b. reaches its peak in midlife.
    c. declines dramatically in midlife.
    d. is replaced by practical problem solving during midlife.

18. During middle adulthood, creativity (p. 504)
    a. becomes less deliberately thoughtful.
    b. is focused more on generating unusual products and less on combining knowledge and experience.
    c. shifts from an egocentric concern with self-expression to more altruistic goals.
    d. is more spontaneous and intensely emotional.

19. Research on the relationship between vocational life and cognitive development shows that (p. 505)
    a. the impact of challenging work on cognitive growth is greatest for young adults.
    b. people in their fifties and early sixties show as many cognitive gains from complex work as do individuals in their twenties and thirties.
    c. the relationship between challenging work and continued cognitive development is less evident in today's middle-aged adults than it was in the middle-aged adults of a generation ago.
    d. cognition has a unidirectional influence on vocational life—that is, cognitive ability affects vocational choice, but vocational life does not affect cognitive development.

20. Adults who return to college for undergraduate and graduate study are most likely to be (p. 506)
    a. women.
    b. under the age of 35.
    c. divorced, single parents.
    d. free of other career and family obligations.

PRACTICE TEST #2

1. Adult-onset hearing loss (p. 484)
    a. is greater among women than men.
    b. is most often caused by a hereditary condition.
    c. is typically first noticeable by a hearing loss at low frequencies.
    d. is minimal in most middle-aged adults, suggesting that severe hearing problems are caused by factors other than biological aging.

2. The _____, or middle supportive layer of skin which consists of connective tissue that stretches and bounces back, giving the skin flexibility, begins to thin during middle adulthood. (p. 484)
    a. hypodermis
    b. epidermis
    c. dermis
    d. flexidermis

3. Hormone therapy (p. 486)
    a. is rarely effective for counteracting menopausal symptoms.
    b. has a range of physical and cognitive risks.
    c. reduces the risk of heart attacks, stroke, blood clots, and breast cancer.
    d. is recommended for all postmenopausal women.

4. Men's climacteric (p. 487)
    a. does not impact reproductive capacity.
    b. causes a decrease in quantity of semen and sperm, although sperm continue to be produced throughout life.
    c. brings an end to reproductive capacity.
    d. leads to serious problems with impotence in approximately 75 percent of men by age 60.

5. The leading causes of death in middle adulthood are (p. 489)
    a. suicide and homicide.
    b. motor vehicle accidents and cancer.
    c. AIDS and heart disease.
    d. heart disease and cancer.

6. Cancer (p. 489)
    a. often results from a complex interaction of hereditary, biological, and environmental factors.
    b. has not yet been linked to genetic causes, and is therefore assumed to result entirely from external factors.
    c. occurs more frequently in women than in men.
    d. is an incurable disease.

7. Osteoporosis (p. 493)
    a. almost always results in slumped-over posture, a shuffling gait, and a "dowager's hump."
    b. is associated with a decline in estrogen production after menopause.
    c. is a natural result of biological aging that cannot be prevented.
    d. occurs more frequently in African-Americans relative to their Asian-American, Caucasian, and Hispanic counterparts.

8. _____ —belief in one's ability to succeed—is vital to adoption and maintenance of an exercise program in midlife. (p. 496)
    a. Physical self-esteem
    b. Physical self-concept
    c. Self-efficacy
    d. Self-control

9. Which group of beginning exercisers is most likely to benefit from a home-based program? (p. 496)
    a. normal-weight individuals
    b. overweight individuals
    c. adults with highly stressful lives
    d. middle-aged women

10. Hardy individuals (pp. 496–497)
    a. use active, problem-centered coping strategies.
    b. view stressful life events as uncontrollable and unmanageable.
    c. deny the occurrence of stressful life events.
    d. are extremely competitive, ambitious, and hostile.

11. In American society, the ideal woman is portrayed as _____, representing the heart of the double standard of aging. (p. 497)
    a. passive and submissive
    b. young and sexually attractive
    c. indecisive and dependent
    d. assertive and competent

12. Which of these tasks most clearly makes use of crystallized intelligence? (pp. 498–499)
    a. learning to speak a foreign language
    b. finding hidden figures in a drawing
    c. articulate expression of ideas and information
    d. creating novel pieces of art work

13. Research on individual and group differences in intelligence reveals that (p. 500)
    a. SES is unrelated to changes in mental abilities during middle adulthood.
    b. changes in mental abilities vary considerably between men and women.
    c. older women are less competent than older men, thereby supporting the double standard of aging.
    d. currently middle-aged adults perform substantially better on cognitive measures than did members of the previous generation when they were the same age.

14. According to the _____ view, age-related slowing of cognitive processing is caused by breaks in the neural connections of the brain, which must be bypassed by forming new, but less efficient, connections. (p. 501)
    a. synaptic pruning
    b. neural network
    c. information-loss
    d. interconnectionist

15. As Shamiya gets older, which type of memory task will probably be the most difficult for her? (p. 502)
    a. recalling meaningful prose
    b. recalling word lists with a strong category-based structure
    c. recalling lists of unrelated words or numbers
    d. recalling information related to her occupation

16. _____ *problem solving,* which requires people to size up real-world situations and analyze how best to achieve goals that have a high degree of uncertainty, continues to show gains in middle adulthood. (p. 503)
    a. Social
    b. Practical
    c. Creative
    d. Situational

17. Expertise tends to develop (p. 503)
    a. in those who are highly educated.
    b. in those who reach the top of administrative ladders.
    c. in those from middle and high SES backgrounds, regardless of education and occupational status.
    d. among individuals from all fields of endeavor, from food service to upper-level administration.

18. During middle adulthood, cognitive gains are most likely to occur in (p. 504)
    a. tasks that rely heavily on information processing skills.
    b. daily activities that require selective attention and simultaneous attention to multiple tasks.
    c. working memory tasks.
    d. areas of extensive experience and expertise.

19. What is the reason most frequently cited by middle-aged women for not finishing their education? (p. 506)
    a. inability to meet academic demands
    b. unsupportive professors and school personnel
    c. career demands
    d. family obligations

20. The most important factor in the success of returning students is (p. 506)
    a. social support.
    b. high intellectual ability.
    c. full-time attendance.
    d. studying at regular times.

CHAPTER 16
EMOTIONAL AND SOCIAL DEVELOPMENT
IN MIDDLE ADULTHOOD

BRIEF CHAPTER SUMMARY

Generativity begins in early adulthood but expands greatly as middle-aged adults face Erikson's psychological conflict of generativity versus stagnation. Highly generative people find fulfillment as they make contributions to society through parenthood, other family relationships, the workplace, volunteer activities, and many forms of productivity and creativity. According to Levinson, middle-aged adults reassess their relation to themselves and the world. At midlife, adults must give up certain youthful qualities, find age-appropriate ways to express others, and accept being older, thereby creating a youth-age balance more in tune with their time of life. Rebuilding the life structure depends on supportive social contexts. Vaillant added that middle-aged adults become guardians of their culture, and the most successful and best adjusted enter a calmer, quieter time of life. Few people experience a midlife crisis, although most must adapt to important events, which often lead to new understandings and goals.

Midlife changes in self-concept and personality reflect growing awareness of a finite lifespan, longer life experience, and generative concerns. At the same time, certain aspects of personality remain stable, revealing that individual differences established during earlier phases persist. Possible selves become fewer and more realistic. Midlifers also become more introspective, and self-acceptance, autonomy, environmental mastery, and coping strategies improve. Both men and women become more androgynous in middle adulthood—a change that results from a complex combination of social roles and life conditions. Despite changes in the organization of personality, little change takes place in basic, underlying personality traits during midlife and beyond.

Because of a declining birthrate and longer life expectancy, the midlife phase of the family life cycle, called "launching children and moving on," has greatly lengthened over the past century. The changes of midlife prompt many adults to focus on improving their marriages. When divorce occurs, midlifers seem to adapt more easily than do younger people. Gains in practical problem solving and effective coping strategies may reduce the stressful impact of divorce. Most middle-aged parents adjust well to departure of children, especially if they have a strong work orientation and parent–child contact and affection are sustained. When family relationships are positive, grandparenthood is an important means of fulfilling personal and societal needs.

Compared with earlier generations, today's adults spend more years not only as parents and grandparents, but also as children of aging parents. The burden of caring for aging parents can be great. Many middle-aged adults become "sandwiched" between the needs of aging parents and financially dependent children. While middle-aged adults often become more appreciative of their parents' strengths and generosity, caring for chronically ill or disabled parents is highly stressful. Sibling contact and support generally declines from early to middle adulthood, although many siblings feel closer, often in response to major life events, such as parental illness. Friendships become fewer and more selective in midlife. Despite negative social changes, such as high rates of marital breakup, single-parent families, and youth crime, supportive ties among younger and older adults remain strong.

Work continues to be a salient aspect of identity and self-esteem in middle adulthood. More so than in earlier or later years, people attempt to increase the personal meaning and self-direction of their vocational lives. Job satisfaction has both psychological and economic significance. Overall job satisfaction improves during midlife, but burnout has become a greater problem in recent years, especially in the helping professions. Vocational development is less available to older workers and many women and ethnic minorities leave the corporate world to escape the glass ceiling, which limits their advancement. Still, radical career changes are rare in middle adulthood. Unemployment is especially difficult for middle-aged individuals, and retirement is an important change that is often stressful, making effective planning important for positive adjustment.

LEARNING OBJECTIVES

After reading this chapter, you should be able to:

16.1   Describe Erikson's stage of generativity versus stagnation and related research findings. (p. 512)

16.2   Discuss Levinson's and Vaillant's views of psychosocial development in middle adulthood, and cite similarities and differences between men and women. (pp. 515–516)

16.3   Summarize characteristics of people who experience a midlife crisis. (p. 517)

16.4   Characterize middle adulthood using a life events approach and a stage approach. (p. 517)

16.5   Describe changes in self-concept and personality in middle adulthood. (pp. 518–520)

16.6   Cite changes in gender identity in midlife. (pp. 520–521)

16.7   Describe stability and change in the "big five" personality traits in adulthood. (pp. 522–523)

16.8   Describe the middle adulthood phase of the family life cycle, and discuss midlife relationships with a marriage partner, adult children, grandchildren, and aging parents. (pp. 524–531)

16.9   Summarize characteristics of midlife sibling relationships and friendships, and discuss relationships across generations. (pp. 531–533)

16.10 Discuss job satisfaction and career development in middle adulthood, paying special attention to sex differences and experiences of ethnic minorities. (pp. 534–536)

16.11 Describe career change and unemployment in middle adulthood. (pp. 536–537)

16.12 Discuss the importance of planning for retirement, noting various issues that middle-aged adults should address. (pp. 537–538)

STUDY QUESTIONS

Erikson's Theory: Generativity versus Stagnation

1.   Define *generativity,* and cite characteristics of the generative adult. (p. 512)

   A. _____

   _____

   B. _____

   _____

2.   In addition to parenting, list four ways adults can be generative. (p. 512)

   A. _____   B. _____

   C. _____   D. _____

3. Explain how generativity brings together personal desires and cultural demands. (p. 513)

Personal desires: _____

Cultural demands: _____

4. What are some characteristics of adults whose resolution of Erikson's midlife conflict is toward stagnation? (p. 513)

_____

_____

5. True or False: Because researchers study generativity in many ways, it is impossible to determine if generativity actually increases in midlife. (p. 513)

6. Having children seems to foster generative development more in (men / women) than their opposite sex counterparts. (p. 513)

A Lifespan Vista: Generative Adults Tell Their Life Stories

1. Cite several themes commonly found in the narratives of highly generative people. (p. 514)

_____

_____

2. What are *themes of contamination*? (p. 514)

_____

3. Explain how generativity and life-story redemption events are connected. (p. 514)

_____

_____

_____

4. True or False: Adults high and low in generativity differ greatly in the number of positive and negative events included in their narratives. (p. 514)

Other Theories of Psychosocial Development in Midlife

Levinson's Seasons of Life

1. Based on Levinson's theory, cite the four-phase sequence that middle-aged adults move through in building a culminating life structure. (p. 515)

_____

_____

_____

_____

2. How do adults differ in their responses to the midlife transition? (p. 515)

_____

_____

3. According to Levinson, what are four developmental tasks that middle-aged adults must confront in order to reassess their relation to themselves and to the external world? (p. 515)

    A. _____

    B. _____

    C. _____

    D. _____

4. What three things must middle-aged adults do in order to create a youth-age balance that is more in tune with their time of life? (p. 515)

5. True or False: Because of the double standard of aging, women find it harder than men to accept being older. (p. 515)

6. How does confronting their own mortality and the actual or impending death of agemates influence awareness in middle adulthood? (p. 516)

    _____

    _____

7. List four ways the image of legacy, which flourishes is midlife, can be satisfied. (p. 516)

    A. _____ B. _____

    C. _____ D. _____

8. Explain how men and women reconcile masculine and feminine parts of the self in middle age. (p. 516)

    Men: _____

    _____

    Women: _____

    _____

9. True or False: Midlife requires that men and women with highly active, successful careers reduce their concern with ambition and achievement and focus more fully on themselves. (p. 516)

10. Explain why supportive social contexts are essential for rebuilding the life structure in middle adulthood. (p. 516)

    _____

    _____

    _____

11. How do opportunities for advancement ease the transition to middle adulthood? (p. 516)

    _____

Vaillant's Adaptation to Life

1. Cite evidence that adults in their late 40s and 50s carry peak responsibility for the functioning of society. (p. 516)

    _____

    _____

    _____

Is There a Midlife Crisis?

1. What is a *midlife crisis*? (p. 517)

    _____

2. How do men and women differ in their responses to midlife? (p. 517)

    Men: _____

    _____

    Women: _____

    _____

3. True or False: Midlife is sometimes experienced as relief rather than crisis. (p. 517)

4. What are some characteristics of adults who experience a midlife crisis? (p. 517)

    _____

    _____

Stage or Life Events Approach

1. Cite evidence that both stage and life events approaches accurately reflect adaptation at midlife. (p. 517)

    _____

    _____

    _____

Stability and Change in Self-Concept and Personality

Possible Selves

1. What are *possible selves,* and how do they change with age? (p. 518)

    A. _____

    B. _____

2. How do possible selves differ from self-concept? (p. 518)

    _____

    _____

Self-Acceptance, Autonomy, and Environmental Mastery

1. Introspection has been consistently shown to (rise/ decline) during the second half of life. (p. 519)

2. Describe three traits which have been found to increase from early to middle adulthood among well-educated adults. (p. 519)

    A. _____

    B. _____

    C. _____

3. Why do Korean middle-aged adults appear to have lower levels of well-being than their North-American counterparts? (p. 519)

_____

_____

_____

Coping Strategies

1. Midlife brings an (increase / decrease) in effective coping strategies. (p. 519)

2. Explain how the coping strategies of middle-aged individuals differ from those of younger individuals. (p. 519)

   Middle-aged: _____

   _____

   Younger: _____

   _____

3. Why might effective coping strategies increase in middle adulthood? (p. 520)

   _____

   _____

Gender Identity

1. Gender identity becomes (more / less) androgynous in midlife. Elaborate on your response. (p. 521)

   _____

   _____

   _____

2. Define *parental imperative theory*. (p. 521)

   _____

   _____

   _____

3. How do social roles influence gender identity in midlife? (p. 522)

   _____

   _____

Individual Differences in Personality Traits

1. List the *"big five" personality traits*. (p. 522)

   A. _____ B. _____

   C. _____ D. _____

   E. _____

2. Which "big five" personality traits show modest declines in midlife? Which ones increase? (p. 522)

A. _____

B. _____

3. True or False: An individual who scores high or low at one age in the "big five" personality traits is likely to do the same from 3 to 30 years later. (p. 522)

4. How do theorists who emphasize change in personality during midlife differ from those who emphasize stability? (pp. 522–523)

_____

_____

_____

Biology & Environment: What Factors Promote Psychological Well-Being in Midlife?

1. Explain how exercise promotes well-being during midlife? (p. 520)

_____

_____

_____

2. What is flow? Why is flow likely to increase in middle adulthood? (p. 520)

A. _____

_____

B. _____

_____

3. In a longitudinal study of 90 men, _____ and _____ in early adulthood were among the best predictors of well-being in middle adulthood. (p. 520)

4. True or False: Friendships are more effective than a good marriage in boosting psychological well-being in midlife. (pp. 520–521)

Relationships at Midlife

1. Why is the middle adulthood phase of the family life cycle often referred to as "launching children and moving on?" (p. 524)

_____

_____

Marriage and Divorce

1. True or False: Middle-aged adults are more likely than individuals in other age groups to experience financial difficulty. (p. 524)

2. True or False: Midlifers seem to adapt more easily to divorce than younger people. (p. 525)

3. Highly educated middle-aged adults are (more / less) likely to divorce. (p. 525)

4. Marital breakup is a strong contributor to the *feminization of poverty.* Explain what this means. (p. 525)

_____

_____

_____

5. List outcomes for middle-aged women who weather divorce successfully. (p. 525)

_____

_____

_____

Changing Parent–Child Relationships

1. True or False: Even when their children are "offtime" in development of independence and accomplishment, middle-aged adults adjust well. (p. 525)

2. Describe how the parental role changes during midlife. (p. 525)

_____

_____

_____

3. Throughout middle adulthood, parents give (more / less) assistance to children than they receive. (p. 526)

4. Once young adults strike out on their own, members of the middle generation, especially mothers, usually take on the role of _____, gathering the family for celebrations and making sure everyone stays in touch. (p. 526)

Grandparenthood

1. On average, American adults become grandparents in their _____, Canadian adults in their _____. (p. 526)

2. List four commonly mentioned gratifications of grandparenthood. (p. 526)

   A. _____

   B. _____

   C. _____

   D. _____

3. How does the grandchild's age affect grandparent–grandchild relationships? (pp. 526–527)

_____

_____

_____

_____

4. Typically, (same-sex / opposite-sex) grandparents and grandchildren are closer, especially _____. (p. 527)

5. As grandchildren get older, distance has (more / less) impact on grandparent-grandchild relationships. (p. 527)

6. Explain how SES and ethnicity influence grandparent-grandchild ties. (p. 527)

SES: _____

_____

Ethnicity: _____

_____

7. Explain how grandparent-parent relations affect grandparent-grandchild relations. (p. 527)

_____

_____

Middle-Aged Children and Their Aging Parents

1. True or False: Adults of past generations were more devoted to their aging parents than are adults of the present generation. (p. 529)

2. True or False: In the non-Western world, older adults often live with their married children. (p. 529)

3. Why are today's middle-aged adults called the *sandwich generation*? (p. 530)

_____

4. Why are women more often caregivers of aging parents? (p. 530)

_____

_____

5. Cite contributions that men make to caring for aging parents. (p. 530)

_____

_____

6. Explain why caring for a chronically ill or disabled parent is highly stressful. (p. 530)

_____

_____

7. What emotional and physical health consequences are associated with parental caregiving? (p. 530)

_____

_____

8. List four ways to relieve the stress of caring for an aging parent. (p. 531)

A. _____

B. _____

C. _____

D. _____

Siblings

1. Sibling contact and support (increase / decline) from early to middle adulthood, yet siblings often feel (closer / less close) during this time of life. (p. 531)

2. True or False: As siblings get older, good relationships often strengthen and poor relationships often worsen. (p. 531)

3. Explain how sibling relationships differ in village versus industrialized societies. (p. 532)

   _____

   _____

   _____

Friendships

1. Briefly describe sex differences in middle-age friendships. (p. 532)

   Men: _____

   _____

   Women: _____

   _____

2. Number of friends (increases / declines) with age. (p. 532)

3. Explain how family relationships and friendships support different aspects of psychological well-being. (pp. 532–533)

   Family: _____

   _____

   Friendships: _____

   _____

Relationships Across Generations

1. True or False: Research findings show that despite social changes, supportive ties among younger and older individuals remain strong. (p. 533)

2. How do middle-aged and older adults differ in their involvement in community activities? (p. 533)

   Middle-Aged: _____

   _____

   Older: _____

   _____

Social Issues: Grandparents Rearing Grandchildren: The Skipped-Generation Family

1. What are *skipped-generation families*? (p. 528)

   _____

2. Cite several reasons for grandparents stepping in and rearing grandchildren. (p. 528)

   _____

   _____

3. Describe challenges grandparents encounter when they raise grandchildren. (p. 528)

_____

_____

_____

Vocational Life

1. Work (does / does not) continue to be a salient aspect of identity and self-esteem in middle adulthood. (p. 534)

2. True or False: Compared with younger employees, older employees have lower rates of absenteeism and show no change in work productivity. (p. 534)

3. What two factors will contribute to the dramatic rise in the number of older workers during the next few decades? (p. 534)

Job Satisfaction

1. Research shows that job satisfaction (increases / decreases) in midlife at all occupational levels. (p. 534)

2. Describe one aspect of job satisfaction that rises with age and one that remains stable. (p. 534)

   Rises: _____

   Remains stable: _____

3. Under what conditions does *burnout* occur, and why is it a serious occupational hazard? (p. 534)

   A. _____

   B. _____

4. How can employers prevent burnout? (p. 534)

   _____

Career Development

1. True or False: Research suggests that training and on-the-job career counseling are more available to older workers. (p. 535)

2. List characteristics of the person and the work environment that influence employees' willingness to engage in job training and updating. (p. 535)

   A. _____

   _____

   B. _____

   _____

3. How do age-balanced work groups foster on-the-job learning? (p. 535)

   _____

4. List factors that contribute to a *glass ceiling* for women and ethnic minorities in the workplace. (p. 536)

_____

_____

_____

_____

Career Change at Midlife

1. What kind of midlife career changes are most common? (p. 536)

_____

2. True or False: When an extreme career shift occurs, it usually signals a personal crisis. (p. 536)

Unemployment

1. True or False: As companies downsize and jobs are eliminated, the majority of people affected are middle-aged and older. (p. 537)

2. Middle-aged adults react (more / less) negatively to unemployment than younger adults. (p. 537)

3. Cite three reasons that middle-aged adults decline more sharply than younger adults in physical and mental health as a result of unemployment. (p. 537)

   A. _____

   _____

   B. _____

   _____

   C. _____

   _____

4. Which forms of social support are most effective for reducing stress and reassuring middle-aged job seekers of their worth? (p. 537)

_____

_____

Planning for Retirement

1. True or False: Most workers report looking forward to retirement. (p. 537)

2. What are some benefits of retirement planning? (p. 537)

_____

_____

3. Less educated people with lower lifetime earnings are (most / least) likely to attend retirement preparation programs. (p. 538)

4. True or False: Financial planning is more important than planning for an active life in promoting happiness after retirement. (p. 538)

ASK YOURSELF . . .

For *Ask Yourself* questions for this chapter, please log on to the Companion Website at www.ablongman.com/berk.

SUGGESTED STUDENT READINGS

Booth, A., & Crouter, A. C. (Eds.). (1998). *Men in families: When do they get involved? What difference does it make?* Mahwah, NJ: Erlbaum. Discusses research on men's involvement in family relationships and their various familial roles as husband, father, and provider.

Ganong, L. H., & Coleman, M. (1999). *Changing families, changing responsibilities: Family obligations following divorce and remarriage.* Mahwah, NJ: Erlbaum. Examines shifts in the rights and duties of individual family members following changes in family structure caused by divorce and remarriage.

Kuttner, R., & Trotter, S. (2002). *Reconnecting parents and children in adulthood.* Tampa, FL: Free Press. Emphasizing a lifespan perspective, this book explores the dynamic relationship between adult children and their parents, including how to negotiate changes in a positive way.

Wassermann, S. (2001). *How to stay close to distant grandchildren.* Vancouver: Hartley & Marks, Inc. Presents a number of practical suggestions for grandparents interested in developing and maintaining close bonds with distant grandchildren. Also addresses frequent grandparent concerns, such as traveling with grandchildren, dealing with the death of a grandparent, and family favoritism.

PUZZLE 16.1 TERM REVIEW

Across

2. _____ imperative theory claims that traditional gender roles are maintained during the active parenting years to help ensure the survival of children

3. _____ selves: future-oriented representations of what one hopes to become and is afraid of becomin

5. Role assumed by members of the middle generation who take responsibilit for gathering the family for celebrations and making sure everyone stays in touch

6. Generativity versus _____: Erikson's psychological conflict of midlife

8. Middle-aged adults who are squeezed between the needs of aging parents and financially dependent children are known as the _____ generation.

9. Glass _____: invisible barrier to advancement up the corporate ladder faced by women and ethnic minorities

10. The _____ crisis refers to inner turmoil, self-doubt, and major restructuring of personality during the transition to middle adulthood

Down

1. _____ of poverty: trend in which women who support themselves or their families have become the majority of the adult poverty population

4. Condition in which long-term job stress leads to emotional exhaustion, a sense of loss of personal control, and feelings of reduced accomplishment

6. _____-generation family: children live with grandparents but apart from parents

7. _____ _____ personality traits: five basic factors into which hundreds of personality traits have been organized: neuroticism, extroversion, openness to experience, agreeableness, and conscientiousness (2 words)

1. Generativity (p. 513)
   a. can only be realized through parenting.
   b. brings together personal desires and cultural demands.
   c. characterizes adults who have become self-centered and indulgent.
   d. prevents some middle-aged adults from making meaningful contributions to society.

2. Compared to men, women (p. 515)
   a. focus more intensely on ambition and achievement in midlife.
   b. perceive themselves as older than their chronological age.
   c. evaluate their lives more positively.
   d. find it more difficult to accept being older.

3. According to Vaillant (p. 516)
   a. well-adjusted men and women enter a calmer, quieter time of life when they reach their fifties.
   b. adults are not ready to "pass the torch" until very late in life.
   c. rapid changes in cultural values initiated by young adults cause many older adults to lose touch with society and subsequently withdraw.
   d. adults focus more on personal goals as they move toward the end of middle age.

4. Sharp disruption and agitation during the midlife transition (p. 517)
   a. are common among most adults.
   b. are more the exception than the rule.
   c. ultimately result in favorable adjustment.
   d. are more common in men.

5. At lunch, Louisa tells a colleague, "I'm thinking about changing jobs. I feel like I'm doing the same thing day after day. Or maybe I can save some money and start a small business in a few years. I've always wanted to do that, and if I don't do it soon, it will never happen." Louisa is discussing (p. 518)
   a. possible selves.
   b. emotion-centered coping.
   c. environmental mastery.
   d. self-acceptance.

6. Effective coping strategies are increasingly used in middle adulthood. For example, middle-aged individuals are more likely to (p. 519)
   a. not care about problems.
   b. "ride" problems out.
   c. look for the "silver lining."
   d. avoid using humor to express ideas and feelings.

7. In a study of well-educated adults ranging in age from the late teens into the seventies, the following three traits increased from early to middle adulthood and then leveled off (p. 519)
   a. self-acceptance, self-concept, and possible selves.
   b. self-acceptance, autonomy, and possible selves.
   c. self-concept, patience, and autonomy.
   d. self-acceptance, autonomy, and environmental mastery.

8. During middle adulthood (p. 521)
   a. women become less confident, self-sufficient, and forceful; men less emotionally sensitive, caring, considerate, and dependent.
   b. women become more confident, self-sufficient, and forceful; men less emotionally sensitive, caring, considerate, and dependent.
   c. both men and women become more confident, self-sufficient, and forceful.
   d. women become more confident, self-sufficient, and forceful; men more emotionally sensitive, caring, considerate, and dependent.

9. Regarding divorce, midlifers (p. 525)
   a. adapt more easily than do younger people.
   b. adapt more poorly than do younger people.
   c. adapt in much the same way as younger people.
   d. often turn their anger toward their children.

10. Which group of middle-aged adults is most likely to divorce? (p. 525)
   a. couples who are still wed to their first spouse
   b. well-educated, financially secure couples
   c. couples whose children recently left home
   d. African-American couples

11. Once young adults strike out on their own, members of the middle generation, especially mothers, often take on the role of (p. 526)
   a. gatekeeper.
   b. kinkeeper.
   c. primary caregiver.
   d. authority figure.

12. Which pair typically has the closest relationship? (p. 527)
   a. grandmother and granddaughter
   b. grandfather and grandson
   c. grandfather and granddaughter
   d. grandmother and grandson

13. Which of the following is true of grandparent-grandchild relationships? (p. 527)
   a. Grandfathers report higher satisfaction with the grandparent role than grandmothers.
   b. Because of family mobility, most grandparents live far away from all of their grandchildren.
   c. The grandparent role is more essential to family maintenance and survival in high-income families than in low-income families.
   d. Compared with grandchildren in intact families, grandchildren in single-parent and stepparent families report engaging in more diverse, higher quality activities with their grandparents.

14. Why do fewer aging adults live with younger generations today than in the past? (p. 529)
   a. Adults today are less devoted to their aging parent than were adults of previous generations.
   b. Many aging adults report a desire to remain independent, which is facilitated by gains in health and financial security.
   c. Adult children often neglect and isolate aging parents and are less appreciative of their parents' strengths and generosity.
   d. Adult children typically live far away from aging parents.

15. When an aging person's spouse cannot provide care, which relative is the next most likely to do so? (p. 530)
   a. an adult son
   b. an adult grandson
   c. an adult daughter
   d. an adult granddaughter

16. As Kiera reached middle age, she was increasingly forced to balance the demands of raising her own children with those of caring for her aging, chronically ill parents. Which term is frequently used to describe experiences such as Kiera's? (p. 530)
    a. kinkeeping
    b. sandwich generation
    c. midlife crisis
    d. family burden

17. A survey of a large, nationally representative sample of American 18- to 90-year-olds revealed that (p. 533)
    a. solidarity between generations is eroding.
    b. the majority of adult children reported feeling tension toward at least one parent.
    c. supportive ties among younger and older individuals remain strong.
    d. most adult children resent caring for an ill parent.

18. Which of the following factors influence willingness to engage in job training and updating in midlife? (p. 535)
    a. supervisor and coworker encouragement
    b. work groups with younger people in them
    c. simplified work tasks
    d. negative stereotypes of aging

19. When an extreme career shift occurs, it is (p. 536)
    a. often a positive vocational decision.
    b. usually an indication of a personal crisis.
    c. usually the result of unemployment.
    d. of little consequence for midlife functioning.

20. Which of the following is true about job loss? (p. 537)
    a. It seldom happens to people at midlife.
    b. Middle-aged adults adjust to it more easily than younger people.
    c. It can disrupt major tasks of midlife, such as generativity.
    d. It often happens to midlifers, but they typically find new jobs quickly.

PRACTICE TEST #2

1. Adults with a sense of stagnation (p. 513)
    a. are well-adjusted and report a high level of life satisfaction.
    b. possess leadership qualities and are open to differing viewpoints.
    c. cannot contribute to the betterment of society because they place their own comfort and security above challenge and sacrifice.
    d. view themselves as role models and sources of wisdom for their children.

2. Rebuilding the life structure during middle adulthood depends on (p. 516)
    a. supportive social contexts.
    b. dramatic revision of family and occupational commitments.
    c. successful confrontation of the double standard of aging.
    d. strengthening of gender-typed characteristics.

3. Middle adulthood is (p. 517)
    a. simply an adaptation to life events, not a stage.
    b. a period of crisis and major restructuring for all adults.
    c. characterized by discontinuity.
    d. a stage because it always brings troubling moments that prompt new understandings and goals.

4. As a young adult, Christian wanted to be a great athlete and a very successful businessman. He has largely attained one of these goals, becoming a highly-paid administrator for a large corporation. As he enters middle adulthood, Christian will probably (p. 518)
   a. strive harder to make his current self match his possible self.
   b. become depressed that he did not achieve all of his goals.
   c. focus less on the business success and more on his athleticism in an attempt to regain his youth.
   d. concentrate more on enhancing personal relationships and being competent at work.

5. Unlike current self-concept, possible selves (p. 518)
   a. do not change with age.
   b. can be defined and redefined by the individual, as needed.
   c. tend to be unstable throughout the lifespan.
   d. are constantly responsive to others' feedback.

6. Which of the following is true of gender identity in middle adulthood? (p. 521)
   a. Both men and women become more androgynous.
   b. Both men and women become strongly gender-typed.
   c. Both men and women show an increase in feminine traits.
   d. Both men and women show an increase in masculine traits.

7. According to parental imperative theory, which of the following occurs to help ensure the survival of children? (p. 521)
   a. Men emphasize nurturance of wife and children.
   b. Women become more goal-oriented.
   c. Parents express the "other-gender" side of their personalities during active parenting years.
   d. Traditional gender roles are maintained during active parenting years.

8. Neuroticism, extroversion, and openness to experience (p. 522)
   a. show a sharp increase from early to middle adulthood.
   b. are common among well-adjusted adults.
   c. show modest declines from the teenage years through middle age.
   d. often transform into agreeableness and conscientiousness.

9. In Southern European countries of Greece, Italy, and Spain, middle-aged parents (p. 525)
   a. do not experience the "launching children" phase of the family life cycle.
   b. encourage their children to leave home during the teenage years.
   c. actively delay their children's departure from the home.
   d. have more conflict-ridden relationships with adult children than do Northern Europeans.

10. When parent–child contact and affection are sustained (p. 526)
   a. parents' life satisfaction declines.
   b. mothers and fathers are able to maintain parental authority.
   c. departure of children from the home is a relatively mild event.
   d. adult children struggle to become independent and accomplished.

11. Compared with adult children who assist in the care of aging parents while maintaining a separate residence, those who live with an ill or disabled parent (p. 530)
   a. experience more stress.
   b. are more well-adjusted.
   c. have less role overload.
   d. rarely find rewards in parental caregiving.

12. In the United States and Canada, in-home care of an ill, aging parent by a nonfamily caregiver is (p. 531)
   a. readily available and government supported.
   b. generally not an option because of its high cost and limited availability.
   c. patterned after the Swedish home-helper system.
   d. rarely used because it does not relieve family caregiver stress.

13. During middle adulthood, many siblings (p. 531)
    a. spend more time together.
    b. report strained relations.
    c. feel closer.
    d. provide each other with more support than at any other time of the lifespan.

14. For both middle-aged men and women (p. 532)
    a. the number of friends declines with age.
    b. the number of friends increases with age.
    c. the number of friends stays about the same with age.
    d. adult friendships are more superficial than they were in earlier years.

15. Burnout occurs more often in (p. 534)
    a. young workers.
    b. helping professions.
    c. high-income professions.
    d. men.

16. Which of the following statements about vocational life is true? (p. 534)
    a. Identity and self-esteem in middle adulthood are unaffected by work.
    b. Older employees have higher rates of absenteeism, turnover, and accidents.
    c. Negative stereotypes of aging have little influence in the workplace.
    d. Job satisfaction increases in midlife at all occupational levels.

17. Women face a glass ceiling because (p. 536)
    a. they are less effective managers than men.
    b. modern businesses realize that the best managers display "masculine" traits.
    c. they have less access to mentors, role models, and informal networks than men.
    d. they are less committed to their careers than men.

18. Midlife career changes (p. 536)
    a. are common.
    b. are usually radical.
    c. typically involve leaving one line of work for another related line of work.
    d. are an easy decision for most middle-aged adults.

19. As companies downsize and jobs are eliminated, the majority of people affected are (p. 537)
    a. young adults.
    b. women.
    c. middle-aged and older.
    d. men.

20. Which of the following is true? (p. 538)
    a. Lower-paid workers are less likely than higher-paid workers to attend retirement preparation programs.
    b. Almost all middle-aged workers plan carefully for retirement.
    c. Retirement planning often results in disappointment after retirement.
    d. Husbands and wives fare better if they plan independently for retirement.

CHAPTER 17
PHYSICAL AND COGNITIVE DEVELOPMENT
IN LATE ADULTHOOD

BRIEF CHAPTER SUMMARY

Vastly different rates of aging are apparent in late adulthood. Dramatic gains in average life expectancy—the number of years that an individual born in a particular year can expect to live—provide powerful support for the multiplicity of factors that slow biological aging, including improved nutrition, medical treatment, sanitation, and safety. A complex combination of genetic and environmental factors combine to determine longevity.

The programmed effects of specific genes and the random cellular events believed to underlie biological aging make physical declines more apparent in late adulthood. Although aging of the nervous system affects a wide range of complex thoughts and activities, research reveals that the brain can overcome some age-related cognitive declines. Changes in sensory functioning become increasingly noticeable in late life. Older adults see and hear less well, and taste, smell, and touch sensitivity may also decline. Hearing impairments are far more common than visual impairments, and many more men than women are affected. Aging of the cardiovascular and respiratory systems becomes more apparent in late adulthood, and as at earlier ages, not smoking, reducing dietary fat, avoiding environmental pollutants, and exercising can slow the effects of aging on these systems. A less competent immune system can increase the elderly person's risk for a variety of illnesses, including infectious diseases, cardiovascular disease, certain forms of cancer, and a variety of autoimmune disorders.

As people age, they have more difficulty falling asleep, staying asleep, and sleeping deeply—a trend that begins after age 30 for men and after age 50 for women. Outward signs of aging, such as white hair, wrinkled and sagging skin, age spots and decreased height and weight become more noticeable in late adulthood. People vary in the aspects of physical aging that matter most to them and problem-centered coping strategies yield improved physical functioning in the elderly. In addition, rapidly expanding assistive technology is available to help older people cope with physical declines.

Physical and mental health are intimately related in late life. The physical changes of late life lead to an increased need for certain nutrients, and exercise continues to be a powerful health intervention. Although sexual desire and frequency of sexual activity decline in older people, longitudinal evidence indicates that most healthy older married couples report continued, regular sexual enjoyment. Illness and disability climb as the end of the lifespan approaches. Cardiovascular disease, cancer, stroke, and emphysema claim many lives, while arthritis and adult-onset diabetes increase substantially. At age 65 and older, the death rate from unintentional injuries is at an all-time high.

When cell death and structural and chemical abnormalities are profound, serious deterioration of mental and motor functions occurs. Alzheimer's disease is the most common form of dementia. Alzheimer's disease comes in two types: familial, which runs in families, and sporadic, which has no obvious family history. With no cure available, family interventions ensure the best adjustment possible for the Alzheimer's victim, spouse, and other relatives. Careful diagnosis of dementia is crucial because other disorders can be mistaken for it. Family members provide most long-term care, especially among ethnic minorities with closely knit extended families.

Individual differences in cognitive functioning are greater in late adulthood than at any other time of life. Although both fluid intelligence and crystallized intelligence decline in advanced old age, plasticity of development is still possible. As older adults take in information more slowly and find it harder to apply strategies, inhibit irrelevant information, and retrieve knowledge from long-term memory, the chance of memory failure increases. Research shows that language and memory skills are closely related. While language comprehension changes very little in late life, retrieving words from long-term memory and planning what to say become more difficult. Finally, traditional problem solving, which lacks real-life context, shows declines.

Cultures around the world assume that age and wisdom go together. Older adults with the cognitive, reflective, and emotional qualities that make up wisdom tend to be better educated and physically healthier and forge more positive relations with others. As in middle adulthood, a mentally active life—above average education, stimulating leisure pursuits, community participation, and a flexible personality—predicts maintenance of mental abilities into advanced old age. And interventions that train the elderly in cognitive strategies partially reverse age-related declines in mental ability. Elders who participate in continuing education through university courses, community offerings, and programs such as Elderhostel, are enriched by new knowledge, new friends, a broader perspective on the world, and an image of themselves as more competent.

LEARNING OBJECTIVES

After reading this chapter, you should be able to:

17.1   Summarize changes in life expectancy during the twentieth and early twenty-first centuries, and discuss gender, SES, and cultural variations in life expectancy. (pp. 547–549)

17.2   Explain age-related changes in the nervous system that take place during late adulthood. (pp. 549–550)

17.3   Summarize changes in sensory functioning during late adulthood, including vision, hearing, taste, smell, and touch. (pp. 550–553)

17.4   Discuss aging of the cardiovascular, respiratory, and immune systems in late adulthood. (pp. 553–554)

17.5   Describe sleep disturbances experienced by older adults. (pp. 554–555)

17.6   Describe changes in physical appearance and mobility in late adulthood. (p. 555)

17.7   Discuss adaptation to the physical changes of late adulthood, including use of effective coping strategies and assistive technology. (p. 556)

17.8   Summarize personal and cultural factors which help older adults to overcome negative stereotypes of aging. (p. 557)

17.9   Discuss health and fitness in late life, with special attention to nutrition, exercise, and sexuality. (pp. 558–561)

17.10 Discuss illness and physical disability in late adulthood, noting risk for arthritis, adult-onset diabetes, and unintentional injuries. (pp. 561–564)

17.11 Discuss common mental disabilities in late adulthood, including Alzheimer's disease, cerebrovascular dementia, and misdiagnosed and reversible dementia. (p. 564–567)

17.12 Summarize health care issues that affect older adults, including health care costs and need for long-term care. (pp. 567–570)

17.13 Explain age-related changes in various types of memory during late life, including deliberate, automatic, associative, remote, and prospective memories. (pp. 570–573)

17.14 Describe changes in language processing in late adulthood, noting factors that explain these changes. (pp. 573–574)

17.15 Summarize changes in traditional and real-life problem solving during late adulthood. (pp. 574–575)

17.16 Describe life experiences that foster the development of wisdom in old age. (pp. 575–576)

17.17 List factors related to cognitive change in late adulthood. (pp. 576–577)

17.18 Discuss the effectiveness of cognitive interventions in late adulthood. (p. 577)

17.19 Describe the types of continuing education programs available to the elderly, and summarize the benefits of participation in such programs. (pp. 577–579)

STUDY QUESTIONS

Physical Development

1. _____ *age* refers to the actual competence and performance of an older adult. (p. 546)

2. Distinguish between *young-old* and *old-old* elderly. (pp. 546–547)

   Young-old: _____

   Old-old: _____

Life Expectancy

1. Define average *life expectancy*. (p. 547)

   _____

   _____

2. In 2000, average life expectancy reached age _____ in the United States and age in Canada. (p. 547)

Variations in Life Expectancy

1. On average, (men / women) can expect to live 4 to 7 years longer than their opposite-sex counterparts—a difference found in almost all cultures. What accounts for this gender gap in life expectancy? (p. 547)

2. List factors which contribute to SES and ethnic differences in life expectancy. (p. 547)

   _____

   _____

   _____

3. Define *active lifespan*. (p. 547)

   _____

   _____

   _____

4. True or False: When researchers compare nations throughout the world, the United States and Canada rank first and second in active lifespan. (p. 547)

Life Expectancy in Late Adulthood

1. During the twentieth century, the number of people age 65 and older (rose / declined) dramatically in the industrialized world. (p. 547)

2. True or False: With advancing age, gender and SES differences in life expectancy increase. (p. 548)

3. Describe the *life expectancy crossover,* which occurs around age 85. (p. 548)

_____

_____

_____

4. Summarize evidence suggesting that heredity affects longevity. (p. 548)

_____

_____

_____

5. True or False: Twin studies suggest that once people pass age 75 to 80, the contribution of heredity to length of life decreases while environmental factors play an increasingly large role. (p. 548)

Maximum Lifespan

1. Define *maximum lifespan.* (p. 548)

_____

_____

_____

2. Cite current estimates of maximum lifespan. (p. 548)

_____

_____

_____

3. Summarize both sides of the controversy regarding whether maximum lifespan figures represent the upper bound of human longevity or whether lifespan can be extended even further. (pp. 548–549)

Represents upper bound: _____

_____

Can be extended further: _____

_____

A Lifepsan Vista: What Can We Learn About Aging from Centenarians?

1. True or False: Recent increases in the number of centenarians in the industrialized world are expected to accelerate in the years to come. (p. 550)

2. Centenarians are more likely to be (men / women). (p. 550)

3. True or False: Less than 20 percent of centenarians have physical and mental impairments which interfere with independent functioning. (p. 550)

4. Describe the health, personality, and activities of robust centenarians. (pp. 550–551)

   Health: _____

   _____

   Personality: _____

   _____

   Activities: _____

   _____

5. True or False: Longevity runs in the families of centenarians. (p. 550)

Physical Changes

Nervous System

1. True or False: Death of neurons causes brain weight to decrease throughout adulthood. (p. 549)

2. In what regions of the brain is neuron loss greatest during late adulthood? (p. 549)

   _____

3. True or False: In healthy older adults, growth of neural fibers takes place at the same rate as in middle-aged adults. (p. 549)

4. Cite three changes in autonomic nervous system functioning in old age. (p. 550)

   A. _____

   B. _____

   C. _____

Sensory Systems

1. What are *cataracts,* and how do they affect vision? (p. 551)

   Definition: _____

   _____

   Impact on vision: _____

   _____

2. Cite two factors which largely account for visual impairments in late adulthood. (p. 551)

   A. _____

   B. _____

3. Depth perception and visual acuity (improve / remain stable / decline) in late life. (p. 551)

4. When light-sensitive cells in the central region of the retina break down, older adults may develop _____, in which central vision blurs and is gradually lost. (p. 552)

5. True or False: Cataracts are the leading cause of blindness in older adults. (p. 552)

6. Explain ways in which visual difficulties impact older people's self-confidence and everyday behavior. (p. 552)

_____

_____

7. List three changes in the ear that cause hearing to decline in late adulthood. (p. 553)

   A. _____

   B. _____

   C. _____

8. Hearing decrements in late life are greatest at (high / low) frequencies. List two additional hearing declines. (p. 552)

   A. _____

   B. _____

9. What hearing difficulty has the greatest impact on life satisfaction? (p. 552)

_____

10. Most older adults (do / do not) suffer hearing loss that is great enough to disrupt their daily lives. (p. 553)

11. Name some ways in which older adults can compensate for hearing loss. (p. 553)

_____

_____

_____

12. List four basic tastes to which older adults experience diminished sensitivity. (p. 553)

   A. _____

   B. _____

   C. _____

   D. _____

13. True or False: Age-related reductions in taste sensitivity are caused by changes in the number and distribution of taste buds. (p. 553)

14. Summarize changes in smell during late adulthood. (p. 553)

_____

_____

_____

15. Older adults experience a sharper decline in touch sensitivity on their (arms and lips / hands). (p. 553)

16. What two factors are thought to account for age-related declines in touch sensitivity? (p. 553)

   A. _____

   B. _____

Cardiovascular and Respiratory Systems

1. List four ways in which the heart muscle changes with advancing age. (p. 553)

   A. _____

   B. _____

   C. _____

   D. _____

2. What changes in the cardiovascular and respiratory systems lead to reduced oxygen supply to body tissues in old age? (p. 554)

   _____

   _____

   _____

Immune System

1. Explain *autoimmune response*. (p. 554)

   _____

   _____

   _____

2. True or False: Age-related declines in immune functioning are the cause of most illnesses among elderly adults. (p. 554)

3. True or False: Increased production of stress hormones undermines immune functioning in late adulthood. (p. 554)

4. Name two factors that protect immune response in old age. (p. 554)

   A. _____

   B. _____

Sleep

1. True or False: Older adults require 2 to 3 more hours of total sleep time per night than do younger adults. (p. 554)

2. Describe sleep difficulties commonly experienced by older adults, and cite two factors that are largely responsible for these sleep problems. (p. 555)

   Sleep difficulties: _____

   _____

   Factors responsible: _____

   _____

3. Summarize three reasons why men experience more sleep disturbances in late life than do women. (p. 555)

A. _____

B. _____

C. _____

Physical Appearance and Mobility

1. Describe changes in the skin during old age. (p. 555)

_____

_____

2. True or False: Both height and weight tend to decline in late adulthood. (p. 555)

3. Name three age-related changes that affect mobility. (p. 555)

A. _____

B. _____

C. _____

Adapting to the Physical Changes of Late Adulthood

1. True or False: Outward signs of aging, such as graying hair, facial wrinkles, and baldness, are closely related to sensory, cognitive, and motor functioning, as well as longevity. (p. 556)

2. Explain how the use of problem-centered coping strategies help older adults adjust to the physical changes of late life. (p. 556)

_____

_____

_____

3. Define *assistive technology,* and provide several examples of assistive technology devices that are available to help older adults cope with physical declines. (p. 556)

Definition: _____

_____

Examples: _____

_____

4. True or False: Many older adults report experiencing prejudice and discrimination. (p. 557)

5. True or False: Despite widespread negative stereotypes of aging, most older adults do not accept them as true of the elderly population or of themselves. (p. 557)

6. Summarize cross-cultural evidence from Inuit and Japanese populations suggesting that positive cultural views of aging contribute to better mental and physical health outcomes among the elderly. (p. 557)

_____

_____

_____

Cultural Influences: Cultural Variations in the Experience of Aging

1. Describe perspectives of aging among the Herero of Botswana, Africa. (p. 558)

2. Explain why elders in Momence, Illinois, a small working-class town, are able to maintain social participation and positions of authority. (p. 558)

3. Contrast the experiences of older adults living in Swathmore, PA with those of elders living among the Herero or in Momence, Illinois, noting reasons for these differences. (p. 558)

Health, Fitness, and Disability

1. The majority of older adults rate their health (favorably / unfavorably). (p. 558)

2. Explain how physical and mental health are intimately related during late life. (p. 559)

3. Summarize SES differences in physical functioning during late life, noting reasons for these differences. (p. 559)

4. True or False: Beyond age 85, women are more impaired than men and are less able to remain independent. (p. 559)

5. Define *compression of morbidity*. (p. 559)

Nutrition and Exercise

1. Describe the physical and environmental conditions which lead to increased risk of dietary deficiencies in late life. (p. 560)

2. True or False: Older adults who take vitamin and mineral supplements show improved health and physical functioning. (p. 560)

3. True or False: Endurance training and weight-bearing exercise are too strenuous for older adults and present more health risks than benefits. (p. 560)

4. Explain how exercise reduces cognitive declines. (p. 560)

_____

_____

_____

5. List several barriers to initiation of an exercise program in late life. (p. 560)

_____

_____

_____

Sexuality

1. Virtually all cross-sectional studies report (maintenance / decline) in sexual desire and frequency of sexual activity in old age. (p. 560)

2. True or False: Most healthy older married couples report diminished sexual enjoyment in late adulthood. (p. 560)

3. (Men / Women) are more likely to withdraw from sexual activity in late life. Why is this the case? (p. 560)

Physical Disabilities

1. List the four leading causes of death in late adulthood. (p. 561)

   A. _____

   B. _____

   C. _____

   D. _____

2. Distinguish between *primary* and *secondary aging*. (p. 561)

   Primary: _____

   Secondary: _____

3. Contrast two forms of arthritis that are common in late life—*osteoarthritis* and *rheumatoid arthritis*. (p. 562)

   Osteoarthritis: _____

   Rheumatoid arthritis: _____

4. Cite evidence that both hereditary and environmental factors contribute to arthritis. (p. 562)

   Heredity: _____

   Environment: _____

5. How can older adults manage arthritis? (p. 562)

_____

_____

6. Explain the cause of adult-onset diabetes. (p. 563)

_____

_____

7. What factors are associated with a risk of developing adult-onset diabetes? (p. 563)

_____

_____

8. What treatments are used to control adult-onset diabetes? (p. 563)

_____

_____

9. Death rate from unintentional injuries is highest during (adolescence and young adulthood / late adulthood). (p. 563)

10. True or False: Older adults have the lowest rates of traffic violations, accidents, and fatalities of any age group. (p. 563)

11. List three factors which contribute to the driving difficulties of older adults. (p. 563)

A. _____

B. _____

C. _____

12. What is the leading type of unintentional injury among the elderly? (p. 563)

_____

13. Explain factors that place older adults at increased risk for falling. (p. 563)

_____

_____

14. True or False: The elderly are at increased risk for serious injury and death after fracturing bones in a fall. (p. 563)

15. Cite several ways to reduce the risk of motor vehicle accidents and falls among the elderly. (p. 564)

A. _____

B. _____

C. _____

Mental Disabilities

1. Define *dementia.* (p. 564)

_____

_____

2. True or False: Approximately 10 percent of adults age 85 and older are affected by dementia. (p. 564)

3. The most common form of dementia is _____, in which structural and chemical brain deterioration is associated with gradual loss of many aspects of thought and behavior. (p. 565)

4. True or False: Alzheimer's disease is the leading cause of mortality in late life. (p. 565)

5. What is usually the first symptom of Alzheimer's disease? (p. 565)

_____

6. List personality changes associated with Alzheimer's disease. (p. 565)

_____

_____

7. Name four symptoms other than memory loss and personality changes that are associated with the progression of Alzheimer's disease. (p. 565)

   A. _____

   B. _____

   C. _____

   D. _____

8. Explain how Alzheimer's disease is diagnosed. (p. 565)

_____

_____

9. Describe two major structural changes in the cerebral cortex associated with Alzheimer's disease. (pp. 565–566)

   A. _____

   B. _____

10. Describe how chemical changes associated with decreased release of neurotransmitters contribute to many of the primary symptoms of Alzheimer's disease. (pp. 565–566)

_____

_____

_____

11. Briefly describe the two types of Alzheimer's disease, familial and sporadic. (p. 566)

   Familial: _____

_____

   Sporadic: _____

_____

12. An abnormality of the _____ gene is the most common known risk factor for sporadic Alzheimer's disease and is present in 50 percent of cases. Explain how this gene is linked to Alzheimer's disease. (p. 566)

13. Other than genetic abnormalities, name some of the biological and environmental risk factors for sporadic Alzheimer's disease. (p. 566)

    Biological: _____

    _____

    Environmental: _____

    _____

14. Cite factors associated with the higher incidence of Alzheimer's disease among African-American elderly. (p. 566)

    _____

    _____

    _____

15. Briefly describe four factors that protect against Alzheimer's disease. (p. 566)

    A. _____

    B. _____

    C. _____

    D. _____

16. True or False: Alzheimer's is a curable disease. (p. 566)

17. Describe interventions that help to ensure the best possible adjustment for Alzheimer's victims and their families. (pp. 566–567)

18. Describe *cerebrovascular dementia*. (p. 567)

19. Summarize biological and environmental influences on cerebrovascular dementia. (p. 567)

    Biological: _____

    _____

    Environmental: _____

    _____

20. True or False: Most cases of cerebrovascular dementia are caused by atherosclerosis. (p. 567)

21. List the warning signs of a stroke. (p. 567)

    _____

    _____

22. Name the disorder that is most often misdiagnosed as dementia, and explain at least one difference between adults with this disorder and those with dementia. (p. 567)

    Disorder: _____

    Difference: _____

23. In addition to the disorder named above in question 22, cite three factors which can lead to reversible symptoms of dementia. (p. 567)

A. _____

B. _____

C. _____

Health Care

1. True or False: The cost of government-sponsored health insurance for the elderly is expected to double by the year 2020 and triple by the year 2040. (p. 567)

2. True or False: Medicare funds 100 percent of older adults medical expenses. (p. 567)

3. Which disorders of aging most often lead to nursing home placement? (p. 569)

_____

_____

4. True or False: Older adults in the Untied States and Canada are less likely to be institutionalized than are those in other industrialized nations. Briefly elaborate on your response. (p. 569)

_____

_____

5. (Caucasian- / African-) Americans are more likely to be placed in a nursing home. Why is this the case? (p. 569)

_____

_____

6. Describe two alternatives which have been recommended to reduce institutionalized care for the elderly and its associated costs. (p. 569)

A. _____

B. _____

7. Summarize ways to improve the quality of nursing home services. (p. 569)

_____

_____

_____

Social Issues: Interventions for Caregivers of Elders with Dementia

1. Describe four needs addressed by the most effective programs for caregivers of older adults with dementia, and provide examples of how such needs are met. (p. 568)

A. _____

B. _____

C. _____

D. _____

1. True or False: Individual differences in cognitive functioning are greater during late adulthood than at any other time of life. (p. 570)

2. Explain how older adults can use *selective optimization with compensation* to sustain high levels of cognitive functioning in late life. (p. 570)

_____

_____

_____

Memory

Deliberate versus Automatic Memory

1. Describe the link between working memory declines and ability to use context cues as a way to aid recall. (p. 571)

_____

_____

2. (Recall / Recognition) memory shows fewer declines in late adulthood. (p. 571)

3. Describe the automatic form of memory known as *implicit memory*. (p. 571)

_____

_____

4. Age differences are greater for (automatic / deliberate) memory. Elaborate on your response. (p. 571)

_____

_____

Associative Memory

1. What are *associative memory deficits*? (p. 571)

_____

_____

2. True or False: Older adults maintain the ability to recognize single pieces of information but have difficulty with tasks that require them to form associations between multiple pieces of information. (p. 572)

Remote Memory

1. True or False: Memory for recent events is more clear than memory for remote events during late life. (p. 572)

2. True or False: People between the ages of 50 and 90 recall intermediate and remote events more readily than recent events. (p. 572)

3. Explain why older adults recall their adolescent and early adulthood experiences more easily than their mid-life experiences. (pp. 572–573)

_____

_____

Prospective Memory

1. What is *prospective memory*? (p. 573)

   _____

   _____

2. Older adults do better on (event-based / time-based) prospective memory tasks. Explain why this is the case. (p. 573)

   _____

   _____

3. Explain why prospective memory difficulties evidenced by older adults in the laboratory setting do not always appear in real life contexts. (p. 573)

   _____

   _____

Language Processing

1. What factors help older adults to maintain their language comprehension skills? (p. 573)

   _____

   _____

2. Describe two aspects of language production that show age-related declines, and note one factor that explains these changes. (p. 573)

   A. _____

   B. _____

   Factor that explains changes: _____

3. Explain two ways in which older adults compensate for difficulties with language production. (pp. 573–574)

   A. _____

   B. _____

Problem Solving

1. (Traditional / Real-life) problem solving declines in old age. Why does this occur? (p. 574)

2. What types of everyday problems are of concern to most older adults? (p. 574)

   _____

   _____

3. Summarize the adaptive problem solving strategies used by older adults to solve problems of daily living. (p. 574)

   _____

   _____

   _____

4. Older adults are (quicker / slower) to make decisions about seeking health care when they are ill than are younger adults. (p. 574)

5. True or False: Older couples are less likely than younger couples to collaborate in everyday problem solving. (p. 575)

Wisdom

1. Define *wisdom,* noting characteristics often used to describe this quality. (p. 575)

_____

_____

2. True or False: Cultures around the world assume that age and wisdom go together. Elaborate on your response. (p. 575)

_____

_____

3. True or False: Research shows that age is more important than life experience in the development of wisdom. (p. 576)

4. In addition to age and life experience, what factor is an important contributor to late-life wisdom? (p. 576)

_____

5. True or False: Wisdom predicts life satisfaction more strongly than do objective life conditions such as physical health, SES, and quality of living environment. (p. 576)

Factors Related to Cognitive Change

1. List four factors that predict maintenance of mental abilities in late life. (p. 576)

   A. _____

   B. _____

   C. _____

   D. _____

2. Explain how retirement can affect cognitive change both positively and negatively. (p. 576)

_____

_____

3. Define *terminal decline,* and note its average length. (p. 576)

   Definition: _____

   Average length: _____

Cognitive Interventions

1. For most of late adulthood, cognitive declines are (rapid / gradual). (p. 577)

2. Summarize findings from the Adult Development and Enrichment Project. (p. 577)

_____

_____

1.   Older adults' participation in continuing education has (increased / declined) over the past few decades. (p. 577)

Types of Programs

1.   Describe characteristics of Elderhostel programs, noting several of the learning opportunities which they offer. (p. 577)

_____

_____

2.   Describe the University of the Third Age and similar programs offered in Europe and Australia. (pp. 577–578)

_____

_____

3.   Summarize three ways to increase the effectiveness of instruction for older adults. (p. 578)

A.   _____

B.   _____

C.   _____

Benefits of Continuing Education

1.   List five benefits of participation in continuing education programs for the elderly. (p. 578)

A.   _____

B.   _____

C.   _____

D.   _____

E.   _____

ASK YOURSELF . . .

For *Ask Yourself* questions for this chapter, please log on to the Companion Website at www.ablongman.com/berk.

SUGGESTED STUDENT READINGS

DeBaggio, T. (2002). *An intimate look at life with Alzheimer's*. New York: Free Press. Written by an individual diagnosed with Alzheimer's, the author examines the highs and lows of everyday life. Instead of focusing solely on limitations of living with a disability, DeBaggio spends a great deal of time raising public awareness

Ellis, N. (2002). *If I live to be a 100*. New York: Crown Publishing. Based on extensive research and a year of interviews, this book highlights the extraordinary lives of centenarians, including their unique life experiences and secrets to living a long, healthy life.

Roszak, T. (2001). *As boomers become elders.* New York: Publishes Group West. As the baby boom generation approaches elderhood, older adults have much more influence in society than ever before. The author explores critical issues for seniors, such as politics, economics, health care, and the potential for older adults to become a rich, cultural resource.

Whalley, L. J. (2001). *The aging brain.* Columbia University Press. Explores age-related changes in brain structure and functioning in late adulthood, including biological and environmental influences, the range of possible treatments for cognitive decline, and future directions for research.

PUZZLE 17.1 TERM REVIEW

Across

3. Life expectancy _____ : age-related reversal in life expectancy of sectors of the population
6. Set of disorders occurring almost entirely in old age; many aspects of thought and behavior are so impaired that everyday activities are disrupted
8. Bundles of twisted threads that are the product of collapsed neural structures are called _____ tangles.
10. _____ lifespan: the number of years of vigorous, healthy life that an individual born in a particular year can expect
11. _____ degeneration is a blurring and eventual loss of central vision due to a break-down of light sensitive cells in the center of the retina
12. Sleep _____ : sleep condition in which breathing stops for 10 seconds or longer, resulting in many brief awakenings
13. Cloudy areas in the lens of the eye that result in foggy vision and (without surgery) eventually blindness
14. _____ lifespan: genetic limit to length of life for a person free of external risk ractors
15. _____ life expectancy: the number of years that a person born in a particular year can expect to live

Down

1. form of arthritis characterized by deteriorating cartilage on the ends of bones of frequently used joints
2. _____ response: abnormal response of the immune system in which it turns against normal body tissues
4. _____ disease is the most common form of dementia in which structural and chemical deterioration in the brain is associated with gradual loss of many aspects of thought and behavior
5. _____ dementia: a series of strokes leaves areas of dead brain cells, producing degeneration of mental abilities
7. _____ plaques: dense deposits of a deteriorated protein surrounded by clumps of dead neurons
9. Form of arthritis in which the immune system attacks the body, resulting in inflammation of connective tissue

PUZZLE 17.2 TERM REVIEW

Across

3. Elders who are _____-old appear physically young for their advanced years

5. _____ memory involves remembering to engage in planned actions at an appropriate time in the future.

6. Compression of _____: public health goal of reducing the average period of diminished vigor before death as life expectancy extends

8. Type of memory deficit that involves difficulty creating or retrievin links between pieces of information

10. Memory without conscious awareness is called _____ memory.

13. Elders who are _____-old show signs of physical decline in late life.

14. _____ technology: an array of devices that permit people with disabilities to improve their functioning

Down

1. _____ memory: recall of events that happened long ago

2. form of cognition that combines breadth and depth of practical knowledge, ability to reflect on that knowledge in ways that make life more bearable and worthwhile, emotional maturity, and creative integration of experience and knowledge into new ways of thinking and acting

4. Selective _____ with compensation strategies that permit older adults to sustain high levels of functioning

7. _____ aging: declines due to hereditary defects and environmental influences

9. _____ age: actual competence and performance of an older adult

11. _____ aging: genetically influenced age-related declines in functioning of organs and systems that affect all members of our species and take place in the context of overall good health

12. _____ decline is a steady, marked decrease in cognitive functioning prior to death.

PRACTICE TEST #1

1. Today, the average life expectancy is approximately (p. 547)
   a. 40 to 45 years.
   b. 55 to 60 years.
   c. 75 to 80 years.
   d. 95 to 100 years.

2. The life expectancy crossover is a phenomenon in which (p. 548)
   a. after age 85, surviving members of ethnic minority groups live longer than members of the white majority.
   b. old-old elderly tend to outlive young-old elderly.
   c. average life expectancy increases steadily from generation to generation.
   d. life expectancy is expected to stabilize and eventually decline in the coming decades because of increased poverty and disease.

3. Ellen is worried about developing cataracts or macular degeneration. What can she do to reduce her risk of developing these conditions? (p. 552)
   a. spend fewer hours working at the computer
   b. wear glasses for reading
   c. eat more fatty foods
   d. take vitamin supplements

4. Which of the following is true of hearing in late adulthood? (p. 552)
   a. Hearing loss in late life is greatest at low frequencies.
   b. Age-related declines in speech perception have the greatest impact on life satisfaction.
   c. Almost all elders suffer from hearing loss that is severe enough to disrupt their daily lives.
   d. Hearing loss has a greater impact on self-care than does vision loss.

5. Aging of the cardiovascular system causes (p. 553)
   a. the heart muscle to become less rigid.
   b. cells within the heart to shrink and multiply.
   c. artery walls to stiffen and accumulate plaque.
   d. the heart muscle to become more responsive to signals from pacemaker cells.

6. Which of the following is true of sleep changes in late adulthood? (p. 554)
   a. Older adults require 3 to 5 more hours of total sleep time per night than do younger adults.
   b. Sleep disturbances are more common in men than women.
   c. Changes in the sensory system are responsible for changes in the timing of sleep during late life (i.e., earlier bedtime and morning awakenings).
   d. Only 5 to 10 percent of elders report problems with insomnia.

7. Mobility declines in late adulthood result from (p. 555)
   a. diminished muscle strength.
   b. visual declines associated with depth perception and acuity.
   c. changes in body structure, particularly height and weight.
   d. age-related changes in the structure of the middle ear, which affects balance.

8. Assistive technology (p. 556)
   a. reverses age-related cognitive declines.
   b. helps to improve the functioning of older people with physical impairments.
   c. is designed to hide the outward signs of aging, such as graying hair and wrinkled skin.
   d. aids older adults with sleep apnea and insomnia.

9. Which of the following is true with regard to group differences in health? (p. 559)
   a. Ethnic and SES variations in health increase dramatically in late adulthood.
   b. Native-American and Canadian Aboriginal populations report better health than do elders from other ethnic groups.
   c. Low-SES elders are more likely to seek medical treatment than their higher-SES counterparts, and they are more compliant with doctors' directives.
   d. After age 85, women are more impaired than men because only the sturdiest men have survived.

10. Which term refers to the public health goal of reducing the average period of diminished vigor before death as life expectancy is extended? (p. 559)
   a. life expectancy crossover
   b. terminal decline
   c. compression of morbidity
   d. selective optimization with compensation

11. Most healthy older married couples report (p. 560)
   a. complete cessation of sexual enjoyment and activity by age 75.
   b. diminished sexual enjoyment and infrequent sexual activity.
   c. continued, regular sexual enjoyment.
   d. slight increases in sexual enjoyment and frequency of sexual activity.

12. The leading cause of death among individuals age 65 and older is (p. 562)
   a. respiratory diseases such as emphysema and pneumonia.
   b. cardiovascular disease.
   c. cancer.
   d. unintentional injuries.

13. Rheumatoid arthritis (p. 562)
   a. is sometimes referred to as "wear-and-tear" arthritis since it affects frequently used joints.
   b. results from an autoimmune response leading to inflammation of connective tissue.
   c. shows little genetic contribution, indicating that environmental causes are to blame for this condition.
   d. responds well to hormone therapy, suggesting that estrogen loss may be involved.

14. The most common form of dementia is (p. 565)
   a. Parkinson's disease.
   b. Alzheimer's disease.
   c. cerebrovascular dementia.
   d. anterograde amnesia.

15. _____, or bundles of twisted threads caused by collapsed neural structures, result in structural change in the memory and reasoning areas of the cerebral cortex. (p. 565)
   a. Neurofibrillary tangles
   b. Amyloid plaques
   c. Neurotransmitters
   d. Cerebrovascular bundles

16. Cerebrovascular dementia (p. 567)
   a. is caused by reduced levels of the neurotransmitters acetylcholine and serotonin.
   b. most often results from severe head injury, which causes brain damage and deterioration of amyloid protein.
   c. results from a series of strokes which leave areas of dead brain cells.
   d. is associated with degradation of the myelin sheathing which surrounds neural fibers.

17. Which of the following is true of cognitive development in late life? (p. 570)
    a. Fluid intelligence is sustained throughout much of late life.
    b. Crystallized intelligence improves in late life as adults learn better ways to compensate for memory and verbal difficulties.
    c. Cognitive improvement and maintenance outweigh cognitive losses in late adulthood.
    d. Individual differences in cognitive functioning are greater in late adulthood than at any other time of life.

18. Which type of memory relates to an individual's ability to create and retrieve links between pieces of information? (p. 571)
    a. implicit
    b. remote
    c. associative
    d. prospective

19. Which of these language abilities remains the most stable as adults grow older? (p. 572)
    a. retrieval of words from long-term memory
    b. planning and organization of speech
    c. understanding the meaning of spoken and written prose
    d. generating the right words to convey a thought

20. The Adult Development and Aging Project (p. 577)
    a. contributed to improved memory and problem solving abilities among elderly participants.
    b. hastened the rate of terminal decline among elderly participants.
    c. provided better strategies for overcoming the physical declines of aging.
    d. was designed to assist caregivers of older adults with Alzheimer's disease.

PRACTICE TEST #2

1. 82-year-old Charlie is vigorous, healthy, and appears physically young for his age. Charlie would be characterized as (p. 546)
    a. young-old.
    b. old-old.
    c. functionally-old.
    d. terminally-old.

2. The probable reason why women live an average of 4 to 7 years longer than men is (p. 547)
    a. less stressful lives.
    b. better access to health care.
    c. more supportive social relationships.
    d. the protective value of females' extra X chromosome.

3. Declines in brain weight throughout adulthood largely result from (p. 549)
    a. shrinkage of the ventricles within the brain.
    b. death of neurons.
    c. myelination of neural fibers.
    d. increased incidence of stroke.

4. The leading cause of blindness among older adults is (p. 552)
    a. glaucoma.
    b. cataracts.
    c. macular degeneration.
    d. neural death in the visual cortex of the brain.

5. Which of the following is true of taste in late life? (p. 553)
   a. Older adults show reduced sensitivity to sweet and salty tastes but retain sensitivity to sour and bitter tastes.
   b. Reduced taste sensitivity is a direct result of changes in the number and distribution of taste buds.
   c. Elder adults are less likely than others to use flavor additives, such as salt, pepper, and sugar, because it makes food less appealing to them.
   d. Reduced taste sensitivity makes food less enjoyable to older adults, which increases the likelihood of dietary deficiencies.

6. Aging of the immune system (p. 554)
   a. causes increased production and responsivity of T-cells.
   b. is the cause of most illnesses among the elderly.
   c. shows little individual variation from one person to the next.
   d. is related to increased malfunction, wherein the immune system is more likely to turn against normal body tissues.

7. Older adults who use _____ coping strategies adapt more favorably to the everyday challenges of aging and show improved physical functioning. (p. 556)
   a. cognition-centered
   b. problem-centered
   c. emotion-centered
   d. avoidant

8. In Western nations (p. 557)
   a. few older adults report experiencing prejudice and discrimination.
   b. negative stereotypes of aging have little impact on older adults' physical and cognitive functioning.
   c. age-related deterioration is viewed as an inevitable feature of late adulthood.
   d. elders are treated with deference and respect.

9. Older adults are generally _____ about their health. (p. 558)
   a. optimistic
   b. pessimistic
   c. indifferent
   d. uninformed

10. Your elderly grandparent is wondering whether or not to take a vitamin-mineral nutritional supplement. What advice should you give? (p. 560)
    a. There is no evidence that supplements offer health benefits.
    b. Supplements are only advantageous to sedentary older adults.
    c. Cognitive enhancers, such as Vitamin E and ginko biloba, are highly effective for improving cognitive functioning.
    d. Supplements are related to improvements in health and physical functioning for most older adults.

11. Physical exercise (p. 560)
    a. does little to slow or diminish age-related declines.
    b. is risky for most older adults, particularly those with a chronic disease.
    c. is common among older adults, with over 75 percent remaining active in late life.
    d. leads to both physical and cognitive gains.

12. Which of these is the best example of primary aging? (p. 561)
    a. farsightedness resulting from stiffening of the lenses of the eye
    b. lung cancer caused by smoking cigarettes
    c. weight gain resulting from a sedentary lifestyle
    d. high blood pressure from prolonged stress in the workplace

13. Which of the following is true of unintentional injuries in late adulthood? (p. 563)
    a. Older adults have the lowest rates of traffic violations, accidents, and fatalities of any age group.
    b. Most older adults do not limit their driving because they fail to recognize their diminished driving abilities.
    c. Falls represent the leading type of accident among the elderly.
    d. Although falls are common among the elderly, they rarely result in serious injuries.

14. The earliest symptom of Alzheimer's disease is (p. 565)
    a. severe memory problems.
    b. disintegration of skilled and purposeful motor movements.
    c. delusions and imaginary fears.
    d. inability to comprehend or produce speech.

15. Sporadic Alzheimer's disease (p. 566)
    a. tends to run in families.
    b. is linked to genes on chromosomes 1, 14, and 21.
    c. is associated with an abnormal gene on chromosome 19, resulting in excess levels of APOE4.
    d. has an earlier onset and a more rapid progression than does familial Alzheimer's disease.

16. Which person is most likely to be placed in a nursing home? (p. 569)
    a. a Caucasian American with Alzheimer's disease
    b. an African-American with cardiovascular disease
    c. a Native American with cancer
    d. an Asian elder with a hip fracture

17. Research on memory capacity in late adulthood shows that (p. 571)
    a. age-related memory declines are greatest for automatic activities, whereas memory for tasks requiring deliberate processing does not change much in old age.
    b. recognition memory suffers less in late adulthood than does recall memory.
    c. older adults recall remote personal experiences more easily than recent ones.
    d. older adults perform better on time-based than event-based prospective memory tasks.

18. Which of the following is true of problem solving in old age? (p. 574)
    a. Older adults solve everyday problems more effectively than complex hypothetical problems.
    b. Problems encountered in late adulthood are nearly identical to those encountered earlier in life.
    c. Older adults view most problems as beyond their control, and consequently, fail to use adaptive coping strategies.
    d. Compared to younger married couples, older married couples are less likely to collaborate in everyday problem solving.

19. Wisdom (p. 575)
    a. is directly related to age, with virtually all older adults showing high levels of wisdom.
    b. is closely linked to life experiences, particularly exposure to and success in overcoming adversity.
    c. is more common in early and middle adulthood than in late adulthood.
    d. shows no relationship to life satisfaction.

20. Elderhostel programs (p. 578)
    a. combine educational programs and recreational activities.
    b. provide direct instruction in compensatory strategies to help elders address cognitive processing declines.
    c. are only beneficial for active, wealthy, well-educated older adults.
    d. are specially designed to meet the needs of elders with little education and few economic resources.

CHAPTER 18
EMOTIONAL AND SOCIAL DEVELOPMENT
IN LATE ADULTHOOD

BRIEF CHAPTER SUMMARY

The final psychological conflict of Erikson's theory, ego integrity verses despair, involves coming to terms with one's life. Adults who arrive at a sense of integrity feel whole, complete, and satisfied with their achievements, whereas despair occurs when elders feel they have made many wrong decisions. In Peck's theory, ego integrity requires that older adults move beyond their life's work, their bodies, and their separate identities. Labouvie-Vief addresses the development of adults' reasoning about emotion, pointing out that older, more psychologically mature adults are more in touch with their feelings. Although researchers do not yet have a full understanding of why older people reminisce more than younger people do, current theory and research indicate that reflecting on the past can be positive and adaptive.

Older adults have accumulated a lifetime of self-knowledge, leading to more secure and complex conceptions of themselves than at earlier ages. During late adulthood, shifts in three personality traits take place. Agreeableness and acceptance of change tend to rise, whereas sociability dips slightly. Although declining health and transportation difficulties reduce organized religious participation in advanced old age, informal religious activities remain prominent in the lives of today's elders.

In patterns of behavior called the dependency-support script and independence-ignore script, older adults' dependency behaviors are attended to immediately and their independent behaviors are ignored. Physical declines and chronic disease can be highly stressful, leading to a sense of loss of personal control—a major factor in adult mental health. Although elders are at risk for a variety of negative life changes, these events actually evoke less stress and depression than they do in younger adults. In late adulthood, social support continues to play a powerful role in reducing stress, thereby promoting physical health and psychological well-being.

In late adulthood, extroverts continue to interact with a wider range of people than introverts and people with poor social skills. Disengagement theory, activity theory, and socioemotional selectivity theory offer explanations for the decline in amount of social interaction in late adulthood. Elders live in contexts—both physical and social—that affect their social experiences and, consequently, their development and adjustment. Communities, neighborhoods, and housing arrangements vary in the extent to which they enable aging residents to satisfy their social needs.

The social convoy is an influential model of changes in our social networks as we move through life. Marital satisfaction rises from middle to late adulthood as perceptions of fairness in the relationship increase, couples engage in joint leisure activities, and communication becomes more positive. Most gay and lesbian elders also report happy, highly fulfilling relationships. Couples who divorce in late adulthood constitute a very small proportion of all divorces in any given year. Compared to divorced younger adults, divorced elders find it harder to separate their identity from that of their former spouse, and they suffer more from a sense of personal failure. Wide variation in adaptation to widowhood exits, with age, social support, and personality making a difference. Siblings, friends, and adult children provide important sources of emotional support and companionship to elders. In addition, older adults with adult grandchildren and great grandchildren benefit from a wider potential network of support. Although the majority of older adults enjoy positive relationships with family members, friends, and professional caregivers, some suffer maltreatment at the hands of these individuals.

Financial and health status, opportunities to pursue meaningful activities, and societal factors (such as early retirement benefits) affect the decision to retire. Retirement also varies with gender, and ethnicity. Most elders adjust well to retirement. Involvement in leisure activities is related to better physical and mental health and reduced mortality. Successful aging, involving maximizing gains and minimizing losses, is best viewed as a process rather than a list of accomplishments. Social contexts that permit elders to manage life changes effectively foster successful aging.

LEARNING OBJECTIVES

After reading this chapter, you should be able to:

18.1   Describe Erikson's stage of ego integrity versus despair. (pp. 584–585)

18.2   Discuss Peck's and Labouvie-Vief's views of development in late adulthood, and describe the functions of reminiscence and life review in older adults' lives. (pp. 585–587)

18.3   Cite stable and changing aspects of self-concept and personality in late adulthood. (p. 587)

18.4   Discuss spirituality and religiosity in late adulthood, and trace the development of faith. (pp. 587–591)

18.5   Discuss individual differences in psychological well-being as older adults respond to increased dependency, declining health, and negative life changes. (pp. 591–594)

18.6   Summarize the role of social support and social interaction in promoting physical health and psychological well-being in late adulthood. (p. 594)

18.7   Describe social theories of aging, including disengagement theory, activity theory, and socioemotional selectivity theory. (pp. 595–596)

18.8   Cite ways in which communities, neighborhoods, and housing arrangements affect elders' social lives and adjustment. (pp. 596–600)

18.9   Describe changes in social relationships in late adulthood, including marriage, gay and lesbian partnerships, divorce, remarriage, and widowhood, and discuss never-married, childless older adults. (pp. 600–604)

18.10 Explain how sibling relationships and friendships change in late life. (pp. 600–604)

18.11 Describe older adults' relationships with adult children, adult grandchildren, and great-grandchildren. (pp. 606–607)

18.12 Discuss elder maltreatment, including risk factors and strategies for prevention. (pp. 607–609)

18.13 Discuss the decision to retire, adjustment to retirement, and involvement in leisure activities. (pp. 609–612)

18.14 Discuss the meaning of successful aging. (pp. 612–613)

STUDY QUESTIONS

Erikson's Theory: Ego Integrity versus Despair

1.   Cite characteristics of elders who arrive at a sense of integrity and those who experience despair. (p. 584)

Integrity: _____

_____

Despair: _____

_____

Peck's Theory: Three Tasks of Ego Integrity

1. Cite three tasks that Peck maintained must be resolved for integrity to develop. (p. 585)

A. _____

B. _____

C. _____

Labouvie-Vief's Theory: Emotional Expertise

1. According to Labouvie-Vief, how do older and more psychologically mature individuals describe their emotional experiences? (p. 585)

_____

_____

2. Explain how older adults' emotional perceptiveness influences their coping strategies. (pp. 585–586)

_____

_____

Reminiscence and Life Review

1. True or False: Older people *reminisce* to escape the realities of a shortened future and the nearness of death. (p. 586)

2. Define *life review,* and explain why it is an important form of reminiscence. (p. 586)

A. _____

_____

B. _____

_____

3. Besides life review, cite three other purposes of reminiscence. (pp. 586–587)

A. _____

B. _____

C. _____

1. Cite three factors that influenced refugees' recollections and assessments of their lifelong experiences. (p. 588)

   A. _____ B. _____

   C. _____

2. Separation and inadequate care had a (more / less) profound impact on temperamentally withdrawn, anxious individuals than on outgoing individuals. (p. 588)

3. Interviewees who were (children / adolescents) were less affected by the absence of close bonds with adults. (p. 588)

4. How did the experiences of British refugees compare with those of Polish and German refugees? (p. 588)

   _____

   _____

   _____

Stability and Change in Self-Concept and Personality

Secure and Multifaceted Self-Concept

1. True or False: Older adults have accumulated a lifetime of self-knowledge, leading to more secure and complex conceptions of themselves than at earlier ages. (p. 587)

2. Explain how a secure and multifaceted self-concept relates to psychological well-being. (p. 587)

   _____

   _____

   _____

Agreeableness, Sociability, and Acceptance of Change

1. Cite three shifts in personality characteristics that take place during late adulthood. (p. 587)

   A. _____ B. _____

   C. _____

Spirituality and Religiosity

1. Older adults attach (great / moderate / little) value to religious beliefs and behaviors. (p. 587–588)

2. True or False: Religious involvement remains fairly stable throughout adulthood. (p. 589)

3. List three factors that may motivate elders to search for inner spiritual resources. (p. 589)

   A. _____ B. _____

   C. _____

4. What three changes occur in adult faith development among adults who reach Fowler's fourth stage? (p. 590)

   A. _____

   B. _____

   C. _____

5. Involvement in both organized and informal religious activities is especially high among _____ elders. (p. 590)

6. Briefly summarize the benefits of religious involvement. (pp. 590–591)

   _____

   _____

7. (Men / Women) are more likely to be involved in religion. What might explain this trend? (p. 591)

   _____

   _____

   _____

Individual Differences in Psychological Well-Being

Control versus Dependency

1. Describe two behavior patterns often used by people when interacting with older adults that serve to reinforce dependent behavior at the expense of independent behavior, regardless of the older person's competencies. (p. 591)

   A. _____

   B. _____

2. What factors influence whether elders will react positively or negatively to caregiving? (pp. 591–592)

   _____

   _____

3. In (Western / Non-Western) societies, many elders fear becoming dependent on others. (p. 592)

Health

1. Summarize the impact of physical health on psychological well-being in late adulthood. (pp. 592–593)

   _____

   _____

   _____

2. True or False: People age 65 and older have the lowest suicide rate of any age group. (p. 593)

3. Cite three factors that help elders to surmount physical impairment. (p. 593)

   A. _____ B. _____

   C. _____

Negative Life Changes

1. True or False: Negative life changes cause less stress for elders than for younger people. (p. 594)

2. Briefly describe sex differences in the coping skills of older adults. (p. 594)

_____

_____

Social Support and Social Interaction

1. Summarize the benefits of social support in late adulthood. (p. 594)

_____

_____

_____

2. Many older adults place a high value on (dependency / independence) and (do / do not) want a great deal of unreciprocated support from people close to them. (p. 594)

3. List two factors that make ethnic minority elders more likely to accept formal support. (p. 594)

   A. _____

   B. _____

4. (Extroverted / Introverted) elders are more likely to maintain high morale. (p. 594)

Social Issues: Elder Suicide

1. Cite sex and age differences in elder suicide. (p. 592)

   A. _____

   B. _____

2. List two reasons why elder suicides tend to be underreported. (p. 592)

   A. _____

   B. _____

3. What two types of events often prompt suicide in late life? (p. 593)

   A. _____

   B. _____

4. List several warning signs of elder suicide. (p. 593)

_____

_____

5. Describe the most effective treatment for depressed, suicidal elders. (p. 593)

_____

_____

6. Cite several reasons why rates of elder suicide have declined during the past 50 years. (p. 593)

_____

_____

A Changing Social World

Social Theories of Aging

1. According to _____ theory, mutual withdrawal between elders and society takes place in anticipation of death. Provide evidence that this theory does not adequately explain the reduced social activity of older people. (p. 595)

_____

_____

2. _____ theory states that social barriers to engagement, not the desires of elders, cause declining rates of interaction. (p. 595)

3. True or False: Consistent with activity theory, studies show that simply offering older adults opportunities for social contact leads to greater social activity. (p. 595)

4. _____ theory states that social interaction does not decline suddenly in late adulthood. Rather it extends lifelong selection processes. (p. 596)

5. According to socioemotional selectivity theory, how do the functions of social interaction change from early to late adulthood? (p. 596)

_____

_____

_____

Social Contexts of Aging: Communities, Neighborhoods, and Housing

1. The majority of senior citizens reside in _____, where they moved earlier in their lives and usually remain after retirement. (p. 596)

2. How do suburban elders differ from inner-city elders? (p. 596)

   A. _____

   B. _____

3. What aspects of smaller communities foster gratifying relationships for older adults? (pp. 596–597)

_____

_____

4. Fear of _____ has a profound, negative impact on older adults' sense of security and comfort. (p. 598)

5. True or False: Older adults are less often targets of crime, especially violent crime, than other age groups. (p. 598)

6. Older adults in Western industrialized nations want to (leave / stay in) the neighborhoods where they spent their adults lives. (p. 598)

7. List three factors that prompt elder relocations. (p. 598)

   A. _____ B. _____

   C. _____

8. Which setting affords the greatest possible personal control for the majority of elders? Under what conditions does this setting pose risks? (p. 598)

   A. _____

   B. _____

9. Although increasing numbers of ethnic minority elders want to live on their own, _____ often prevents them from doing so. (p. 598)

10. Cite factors that contribute to rising poverty rates among elderly women. (p. 599)

    _____

    _____

11. Identify three types of residential communities available to North American senior citizens. (pp. 599–600)

    A. _____ B. _____

    C. _____

12. List three positive effects of residential communities on physical and mental health. (pp. 599–600)

    A. _____

    B. _____

    C. _____

13. Which residential setting represents the most extreme restriction of autonomy? (p. 600)

    _____

14. How do North American nursing homes differ from European facilities? (p. 600)

    _____

    _____

Biology & Environment: Aging, Time Perception, and Social Goals

1. True or False: Socioemotional selectivity theory underscores that our time perspective plays a crucial role in the social goals we select and pursue. (p. 597)

2. How do findings on the social perspectives of men with AIDS symptoms support socioemotional selectivity theory? (p. 597)

   _____

   _____

   _____

3. Mainland Chinese elders express a (stronger / weaker) desire for familiar social partners because they perceive their future as (more / less) limited. (p. 597)

Relationships in Late Adulthood

1. How does the *social convoy* support adaptation to old age? (p. 600)

   _____

   _____

Marriage

1. Provide three reasons why marital satisfaction increases from middle to late adulthood, when it is at its peak. (p. 601)

   A. _____

   B. _____

   C. _____

2. When marital dissatisfaction is present, it takes a greater toll on (men / women), who tend to confront marital problems and try to solve them. (p. 601)

Gay and Lesbian Partnerships

1. True or False: Most elderly gay and lesbian couples report happy, highly fulfilling relationships. (p. 601)

2. What unique challenges do aging gays and lesbians face? (pp. 601–602)

   _____

   _____

   _____

Divorce and Remarriage

1. Although rare, divorce in late adulthood is increasing. What reasons do men and women give for initiating divorce in late life? (p. 602)

   Men: _____

   Women: _____

2. Following divorce, older adults find it (easier / harder) to separate their identity from that of their former spouse, and they suffer (more / less) from a sense of personal failure. (p. 602)

3. Why do women suffer more than men from late-life divorce? (p. 602)

_____

_____

4. List three reasons why late adulthood remarriages are more frequent after divorce than widowhood. (p. 602)

   A. _____

   B. _____

   C. _____

Widowhood

1. True or False: Ethnic minorities with high rates of poverty and chronic disease are more likely to be widowed. (p. 602)

2. When widowed elders relocate due to financial or physical difficulties, they usually choose to move (closer to / in with) family. (p. 603)

3. The greatest problem for recently widowed elders is _____. (p. 603)

4. Cite two characteristics that contribute to resiliency in widowed elders. (p. 603)

   A. _____   B. _____

5. (Men / Women) find it more difficult to adjust to widowhood. What accounts for this gender difference? (p. 603)

_____

_____

Never-Married, Childless Older Adults

1. Cite examples of alternative, meaningful relationships formed by adults who remain single and childless throughout life. (pp. 603–604)

_____

_____

2. In a large, nationally representative sample of Americans over age 70, childless (men / women) without marital partners were far more likely to feel lonely. (p. 604)

Siblings

1. Both men and women perceive bonds with (sisters / brothers) to be closer. (p. 604)

2. Under what circumstances are elders likely to turn to siblings for assistance? (p. 604)

_____

3. Cite the benefits of joint reminiscing between siblings in late adulthood. (p. 605)

_____

_____

_____

Friendships

1. List four functions of elder friendships. (pp. 605–606)

    A. _____

    B. _____

    C. _____

    D. _____

2. True or False: Friendship formation continues throughout life. (p. 606)

3. Why do elders tend to report more intergenerational friendships than in earlier years? (p. 606)

    _____

4. What are *secondary friends*, and who is more likely to have them? (p. 606)

    A. _____

    B. _____

Relationships with Adult Children

1. As with other ties, the (quality / quantity) of interactions between elders and their adult children affects older adults' life satisfaction. (p. 606)

2. How do warm bonds between elders and their adult children foster psychological well-being? (p. 606)

    _____

    _____

3. (Moderate / Extensive) support from adult children is psychologically beneficial to elders. (p. 606)

4. Cite sex differences in older parent-adult child interaction. (p. 606)

    Daughters: _____

    Sons: _____

Relationships with Adult Grandchildren and Great-Grandchildren

1. The majority of grandchildren (do /do not) feel obligated to assist grandparents in need. Grandparents often expect _____ but not practical help from grandchildren. (p. 607)

2. List factors that influence the quality of grandparent-adult grandchild relationships. (p. 607)

    _____

    _____

    _____

3. Longitudinal research reveals that as grandparents and grandchildren move through life, contact (increases / declines). (p. 607)

Elder Maltreatment

1. List and briefly describe four forms of elder maltreatment. (pp. 607–608)

    A. _____

    B. _____

    C. _____

    D. _____

2. _____ is the most common form of elder abuse, followed by _____.
    (p. 608)

3. Perpetrators of elder abuse usually (are / are not) family members. (p. 608)

4. List five risk factors that contribute to the likelihood of elder abuse. (p. 608)

    A. _____

    B. _____

    C. _____

    D. _____

    E. _____

5. Why is preventing elder maltreatment by family members especially challenging? (p. 608)

    _____

    _____

6. Identify several components of elder maltreatment prevention programs. (pp. 608–609)

    _____

    _____

    _____

7. How can societal efforts reduce the incidence of elder abuse? (p. 609)

    _____

    _____

Retirement and Leisure

1. Cite several trends in the retirement process in Western industrialized nations. (p. 609)

    _____

    _____

The Decision to Retire

1. What is usually the first consideration in the decision to retire? List additional considerations. (p. 609)

   First: _____

   Additional: _____

   _____

   _____

2. Why do women tend to retire earlier than men? What is the exception to this trend? (p. 610)

   A. _____

   B. _____

Adjustment to Retirement

1. True or False: For most people, mental health is fairly stable from the pre- to post-retirement years. (pp. 610–611)

2. Cite workforce and psychological factors that predict retirement satisfaction. (p. 611)

   Workforce: _____

   _____

   Psychological: _____

   _____

3. How can retirement enhance marital satisfaction? How does marital satisfaction, in turn, influence adjustment to retirement? (p. 611)

   A. _____

   B. _____

Leisure Activities

1. What is the best preparation for leisure in late life? (p. 611)

   _____

2. List several benefits of involvement in leisure activities. (p. 611)

   _____

   _____

3. Why does the frequency and variety of leisure pursuits tend to decline in late adulthood? (p. 611)

   _____

4. List four characteristics of elders who become involved in volunteer work. (p. 612)

   A. _____   B. _____

   C. _____   D. _____

5. Older adults report (less / more) awareness of public affairs and vote at a (lower / higher) rate than do other adults. (p. 612)

Successful Aging

1. Define *successful aging,* and cite characteristics of successful agers. (p. 612)

   A. _____

   B. _____

2. How have views of successful aging changed in recent years? (p. 612)

   _____

   _____

3. List eight ways in which older adults realize their goals. (pp. 612–613)

   A. _____

   B. _____

   C. _____

   D. _____

   E. _____

   F. _____

   G. _____

   H. _____

4. Cite societal contexts that permit elders to manage life changes effectively. (p. 613)

   _____

   _____

   _____

ASK YOURSELF . . .

For *Ask Yourself* questions for this chapter, please log on to the Companion Website at www.ablongman.com/berk.

SUGGESTED STUDENT READINGS

Beisgen, B. A., Kraitchman, M. C., & Ellis, A. C. (2003). *Opportunities for successful aging.* New York: Springer Publishing. Examines the experiences of elders in a wide range of settings, including assisted living facilities, adult day living centers, residential facilities, and recreational programs.

Eyetsemitan, F. E., & Gire, J. T. (2003). *Aging and adult development in the developing world: Applying western theories and concepts.* West Point, CT: Greenwood Publishing. A collection of chapters highlighting the influence of environmental contexts on the aging process. According to the authors, Western theories of aging may be inappropriate for understanding the experiences of elders in developing societies.

Heilbrun, C. G. (1998). *The last gift of time: Life beyond sixty.* New York: Ballantine. Written by a distinguished author and critic, this book explores the ups and downs of life after age 60, including changing relationships, emotional and intellectual insights, and unexpected pleasures and disappointments that accompany the aging process.

McFadden, S. H., & Atchley, R. C. (Eds.). (2001). *Aging and the meaning of time: A multidisciplinary exploration.* New York: Springer. Describes the meaning of aging and how perception of time influences how elders confront their own mortality.

Moore, A. J., & Stratton, D. C. (2001). *Resilient widowers: Older men speak for themselves.* New York: Springer Publishing. Based on a five-year study of 51 widowers, this book examines widowhood in the context of life experience, including grief and adjustment, living alone, remarriage, and the importance of social support.

Vaillant, G.E. (2002). *Aging well: Surprising guideposts to a happier life from the landmark Harvard Study of Adult Development.* Boston: Little Brown. Based on a longitudinal study of 824 participants followed from adolescence through old age, this book explores the multitude of factors contributing to resilience across the lifespan. Vaillant concludes that individual lifestyle choices perhaps play a greater role in successful aging than genetics, wealth, race, and gender.

PUZZLE 18.1 TERM REVIEW

Across

3. _____ aging: gains are maximized and losses are maximized

5. _____-ignore script: pattern of interaction in which elders' independent behaviors are largely ignored, leading them to occur less often

7. According to _____ theory, declines in social interaction during late adulthood are due to a mutual withdrawal between elders and society in anticipation of death.

9. _____ housing: housing for elderly that adds a variety of suppot services

10. The process of telling stories about people and events from the past and reporting associated thoughts and feelings

12. _____ _____ communities: housing for elderly that offers a range of options, from independent or congregate housing to full nursing home care (2 words)

Down

1. Life _____ : process of calling up, reflecting on, and reconsidering past experiences and contemplating the meaning with the goal of achieving greater self-understanding

2. According to _____ theory, declines in social interaction during late life are due to failure of the social environment to offer opportunities for social contact not the desires of elders.

4. _____ selectivity theory: declines in social interaction late adulthood are due to physical and psychological changes, which lead elders to emphasize the emotion regulating function of interaction.

6. Social _____ : views the individual within a cluster of relationships moving throughout life

8. _____-support script: pattern of interaction in which elders' dependency behaviors are attended to immediately, thereby reinforcing those behaviors

11. _____ friends: people who are not intimates but with whom the individual spends time occasionally

13. Ego _____ versus despair: Erikson's psychological conflict of late adulthood

402

PRACTICE TEST #1

1. According to Erikson, adults who arrive at a sense of integrity (p. 584)
   a. feel they have made many wrong decisions throughout their lives.
   b. feel whole, complete, and satisfied with their achievements.
   c. feel contempt toward themselves and others.
   d. dealt with significant psychological problems early in life.

2. In one study, when asked to relate personal experiences in which they were happy, angry, fearful, and sad, and to indicate how they knew they felt the emotion (p. 585)
   a. younger adults emphasized how they did feel rather than how they should feel.
   b. older adults emphasized how they should feel rather than how they did feel.
   c. older adults gave vivid descriptions that viewed both mind and body as contributing to feeling states.
   d. younger adults gave vivid descriptions that viewed both mind and body as contributing to feeling states.

3. Compared to young adults, elders (p. 585)
   a. feel emotion superficially.
   b. have poor emotional self-regulation.
   c. are more able to interpret negative events in a positive light.
   d. are less able to separate emotional interpretations from objective aspects of situations.

4. In advanced old age, the majority of older adults regard themselves as (p. 587)
   a. much different than they were in middle adulthood.
   b. helpless and unable to lead a fulfilling life.
   c. rigid and pessimistic.
   d. very much the same person they have always been.

5. Longitudinal research suggests that religious involvement (p. 589)
   a. declines sharply in late adulthood.
   b. remains fairly stable throughout adulthood.
   c. is especially low among low-SES ethnic minority elders.
   d. has little impact on physical and psychological well-being.

6. Compared to her 85-year-old brother, 82-year-old Jada is more likely to report (p. 594)
   a. a higher sense of psychological well-being.
   b. a similar sense of psychological well-being.
   c. a lower sense of psychological well-being.
   d. higher self-esteem.

7. Having an extraverted personality is linked to (p. 594)
   a. low self-esteem and depression in late life.
   b. loneliness in old age, since opportunities for social interaction are limited.
   c. high morale in old age.
   d. decreased commitment to social relationships.

8. Compared to younger adults, older adults place greater emphasis on (p. 596)
   a. seeking affirmation from social partners.
   b. information seeking and future contact as a basis for selecting social partners.
   c. the emotional quality of their social interactions.
   d. increasing the size of their social networks.

9. Both urban and rural older adults report greater life satisfaction when (p. 597)
   a. many senior citizens reside in their neighborhood.
   b. many children reside in their neighborhood.
   c. few people reside in their neighborhood.
   d. many young adults reside in their neighborhood.

10. Although increasing numbers of ethnic minority elders want to live on their own, _____ often prevent(s) them from doing so. (p. 598)
    a. pride
    b. cultural values
    c. their children
    d. poverty

11. Residential communities for the aged (pp. 599–600)
    a. often have positive effects on physical and mental health.
    b. reduce elders' physical mobility and social participation.
    c. are more likely to foster favorable adjustment if they are large facilities.
    d. work best when elders can get to know people with values and goals unlike their own.

12. Marital satisfaction (p. 601)
    a. rises from middle to late adulthood.
    b. remains stable from middle to late adulthood.
    c. declines from middle to late adulthood.
    d. has little impact on psychological well-being in late adulthood.

13. Elderly gay and lesbian couples typically (p. 601)
    a. have great difficulty achieving a sense of integrity.
    b. experience less hostility and discrimination than younger gay and lesbian couples.
    c. report happy, highly fulfilling relationships.
    d. turn to family members and friends instead of their partners for social support.

14. Compared with widowed women, divorced older women may be more motivated to remarry because of (p. 602)
    a. greater fear of living alone.
    b. more extreme economic circumstances.
    c. greater desire for companionship.
    d. greater interest in a male role model for their children.

15. Compared with younger adults, elders who must cope with the death of a spouse typically show (p. 603)
    a. the same type and intensity of reactions.
    b. a less intense but longer-lasting reaction.
    c. less resiliency in the face of loneliness.
    d. fewer problems adjusting to the death.

16. Elderly women mention _____ as a primary aspect of close friendship. (p. 605)
    a. living assistance
    b. acceptance
    c. links with the larger community
    d. common activities

17. The kind of assistance that elders most often receive from their adult children is (p. 606)
    a. advice and emotional support.
    b. help with day-to-day living tasks.
    c. financial assistance.
    d. assistance with medical emergencies.

18. Which of the following is the most common form of elder maltreatment? (p. 608)
    a. physical neglect
    b. financial abuse
    c. psychological abuse
    d. physical abuse

19. Women are more likely to retire earlier than men because they tend to be (p. 610)
    a. better off financially.
    b. in better health.
    c. in unstimulating work environments.
    d. more responsive to family events.

20. Recent views of successful aging focus on the (p. 612)
    a. achievements of individuals with outstanding life accomplishments.
    b. processes people use to reach personally valued goals.
    c. social lives of successful and unsuccessful agers.
    d. identification of a single set of standards for aging well.

PRACTICE TEST #2

1. At age 80, Barbara can't face the idea that she will die and the world will go on. She has children and grandchildren but has little interest in their lives. According to Peck, Barbara needs to work on (p. 585)
    a. body transcendence.
    b. ego transcendence.
    c. ego differentiation.
    d. future differentiation.

2. In reminiscing, Marty draws on the past for effective problem-solving strategies, Marty is engaging in
    _____ reminiscence, which makes life _____ (p. 587)
    a. self-focused; lonely and depressing
    b. other-focused; fun and engaging
    c. knowledge-based; rich and rewarding
    d. life-review; reflective and enjoyable.

3. During late adulthood, self-concept becomes (p. 587)
    a. more insecure.
    b. more complex and multifaceted.
    c. less self-accepting.
    d. simpler and more streamlined.

4. Which of the following are linked to religious involvement in late adulthood? (p. 591)
    a. feeling more distant from family and friends
    b. increased financial well-being
    c. longer survival
    d. poorer physical functioning

5. Dependency–support and independence–ignore scripts (p. 591)
    a. reinforce dependent behavior.
    b. reinforce independent behavior.
    c. foster well-being and autonomy.
    d. are unaffected by one's social and cultural contexts.

6. Compared with people of other age groups, elders have the (p. 592)
    a. lowest suicide rate.
    b. highest suicide rate.
    c. lowest rate of depression.
    d. lowest rate of suicide but highest rate of depression.

7. Ethnic minority elders are more likely to accept agency-provided support services when they are (p. 594)
   a. connected to a familiar neighborhood organization, such as the church.
   b. arranged and paid for by their adult children.
   c. delivered by people they do not know.
   d. motivated by obligation rather than care and concern.

8. According to disengagement theory, declining rates of interaction in late adulthood are caused by (p. 595)
   a. social barriers to engagement.
   b. life-long selection processes.
   c. the desire of elders to reduce social interaction.
   d. mutual withdrawal between elders and society in anticipation of death.

9. Which of the following is the primary reason that elders residing in small and mid-sized communities are more satisfied with life than elders living in urban areas? (p. 598)
   a. children tend to live closer
   b. more opportunities for interaction with others of the same ethnic background
   c. greater participation in local politics
   d. lower crime rates

10. Which of the following statements about crime against the elderly is accurate? (p. 598)
    a. Older adults are more often the targets of crime, especially violent crime, than other age groups.
    b. Older adults are less often targets of crime, especially violent crime, than other age groups.
    c. Older adults living in high-SES neighborhoods are frequently targets of crime.
    d. Compared to women, older men are more often the targets of petty crime, such as pickpocketing.

11. The majority of older adults in Western nations want to live (p. 598)
    a. in their own homes and neighborhoods, and 90 percent of them do.
    b. in their own homes and neighborhoods, but only 50 percent do.
    c. in a warmer climate like that found in Florida and Arizona.
    d. with their children or other family members.

12. In nursing homes (p. 598)
    a. social partners are abundant, and social interaction is high.
    b. personal control over social experiences is low.
    c. interaction with people in the setting predicts high life satisfaction.
    d. residents with physical impairments are less depressed than their community-dwelling counterparts.

13. When marital dissatisfaction is present in late adulthood, it (p. 601)
    a. takes a greater toll on men than on women.
    b. takes a greater toll on women than on men.
    c. affects men and women similarly.
    d. often results in domestic violence.

14. When asked about the reasons for divorce (p. 602)
    a. elderly men typically mention difficulty adjusting to spending more time with their spouse following retirement.
    b. elderly women typically mention boredom with the relationship and a desire to form new, more rewarding relationships.
    c. both elderly men and women mention interest in a younger partner.
    d. elderly men typically mention lack of shared interests and activities, while elderly women typically mention their partner's refusal to communicate and emotional distance.

15. Same-sex friendships are key in the lives of (p. 604)
    a. never-married elderly men.
    b. married elderly men.
    c. never-married elderly women.
    d. married elderly women.

16. In late adulthood, sibling relationships (p. 604)
    a.   are closer with brothers.
    b.   become more emotionally distant.
    c.   more often involve direct assistance than socializing.
    d.   involve increased levels of support when siblings live close to each other.

17. Longitudinal research reveals that as grandparents and grandchildren move through life (p. 607)
    a.   contact and affection decline.
    b.   contact and affection increase.
    c.   contact declines but affection increases.
    d.   contact increases but affection declines.

18. Elder maltreatment is more common when caregivers (p. 608)
    a.   are emotionally and financially independent.
    b.   have a history of family violence.
    c.   are not related to the victim.
    d.   work in nursing homes, even those with good working conditions.

19. Retirement (p. 611)
    a.   usually causes physical health problems.
    b.   provides much desired relief for people highly dedicated to their careers.
    c.   generally leads to a rise in marital satisfaction.
    d.   results in a decline in quality of social support.

20. Involvement in leisure activities (p. 611)
    a.   is related to better physical and mental health and reduced mortality.
    b.   is related to better physical health but has relatively little impact on mental health.
    c.   does not change much over the course of late adulthood.
    d.   is greater for elders in ordinary homes than retirement communities.

CHAPTER 19
DEATH, DYING, AND BEREAVEMENT

BRIEF CHAPTER SUMMARY

When asked how they would like to die, most people say they want death with dignity—either a quick, agony-free end during sleep or a clear-minded final few moments in which they can say farewell and review their lives. In reality, death is the culmination of a straightforward biological process. Death is long and drawn out for three-fourths of people—many more than in times past, due to life-saving medical technology. In general, dying takes place in three phases: the agonal phase, clinical death, and mortality. In most industrialized nations, brain death is accepted as the definition of death. However, the thousands of patients who remain in a persistent vegetative state reveal that the brain-death standard does not always solve the dilemma of when to halt treatment to the incurably ill. Because most people will not experience an easy death, we can best ensure death with dignity by supporting dying patients through their physical and psychological distress, being candid about death's certainty, and helping them learn enough about their condition to make reasoned choices about treatment.

Between ages 7 and 10, most children grasp the three components of the death concept—permanence, universality, and nonfunctionality. Although children usually have an accurate conception of death by middle childhood, there are wide individual differences, and ethnic variations suggest that religious teachings also affect children's understanding of death. While parents often worry that discussing death candidly with children will fuel their fears, children with a good grasp of the facts of death have an easier time accepting it. Direct explanations that fit the child's cognitive maturity work best. Adolescents can easily voice the permanence, universality, and nonfunctionality of death, but their understanding is largely limited to the realm of possibility. And because teenagers have difficulty integrating logical insights with the realities of everyday life, their understanding of death is not yet fully mature. By encouraging adolescents to discuss concerns about death, adults can help them build a bridge between death as a logical concept and their personal experiences. In early adulthood, many people brush aside thoughts of death, perhaps prompted by death anxiety or relative disinterest in death-related issues. Overall, fear of death declines with age, reaching its lowest level in late adulthood and in adults with deep faith in some form of higher being.

According to Kübler-Ross, dying people typically express five responses, initially proposed as stages: denial, anger, bargaining, depression, and acceptance. But rather than stages, the five reactions Kübler-Ross observed are best viewed as coping strategies that anyone may call on in the face of threat. A host of contextual variables—nature of the disease; personality and coping style; family members' and health professionals' truthfulness and sensitivity; and spirituality, religion, and cultural background—affect the way people respond to their own dying and, therefore, the extent to which they attain an appropriate death.

Although the overwhelming majority of people want to die at home, caring for a dying patient is highly stressful. Hospital dying takes many forms and each pattern is affected by the physical state of the dying person, the hospital unit in which it takes place, and the goal and quality of care. Whether a person dies at home or in a hospital, the hospice approach strives to meet the dying person's physical, emotional, social, and spiritual needs and emphasizes quality of life over life-prolonging measures.

The same medical procedures that preserve life can prolong inevitable death, diminishing the quality of life and personal dignity. In the absence of national consensus on passive euthanasia, people can best ensure that their wishes will be followed by preparing an advanced medical directive—a written statement of desired medical treatment should they become incurably ill. Although the practice has sparked heated controversy, public support for voluntary euthanasia is growing; slightly less public consensus exists for assisted suicide.

Although many theorists regard grieving as taking place in orderly phases of avoidance, confrontation, and restoration, in reality, people vary greatly in behavior and timing and often move back and forth between these reactions. Like dying, grieving is affected by many factors, including personality, coping style, and religious and cultural background.

Circumstances surrounding the death—whether it is sudden and unanticipated or follows a prolonged illness—also shape mourners' responses. When a parent loses a child or a child loses a parent or sibling, grieving is generally very intense and prolonged. People who experience several deaths at once or in close succession are at risk for bereavement overload, leaving them emotionally overwhelmed and unable to resolve their grief. Preparatory steps can be taken to help people of all ages cope with death more effectively. Today, instruction in death, dying, and bereavement can be found in colleges and universities; training programs for doctors, nurses, and helping professionals; adult education programs; and a few elementary and secondary schools.

LEARNING OBJECTIVES

After reading this chapter, you should be able to:

19.1 Describe the physical changes of dying, with special attention to the three phases of death. (pp. 620–621)

19.2 Discuss the controversy over how to define death, noting cross-cultural perspectives. (pp. 621–622)

19.3 Explain ways to promote death with dignity. (p. 622)

19.4 Discuss age-related changes in conception of and attitudes toward death. (pp. 622–626)

19.5 Explain the concept of death anxiety, citing personal and cultural variables related to apprehension about death. (pp. 626–627)

19.6 Describe and evaluate Kübler-Ross's stage theory of dying. (pp. 627–628)

19.7 List goals associated with an appropriate death, and summarize contextual factors that influence a person's adaptation to death. (pp. 628–631)

19.8 Discuss the benefits and drawbacks of dying at home versus in a hospital, and explain how the hospice approach aims to improve quality of life for dying patients and their families. (pp. 631–633)

19.9 Discuss ethical and legal controversies surrounding euthanasia and assisted suicide. (pp. 633–639)

19.10 Describe the phases of grieving, and discuss personal and situational variables that influence mourners' responses to the loss of a loved one. (pp. 639–642)

19.11 Explain the concept of bereavement overload, and describe bereavement interventions aimed at helping mourners recover from grief. (pp. 642–645)

19.12 Explain how death education can help people cope with death more effectively. (p. 645)

STUDY QUESTIONS

How We Die

Physical Changes

1. True or False: The overwhelming majority of people experience a quick, agony-free death. Elaborate on your response. (p. 620)

    _____

    _____

    _____

2. Describe the three phases of dying—the agonal phase, clinical death, and mortality. (p. 621)

Agonal phase: _____

_____

Clinical death: _____

_____

Mortality: _____

_____

Defining Death

1. What definition of death is currently used in most industrialized nations? (p. 621)

_____

_____

2. Describe the definition of death used by doctors in Japan, citing cultural beliefs which have led them to use a different definition than that used in other industrialized nations. (p. 621)

_____

_____

_____

3. Explain why the brain death standard does not solve the dilemma of when to halt treatment. (p. 621)

_____

_____

_____

Death with Dignity

1. Summarize three ways in which we can foster dignity in death through the ways in which we communicate with and care for the dying person. (p. 622)

A. _____

_____

B. _____

_____

C. _____

_____

Childhood

1. List and describe the three concepts on which a realistic understanding of death is based. (p. 623)

    A. _____

    _____

    B. _____

    _____

    C. _____

    _____

2. How do preschoolers make sense of death when they are not given a clear explanation? (p. 623)

    _____

    _____

3. By what age do most children grasp the three components of the death concept, and in what order do they learn these components? (p. 623)

    Age: _____

    Order: _____

4. Explain how factors such as experience with death and religious teaching affect children's conception of death. (pp. 623–624)

    Experience with death: _____

    _____

    Religious teaching: _____

    _____

5. True or False: Discussing death honestly and directly is likely to increase children's fears. Elaborate on your response. (p. 624)

    _____

    _____

    _____

Adolescence

1. True or False: Adolescents' understanding of death is not yet fully mature. (p. 624)

2. Cite examples of adolescents' reasoning and behavior which suggest that they have difficulty integrating logic and reality when reflecting on death. (p.)

_____

_____

_____

3. List three reasons why adolescents have difficulty integrating logic and reality in the domain of death. (p. 625)

   A. _____

   B. _____

   C. _____

4. Describe five ways to discuss concerns about death with children and adolescents. (p. 625)

   A. _____

   _____

   B. _____

   _____

   C. _____

   _____

   D. _____

   _____

   E. _____

   _____

Adulthood

1. Trace age-related changes in the conception of death from early to late adulthood. (p. 625)

   Early adulthood: _____

   _____

   Middle adulthood: _____

   _____

   Late adulthood: _____

   _____

Death Anxiety

1. What is *death anxiety*? (p. 626)

   _____

   _____

2. Research reveals (few / large) individual and cultural differences in the anxiety-provoking aspects of death. (p. 626)

3. Identify two personal factors that minimize death anxiety. (p. 626)

   A. _____

   _____

   B. _____

   _____

4. True or False: Death anxiety increases with age, reaching its peak in late adulthood. (p. 626)

5. What is *symbolic immortality,* and how does it affect death anxiety? (p. 626)

   Definition: _____

   _____

   Affect on death anxiety: _____

   _____

6. Cross-cultural studies show that (men / women) are more anxious about death. (p. 626)

7. Explain the link between mental health and death anxiety. (p. 626)

   _____

   _____

8. True or False: Children rarely display death anxiety. (pp. 626–627)

Thinking and Emotions of Dying People

Do Stages of Dying Exist?

1. List and describe Kübler-Ross's five stages of dying, and explain how family members and health professionals should react at each of the first four stages. (p. 628)

   A. _____

   Reactions: _____

   _____

   B. _____

413

Reactions: _____

_____

C. _____

Reactions: _____

_____

D. _____

Reactions: _____

_____

E. _____

Reactions: _____

_____

2. True or False: Kübler-Ross viewed her five stages as a fixed sequence which is universally experienced by all individuals. (p. 628)

3. Summarize criticisms of Kübler-Ross's theory. (p. 628)

_____

_____

_____

Contextual Influences on Adaptations to Dying

1. Define *appropriate death.* (p. 629)

_____

_____

_____

2. Cite five goals associated with a good death. (p. 629)

A. _____

B. _____

C. _____

D. _____

E. _____

3. True or False: Dying people display similar reactions, regardless of the nature of their disease. (p. 629)

4. True or False: The way an individual views stressful life events and has coped with them in the past is closely related to that individual's view of dying. (p. 629)

5. A candid approach, in which those close to and caring for the dying person acknowledge the terminal illness, is (ill-advised / recommended). (p. 629)

6. True or False: In certain ethnic groups, it is common for doctors to withhold information about a dying patient's prognosis. (p. 630)

7. Cite three factors that are key to nurses' success in meeting the needs of dying patients and their families. (p. 630)

   A. _____

   B. _____

   C. _____

8. Describe five strategies for effective communication with dying people. (p. 630)

   A. _____

   B. _____

   C. _____

   D. _____

   E. _____

9. Explain how Buddhist practices and beliefs foster an acceptance of death. (p. 630)

   _____

   _____

10. Describe how Native-American and Inuit cultural attitudes shape people's experiences with death. (pp. 630–631)

   Native-American: _____

   _____

   Inuit of Canada: _____

   _____

A Place to Die

Home

1. Summarize the advantages and disadvantages of dying at home. (p. 631)

   Advantages: _____

   _____

   Disadvantages: _____

   _____

2. Explain why family members report more prolonged psychological stress following a home death when compared to family members whose loved one died elsewhere. (p. 631)

   _____

   _____

   _____

Hospital

1. Name two things that emergency room staff can do to help family members cope with the sudden loss of a loved one. (p. 632)

   A. _____

   B. _____

2. Patients with (cancer / cardiovascular disease) account for most cases of prolonged dying. (p. 632)

3. Explain the conflict of values between dying patients and health professionals in hospital settings, especially in intensive care units. (p. 632)

   _____

   _____

4. True or False: The majority of American hospitals have comprehensive treatment programs to ease physical, emotional, and spiritual pain at the end of life. (p. 632)

5. Most doctors and nurses (are / are not) specially trained in managing pain in dying patients. (p. 632)

The Hospice Approach

1. Describe the hospice approach, noting its seven main features. (p. 632)

   Description: _____

   A. _____

   B. _____

   C. _____

   D. _____

   E. _____

   F. _____

   G. _____

2. Define *palliative care.* (p. 632)

   _____

   _____

3. True or False: Hospice programs offer a continuum of care, with some patients receiving services in the home while others receive services in hospitals or nursing homes. (p. 633)

4. Government health care benefits in the United States and Canada (do / do not) cover hospice care. (p. 633)

5. Explain how hospice care contributes to improved family functioning. (p. 633)

   _____

   _____

6. The majority of North Americans (are / are not) familiar with the philosophy of the hospice approach. (p. 633)

The Right to Die

Passive Euthanasia

1. The United States and Canada (do / do not) have uniform right-to-die policies for cases involving terminal illness or persistent vegetative state. (p. 634)

2. Distinguish between *passive* and *active euthanasia.* (p. 634)

   Passive: _____

   _____

   Active: _____

   _____

3. True or False: When there is no hope of recovery, the majority of Americans and Canadians support the patient's or family members' right to end treatment. (p. 634)

4. Passive euthanasia (is / is not) widely practiced as part of ordinary medical procedure, in which doctors exercise professional judgment. (p. 634)

5. (Religion / Ethnicity) strongly contributes to people's views of passive euthanasia. (p. 634)

6. In the absence of a national consensus on passive euthanasia, how can people best ensure that their wishes will be followed should they become terminally ill or fall into a persistent vegetative state? (pp. 634–635)

   _____

   _____

   _____

7. Name and describe two types of advance directives recognized in the majority of U.S. states. (pp. 634–635)

   A. _____

   _____

   B. _____

   _____

8. Cite two reasons why living wills do not guarantee personal control over treatment. (p. 635)

   A. _____

   _____

   B. _____

   _____

9. The durable power of attorney for health care is (more / less) flexible than the living will. Explain why this is the case. (p. 635)

   _____

   _____

   _____

10. True or False: Over 70 percent of North Americans have executed a living will or durable power of attorney. (pp. 635–636)

11. What is a health care proxy, and how does it help to ensure that a patient's medical wishes are obeyed? (p. 636)

_____

_____

Voluntary Active Euthanasia

1. True or False: Voluntary active euthanasia is a criminal offense in most countries, including the United States and Canada. (p. 636)

2. True or False: Only about 20 percent of people in Western nations approve of voluntary active euthanasia. (p. 636)

3. Summarize opponents' concerns about voluntary active euthanasia. (p. 636)

_____

_____

_____

Assisted Suicide

1. True or False: Assisted suicide is legal in many Western European countries. (p. 638)

2. Describe Oregon's Death with Dignity Act. (p. 638)

_____

_____

_____

3. True or False: 75 percent of North Americans are opposed to assisted suicide. (p. 638)

4. Under what four conditions did a panel of medical experts conclude that assisted suicide is warranted? (p. 638)

A. _____

B. _____

C. _____

D. _____

Social Issues: Voluntary Active Euthanasia: Lessons from Australia and the Netherlands

1. Summarize the debate over the euthanasia statute in Australia's Northern Territory. (p. 637)

_____

_____

_____

_____

2. List the conditions under which voluntary active euthanasia is legal in the Netherlands. (p. 637)

_____

_____

_____

3. True or False: Some Dutch doctors have admitted to actively causing death in patients who did not ask for it. (p. 638)

Bereavement: Coping with Death of a Loved One

1. Distinguish between bereavement, grief, and mourning. (p. 639)

Bereavement: _____

Grief: _____

Mourning: _____

Grief Process

1. Match each of the following phases of grief with the appropriate description. (pp. 639–640)

_____ Bereaved individual must balance emotional
consequences of his/her loss with attending to life
changes associated with the loved one's death

1. Avoidance
2. Confrontation
3. Restoration

_____ A numbed feeling serves as "emotional anesthesia"

_____ Mourner confronts the reality of the loss and
experiences a cascade of emotional reactions

_____ Bereaved individual yearns for the deceased and
obsessively reviews the circumstances of the death

_____ Mourner may show a variety of behavioral changes,
including absentmindedness, poor concentration, self-
destructive behavior, and/or depression

_____ Emotional energy shifts toward life-restoring pursuits

_____ The bereaved person experiences shock followed by
disbelief and is unable to comprehend the death

Personal and Situational Variations

1. Explain differences in grieving when the death is sudden and unexpected versus prolonged and expected. (p. 640)

Sudden and unexpected: _____

_____

Prolonged and expected: _____

_____

2. Define *anticipatory grieving*. (p. 640)

_____

_____

3. Compared with survivors of other sudden deaths, people grieving a suicidal loss are (more / less) likely to blame themselves for what happened. (p. 640)

4. List three reasons why the death of a child is the most difficult loss that an adult can face. (p. 641)

   A. _____

   B. _____

   C. _____

5. True or False: A child's death typically leads to a marital breakup, regardless of prior marital satisfaction. (p. 641)

6. Why is the loss of a family member likely to have long-standing consequences for children? (p. 641)

   _____

   _____

   _____

7. List the physical, behavioral, and emotional symptoms often displayed by children who are grieving the loss of a parent or sibling. (p. 641)

   _____

   _____

   _____

8. True or False: When children maintain mental contact with a deceased parent or sibling by dreaming about or speaking to them, this hinders the child's ability to cope with the loss. (p. 641)

9. Describe the link between cognitive development and children's ability to grieve, noting how adults can help young children better understand the person's death. (p. 641)

   _____

   _____

   _____

10. Grief-stricken (school-age children / adolescents) tend to keep their grieving from both adults and peers, often leading to depression and attempts to escape the grief through acting out behavior. (p. 641)

11. Younger adults display (more / fewer) negative outcomes than do older adults following the death of a spouse. Why is this the case? (p. 641)

   _____

   _____

12. Describe *bereavement overload,* and note how it impacts ability to cope with grief. (p. 642)

   Description: _____

   _____

   Impact: _____

   _____

13. Identify three groups of individuals who are at increased risk for bereavement overload. (pp. 642–643)

A. _____

B. _____

C. _____

Bereavement Interventions

1. Describe five suggestions for resolving grief following the death of a loved one. (p. 644)

A. _____
_____

B. _____
_____

C. _____
_____

D. _____
_____

E. _____
_____

2. Self-help groups that bring together mourners who have experienced the same type of loss
(are / are not) effective for reducing stress. (p. 644)

3. List characteristics of bereavement interventions for children and adolescents. (pp. 644–645)

_____
_____
_____

4. Cite four instances in which grief therapy may be necessary in order to help the mourner overcome his/her loss.
(p. 645)

A. _____

B. _____

C. _____

D. _____

Cultural Influences: Cultural Variations in Mourning Behavior

1. Describe differences in mourning behaviors and beliefs about death in the following religious and cultural groups:
(p. 642)

Christians: _____
_____

Jews: _____

_____

Quakers: _____

_____

Balinese of Indonesia: _____

_____

Tribal and village cultures: _____

_____

2. Summarize the benefits of Internet memorials. (p. 643)

_____

_____

_____

Death Education

1. List the four goals of death education. (p. 645)

A. _____

B. _____

C. _____

D. _____

2. True or False: Compared to lecture style programs, experiential programs that help people confront their own mortality are more likely to heighten death anxiety. (p. 645)

ASK YOURSELF . . .

For *Ask Yourself* questions for this chapter, please log on to the Companion Website at www.ablongman.com/berk.

SUGGESTED STUDENT READINGS

Becvar, D.S. (2001). *In the presence of grief: Helping family members resolve death, dying, and bereavement issues.* New York: Guilford. Based on personal accounts and contemporary research, this book explores the many contexts in which death may occur. Additional topics include: death of a child, sibling, parent, and spouse; funerals and other rituals; and strategies for practitioners working with bereaved families.

Duncombe, P.W., & Titus, A.G. (2000). *When death comes suddenly: First –person accounts of surviving the loss of family members.* New York: Vantage Press. A collection of narratives highlighting the different aspects of experiencing a sudden death, including emotional reactions, the grieving process, and the role of social workers, psychologists, and clergy.

Dworkin, G., Bok, S., & Frey, R.G. (1998). *Euthanasia and physician assisted suicide: For and against.* New York: Cambridge University Press. Presents moral issues involved in doctors assisting patients to die with dignity and the ongoing debate between the medical profession, ethicists, and general public regarding euthanasia and physician-assisted suicide.

Pojman, L .P. (2000). *Life and death: Grappling with the moral dilemmas of our time (2nd ed.).* Belmont, CA: Wadsworth. Presents a range of moral issues surrounding matters of life and death, including suicide, euthanasia, abortion, and the death penalty.

Webb, N.B. (Eds.). (2002). *Helping bereaved children: A handbook for practitioners.* New York: Guilford. Examines the impact of violence on children and ways in which schools and communities should approach incidents of murder, bombings, and terrorist attacks.

PUZZLE 19.1 TERM REVIEW

Across

1. _____ death: irreversible cessation of all activity in the brain and brain stem
4. Persistent _____ state: cerebral cortex no longer registers electrical activity, but the brain stem remains active
6. _____ euthanasia: withholding or withdrawing life-sustaining treatment, permitting the patient to die naturally
8. _____ will: written statement specifying the treatments a person does or does not want in case of terminal illness, coma, or other near-death situation
9. Phase of dying in which an individual passes into permanent death
10. Durable power of _____ for health care: written statement that authorizes another person to make health care decisions on one's behalf in case of incompetence
11. Practice of ending the life of a person suffering from an incurable condition

Down

2. _____ medical directive: written statement of desired medical treatment should a person become incurably ill
3. Voluntary _____ euthanasia: practice of ending a patient's sufffering, at the patient's request, before a natural end to life
5. _____ death: a death that makes sense in terms of the person's pattern of living and values, and at the same time, preserves or restores significant relationships and is as free of suffering as possible
7. _____ death: phase of dying in which heartbeat, circulation, breathing, and brain functioning stop, but resuscitation is still possible

PUZZLE 19.2 TERM REVIEW

Across

4. Culturally specified expression of a bereaved person's thoughts and feelings
6. Component of the death concept specifying that all living things will eventually die
8. Intense physical and psychological distress following a loss
10. _____ grieving: acknowledging that the loss is inevitable and preparing emotionally for it
11. _____ care: aimed at relieving pain and other symptoms in terminally ill patients in order to protect the person's quality of life rather than prolonging life
12. _____-_____ model of coping: oscillation between dealing with emotional consequences of loss and attending to life changes

Down

1. Component of the death concept specifying that once a living thing dies, it cannot be brought back to life
2. Phase of dying in which gasps and muscle spasms occur during the first moments in which the body cannot sustain life anymore
3. Component of the death concept specifying that all living functions cease at death
5. Comprehensive program of support services that focuses on meeting terminally ill patients' physical, emotional, social, and spiritual needs and that offers follow-up bereavement services to families
7. Death _____: fear and apprehension of death
9. The experience of losing a loved one by death

PRACTICE TEST #1

1. Brianna was found unconscious in a swimming pool. Her heartbeat and breathing had stopped, yet the paramedics were able to revive her. Brianna was in the _____ phase of dying. (p. 621)
    a. agonal
    b. clinical death
    c. mortality
    d. anticipatory

2. Which definition of death is currently used in most industrialized nations? (p. 621)
    a. loss of heartbeat and respiration
    b. lack of activity in the cerebral cortex, even if the brain stem remains active
    c. irreversible cessation of all activity in both the brain and brain stem
    d. muscle spasms indicating that the body can no longer sustain life

3. Death with dignity refers to (p. 620)
    a. a quick, agony-free death during sleep.
    b. receiving sufficient medication so that the individual does not suffer during a long, drawn out death.
    c. death in the home, where the individual is likely to be most comfortable.
    d. being well-informed about one's condition and being assured of support and compassionate care.

4. Which of these aspects of the death concept is most difficult for children to comprehend? (p. 623)
    a. People die at different ages and from different causes.
    b. Dead people will not wake up or come back to life.
    c. Dead people can no longer eat, breath, move, think, or feel.
    d. All living things will eventually die.

5. Parents can enhance children's understanding of death by (p. 623)
    a. providing direct explanations that fit the child's level of cognitive maturity.
    b. using child-friendly clichés to explain death, such as by saying "Grandpa went on a long trip."
    c. emphasizing scientific evidence rather than religious beliefs.
    d. avoiding discussions of death until children are old enough to grasp all elements of the death concept.

6. Teenagers' understanding of death is often not evident in their behavior because (p. 625)
    a. they cannot yet explain the permanence and nonfunctionality of death.
    b. the dividing line between life and death becomes more clear in adolescence than it was in childhood.
    c. they fail to formulate personal theories about life after death.
    d. the adolescent personal fable leads them to believe that they are beyond the reach of death.

7. Kübler-Ross's phases of dying (p. 628)
    a. should be viewed as a fixed sequence displayed by all individuals.
    b. provide an exhaustive list of people's responses to death.
    c. are best viewed as coping strategies that can be called on in the face of threat.
    d. do not accurately represent people's reactions to their impending death.

8. Recent theorists propose _____ as an alternative to Kübler-Ross's phases. According to this perspective, death should make sense in terms of the individual's pattern of living and values, it should preserve and restore significant relationships, and it should be as free of suffering as possible. (p. 628)
    a. agonal death
    b. appropriate death
    c. functional death
    d. anticipatory death

9. In communicating with a dying person, it is best to (p. 630)
   a. give somewhat misleading information about the diagnosis and the course of the disease in order to reduce anxiety.
   b. avoid discussing death-related issues.
   c. discourage the person from maintaining hope, since favorable outcomes are not realistic.
   d. listen attentively and accept the person's feelings.

10. Which group emphasizes the circular relationship between life and death, in which death is viewed as an important means of making way for others? (pp. 630–631)
    a. Buddhists
    b. Native Americans
    c. Inuits of Canada
    d. African-Americans

11. One drawback of dying in a hospital is (p. 632)
    a. the high physical, psychological, and financial demand on caregivers.
    b. family members experience more prolonged psychological distress than do family members whose loved ones died at home.
    c. privacy and communication with family members are secondary to monitoring the patient's condition.
    d. the extreme emphasis on palliative care.

12. A hospice is (p. 632)
    a. a home for dying patients.
    b. a type of hospital specially designed to meet the needs of dying patients.
    c. a religious facility intended to address the unique spiritual issues confronting dying patients.
    d. a comprehensive program of support services for terminally ill patients and their families.

13. Palliative care is aimed at improving the quality of remaining life by (p. 632)
    a. relieving pain and other symptoms, such as nausea, insomnia, and depression.
    b. providing rich social supports.
    c. reducing death anxiety while fostering a sense of dignity and self-worth.
    d. promoting a strong sense of spirituality.

14. In passive euthanasia (p. 634)
    a. medical personnel focus on relieving pain in order to protect the quality of life in terminally ill patients.
    b. experimental medical procedures are utilized in an effort to prolong life in patients who would otherwise have no hope of survival.
    c. doctors or loved ones act directly, at the patient's request, to end suffering before a natural end to life.
    d. life-sustaining treatment is withheld or withdrawn, permitting a patient to die naturally.

15. A living will (p. 634)
    a. guarantees personal control over medical decision-making.
    b. is a legally-binding document which must be followed by medical personnel.
    c. often does not cover people in a persistent vegetative state or elders with chronic problems, such as Alzheimer's disease, which are not classified as terminal.
    d. is more flexible than a durable power of attorney for health care.

16. Approximately _____ percent of North Americans support a patient's right to die through passive euthanasia, voluntary active euthanasia, or assisted suicide. (p. 634)
    a. 1 to 2
    b. 10 to 30
    c. 40 to 60
    d. 70 to 90

17. During the confrontation phase of the grief process (p. 639)
    a. the bereaved person experiences a numbed feeling that serves as "emotional anesthesia."
    b. the death is too much for survivors to comprehend.
    c. the mourner recognizes the reality of the loss and often experiences a cascade of emotional reactions.
    d. the bereaved individual shifts his/her emotional energies toward life-restoring pursuits.

18. During which phase of the grief process do mourners use the dual-process model of coping, in which they shift back and forth between dealing with the emotional consequences of loss and attending to life changes? (p. 640)
    a. anticipatory
    b. avoidance
    c. confrontation
    d. restoration

19. Children and adolescents who experience the loss of a parent or sibling (p. 641)
    a. adjust quickly because they cannot yet comprehend the permanency of the loss.
    b. respond best when adults use clichés and misleading statements to explain the death.
    c. should be discouraged from maintaining mental contact with the deceased, such as by thinking and dreaming about the person or speaking to them regularly.
    d. often experience persistent depression, anxiety, and angry outbursts.

20. Death education programs are least effective when the format involves (p. 645)
    a. role-playing.
    b. discussions with terminally ill patients and their families.
    c. visits to mortuaries and cemeteries.
    d. lectures conveying factual information about the dying process.

PRACTICE TEST #2

1. About _____ percent of people experience a quick, agony-free death. (p. 620)
    a. 5
    b. 20
    c. 45
    d. 80

2. The term used by the medical profession for individuals whose brain stems continue to function but who show no electrical activity in the cerebral cortex is (p. 621)
    a. brain death.
    b. persistent vegetative state.
    c. imminent mortality.
    d. cortical death.

3. Compared with earlier generations, today's children and adolescents in industrialized nations are (p. 622)
    a. more comfortable dealing with death due to their greater role in helping to care for dying family members.
    b. more accepting of death due to frequent images of death seen in television shows, movies, and news reports.
    c. less likely to experience death anxiety due to their heightened religious awareness.
    d. more insulated from death since they are more likely to reach adulthood without experiencing the death of someone they know well.

4. Children usually master an understanding of death by age (p. 623)
    a. 2 to 3.
    b. 5 to 6.
    c. 7 to 10.
    d. 12 to 15.

5. At what stage of life are individuals most likely to think and talk about death? (p. 625)
    a. childhood and adolescence
    b. early adulthood
    c. middle adulthood
    d. late adulthood

6. Among elders in Western cultures, the most important factor in reducing death anxiety is (p. 626)
    a. a spiritual sense of life's meaning.
    b. commitment to an organized religion.
    c. the conviction that there is an afterlife.
    d. good physical health for one's age.

7. Death anxiety (p. 626)
    a. increases with age.
    b. declines with age.
    c. is unrelated to age.
    d. is an individual trait that remains stable from childhood into late adulthood.

8. According to Kübler-Ross once a dying patient has reached the stage of acceptance, he/she will often (p. 628)
    a. appear cheerful and eager for death.
    b. become more sociable and outgoing.
    c. feel no hope at all of avoiding death.
    d. withdraw from most or all people.

9. Family members are most likely to deny a loved one's impending death because (p. 629)
    a. as long as the person looks physically healthy, they can forget that he/she is dying.
    b. the dying person becomes agitated whenever the topic of death is discussed.
    c. they want to avoid bringing closure to the relationship and dealing with fears and regrets.
    d. they are often poorly informed about the nature of the disease and the certainty of death.

10. When a dying person feels a strong sense of spirituality, it tends to produce (p. 630)
    a. less fear of death and more acceptance of dying.
    b. more anger at God for not preventing one's death.
    c. confusion and distress about what dying really means.
    d. anger and resentment toward those who go on living.

11. 70 to 80 percent of North Americans would prefer to die (p. 631)
    a. at home.
    b. in a hospital.
    c. in a hospice.
    d. in a doctor's office.

12. The central belief of the hospice approach is that (p. 632)
    a. medical choices should be made by an objective third party in order to ease the psychological strain on the dying person and his/her family.
    b. quality of life is the most important issue surrounding a person's journey toward death.
    c. terminally ill patients should always be able to die in their homes.
    d. contact with family members should be secondary to monitoring the condition of the dying patient.

13. About 50 percent of patients dying of _____ choose a hospice approach. (p. 633)
    a. cardiovascular disease
    b. AIDS
    c. respiratory illnesses, such as emphysema and pneumonia
    d. cancer

14. In the United States today, use of passive euthanasia for terminally ill patients and those in a persistent vegetative state is considered (p. 634)
    a. immoral and unethical.
    b. an extreme procedure that must be approved by the courts.
    c. permissible only for the most elderly patients.
    d. an ordinary part of normal medical practice.

15. In a(n) _____, people specify the treatments that they do or do not want in case of a terminal illness, coma, or other near-death situation. (p. 635)
    a. medical waiver
    b. durable power of attorney for health care
    c. living will
    d. assisted suicide

16. Which U.S. state passed the Death with Dignity Act, which allows physicians to prescribe drugs so that terminally ill patients can end their own lives? (p. 638)
    a. California
    b. Oregon
    c. New York
    d. Florida

17. After Jayda's sister died, she experienced intense physical and psychological distress. Jayda was experiencing (p. 639)
    a. bereavement.
    b. mourning.
    c. grief.
    d. dual-process coping.

18. Adjusting to death is easier when (p. 640)
    a. the survivor understands the reasons for the death.
    b. the death is sudden and unanticipated.
    c. the death is the result of a suicide.
    d. a person experiences several deaths in close succession.

19. Which group tends to adjust best following the loss of an intimate partner? (p. 641)
    a. young adults
    b. middle-aged adults
    c. elderly adults
    d. gay and lesbian adults

20. One of the best ways to help a grieving person is by (p. 644)
    a. giving advice aimed at hastening recovery.
    b. discussing one's own experiences with death.
    c. encouraging the person to spend some time alone.
    d. listening and "just being there."

PUZZLE 1.1

PUZZLE 1.2

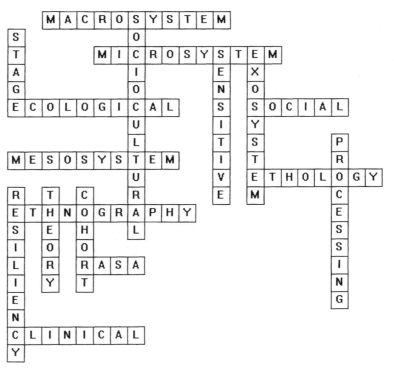

PUZZLE 1.3

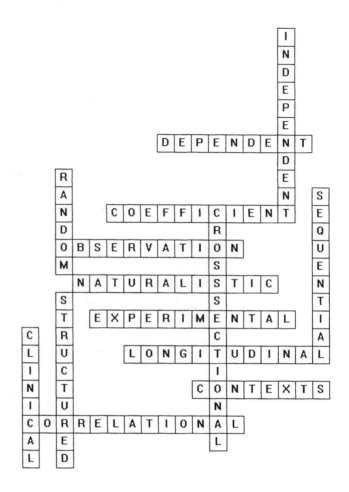

PUZZLE 2.1

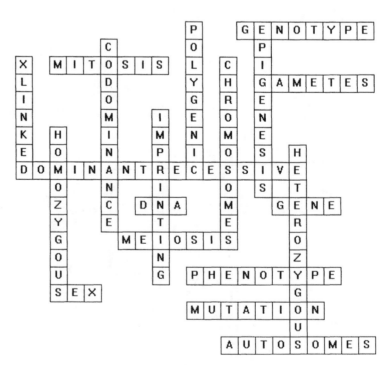

PUZZLE 2.2

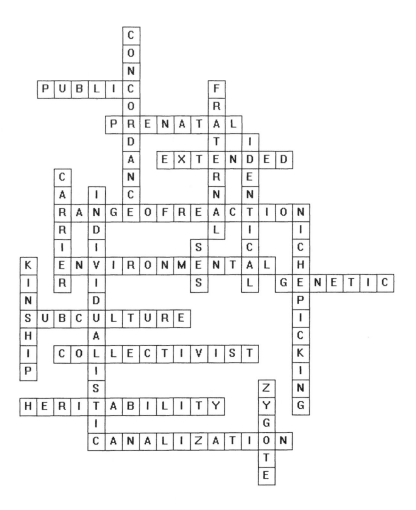

PUZZLE 3.1

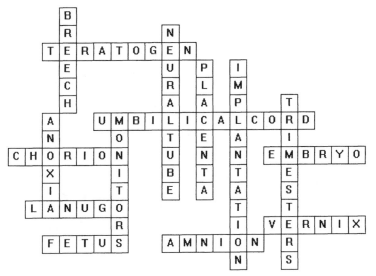

PUZZLE 3.2

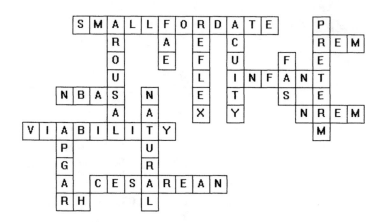

PUZZLE 4.1

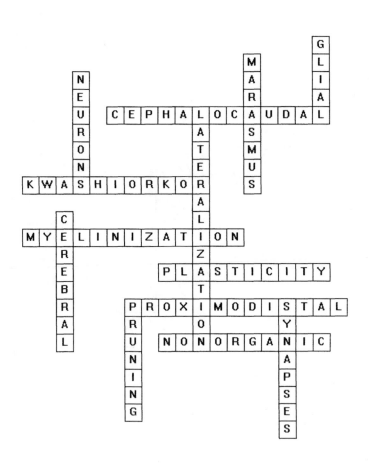

PUZZLE 4.2

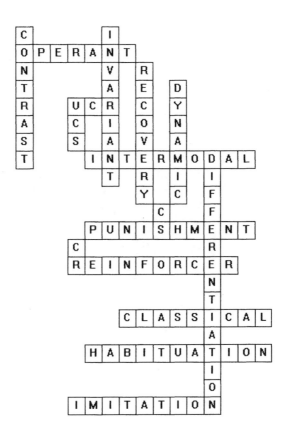

PUZZLE 5.1

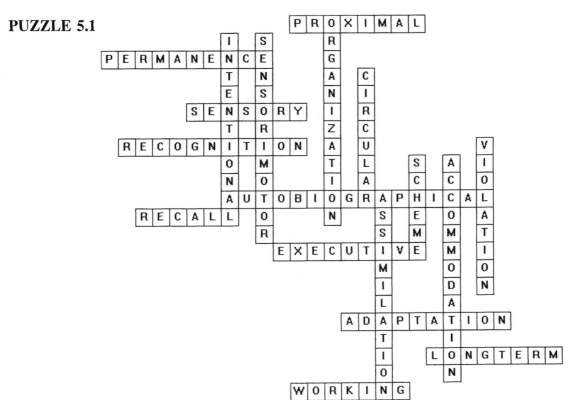

PUZZLE 5.2

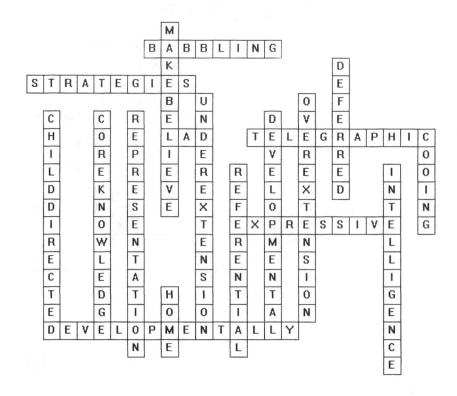

PUZZLE 6.1

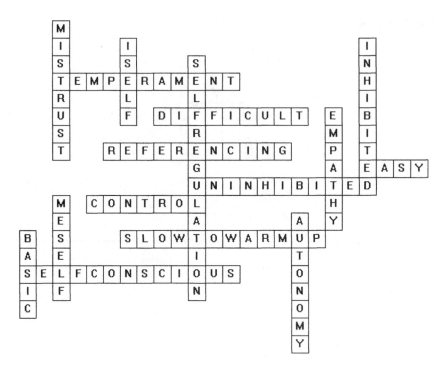

PUZZLE 6.2

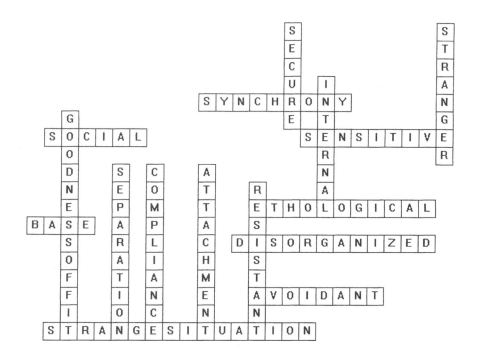

PUZZLE 7.1

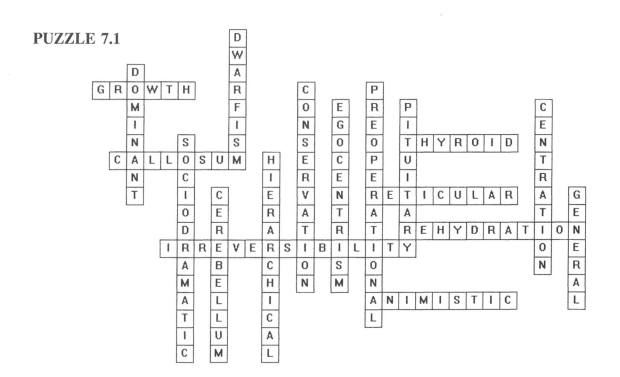

PUZZLE 7.2

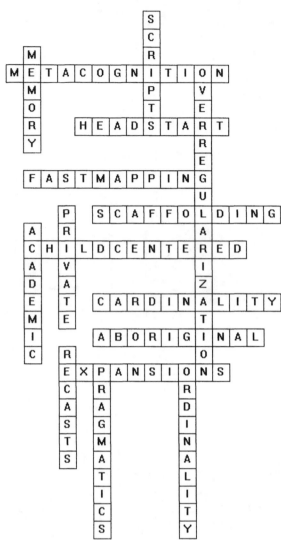

PUZZLE 8.1

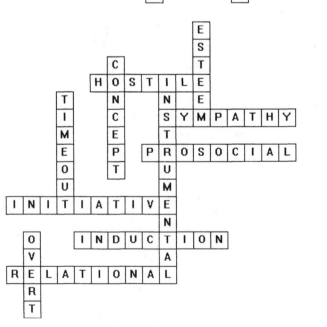

A-8

PUZZLE 8.2

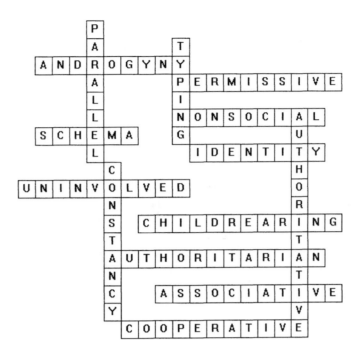

PUZZLE 9.1

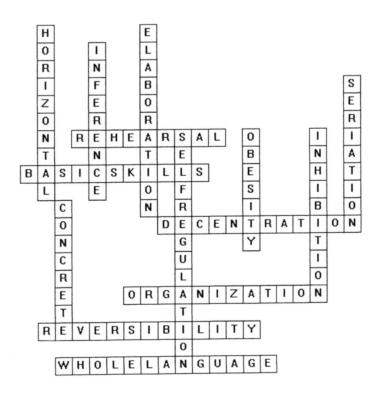

PUZZLE 9.2

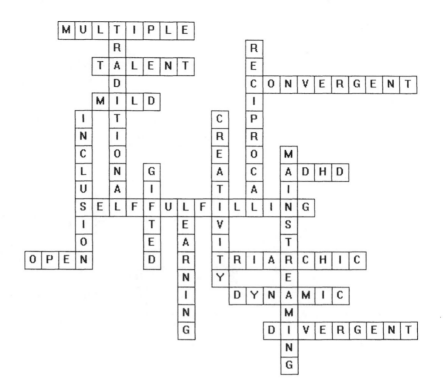

PUZZLE 10.1

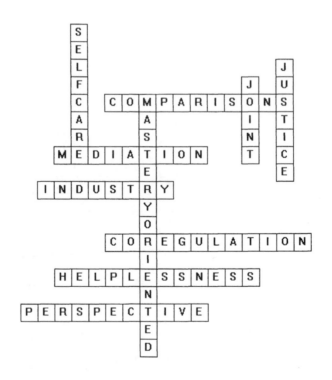

PUZZLE 10.2

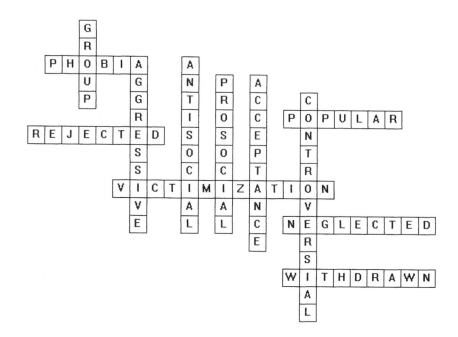

PUZZLE 11.1

PUZZLE 12.1

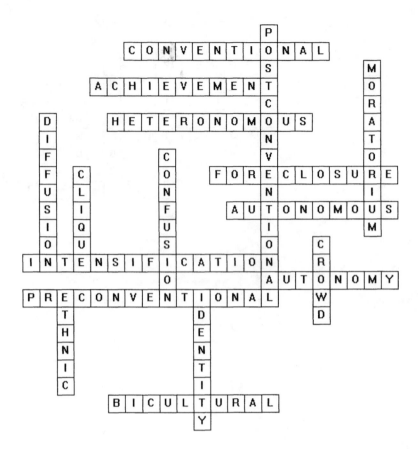

PUZZLE 13.1

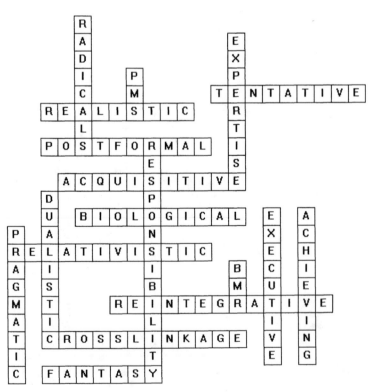